THE BRITISH AND GERMAN BANKING SYSTEM:
A COMPARATIVE STUDY

PREPARED BY
ECONOMISTS ADVISORY GROUP LTD.

FOR
THE ANGLO-GERMAN FOUNDATION

The Anglo-German Foundation for the Study of Industrial Society was established by an inter-governmental agreement between the Federal Republic of Germany and the United Kingdom following a generous initiative of the German Federal Government which was given expression during a state visit to Britain of the then Federal President, the late Dr. Gustav Heinemann. It was incorporated by a Royal Charter granted on the 5th December 1973. The Patrons of the Foundation are HRH The Prince Philip, Duke of Edinburgh, and Prof. Dr. Karl Carstens, President of the Federal Republic of Germany.

Financial support for the Foundation is now provided by both Governments, which each appoint six Members to the Board of Trustees.

The Foundation initiates and supports the study of the social, economic and political problems of Western industrial society, drawing particularly on the resources of the two countries in tackling common problems. A major part of the programme is concerned with the dissemination by publication, conferences or seminars of the results of such studies.

The opinions expressed in this report are entirely those of the authors.

ISBN   0 905492 35 8   Price £9.50

CONTENTS

LIST OF TABLES

Page

FOREWORD

by

Prof.Dr.Dr.h.c. N. Kloten

President Landeszentralbank in Baden-Württemberg

In the United Kingdom there is a good tradition of examining from time to time by means of a commission of enquiry how successful the British banking system has been in a changing economic environment and under altered international competitive conditions. In the Federal Republic of Germany, by contrast, committees of experts are set up as the need arises to comment on outstanding questions of bank supervision, forthcoming legislation, and some aspects of the economic power wielded by banks. The two latest reports of this kind on the banking systems of the United Kingdom and Germany, i.e. the Wilson Report and the report of the Gessler Commission (commission of enquiry into "Basic banking questions"), have contributed a great deal to the present comparative study; in particular the questions raised in it owe much to these reports.

This comparison of the British and German banking systems fills a gap through the very wealth of the information it provides on their structures, modes of operation, development trends, and current problems. But a more important feature is that the German banking system is considered from the point of view of the Wilson Report and the British banking system from the angle of the report of the Gessler Commission; thus each system is subjected to unaccustomed questions driving from the standpoint of the other system. The special attraction of this method is obvious. The British and German banking systems are - at least in terms of their historical roots - the purest examples in the world of the realisation of two different concepts: the specialised banking system in the United Kingdom and the "universal" (i.e. multi-purpose) banking system in Germany. This polarisation means virtually that nowhere in the study are the two systems analysed separately from each other; instead they are always described and assessed on a comparative basis.

The outcome corresponds to that of the Wilson report and of the report of the Gessler Commission, both of which advocate the basic retention of the present banking system in their respective countries. Thus the study does not leave the reader with the impression that one system is inherently superior to the other. In principle both systems enable the central banks to conduct an efficient monetary policy. Accordingly the varying degrees of success in maintaining stability in the two countries are not a corollary of the particular technical features of the two banking systems; they both provide thoroughly comparable opportunities in the field of economic policy, i.e. give the central banks a chance to realise their monetary objectives.

The fact that the success of the two countries in maintaining stability differed so markedly is attributable to their divergent outlook with respect to monetary theory and their varying concepts in the field of monetary policy (the changes in which in both countries since the Second World War are described with great understanding), and even more to the way in which the monetary priorities were set and functions assigned to the individual policy areas. In Britain, where inflation was long interpreted as being a consequence of cost pressure (especially wage cost pressure), high priority was given to incomes policy in the form of wage guidelines and - as a complement to this, to gain the trade unions' support - price controls. Monetary policy, relieved of the burden of combating inflation, strove by means of interest rate measures to maintain the external value of sterling and achieve balance of payments equilibrium. Demand management was primarily a matter for fiscal policy. Monetary policy in Germany, by contrast, always felt committed to its statutory mandate to keep the value of money stable, and hence felt responsible for fighting inflation. But there inflation was not considered to be a purely monetary phenomenon; in order to guarantee monetary stability it was not thought sufficient to bring the money supply into line with potential supply in real terms.

The functional role of wage settlements for the price level
and the stabilising effect of sound fiscal policies were
always recognised, if not invariably acted upon. "The
German willingness to use monetary policy to control inflation
shows a clear difference of view to the UK where, until
relatively recently, the money supply was regarded as
little more than a useful indicator reflecting, rather than
causing, trends in wages and prices" (p. 368). From the
German point of view these monetary policy standpoints also
reflect the institutional autonomy of the Bundesbank on the
one hand and the administrative integration of the Bank
of England in the government on the other hand. But from the
British point of view they are, rather, an outcome of the
social consensus about the order of importance of the overall
economic objectives; it is this consensus that determines
whether there should be more or less monetary stability
and thus, in the final analysis, the actual degree of
independence enjoyed by the central banks in the field of
monetary policy.

The authors deserve high praise for their capacity
to appreciate the special features of two banking systems
as well as the historical and intellectual specifics of
British and German monetary policy. The same applies
unreservedly to the technical quality of the comparison,
to the masterly selection of facts, and to evaluation of the
literature. In all cases an attempt has been made to make
the banking, national accounts, and flow of funds statistics
comparable or to point out and quantify the differences. In
addition to the many useful details, the chief merit of the
study is the light it sheds on macro-economic relationships
and on the interaction of all the elements in the respective
banking systems; in this way both problems and solutions
become very plain.

PREFACE BY EAG

The principal aims of this study were to compare the structure and operation of the domestic banking systems of the United Kingdom and the Federal Republic of Germany, and to consider the relationships that might exist between the functioning of the two systems and the performance of the respective economies. The study, therefore, touches only marginally on international aspects of banking. Chapters 1 and 2 describe the main features of the two banking systems. Chapters 3 to 7 discuss the supply of savings and the finance of industrial and commercial companies, small business and the public sector, including the vexed question of the relationship between banks and industrial management. Chapter 8 discusses the role of the banks in the organised markets for short- and long-term finance, and Chapter 9 the relationship between the monetary experience of the two countries and their very different inflation rates. Finally, Chapter 10 discusses some recent developments in banking supervision.

Research work was carried out by an EAG team under the direction of Professor E.V. Morgan, who has edited this report. Other members of the team were Messrs. G. Bannock, A. Doran and R.L. Harrington (UK) and Professor K.H. Hennings, U. Arnold, B. Elfers, U. Hagerberg and E. Wagner (Germany).

Individual Chapters have been written by those whose names appear at their head; they naturally reflect the views of their authors, though we have tried to attain as much consensus and consistency as possible. Authors have, of course, drawn heavily on research by other members of the team, particularly on a series of working papers by Professor K.H. Hennings. These papers contain additional material that has not been used here for reasons of space; they are listed at the end of this report, and photostat copies can be provided on application to us.

We should like to express our gratitude to the Anglo-German Foundation for its financial support and to the many bankers and businessmen who have given their time to help us in interviews. Needless to say, responsibility for any errors and omissions and for the opinions expressed rests with the editor and authors.

ECONOMISTS ADVISORY GROUP LTD.
December 1980

Note on Statistics

One billion (bn.) = 1,000 million.
- = zero or less than half last digit.
Figures may not sum exactly to totals because of rounding.

INTRODUCTION

The British and German banking systems both have long
histories, and they have grown up in very different political
and economic environments. It is not surprising, therefore,
that there should be many differences in structure and methods
of operation between the two systems, and it is often difficult
to assess how far these differences are of real economic
significance and how far they are merely a matter of adapting
to different circumstances. The systems of both countries
are continuously evolving and in some areas change is going
on at a very rapid pace. These matters are discussed at
some length in the body of this report, so readers may find
it convenient to have a brief summary of our more important
conclusions.

Structure and organisation

The UK banking system is more narrowly defined and
more highly concentrated, both in numbers and geographically,
than that of Germany. There is no close equivalent to the
German co-operative banks in Britain. Savings banks are much
less developed in Britain and are outside the official
definition of the banking system, as are building societies.
The five major London clearing banks do between 55 and 60
per cent of all UK banking business. In Germany, the
"big three" which have nationwide branch networks do just
over 10 per cent of all business; a further 15 per cent is
shared between about 190 regional and private banks; nearly
40 per cent is done by local authority savings banks and their
central institutions and nearly 15 per cent by co-operative
banks and their central institutions; the remainder is in the
hands of mortgage banks, hire purchase banks, and a few
specialist institutions. We believe that this diversity
among German banks has promoted competition and has helped
in the mobilisation of savings and in the finance of small
and medium-sized business.

German commercial banks, savings banks and co-operative
banks all act to a greater or lesser degree as "Universalbanken";
they provide not only the payments, deposit and lending,
and foreign exchange services associated with the British
clearing banks, but also the financial advice, new issue,and
fund management services still mainly provided in the UK by
merchant banks, issuing houses and stockbrokers. This
"universality" has come about as a result of strong competition
between different types of bank. Originally commercial
banks were concerned mainly with business finance, savings
banks with the mobilisation of local savings largely for the
finance of the public authorities that founded them, and
co-operative banks with the provision of small loans for
farmers and artisans. With the passage of time, however,
savings banks and co-operative banks have moved increasingly
into general business finance and commercial banks have
competed to a growing extent for small household savings.
In Britain a similar competitive process is taking the
clearing banks, directly or through subsidiaries, into "merchant
banking" business; they are also beginning to move into housing
finance in competition with the building societies and the
Trustee Savings Banks are beginning to move into ordinary
banking business. There is still, however, a lot more
specialisation in the UK than in Germany.

A far larger proportion of total savings flows through
the banking system in Germany than in the UK. A counterpart
of this is the much greater importance of the building
societies in the UK. Life assurance funds are also more
important in Britain, and Germany has no equivalent of UK
pension funds. Pensions are normally financed either on
a "pay as you go" basis or by "balance-sheet funding", whereby
pension liabilities are recorded in the balance-sheets of the
companies concerned but without any separate fund being
established.

Life assurance and pension funds are the two main channels
by which savings in Britain reach the long-term market for
both government and company securities. The relative weakness
of these institutions in Germany is associated with smaller

long-term capital markets and a greater reliance - both by
public authorities and business - on long-term bank finance. There
has probably been a two-way interaction of cause and effect;
the relative weakness of other sources of finance leads to
greater reliance on the banks, but the wide range of
finance offered by the banks and their close relationships with
their customers may have inhibited the growth of other markets.

Another respect in which the two countries differ is
in the constitution, organisation, and operation of their
central banks. The Bank of England is legally subordinate
to the government, which has statutory powers to issue directives
to it; the statute setting up the Deutsche Bundesbank
specifically declared its independence of the government. It is
hard to tell how significant this legal difference is, since
officials of the Treasury and the central bank seem to
co-operate fairly closely in both countries. We believe
however that the German legislation reflects a recognition
by government and public opinion of the need for a monetary
policy aimed primarily at protecting the value of the
currency by curbing inflation. During most of the period we
have studied, this recognition does not seem to have been present
in Britain.

Because of its federal origins the Bundesbank has
branches in each of the Länder capitals and in most other
important cities and towns. The Bundesbank branches play an
important part in the operation of the system, providing a
clearing service for other banks and also undertaking open-
market operations. The Bank of England established branches
in major provincial centres as long ago as 1826 and a few
still remain, but their functions are very minor.

This difference in the organisation of the central banks
provides one of the reasons for the relatively undeveloped
state of short-term capital markets in Germany. Another is
the activities of the central institutions of the savings banks
and co-operative banks. These institutions provide an additional
clearing service, take deposits from members who have funds in

excess of their requirements and, in the case of the saving
banks, make loans to members who are short of funds.

The mobilisation of savings

Germany has experienced a higher ratio of saving to
national income than Britain. In both countries the ratio
has fallen since 1973, largely because of financial deficits
in the public sector. Household saving has become an
increasingly large proportion of total saving in both countries.
The state has offered incentives to household saving in both
Britain and Germany, though there are significant differences
between the two systems. British incentives are all in the
form of tax reliefs; building societies get some tax advantages
but the main beneficiaries are savings through the government-
sponsored National Savings movement and through life assurance
and pension funds. Savings held in banks get no tax concessions
and the banks feel, rightly in our opinion, that they are
discriminated against. Tax concessions to savings are
available in Germany, but the main incentive has been the
payment of premiums on medium-term savings (usually a minimum
of 6 to 7 years) with banks and building societies. The
limited evidence available suggests that these incentives have
not had much effect on the total volume of saving in either
country, but that they have exerted a considerable influence
on the ways in which savings are held and, hence, on the
development of banks and other institutions.

There is intense competition for household savings
between German banks, which shows itself in the variety of
different savings media offered, in extensive market
research, and in widespread advertising of the interest rates
and premiums offered to depositors. There is much less
evidence of this kind of competition in the UK, though
it has increased somewhat as a result of the high interest
rates of the past two years.

A difference between the two countries that we regard
as very important is the ability of German banks to attract
household savings into medium - and long-term savings deposits
and savings bonds. For example in the years 1975-77, 16 per
cent of net acquisitions of financial assets (NAFA) by British
households went into bank deposits, but these were almost all
at sight or 7 days notice. In Germany only 4 per cent of
house-hold NAFA went into short-term deposits but 45 per cent
went into long-term deposits and various kinds of bank bonds.
This massive inflow of medium - and long-term household
savings enables German banks to provide large-scale finance
both to industry and government without generating an
inflationary rise in the money stock. In our view this is
probably the biggest single advantage derived by the German
economy (relative to the British) from its banking system.

Finance for industry and commerce

The German economy has a much larger proportion,
compared to the British, of unincorporated business and private
companies (GmbH) and a smaller proportion of listed public
companies. Moreover, among listed companies equity, capital
usually forms a smaller proportion of total balance-sheet
liabilities. This relative weakness of the equity base has
caused some concern in Germany. Again, causal relationships
may work both ways. Small firms everywhere find access to
the long-term capital market difficult or impossible and this,
together with the limitations already noted of the German
capital market, encourages reliance on the banks. On the
other hand, some German critics argue that their banks
discourage companies from going to the market in order, as
one of them put it to us, "to hang on to the goodies".

British banks are often criticised for making fewer
medium-term loans than their German opposite numbers.
The absolute volume of medium-term lending by German banks is
much larger because of the greater amount of total lending.
Ten years ago it would also have been true that German banks

made a higher proportion of their loans at medium-term, but this gap has narrowed greatly. About half of UK banks lending to the company sector is now medium-term (two years or more); no strictly comparable figures are available for Germany, but the proportion is probably rather over 55 per cent.

The cost of borrowing differs between the two countries because of different levels of interest rates, which are partly the result of differing rates of inflation. If the margin above the central bank rediscount rate is taken as a measure, there is not much difference between the two countries. Since the Bank of England's MLR has on average been well above the rediscount rate of the Deutsche Bundesbank, British borrowers have generally faced higher nominal charges. However, the real cost of borrowing, after allowing for inflation, has often been lower in the UK. It should also be noted that German lending is normally secured whereas a large part of British bank loans are unsecured.

We found bankers in both countries unwilling to talk, except in very general terms, about the criteria used in assessing applications for loans. Our impression is, however, that when faced with similar situations there is no great difference between banks in the two countries. The possible exceptions to this are small firms (discussed below) and rescue operations for firms in financial trouble.

Banks and industrial management

Many British commentators have drawn attention to the role of German banks as shareholders in industrial and commercial companies and to their representation on supervisory boards; some of them have concluded that German banks exercise more influence on company management than do British banks, and have suggested that this may be one of the reasons for the generally superior performance of German industry.

German banks are beneficial owners of only about 8 per cent of all ordinary shares of German companies, but they can also exercise voting rights in respect of shares (about half the total) deposited with them by customers. British banks own less than 1 per cent of all UK equities, and there is no British equivalent to the German security deposit system. British banks do, however, manage substantial funds on behalf of unit trusts, insurance and pension funds, charities, and wealthy individuals. They can exercise voting rights in respect of shares owned by these funds, but the proportion of all voting rights which they control is probably less than half that controlled by German banks.

It is quite common in Britain (though less so than in Germany) for one person to sit on the board of a bank and of one or more industrial companies. In Germany, however, it is generally full-time bankers who sit as members of part-time supervisory boards of industrial and commercial companies; in Britain it is usually a case of full-time industrialists being invited to act as part-time directors of banks.

There is no doubt that German banks have greater potential power than British banks over industrial and commercial companies, but we found no evidence that this potential was actually used to influence long-term corporate planning, still less day to day management, of viable companies. German banks do appear to be rather more willing to mount rescue operations for companies threatened with bankruptcy, and in such cases there may well be a greater involvement with management. In general, however, we found no evidence that British companies have suffered from their relatively "arm's length" relationship with their bankers, and we certainly do not believe that differences of this kind can have any bearing on the relative performance of the two economies.

Small firms

There is no generally accepted definition of "small" in this context, and banks do not record their lending according to any measure of customer size. It is impossible, therefore, to produce comparable statistics for bank lending to small firms, but it is quite clear that such lending is much larger, both in absolute terms, and as a proportion of all lending, in Germany. This is partly because of the greater importance of small business in the German economy, but differences in structure between the two systems are also relevant. Lending to small firms is done more by savings banks and co-operative banks than by the big commercial banks, and there is, as one would expect, a relationship between size of bank and size of loan. We believe that the existence of a large number of small local savings banks and co-operative banks, each centred in its locality, has been generally helpful to small firms.

German credit guarantee associations have no counterpart in the UK, though they have in some other countries. They have been criticised for bureaucracy and excessive caution and they certainly cover only a small fraction (we estimate about 0.3 per cent) of all bank lending to the "Mittelstand". However they are more important in relation to the very small firms of the "Handwerk" sector.

Subsidies on loans to small firms through the banking system are available both from federal funds and from the Länder, but they appear to apply only to about 3 per cent of all lending to the "Mittelstand".

Banks and public sector finance

Both Britain and Germany have experienced large public sector financial deficits since the early seventies. These have generally been greater in proportion to national income, though not always in absolute amount, in Britain. There have been marked differences in the way in which deficits have been financed and in the involvement of the banking system.

British borrowing has been much more centralised, with the central government covering its own needs, almost all those of the public corporations, and a large part of those of local authorities. In Germany the central government, the two major public corporations (the railways and the post office), and individual Länder and local authorities all make their own arrangements.

In the decade 1970-1979, the federal government raised over 60 per cent of its loans from banks, the Länder governments over 80 per cent, and local authorities over 100 per cent (making net repayments of other debt). The British government, particularly since 1971, has tried to minimise its bank borrowing by selling long-term debt to the non-bank private sector, and the proportion borrowed from the banks over the decade as a whole was less than 30 per cent.

Despite this difference the impact of public sector borrowing on the money supply has been a chronic problem in Britain, whereas no such worries appear to have arisen in Germany. We believe this is mainly due to three reasons: first, the smaller size of the German deficit in relation to national income; secondly, the power of the German banking system, already noted, to mobilise large amounts of medium-term savings; and thirdly, differences in techniques of monetary control. In the UK bank lending to the government is largely in the form of Treasury bills and very short-dated government bonds, which form "reserve assets" and so enhance the power of the banks to lend also to the private sector. In Germany, bank reserves are in the form of balances with the Bundesbank, so that lending to the public sector does not have this effect.

Banks and capital markets

British short-term capital markets are much more highly developed than those of Germany and are dominated by the banks. The reasons for the relative lack of such markets in Germany are largely in the structural differences already noted; the regional organisation of the Bundesbank, and the facilities provided for members by the central institutions of the savings banks and co-operative banks which reduce the need for organised markets in short-term assets.

Nevertheless British banks probably enjoy better facilities than banks in Germany, and most other countries, for maintaining liquidity without sacrificing income, and for matching the maturity pattern of assets and liabilities. The markets do, however, pose some problems for the monetary authorities in relation to the liquidity of the system as a whole.

The German banks are much more involved than their British counterparts in both the primary and secondary markets for long-term securities. In the primary market the costs of new issues in the two countries appear to be very similar. In the secondary market the British system of "single capacity" seems to have advantages in avoiding potential conflicts of interest, maintaining a continuous market and enabling some bargains to be made that would be difficult or impossible under the German system.

The British secondary market has been compared unfavourably with the German for its alleged "over activity" and volatility, but such comparisons are based largely on misunderstanding. An implication of "single capacity" is that bargains are marked twice, one when a jobber buys and once when he sells; if allowance is made for this, turnover rates in equities are very similar in the two countries. Turnover in British government securities is high, but this is mainly due to the techniques of debt management operated by the Bank of England.

It is difficult to measure "volatility", but an examination of cyclical movements in share prices shows that the number of cylces has been roughly the same in the two countries, but the amplitude of fluctuations has been rather greater in the UK. We believe that this can be largely explained by the greater variations in inflation rates, interest rates and government policy in Britain, but the German banks' policy of supporting the shares of companies for which they act as banker may have had a stabilising influence.

Monetary policy and inflation

It is well known that, over the past twenty years, Britain has had one of the highest inflation rates among developed industrial countries, and Germany one of the lowest. The causal relationship between money and inflation is still a matter of controversy, but the German authorities have generally shown a greater determination to control inflation and a stronger belief in the need to control the growth of the money stock as a means to that end.

Monetary expansion has been more rapid in Britain than in Germany, but the difference has been less than the difference in inflation rates. Hence, the "velocity of circulation" of money (the ratio of national income to the money stock) has risen in Britain and fallen in Germany. Between the early sixties and the late seventies the ratio of GNP to the broadly defined money stock, M_3, rose from about 2.8 to 3.2 in Britain and fell from 2.6 to 2.0 in Germany. A rise in the velocity of circulation implies a fall in "demand for money" (i.e. the amount, relative to its income, that the public wishes to hold in money balances). The contrasting experience of the two countries may be largely due to the higher interest rates prevailing in Britain, but the differences in the degree of bank competition for savings already mentioned may also have played a part.

The attempts of the Deutsche Bundesbank to control
the expansion of the German money stock have been hampered
during much of the period under study by strong inflows of
money from abroad. For this and other reasons the
Bundesbank has now always attained its monetary targets but
it has been more successful in this respect than has the
Bank of England. We believe that this is due partly to
the higher priority given to monetary restraint by German
politicians and public opinion, and partly to differences
in the methods of operation of the two central banks.

The difference in the form in which commercial
banks have to hold required reserves has already been
mentioned. There are many other differences between the
instruments used by the two central banks and in their
methods of operation, which are discussed in Chapters 1,
2 and 9. It must also be borne in mind that the two banks
operate in very different systems of financial markets, so
it does not necessarily follow that methods that work well
in one setting would transplant successfully to the other.
Within its own setting, however, the Bundesbank has exerted
a more effective influence in the growth of the money stock
than has the Bank of England.

Banking supervision

Germany has had a formal system of banking supervision
since 1934, which is operated by a supervisory authority
independent of, though working closely with, the Bundesbank.
In Britain the Bank of England has for a long time kept an
informal watch on the banking system but a formal process of
supervision is only now being worked out following the passage
of the 1979 Banking Act. Both countries have responded to
the growing complexity and increasing risks of banking by
laying down standards for capital, liquidity, and foreign
exchange exposure. The British rules have still not been
fully worked out but it seems likely that the system will be
rather less formal than the German. The main types of German

banks have recently established, through their respective
associations, schemes of mutual self-help to prevent bank
failures. No formal scheme of this kind operates in Britain,
though the Bank of England has organised 'ad hoc' support
operations such as the 1973-74 "lifeboat", when they have
been needed. The mutual support arrangements in Germany
largely eliminate the need for deposit insurance; neither country
has an insurance scheme at present, though one will shortly
be set up in Britain under the provisions of the 1979 Act.

Conclusions

Many of the differences between the British and German
systems are the results of adaptation to differences in
economic and political environment, and some of the
criticisms of the British system that have been made seem
by us misplaced. British banks can no longer be fairly
criticised for putting too little of their resources into
medium-term lending, and British industry does not seem to
be at a disadvantage in relation to the cost of borrowing
or the lending criteria operated by the banks. German banks,
because of their "universality", have closer contacts with
their industrial customers than do their British counterparts,
but German industry does not derive any great advantages, and
suffers some disadvantages, from this relationship. Finally,
in spite of the big differences in bank control of equity,
voting rights, and board membership, we found no evidence of
either British or German banks attempting to influence the
normal management decisions of industry.

Both long-term and short-term capital markets are
generally more developed in the UK and we believe that this
is an advantage to banks, industry, and the public. On
the other hand German banks seem to have been more active in
competition among themselves and with other institutions
for household savings and have been conspicuously successful
in attracting savings into medium-term saving accounts and
bonds. This has enabled the banking system to undertake a

large volume of lending both to industry and government without
an undue expansion of the money stock, and may also have
helped to bring about a fall in the velocity of circulation.
The German authorities and German public opinion have given
a higher priority to the control of inflation, and have shown
a clearer recognition that the control of inflation requires
restraint of the rate of growth of the money stock. Finally
the Deutsche Bundesbank seems to us to have used the available
instruments of monetary control more effectively than the
Bank of England. In these ways differences in the two
banking systems seem to us to have had an important bearing
on the different course of inflation in the two countries.

CHAPTER 1: THE STRUCTURE OF THE UK BANKING SYSTEM
By E. Victor Morgan

1. DEFINITIONS

Until the passage of the 1979 Banking Act, there had
been no general legal definition of a bank, though a number
of administrative definitions had evolved, e.g. for exchange
control, for the operation of reserve asset requirements and
for the compilation of statistics. The 1979 Act defines
deposits and provides that deposits may only be accepted by
firms or institutions in one of three categories:-

> Banks,
>
> Other licenced deposit-taking institutions, and
>
> Members of exempted categories, which include
> savings banks, building societies, local authorities
> and stockbrokers.

The Bank of England is required to compile a register of
banks, and is also responsible for licencing other deposit-
taking institutions. The Act lays down guidelines that the
Bank shall take account of when deciding whether or not to
register an institution as a bank. These include having a
"high reputation and standing in the financial community";
providing, "either a wide range of banking services, or a
highly specialised banking service"; and meeting minimum
requirements as to net assets.

The main banking statistics published in the Bank of
England's Quarterly Bulletin under the heading "Banks in the
United Kingdom" relate to all banks that observe the current
12.5 per cent reserve ratio. The "banking sector" as defined
for national accounts purposes and some Bank of England
statistics includes the "Banking Department" of the Bank of
England and firms in the London Discount Market. Both of
these definitions exclude a large number of other
institutions that accept deposits from the public and which
would be classified as banks in Germany.

TABLE 1.1: DISTRIBUTION OF DEPOSITS BETWEEN BANKS AND OTHER
INSTITUTIONS £m. Dec.

Percentages of total in brackets

	1962	1971	1976 [3]	1980 (Sep)
BANKS [1]				
London clearing banks	7,168 (44.4)	10,779 (31.9)	21,760 (31.4)	36,198 (29.5)
Scottish clearing banks and N. Ireland banks	886 (5.4)	1,348 (4.0)	2,929 (4.2)	4,972 (4.1)
Other banks in UK [2]	431 (2.7)	2,994 (8.9)	8,635 (12.5)	18,042 (12.3)
TOTAL BANKS	8,485 (52.5)	15,121 (44.8)	33,324 (48.2)	59,212 (48.2)
Building societies	3,510 (21.7)	12,176 (36.1)	26,271 (38.0)	47,334 (38.6)
National Savings Bank	1,760 (10.9)	1,831 (5.4)	2,199 (3.2)	3,449 (2.9)
Trustee Savings Banks	1,529 (9.5)	2,797 (8.3)	4,217 (6.1)	5,442 (4.4)
Local authorities	662 (4.1)	1,300 (3.8)	2,868 (4.1)	6,121 (5.0)
Finance houses	202 (1.3)	548 (1.6)	317 (0.5)	1,244 (1.0)
TOTAL	16,148	33,773	69,196	122,802

Note: 1. For 1962, "current and deposit accounts"; subsequently
sterling deposits of UK non-bank residents.

2. Including National Giro.

3. Coverage of series increased in 1976.

Source: Committee of London Clearing Bankers' Stage 1 evidence to
Wilson Committee, Table 1 and Financial Statistics.

Table 1.1 based on evidence submitted to the Committee to Review the Functioning of Financial Institutions (Wilson Committee) shows the relative positions of banks and other deposit taking institutions. Salient features of the Table are:

-   More than half of all deposits are in the hands of institutions not classified as banks. During the 1960's the banks were growing more slowly than other institutions and their share of deposits was falling, but this trend has been reversed since the change in monetary policy in 1971.

-   Much of the growth in banking since 1971 has been in the "other banks" group.

-   The building societies have maintained a very rapid growth rate.

This Chapter first considers the institutions classified by the Bank of England as banks. This is followed by a brief description of other deposit taking institutions; of the discount houses; and of the various short-term financial markets in the banking system. Finally, we outline briefly the role of the Bank of England as the central bank.

2.   BANKS IN THE UNITED KINGDOM

The Bank of England, since 1975, publishes balance-sheet figures for banks in the UK in the nine groups shown in Tables 1.2-1.4. Table 1.2 shows gross deposits of each group in sterling and in other currencies, and Table 1.3 shows deposits net of inter-bank deposits. An outstanding feature of the Tables is the importance of foreign currency business; gross deposits in overseas currencies are more than double the value of sterling deposits. The foreign currency business of London has been growing very rapidly in the past twenty years, and the figures have also been swollen at times by the depreciation of sterling, since foreign currencies are converted into sterling (for statistical purposes) at the current exchange rate. Foreign currency business, though subject to general surveillance by the Bank of England, is

TABLE 1.2: BANKS IN THE UK DEPOSITS 15/10/80

	STERLING		OTHER CURRENCY	
	£m	Per cent of total	£m	Per cent of total
BRITISH BANKS				
London clearing banks	41,183	47.3	10,664	5.8
Scottish clearing banks	4,691	5.4	1,315	0.7
N. Ireland banks	1,339	1.5	13	–
Accepting houses	4,837	5.6	5,983	3.2
Other	16,442	18.9	21,441	11.2
	68,492	78.7	39,416	21.5
OVERSEAS BANKS				
American	8,469	9.7	50,505	27.3
Japanese	824	0.9	37,153	20.1
Other	8,249	9.5	48,441	26.2
	17,542	20.1	136,099	73.6
Consortium banks	1,050	1.2	9,528	5.1
	87,084		185,042	

Source: Bank of England Quarterly Bulletin, Dec. 1980, Table 3.

TABLE 1.3: BANKS IN THE UK DEPOSITS (EXCLUDING INTER-BANK) 15/10/80

	STERLING		OTHER CURRENCIES	
	£m	Per cent of total	£m	Per cent of total
BRITISH BANKS				
London clearing banks	39,605	56.3	8,883	6.2
Scottish clearing banks	4,526	6.4	802	0.6
N. Ireland banks	815	1.2	5	-
Accepting houses	3,588	5.1	4,120	2.9
Other	10,870	15.5	15,016	10.4
	59,404	84.5	28,826	20.0
OVERSEAS BANKS				
American	5,313	7.6	41,262	30.7
Japanese	239	0.3	26,538	18.4
Other	4,899	7.0	38,838	26.9
	10,451	14.9	109,638	76.0
Consortium banks	450	0.6	5,832	4.0
	70,305		114,085	

Source: Bank of England <u>Quarterly Bulletin</u>, Dec. 1980, Table 3.

not subject to reserve ratios and other instructions of monetary policy that apply to sterling business. Since the main object of this study is to compare the domestic operations of the UK and German systems, we shall be only indirectly concerned with foreign currency business.

Comparison of Tables 1.2 and 1.3 shows that over 20 per cent of deposits are held by one bank with another. Some of these holdings arise simply for working convenience; e.g. non-clearing banks usually hold working balances with a clearer who handles their cheques. However, most of them are "bought" in the various money markets described on pages 25 - 30 below. On the whole, overseas banks use these markets rather more than British banks and the London clearing banks use them less than others. Hence Table 1.3 shows British banks having 84.5 per cent of non-bank sterling deposits against only 78.7 per cent of total deposits in Table 1.2. The London clearing banks have less than half of total deposits but 56 per cent of non-bank deposits.

Table 1.4 shows the advances of the nine groups and it is clear that their market shares do not differ greatly from those of non-bank deposits. Whatever measure is used the clearing banks still have much the largest share of sterling business.

The Clearing Banks

The Radcliffe Report (1959) stated that "nearly all the domestic banking business of England and Wales is in the hands of the eleven banks that are members of the London Bankers' Clearing House".[1] A number of important changes have occurred during the past 20 years.

---

1. Committee on the Working of the Monetary System, HMSO, London 1959, Cmnd. 827 paragraph 126.

TABLE 1.4: BANKS IN THE UNITED KINGDOM STERLING ADVANCES 15/10/80

	£m	Per cent of total
BRITISH BANKS		
London clearing banks	29,868	55.6
Scottish banks	3,694	6.9
N. Ireland banks	874	1.6
Accepting houses	1,890	3.5
Other	7,876	14.6
	44,202	82.3
OVERSEAS BANKS		
American	5,119	9.5
Japanese	528	1.0
Other	3,322	6.2
	8,969	16.7
Consortium banks	541	1.0
	38,744	

Source: Bank of England _Quarterly Bulletin_, June 1979,
         Table 3.

Firstly, a series of mergers has reduced the eleven banks to six, of which one (Coutts & Co.) is very small and is a subsidiary of National Westminster. A similar merger movement has occurred in Scotland, where the number of banks has been reduced from six to three. One Scottish bank (Clydesdale) is wholly owned by the Midland, while Williams and Glyn's (the smallest of the London clearers, apart from Coutts) is owned by the Scottish National and Commercial Banking Group. Lloyds Bank have a minority shareholding in the National and Commercial Banking Group and Barclays in the Bank of Scotland. Of the four banks operating in Northern Ireland two have headquarters in the Republic and the other two are owned respectively by Midland and National Westminster.

Secondly, the Clearing Banks have had to face growing competition in domestic business from other British banks and from a rapidly growing number of overseas banks with branches in London. Changes in statistical definitions make it impossible to calculate the resulting loss of market share precisely but sterling deposits held by the Clearing Banks themselves fell from about 85 per cent of all UK bank deposits in the early 1960's to under 63 per cent in 1973. There was a sharp recovery in 1974 followed by gradual decline to about 58 per cent in 1979.

Thirdly, the Clearing Banks reacted, as will be shown in subsequent Chapters, both by increasing the range of services offered within the parent company and by acquiring or forming subsidiaries. At the time of the Clearing Banks Stage One evidence to the Wilson Committee (December 1976), deposits with these subsidiaries formed about 20 per cent of the group total.

The Clearing Banks are (apart from the Bank of England) the oldest element in the UK banking system. Some of them can trace an ancestry back to the 17th Century and most to the early nineteenth Century. The English banks started as small local institutions and expanded to their present position partly by internal growth but mainly by amalgamations.

The Clearing Banks have three important and closely related characteristics that distinguish them from the rest of the system. They operate nationwide branch networks; they administer the national payments system by clearing cheques and by taking-in and paying-out notes and coin; and they accept deposits in very small as well as large amounts. Hence, these operations are often called "retail banking".

The terminology used to describe deposits is rather confusing, partly because of the need to adapt to rapid changes of practice. The official statistics published by the Bank of England now refer only to "sight deposits" and "time deposits". The banks themselves, in their evidence to the Wilson Committee, distinguish between "branch retail deposits" and "wholesale deposits". Retail deposits comprise "current accounts" (sight deposits) that can be withdrawn on demand, and on which no interest is paid, and "deposit accounts", on which interest is paid and which formally require 7 days notice of withdrawal.[1] However, "it is currently normal in practice for the banks to waive this requirement, adjusting interest payments in lieu of notice".[2] Wholesale deposits comprise larger amounts committed for a longer time and either deposited directly with the banks or acquired through the market.

The interest cost of branch retail deposits is much lower than that of wholesale deposits since interest on deposit accounts is below money market rates and no interest at all is paid on current accounts, though customers keeping a sufficient credit balance are relieved of normal charges for the management of their account. This effect on the Clearing Banks' costs is sometimes called an "endowment" effect. Against the benefits of "endowment" have to be set the costs of maintaining the branch network (less branch revenue from charges) and of keeping some £800m. of notes

1. The Scottish banks have slightly different definitions.
2. Wilson Committee Evidence on the Financing of Industry and Trade, HMSO, London 1978, Vol. 3 p.118.

and coin in branch safes and tills. Whether the real cost
of branch deposits is, on average, lower than that of
wholesale deposits is doubtful. What is certain is that
their relative cost varies with the level of interest rates.
Since a large part of the cost of retail deposits is
invariant to interest rate changes the "endowment effect" is
more valuable when money is dear than when it is cheap.
Hence the competitive position of the Clearing Banks against
others who have no retail deposits is strongest in periods
of high interest rates.

The evidence of the Committee of London Clearing Bankers
to the Wilson Committee shows that branch retail deposits have
been growing less rapidly than the rise in prices. Between
1972 and 1976 the rise was only 157 per cent compared with
a rise of 201 per cent in the index of retail prices. The
ratio of current to deposit accounts within the total varies
with interest rates but there has been a strong downward
trend; in the three years 1962-64 current accounts formed
61.8 per cent of all retail deposits; in 1974-76 only
33.8 per cent. Wholesale deposits have been growing much
faster than retail deposits and, by 1976, they accounted for
over 40 per cent of all sterling deposits of the London
Clearing Banks.

The banks' evidence to the Wilson Committee gives some
information not previously available about the maturity
structure of deposits. On 16th February 1977 the
percentage distribution for the parent banks and their
subsidiaries was as follows:

	Per cent of total
Sight	39
Less than 8 days	37
8 days - 3 months	16
3 - 12 months	6
Over 12 months	2

Little information is available about the maturity structure
of non-clearing bank deposits (which are largely wholesale)
but the Wilson Report states that "three-quarters of

wholesale deposits have a maturity of less than three months, and only about 5 per cent of such deposits are for periods in excess of one year".[1] The relative lack of medium-term deposits seems to be a significant feature of the UK compared to Germany.

Information about the sources of deposits by sector is only available for the banking system as a whole (see page 41 and Table 1.12).

The main sterling assets of the London Clearing Banks are shown in Table 1.5. Direct lending to the public sector takes place by the purchase of Treasury bills, by the making of loans to local authorities, through the market by investments in government securities, and by advances. In addition the banks' holdings of notes and coin, balances with the Bank of England, and Special Deposits represent indirect lending to the government, and part of call money and other market loans is on-lent to the public sector through the discount market and other banks. Direct lending to the private sector is represented in the Table by discounts of "other bills" and by advances, and again there is some on-lending by other banks and by discount houses.

There have been some major changes in lending over the past 20 years. Again statistical difficulties preclude exact measurement but the broad pattern is plain. The most dramatic change has been the rise in the relative importance of advances from about 30 per cent of sterling lending at the time of the Radcliffe Report to about 68 per cent. Market loans have increased in importance with the growth of the various "secondary" money markets (see pages 25-30) and there has been a significant, though limited, revival in the use of commercial bills. There has also been a rise in the item described as "other investments" linked with the growth of subsidiary companies.

---

1. Report of Committee to Review the Functioning of Financial Institutions (hereafter referred to as the Wilson Committee) Cmnd 7937. HMSO London, June 1980.

TABLE 1.5: STERLING ASSETS OF LONDON CLEARING BANKS 15/10/80

	£m	Per cent of total
Notes and coin	885	2.0
Balances with Bank of England	483	1.1
Special deposits and supplementary special deposits	-	-
Call money	2, 22	4.8
Other market loans:		
UK banks (including sterling CDs)	5,690	13.0
Local authorities	391	0.9
Other (including overseas)	105	0.2
Bills:		
.Treasury bills	454	1.0
Other bills	1,095	2.5
Investments:		
UK government securities	1,108	2.5
Other	1,683	3.8
Advances:		
UK public sector	403	0.9
UK private sector	26,535	60.5
Overseas	2,930	6.7
	43,884	

Source: Bank of England Quarterly Bulletin, Table 3.2.

The counterpart to these increases has been a sharp decline in the relative importance of Treasury bills and government securities. The former have fallen from around 17 per cent of total lending at the time of the Radcliffe Report to only about 1 per cent, and the latter from about 28 per cent to 2.5 per cent.

These changes reflect a marked change in the role of bank finance as between the public and private sectors. From the early post-war years until the late 1960's lending to the private sector was generally restricted by quantitative controls, but no such constraints were imposed on public sector borrowing. Since 1971 quantitative restrictions have been removed and, though there are no formal rules, the authorities have made increasingly successful efforts to finance public borrowing by the sale of securities to non-bank holders. As a result direct lending to the public sector now forms only about 8 per cent of the clearing banks' sterling assets compared with about 45 per cent twenty years ago. The corresponding figure for direct lending to the UK private sector has risen from about 30 per cent to 63 per cent.

The Bank of England's quarterly analysis of bank advances relates to the system as a whole, but the clearing banks gave figures (including subsidiaries) to the Wilson Committee. The percentage of sterling advances to the UK private sector (other than banks) going to the main categories of economic activity in 1976 were:

	Per cent of total
Manufacturing	27.3
Other production	13.5
Services	24.8
Financial	13.9
Personal	20.4

The main instrument of lending is the overdraft, though there has been a substantial growth of term lending both directly by the clearing banks and through their subsidiaries over the past ten years. As already stated, there has also

been a revival of bill finance. Here the clearing banks
contribute both by purchasing commercial bills (shown in
Table 1.5) and granting acceptance credits. In giving an
acceptance credit a bank, in effect, guarantees a loan
rather than actually making it so that acceptances are shown
as an "off balance-sheet" item. The clearing banks provide
finance through their subsidiaries by hire purchase, leasing,
and factoring, and also operate unit trusts. (These matters
will be discussed in more detail in Chapter 4).

Wholesale Banks

The term "wholesale banks", though not an official one,
is now widely used to describe British banks other than the
London and Scottish clearers and the Northern Ireland banks,
and overseas banks. Their figures are reported under the
last six headings of Tables 1.2-1.4.

In many ways the most distinctive group are the
accepting houses. Most of these firms had their origin in
19th Century merchant houses which had obtained a high
reputation as traders and whose bills could therefore be
discounted at favourable rates. They began their financial
business by accepting bills (in return for a commission) on
behalf of less well-known traders; from this base they
expanded it into a variety of banking businesses and their
trading activities were gradually abandoned.

Accepting houses now have three major activities which
are normally organised in separate divisions:

    Banking
    Corporate finance, and
    Fund management.

Their banking business is broadly similar to that of other
wholesale banks, though acceptance business is still more
important than for other banks, and about half of all private
sector bills in the market bear their names. They have

also played a prominent part in organising syndicated loans
in which a number of banks contribute to the finance of
large projects. Their corporate finance activities include
financial advice to companies, the negotiation of mergers
and take-overs,and the arrangement of new security issues.
As fund managers, accepting houses manage security portfolios
on behalf of pension funds, charities,and wealthy individuals,
and also operate unit trusts. Some merchant banks also
provide finance through leasing and factoring (generally
through subsidiary companies) and some also have subsidiaries
providing "venture capital" for small firms. Only the banking
activities of accepting houses are subject to reserve
requirements and are covered in the Bank of England statistics.

Until 1972 the Bank of England was opposed to mergers
between the accepting houses and clearing banks. This official
discouragement was withdrawn in 1972 but the change has, so
far, had little effect. One member of the Accepting Houses
Committee, Samuel Montagu & Co., is owned by the Midland
Bank, but the other clearers have preferred to develop their
own merchant banking subsidiaries.

The group described as "other British Banks" comprises
the subsidiaries of the clearing banks specialising in
wholesale banking and in international business,together
with a number of smaller wholesale banks that are not members
of the Accepting Houses Committee. Sterling assets of
accepting houses and other British banks are shown in
Table 1.6.

A few European and American banks have had branches
in London since the 19th Century, but the major expansion
in their numbers and the volume of their business has
occurred in the past 20 years. At the end of 1950 there
were only 53 branches and representative offices of overseas
banks - by 1960 the figure had risen to only 77, but by 1976
it was 255. Approximately 240 foreign banks are currently
listed by the Bank of England.

The growth of overseas banking has been closely linked
to the development of the Euro-currency markets and to the
growth of multinational companies in industry and trade. A
substantial part of the sterling operations of overseas
banks in the UK consists of providing banking services to UK
branches or subsidiaries of overseas companies, but they are
participating to an increasing extent in ordinary
domestic business. In some directions they have brought new
techniques and new attitudes which have influenced their
British competitors, and so have an importance greater than
their actual share of business.

A very recent development is shown in the last group
of the Bank of England statistics - consortium banks. These
are banks that are owned by a group of other banks usually
drawn from several different countries.

Despite their diversity of origin, wholesale banks
have a large number of features in common, many of which
can be seen in Tables 1.2-1.4, and in Tables 1.6 and 1.7,
which show the sterling assets of British and overseas
wholesale banks. Their main characteristics can be
summarised as follows:

> Foreign currency business forms by far the largest
> part of their activities, especially for overseas
> banks. Table 1.3 shows that British wholesale
> banks held about £14 bn. of sterling non-bank deposits
> and £19 bn. of foreign currency deposits. For
> overseas banks the figures were £10bn. and £110 bn.
> Banks can switch foreign currency deposits into
> sterling and vice-versa, so that the amount of
> their sterling lending need not coincide with the
> amount of their sterling deposits. This is one of
> the ways in which the UK may either borrow from or
> lend to other countries.

> Wholesale banks are not members of the Clearing House
> and play very little part in the domestic payments
> system. The limited cheque-paying facilities that
> they provide are operated through accounts with the
> clearing banks.

TABLE 1.6: STERLING ASSETS OF ACCEPTING HOUSES AND OTHER
           BRITISH BANKS 15/10/80

	£m	Per cent of total
Notes and coin	31	0.1
Balances with Bank of England	9	-
Special deposits and supplementary special deposits	-	-
Call money	1,118	4.6
Other market loans:		
UK banks (including sterling CDs)	7,733	31.9
Local authorities	1,975	8.2
Other (including overseas)	1,417	5.8
Bills:		
Treasury bills	207	0.9
Other bills	499	2.1
Investments:		
UK government securities	837	3.5
Other	665	2.7
Advances:		
UK public sector	327	.3
UK private sector	8,879	36.6
Overseas	560	2.3
TOTAL	24,257	

Source: Bank of England Quarterly Bulletin, Dec. 1980, Tables 3.5 and 3.6.

TABLE 1.7: STERLING ASSETS OF OVERSEAS BANKS 15/10/80

	£m	Per cent of total
Notes and coin	12	-
Balances with Bank of England	3	-
Special and supplementary deposits	-	-
Call money	1,137	6.1
Other market loans:		
UK banks (including sterling CDs)	4,816	25.8
Local authorities	1,265	6.8
Other (including overseas)	1,167	6.2
Bills:		
Treasury bills	319	1.7
Other bills	338	1.8
Investments:		
UK government securities	441	2.4
Other	223	1.2
Advances:		
UK public sector	1,062	5.7
UK private sector	7,208	38.6
Other	699	3.7
TOTAL	18,690	

Source: Bank of England Quarterly Bulletin, Dec. 1980, Tables 3.7 to 3.9.

Nearly all of them operate from London and, though a few have a small number of branches, they make no attempt to maintain a national branch network.

These characteristics imply that wholesale banks do not need large amounts either of notes and coin or balances with the Bank of England, and Tables 1.6 and 1.7 show that their holdings are very small in relation to those of the clearers.

Deposits are taken in relatively large amounts and so
come mainly from companies rather than individuals.
Sight deposits are a small proportion of the total,
only about 17 per cent compared with 40 per cent for
the clearers. Time deposits are generally of fixed
term and, though maturity statistics are not available,
the average term is generally believed to be longer
than for the clearers.

As can be seen from Tables 1.6 and 1.7, the wholesale
banks make very extensive use of the inter-bank loan
market and of certificates of deposit, and also have
substantial funds on temporary loan to local
authorities.

Relative   to the clearers, wholesale banks are more
important in advances to the public sector, but
advances to the private sector are comparatively small
37 per cent of sterling assets for British banks and
39 per cent for overseas banks, compared with 60 per
cent for the London clearing banks.

Statistics of advances by maturity are not available
but it is generally accepted that they comprise a
smaller proportion of overdrafts and a larger
proportion of medium term loans than those of the
clearers.

3.   OTHER DEPOSIT-TAKING INSTITUTIONS

Building Societies

     As shown in Table 1.1 the resources of building
societies have grown more rapidly than those of any other
deposit-taking institutions except wholesale banks over the
past two decades. The societies are a form of savings
bank specialising in the finance of house purchase. The
first building society is said to have been founded by a
Birmingham publican in 1775 but the movement has its roots
in the striving for mutual self-help among skilled workers
in the Industrial Revolution, which also produced the
trustee savings banks, the co-operative movement, the
friendly societies,and the craft unions. These origins are
still reflected in the fact that the societies operate under
the supervision of the Chief Registrar of Friendly Societies,
whose reports are a main source of statistical information.

The number of societies has been falling steadily,
mainly as a result of mergers, from nearly 2,800 in 1890
to 480 in 1970 and 326 in 1978. They range from large
organisations with a nationwide branch network to tiny ones
operating from single offices in small provincial towns.
The five largest societies account for rather over half of
total resources. The societies are, like other friendly
societies, mutual non-profit organisations and any surplus,
after paying management expenses and tax, is credited to
reserve. The gap between borrowing and lending rates is
set at the minimum regarded as necessary to cover expenses
and maintain reserves at a prudent level.

The main liabilities of the societies are "shares"
and "deposits". The technical difference between them is
that "shareholders" are legally members of the society
whereas "depositors" are creditors. Depositors would,
therefore, take precedence for repayment if a society went
into liquidation, and so they receive a slightly lower rate
of interest. Deposits form less than 4 per cent of total
liabilities, and shares are virtually equivalent to deposits
in other institutions. They form a highly liquid asset.
Where notice of withdrawal is formally required it is
frequently waived and, in practice, amounts up to £100 can be
withdrawn on demand, and larger sums within a few days.
However, some societies have recently sought longer-term
funds by offering shares and bonds for fixed periods of up
to five years.

Over 99 per cent of shares and deposits come from the
personal sector, and about 80 per cent of resources are employed
in housing finance, nearly all of it in mortgage loans to
the personal sector. Housing finance is also available from
banks, insurance companies, and local authorities, but the
building societies dominate the market, providing nearly 83
per cent of lending for house purchase to the personal
sector in 1979. The remaining assets of the societies,

apart from premises and cash, are distributed between deposits
with, and mortgages of, local authorities and short- and
medium-term government securities (see Table 1.8).

This concentration of housing finance in the hands
of the building societies means that it is largely
separate from other financial markets, though it cannot be
insulated from them. The societies are in competition with
other institutions in the markets for gilt-edged stock and
local authority debt but the main point of contact with the
rest of the financial system is in competition for deposits.

The Building Societies Association makes recommendations
on the rates that societies should pay on shares and deposits
and charge on mortgages. However, only 228 of the 326
societies are members of the association; the recommendations
are not mandatory and a substantial minority of members
either do not comply or do so only after considerable delay.
The recommended rate has recently come in for some criticism
and the Wilson Committee has recommended its abolition.

Building society rates are generally "sticky", partly
because of the administrative problems of changing rates on
about 20 million share accounts and over 4½ million mortgage
accounts. When the societies lag behind rates in more
volatile sections of the market, the inflow of new money
falls off and new mortgages are 'rationed'. There has been
a more general reluctance to raise rates to the high levels
of recent years (partly because of government pressure) and
the tendency for the supply of funds to fall short of demand
has become chronic. Many societies keep demand in line with
their available resources by imposing conditions on loans,
e.g. that borrowers must have saved with the society for a
certain time or accumulated a minimum balance.

The societies are not subject to reserve requirements
or any of the other controls imposed on the banking system,
but the movement has been increasingly subject to informal
pressure from government. Mortgage rates are politically

TABLE 1.8: BUILDING SOCIETIES LIABILITIES AND ASSETS END- 1977

LIABILITIES	£m	Per cent	ASSETS	£m	Per cent
Shares and deposits:			Mortgages	36,986	80.2
To persons	42,422	92.0	Short-term assets	2,470	5.4
Other	349	0.8	Government securities	4,027	8.7
Reserves	1,634	3.5	L.A. long-term debt	1,783	3.9
Other[1]	1,701	3.7	Other[2]	860	1.9
	46,126			46,126	

Note: 1. Including accrued interest

2. Excluding land building and equipment, £441m. at end-1977.

Source: Financial Statistics, Dec. 1980, Table 8.7.

sensitive and governments have tried to minimise increases.
They have also tried at times to influence the volume of
lending as a means of influencing house prices and the
construction industry; for example, in 1978,societies were
urged to restrain their lending in the hope of checking a
rapid rise in house prices.

Building societies receive special tax treatment which,
though it involves no net cost to the state, gives them some
competitive advantage. Interest is paid to members tax free
and the societies pay tax at what is known as a "composite
rate". This rate is calculated so as to make the total
payment equal to what the revenue would have received if
interest had been paid gross and each recipient taxed at the
appropriate individual rate. About a fifth of building
society share-holders have incomes below the tax exemption
limits so the arrangement has the paradoxical effect of
subsidising better-off members at the expense of the worse
off. It also gives the societies a slight competitive edge
over the banks in competing for the savings of the better-
off section of the community.

Savings banks

The trustee savings banks had their origins in the
second decade of the nineteenth century and, after a century
and a half in which their functions changed little, they are
now undergoing a radical transformation. The original banks
were small local organisations, their operations were
supervised by local boards of trustees, but their funds were
all deposited with the National Debt Commissioners, and
interest and principal were guaranteed by the government.
After 1870 the banks were able to form "special investment"
departments, where they enjoyed greater freedom of investment and could pay rather higher rates of interest.
However, they were still allowed to place funds only in the
public sector, and they offered no overdraft or cheque-
paying facilities.

Acts of Parliament of 1969 and 1976 paved the way for far-reaching changes both in structure and activities. The local banks amalgamated into 17 regional banks which, between them, have about 1,650 branches. A Central Board exercises general powers of supervision and operates a Central Trustee Savings Bank (which acts as banker and clearing agent for the regional banks), a unit trust company, and an insurance company. Cheque book accounts had been introduced in 1968 and in 1976 term deposits for periods of six months to four years, and amounts from £1,000 to £25,000 were accepted. Personal loans and overdrafts were introduced in 1977 and bridging loans for house purchase and loans for home improvement in 1978. In 1979 the banks began to make small commercial loans and they will shortly enter the mortgage business. Other facilities recently offered include cheque cards and credit cards. Over the next few years it is expected that the few remaining restrictions on their activities will be removed and that sums deposited with the National Debt Commissioners will be repaid, enabling the TSBs to participate in the full range of activities performed by the clearing banks. Meanwhile they enjoy exemption under the 1979 Banking Act and are not subject to reserve requirements.

The other major savings bank is the National Savings Bank (formerly the Post Office Savings Bank) founded in 1861. So far it has not gone the way of the TSBs but continues to operate on traditional lines. Its funds are employed wholly in the public sector and it does not provide cheque-paying facilities, though these are available through the National Giro which is also operated by the Post Office.

Finance houses

This is the name given to a group of companies that originally specialised in hire-purchase finance. Some of the oldest began with the finance of railway wagons and then moved on to commercial road vehicles, cars, and consumer

durables. More recently they have moved into other forms
of financing including term-loans, leasing, factoring, and
block discounting. In 1971 several of the larger ones
agreed to conform to the new banking reserve requirements
and have since been classified as banks. Of the remainder
eight large companies not classified as banks have,
nevertheless, agreed with the Bank of England on rather
less stringent reserve requirements, but many small companies
are not subject to this form of control at all.

4.   SHORT-TERM FINANCIAL MARKETS

London's traditional short-term markets, going back to
the early nineteenth century, were in loans at call or short
notice from the banks (the money market) and in bills of
exchange. The main participants in the markets were the
clearing banks and discount houses, with the Bank of England
acting as lender of last resort. The growth of wholesale
banking in the last twenty years has been associated with the
growth of new markets, sometimes called "parallel money
markets". The most important of these are in inter-bank
deposits (both sterling and foreign currency), negotiable
certificates of deposit (both sterling and foreign currency),
and local authority temporary debt. At first the clearing
banks confined themselves largely to the old markets and the
new wholesale banks to the new markets, but now all banks
operate in the whole range of markets though, as already
noted, the wholesale banks still make more use than the
clearers of the inter-bank and C.D. markets. The discount
houses are a key element in all these markets so they will
be described briefly; the salient features of individual
markets will then be noted, and the working of the whole
system will be discussed more fully in Chapter 8.

The discount houses

The statistics relating to discount houses are
presented by the Bank of England under the slightly
misleading heading of "The Discount Market". The figures
cover 11 firms that are members of the London Discount
Market Association together with two "discount brokers" and
the so-called "money trading departments" of five banks.
The brokers do a similar business to the members of the
Association though on a smaller scale. The "money trading"
departments are special sections of the banks in question
that specialise in supplying bills and other short-term
assets to other banks; their activities are kept separate
from the companies' general banking business and their
figures are not included in the banking tables presented
earlier in this chapter.

The main liabilities and assets of the discount market
are shown in Table 1.9. The discount houses take wholesale
deposits from the public, but about 85 per cent of their
borrowed funds are provided by the banks, almost all in
loans repayable overnight or at call. Their assets consist
of bills, funds lent in the parallel money markets,
government securities, mostly in the range of one to five
years to maturity, and local authority securities. The
houses are active dealers in these assets and earn their
living partly from the (very narrow) margin between the
interest rates at which they borrow and lend and partly by
dealing profits. The proportion of different assets in their
portfolio varies considerably from time to time.

TABLE 1.9: DISCOUNT MARKET ASSETS AND BORROWED FUNDS
        15/10/80

	£m
BORROWED FUNDS	
Sterling:	
Bank of England	21
Other UK banking sector	4,482
Other UK	222
Overseas	21
Other currencies	101
TOTAL	4,746
ASSETS	
Sterling:	
Bills:	
Treasury	353
Other public sector	127
Other	2,046
Funds lent:	
UK banking sector	106
CDs	717
Local authorities	145
Other	61
Investments	
Government securities	857
Local authority securities	385
Other	12
Other sterling	13
Other currencies	151
TOTAL	4,869

Source: Bank of England Quarterly Bulletin, Dec. 1980, Table 2

The main functions of the discount houses can be summarised as follows:

i. They act as intermediaries between the Bank of England and the rest of the banking system. In most other countries, including Germany, commercial banks can borrow directly from the central bank. In Britain there is a long tradition that banks do not do this, but instead call in loans from the discount market if they need to replenish their reserves. The discount houses have the right of access to the Bank of England as lender of last resort and, if a bank calls in a loan, and a discount house cannot find another outside lender, it borrows from the Bank of England. The role of the discount houses in relation to monetary management has been somewhat complicated by the reserve asset rules introduced in 1971 and this will be discussed in Chapter 9.

ii. They perform a service to the banks by supplying them with liquid assets of the kind and maturity they need. For example the discount houses portfolio of Treasury bills will range from some that are newly issued and are not due for payment for nearly three months to some that are due in a few days. They will sell any of these at an appropriate price so that banks can adjust the maturity of their own bill portfolios as they wish by purchases from the market. Similar arguments apply to the other assets shown in Table 9.

iii. In relation to government borrowing by the sale of Treasury bills, the discount houses perform the technical function known as "covering the tender". Each week the Bank of England announces the amount of intended sales in the following week's tender and the discount houses put in bids (arranged on a quota system related to their size) the total of which equals the amount on offer. Until 1971 the houses agreed on a common price at which they tendered but since then, each house has fixed its own price. However the Treasury still gets the issue underwritten.

iv. In relation to commercial bills the discount houses have to assess the credit-worthiness of those on whom bills are drawn. In many cases, where bills are accepted by an accepting house or a bank, this presents no problem, but the houses also discount a substantial amount of so-called "trade bills" that do not have a bank acceptance.

v. The discount houses also act as "market-makers". By holding a stock of assets and being willing to deal either way, they tend to be net buyers when there is excess supply in the rest of the market and net sellers when there is excess demand. They thus ensure

that a seller can always find a ready buyer (and
vice-versa) and help to stabilise prices. They
perform this function in the markets for bills,
certificates of deposits,and negotiable local authority
authority bonds. In the early post-war years they
were also important in this respect in the market
for short-term government securities, but their
activities in this market have declined since 1971.

vi.   Finally, the discount houses have subsidiaries that
      act as brokers in the parallel money markets and in
      the foreign exchange market.

The markets

In the market for loans at call and short notice
(often called "the money market") the borrowers are the
discount houses and, to a lesser extent, jobbers on the
Stock Exchange. The lenders are the banks (see Tables 1.5
to 1.7),with the Bank of England as lender of last resort.
A feature of the market is that all loans are secured, the
borrower depositing bills or other securities with the
lender as collateral. Transactions in the market are
settled by drafts on accounts at the Bank of England and
this, together with the Bank's role as lender of last resort,
means that the market is, indirectly, a market in balances
at the central bank. It fulfills the same function, though
in a different way, as the Federal Funds market in New York.

In the market for bills the borrowers are the central
government, local authorities, and companies in the private
sector. The discount houses buy (discount) bills and either
hold them to maturity or re-sell them to banks and others.
Until recently the banks were almost the only purchasers but
non-bank holders now have significant amounts of both
Treasury and commercial bills.

The "parallel money markets" differ from the traditional money market in that loans are all unsecured. In the
inter-bank market, as its name implies, both borrowers and

lenders are banks. The market has two main functions.
Firstly, it enables banks to match the total amount of their
borrowing and lending; a bank that wants to lend more
than the amount of its deposits can "buy" extra deposits in
the market, while a bank that has more deposits than it
wants to lend can "sell". Secondly, it helps banks to match
the maturity structure of loans and deposits; for example,
a bank whose loans were "too long" in relation to its
deposits could lend on short-term and borrow on longer-term
in the market.

The market in certificates of deposit serves a
similar purpose, but with two differences. The existence of
a negotiable certificate, as distinct from a mere book-entry,
means that a lender can recover his money before the deposit
is due for repayment by selling his certificate. Certificates
also provide a convenient liquid asset for non-bank holders
and about 25 per cent of all sterling certificates are held
outside the banking system.

The temporary debt of local authorities, consisting of
deposits with original maturities ranging from overnight to a
year, provides a close substitute for CDs. The banks and
discount houses are substantial holders but so, too, are
savings banks, building societies, other financial
institutions, and industrial and commercial companies.

There are also smaller markets in finance house
deposits and in inter-company loans. The latter is newer
and less highly organised than those described above, and
no statistics are available.

Figures for the volume of assets in the main markets
are given in Table 1.10.

TABLE 1.10: SHORT-TERM STERLING MARKET INSTRUMENTS IN THE U.K.

£m

	1967	end of 1972	1979
Money at call with discount market	1,662	2,530	4,435
Treasury bills	3,156	1,719	2,480
Commercial bills	725	1,188	5,580
Local authority bills)	1,758	240	599
Local authority temporary debt)		2,145	5,135
Deposit with financial houses	591	437	1,117
Inter-bank deposits	1,309	5,068	16,433
Sterling CDS	–	4,934	3,692
Other market loans by banks	–	–	5,314
Total	9,201	18,261	44,785

Source: Wilson Committee Report, Cmnd. 7937, p.510. For reasons explained in detail in the source, figures for earlier years are not strictly comparable with 1979.

5.   THE BANK OF ENGLAND AND MONETARY POLICY

Since 1946 the Bank of England has been state-owned
and the governor and court of directors are appointed by the
Crown, i.e. by the government of the day. The constitutional
position of the bank is in sharp contrast to that of
the Deutsche Bundesbank. The 1946 Bank of England Act
ensures that the Bank shall be subordinate to the Treasury
by providing that, "The Treasury may, from time to time,
issue such directions to the Bank as, after consultation
with the Governor of the Bank, they think necessary in the
public interest". In practice there is a very close working
relationship between senior officials of the Treasury and
the Bank and, so far as is known, the power of direction has
never been used. However, its mere existence ensures that
the government has the last word if any disagreement arises.

The Bank administers the note issue which since 1931
has been inconvertible and since 1939 has been "backed"
only by government securities. The amount of the issue is
fixed by Treasury orders which require the periodic approval
of Parliament but this is given automatically and the actual
amount of notes in circulation varies with the needs of the
public. The issue is handled by a separate department of
the Bank (the Issue Department). This is a relic of the past
when issues above a certain fixed amount had to be backed by
gold, but it is now only an accounting convention. The main
economic significance of the way in which the note issue is
handled is that the Issue Department receives government
securities as "backing" for notes issued. The interest on
these securities, after deducting the expenses of the note
issue, is returned to the Treasury, but the Bank has a
portfolio of more than £7,500 million which it can use in
its debt management operations.

As financial agent for the government the Bank keeps
the Exchequer account, receiving government revenue and
making payments. The size of government transactions is such
that the operation of this account gives the Bank great power

over the money market. The Bank arranges the Treasury bill
tender and the issue of new quoted securities, and maintains
the registers in which holdings of government debt are
recorded. However, the government can borrow from the
public not only by selling newly issued securities but also
by selling from the Bank's own portfolio mentioned in the
last paragraph.

The Bank operates the Exchange Equalisation Account
as agent for the government, holding the central reserve of
gold and foreign currencies and intervening in the foreign
exchange markets when rates deviate from desired levels. It
also undertakes the administration of exchange control regulations.

The responsibility of lender of last resort, which the
Bank has recognised for more than a century, has given it a
long-standing interest in the solvency and liquidity of the
banking system. At first this interest was concentrated
mainly on the accepting houses and the discount market, with
which the Bank has particularly close relations, but it has
now extended in an informal way over the whole banking system
and to the securities industry. Its supervisory role in
relation to the banks is discussed in Chapter 10.

During the difficult times of the late twenties and
early thirties the Bank became directly involved in
providing and arranging financial assistance for firms and
industries that were in trouble, including cotton, steel,
and shipbuilding. This had led to continuing contacts with
industry and to the Bank taking the initiative in a number
of matters e.g. the formation of Finance for Industry and
Equity Capital for Industry and the encouragement of
medium-term lending by the banks.

Though all these functions are important, our main
concern in this chapter is with the Bank's role as the
agent through which the government carries out its monetary
policy. Before describing the instruments of this policy

it is necessary to note an important change in objectives
that has taken place over the past fifteen years. Until the
mid-1960s the government and the Bank (often described
collectively as "the authorities") were not concerned with
regulating the amount of money in circulation but rather
with the level of interest rates and the availability of
credit to the private sector. The level of interest rates
was influenced by the terms on which government securities
were issued and on which sales were made from the Banks'
portfolio, and the volume of bank lending to the private
sector was restrained, when necessary, by direct controls
over the banks. From the late 1960s there was a growing
belief in the importance of regulating the total money
supply, defined for this purpose as notes and coin in the
hands of the public, plus UK residents' sterling deposits
with the banking system (generally known as "sterling M3").
This change culminated in the announcement, in 1976, of a
target rate of expansion for sterling M3, and this target
is now regularly set by the Chancellor of the Exchequer
and announced in his budget speech.

     The movement towards control of the money supply as
the main objective of monetary policy was accompanied by a
growing realisation of the disadvantages of direct controls
over the banks and a desire to stimulate more active
competition. These changes in the climate of opinion led
to a major change in 1971, announced by the Bank of England
in a paper entitled Competition and Credit Control (C.C.C.).
The main changes were in Bank of England operations in the
gilt-edged market, cartel agreements among banks, and
reserve requirements. They can be summarised as follows:-

i.   Prior to 1971 the Bank acted as "jobber of last
        resort" in the gilt-edged market; it was always
        willing to buy government stock at a price of its own
        choosing but which, in fact, did not differ much from
        that ruling in the market. This commitment often
        involved the Bank in purchases which largely offset
        the sale of new securities. Net borrowing by gilt-
        edged sales was thus relatively small, and the
        government was heavily dependent on the banking system.
        In 1971 it was announced that, "the Bank is not

prepared, as a general rule, to buy stock outright except in the case of stocks with one year or less to maturity"[1] The Bank reserves the right to deal either way at its own discretion but, in fact, re-purchases of government stocks have been much smaller; net sales to the non-bank public have been much larger; and, as already noted, the role of the banks in the finance of the public sector has been much reduced.

ii.   Prior to 1971 there had been a number of agreements on interest rates; the clearing banks agreed on maximum rates for deposits, on minimum rates for overdrafts, and on rates charged on certain loans to the discount market; and the discount houses agreed the rate at which they would tender for Treasury bills. All these agreements were abandoned.

iii.   Reserve requirements before 1971 applied only to the clearing banks, which were required to hold 8 per cent of their deposits in notes, coin and balance with the Bank of England, and a further 20 per cent in a defined group of liquid assets. The new system applied to all banks, and required them to keep a minimum of 12.5 per cent of "eligible liabilities" (broadly equivalent to sterling deposits) in "reserve assets". The following items qualify as "reserve assets":-

> Balances with the Bank of England
> Money at call.
> UK and N. Ireland Treasury bills.
> Other bills eligible for discount at the
>   Bank of England
> British government stocks with one year
>   or less to run to maturity

The clearing banks are required to keep 1.5 per cent of eligible liabilities in balances with the Bank of England, and bills other than Treasury bills count as reserve assets only up to 2 per cent of eligible liabilities. With these exceptions banks are free to choose the allocation of reserves between different categories of reserve asset.

The new system also provided reserve requirements for discount houses and finance houses. There have been several modifications to the system since 1971, the most important of which are mentioned below.

---

1.   Bank of England _Quarterly Bulletin_, June 1979, p. 138

The effect of the changes has been to leave the authorities with six potential methods of influencing the growth of the money stock:-

> Control of the reserve base.
> Influence over interest rates.
> Special deposits.
> Supplementary special deposits.
> Public borrowing and debt management, and
> Direct controls.

If the authorities could determine the amount of reserve assets in the hands of the banks, the 12.5 per cent ratio would enable them automatically to set a ceiling on the amount of "eligible liabilities" which form by far the largest part of sterling M3. In fact, the Bank says that it does not operate in this way. A recent article in the Quarterly Bulletin states that:-

> ".... there has been no attempt to use this ratio as a device for imposing a ceiling on the stock of eligible liabilities. As before (1971) the Bank of England has chosen - through its open-market operations and lender of last resort facilities - to concentrate on influencing short-term interest rates, being prepared always to provide funds requested by the banking system but on interest-rate terms of its own choosing".[1]

Similar statements have been made by senior Bank officials on several occasions, but it is difficult to reconcile them completely with other evidence. For example the Bank's Annual Report for 1978-79 refers to a "tight reserve asset position" arising in June and July "as a result of large sales of gilt-edged stocks by the authorities", and describes the reduction of special deposits at that time as "a technical smoothing operation for relieving pressures on the reserve asset position of the banking system and on interest rates". Special deposits (see below) are essentially a means of influencing the banks' stock of reserve assets and it is difficult to see why the Bank

---

1. In D.K.W. Foot, C.A.E. Goodhart and A.C. Hotson, Monetary Base Control. BEQB June 1979, p. 150.

should have used this device as vigorously as it has unless it attached some importance to the size of the reserve assets base.

The Bank has many ways of influencing interest rates, at least in the short-term. Its published Minimum Lending Rate (MLR), formerly called Bank rate, is an indication of the terms on which it will act as lender of last resort. By varying the size of the Treasury bill offer relative to government payments, it can influence the net inflow or outflow of funds between the money market and the Exchequer account. It can generate similar flows to or from the money market by its own purchases or sales of securities (open-market operations) and it can vary the terms on which new issues of government stock are made and on which it is prepared to deal from its own portfolio.

Changes in interest rates can influence the growth of the money stock in various ways. For example a rise in interest rates may reduce the demand for bank loans, particularly if bank lending rates rise relative to those of other financial institutions. And a rise in interest rates may reduce the public's desire to hold bank deposits, especially if bank deposit rates rise less than the yield on other assets. The statement quoted above indicates that the Bank regards operations on interest rates as its main instrument of control, but the relative merits of this technique compared with operations on the reserve base are a matter of controversy.

"Special deposits" were first used in the early 1960s and continued after the introduction of C.C.C. The Bank calls for these deposits from banks as a percentage of their eligible liabilities. They bear interest at the average Treasury bill rate, so there is little financial penalty in having to make them, but they do not rank as reserve assets. The Bank lends funds deposited in this way to the government, which has that much less need to issue Treasury bills (which are reserve assets). The net effect of a call for special deposits is, therefore, to transfer part of banks' assets from the reserve to the non-reserve category, while a release of special deposits reverses this process.

"Supplementary special deposits" were first introduced in 1973 and have been used intermittently since that time. When the scheme is in operation the Bank announces, for some months ahead, a penalty-free rate of growth of "interest-bearing eligible liabilities" (IBELs). Any bank that exceeds this growth rate has to make deposits with the Bank on a scale that rises rapidly to 50 per cent of the excess. Unlike ordinary special deposits, supplementary special deposits are non-interest-bearing, so they involve a substantial financial penalty. The scheme thus reduces the ability of the banks to compete with one another and with other financial institutions for deposits.

The authorities can exert a direct influence on the public sector's demand for bank finance both through the total amount of public borrowing and the way in which it is managed. Other things being equal, the greater the total public sector borrowing requirement (PSBR), the greater the need for bank finance, and the present government attaches great importance to reducing the PSBR as a means of curtailing the growth of the money supply. However, it is also possible to vary the public sector's demand for bank finance within a given PSBR by varying the terms on which different types of security are offered. For example, a rise in interest rates on securities that appeal mainly to non-bank holders will normally bring in more funds from these sources and so reduce the need to borrow from the banks. These relationships are discussed in Chapters 7 and 9.

Finally, the Bank retains the power given by the 1946 Act to issue, with the approval of the Treasury, directives to the banks. In fact the Bank's requirements take the form of requests rather than directives but, because of the underlying power of directions, its requests have virtually

the force of law. Before 1971, this power was frequently
used to impose ceilings on bank lending to the private
sector. This has not been done since the introduction of
C.C.C., but the Bank regularly issues guidelines on sectors
of the economy that should be given high and low priority
for bank loans.

The working of the British system of monetary control
is the subject of much controversy. A recent discussion
paper issued by the Treasury and the Bank of England[1]
announced the ending of supplementary special deposits in
June, and also indicated the authorities' ultimate intention
to extend to all banks the obligation, at present confined
to the London Clearing Banks, to keep balances with the Bank
of England, abolishing the present reserve asset
requirements   and introducing new liquidity rules for
prudential purposes. At the time of writing (October 1980)
it is uncertain when these changes will be made and what,
if any, other control instruments will be introduced.

6.   THE BANKS AND THE ECONOMY

It is well known that British banks form a smaller
part of the total financial system than German banks. This
is partly because of the narrow definition of the banking
sector in Britain, but also because of the greater importance
of building societies and long-term financial institutions.
Table 1.1 shows that the banks' share in the liabilities of
all deposit taking institutions fell from 52.5 per cent in
1962 to 48.2 per cent in 1980. Table 1.11 presents a
broader picture including the main long-term financial
institutions. Financial intermediation (measured by the
annual increase in the liabilities of these institutions to
non-financial sectors) has risen sharply in relation to GDP
since the 1960's. This is the counterpart of the rise in

---

1.   Monetary Control. Cmnd. 7858, HMSO, March 1980.

TABLE 1.11: SHARES OF FINANCIAL INSTITUTIONS IN ADDITIONS TO LIABILITIES TO NON-FINANCIAL SECTORS

	1963-1967		1973-1977		1978		1979	
	Per Cent of Total	Per Cent of GDP	Per Cent of Total	Per Cent of GDP	Per Cent of Total	Per Cent of GDP	Per Cent of Total	Per Cent of GDP
Banking sector	23	1.8	28	3.1	27	3.1	30	3.6
Savings banks (investment associations)	5	0.4	2	0.2	4	0.4	4	0.5
Building societies	26	2.0	30	3.4	27	3.0	26	3.1
Finance houses	1	0.1	-	-	-	-	1	0.1
Life assurance companies and Pension funds	43	3.3	38	4.3	41	4.6	40	4.9
Unit trusts	3	0.2	1	0.1	1	0.1	-	-
TOTAL		7.8		11.1		11.2		12.2

Source: Wilson Committee Report. Cmnd. 7937 p.65.

personal savings discussed in Chapter 3. The banks' share
in the total rose sharply during the 1960's but has since
fluctuated in the range of 27-30 per cent without any
definite trend.

Table 1.12 shows the assets and liabilities of the
banking system by non-bank sectors. The total of the assets
column (loans made and securities held by the banks) exceeds
the liabilities (deposits by the non-bank public) because
the former includes assets acquired with the banks' own
funds. It is apparent that all the main sectors of the
economy are both substantial holders of bank deposits and
substantial borrowers. A significant part of the banks'
business thus consists of channelling funds from surplus to
deficit units within each sector. However, there are also
very large movements of funds between sectors through the
banking system. The Table shows the amounts outstanding,
which represent the cumulative results of all past
transactions; annual flows will be discussed in later
Chapters. Though public borrowing from the banks has been
reduced in recent years, the public sector is still a large
net debtor, as is the company sector. In the personal
sector, "Persons, households and individual trusts" relate
to individuals in their non-business capacity, while "other"
consists mainly of non-corporate business. A notable
difference between corporate and non-corporate business is
that unincorporated firms as a group hold deposits that
substantially exceed their bank borrowing. Persons not
engaged in business are very large net creditors and the
biggest inter-sector flow is from this group to the business
and public sectors.

TABLE 1.12: STERLING ASSETS AND LIABILITIES OF UK BANKS BY SECTOR, END-1978

	DEPOSIT LIABILITIES		ASSETS	
	£m.	% of Total	£m.	% of Total
PUBLIC SECTOR:				
- Central government	592	1.2	8,273	14.9
- Local authorities	330	0.7	4,441	8.0
- Public corporations	376	0.8	764	1.4
Total public sector	1,298	2.7	13,478	24.3
PERSONAL SECTOR				
- Persons, households and individual trusts	17,554	36.1	6,512	11.8
- Other	6,620	13.7	4,268	7.7
Total personal sector	24,174	49.8	10,780	19.5
Industrial and commercial companies	11,884	24.4	22,579	40.8
Other financial institutions	5,801	11.9	3,404	6.2
Overseas	5,476	11.3	5,089	9.2
TOTAL	48,633		55,330	

Source: Wilson Committee Report. Cmnd. 7937, p.p. 398 and 400.

CHAPTER 2: THE STRUCTURE OF BANKING IN WEST GERMANY

by K. H. Hennings

1. THE BANKS

Introduction

The German[1] banking system is characterized by a number of features which set it apart from those of other countries. There are more banks per head of the population than in most other countries: there are more than 5,500 independent banks with almost 39,000 branches. On average, therefore, there is one bank for every eleven thousand inhabitants, and either a bank or a bank branch for every 1,400 inhabitants. Naturally most of these banks are to be found in large cities, but smaller centres and rural areas are on the whole well served. Frankfurt has emerged as the main financial centre, but there are minor ones as well (in Düsseldorf, Hamburg and Munich), and Frankfurt does not play the dominant role of London in the British system.

Another important feature is that, within the German banking sector, public, private, and co-operative institutions exist side by side and behave in roughly the same way. The very decentralized nature of public involvement in the financial sector and the traditional independence of German public institutions imply that, although there is a large number of publicly owned banks, they can and do behave like private or co-operative banks.

Yet another feature, often commented upon, is that the German financial system is dominated by Universalbanken which, like financial supermarkets, "offer almost all bank services under one roof, and which are characterized by the combination

---

1. For the sake of convenience, "German" and "West German" are used as synonyms.

44.

of the business of deposit taking and loan making with the business of trading in securities, including the ownership of investments in other bank and non-bank firms".[1]
Specialist banks exist, and so do specialist non-bank financial intermediaries. But they play an important role only where legal or other institutional barriers prevent competition from Universalbanken. Even where this is the case most Universalbanken can refer their customers to wholly-or partly-owned subsidiaries; they can therefore still offer the full range of financial services.

This dominance of Universalbanken is not a new development.[2] Ever since the middle of the nineteenth century the industrialization of the German economy was accompanied by the growth of this type of banking firm. This was the consequence not so much of the scarcity of capital, but rather of a combination of facts: existing capital markets were geared to the handling of public rather than private debt, savers preferred public bonds to private shares or bonds, and firms with capital intensive production methods often found it difficult to obtain corporate status. As a consequence the existing (mainly private) banking houses were reluctant to expand their operations to the financing of industrial undertakings. The gap was filled by newly created banks, many of them founded by industrialists, often with government help. Later foundations often had the active help of long established private bankers but the private bankers had lost the initiative and with it their dominating role in the banking sector to the Universalbanken. Moreover, close links had been established between industry and commerce and the banking sector, much closer indeed than is compatible with "banking at arm's length". The necessity to finance the First World War by credit creation was a further stimulus for the growth of Universalbanken, as was the banking crisis of 1931 which led to compulsory and partly government financed take-overs of ailing banks by both private and public banks. Finally, the intitial scarcity of capital after the Second World War and the exigencies of the reconstruction period

1. See Bericht (1979), para. 148.
2. For what follows see Pohl (1977), Buschgen (1970), pp. 20-43, and Weber (1902)

provided yet another rationale for the continued existence
of banks that combined deposit banking with industrial
investment business.

In spite of this long tradition, the existence of
Universalbanken has not been uncontroversial. Critics have
pointed out that the combination of deposit banking with
security trading creates a conflict of interest which all
too often is decided against the interests of small savers.
They have argued that this type of bank provides undue
opportunities to use insider information and to manipulate,
or at least manage, stock market prices and that the
accumulation of bank and non-bank investments in the hands
particularly of a few large banks gives them too much
economic power for comfort.[1] On the contrary, defenders
of the existing system have pointed out that this type of bank
provides a number of advantages:

(i)   Universalbanken allow easy access to banking services
and therefore help to create an efficient system of
financial intermediation. This is true particularly
when small savers need to be educated in the use of
more sophisticated financial services.

(ii)   In a country with dispersed industrial centres,
Universalbanken with their typically large branch
networks provide a decentralized financial system
which again makes for an efficient system of
financial intermediation.

(iii)   Because of their supermarket nature, Universalbanken
have lower costs when acquiring new customers, or new
information.

(iv)   There are also internal cost advantages because of
the possibility of mixed calculation and because of
scale effects. Against this have to be set the
possible cost advantages from specialization and
division of labour but it is argued that these are
small for large firms such as the majority of
Universalbanken.

(v)   Finally, it is argued that the diversification of
risks that comes with the large all-encompassing
nature of Universalbanken makes for stability for
both profits and business policy and that this improves
the efficiency of the banking sector.

---

1.   For the pros and cons compare Moesch and Simmert (1976)
or Buschgen (1970) and (1971). See also Bericht (1979)

The latest attempt to solve the issue is the report
of the so-called Gessler commission, a committee of experts
called by the Federal Minister of Finance who reported in
1979 after four and a half years of deliberation.[1] Their
arguments deserve more space than can be afforded in this
context. Suffice it to say, therefore, that on balance they
came out in favour of Universalbanken even though they
recommended a number of changes, most importantly a limitation
of bank holdings of long-term non-bank investments.

As mentioned above, there are specialist banks in the
sense that legal provisions restrict them to certain types
of banking business. Yet less than 300 of the more than 5,500
independent banks in Germany fall into this category. All
the others are legally able to pursue all kinds of banking
business. Most of them actually do, although there are (as
will be seen below) variations between banks. The number
of banks which have in effect specialized in only a few kinds
of banking business is difficult to determine but is considered
to be small. Quite a few of the remaining private bankers
fall into this category, but the force of competition is
such that even they attempt to provide the full range of
banking services if asked to do so.

A further feature characterizing German banking is
the co-existence of public supervision with strong
competition. As in many other countries, public supervision
of the banking sector was introduced after the banking
crisis of 1931. The German system of supervision, described
in Chapter 10, is considerably stricter and more detailed
than that of the UK. Nevertheless, there is a considerable
degree of competition in German banking, especially since
the abandonment of the interest rate cartel in 1967. As
will be seen below this has led over the last twenty years
to a broadening of the spectrum of banking services offered
by almost all banks, and especially by those which tended
to concentrate their business on particular types of banking

---

1.   See Bericht (1979)

or particular groups of clients.

Another aspect in which the German banking system differs from that of the UK and many others is in its payments mechanism. A much higher proportion of payments than elsewhere is effected by direct credit transfers. There exist extended giro networks among both the savings banks and the credit co-operatives, the Post Office offers another giro network service, and finally all banks can make use of the fact that they all have accounts with the Bundesbank, so that the Bundesbank in effect offers another giro network. As all these systems are integrated and relatively cheap to use, direct credit transfers are resorted to much more frequently than (say) cheques. Cheques that cannot be cleared within the branch network of one of the large banks, or within such banking groups as the savings banks or the credit co-operatives, will normally be cleared by way of the Bundesbank.

The Banking Sector: An Overview

The Kreditwesengesetz defines a bank as a firm which engages in one or more of the following forms of banking business, provided such business requires a commercially organized framework (e.g. bookkeeping, a permanent office, etc.):

(i)   deposit taking, no matter whether interest is paid or not;

(ii)   money lending;

(iii)   purchasing cheques or bills of exchange;

(iv)   trading in securities for others;

(v)   safekeeping and looking after securities for others;

(vi)   operating investment funds;

(vii)   trading in credit;

(viii) offering guarantees for borrowers or lenders;

(ix)   operating giro networks.

Other types of business can be included in this list if necessary. No use has so far been made of this provision, however. In consequence such forms of business as factoring or financial leasing do not yet qualify as banking business so that non-banks can pursue them.

Certain institutions are exempted from the provisions of the Kreditwesengesetz and therefore do not qualify as a bank, even though they pursue business which is listed above. Among these are insurance companies and social security institutions, the post office, and a number of public institutions. Most of the latter would normally qualify as non-bank financial intermediaries. A few, however, are indisputably banks (such as the Deutsche Bundesbank, which is exempted from supervision by the BAK), and are included in the discussion below; they are also included in the statistical data prepared by the Deutsche Bundesbank.

On the other hand, not all institutions that are banks according to the legal definition are also "reporting banks" in the sense that they are included in the Bundesbank statistical data on banking. Among the non-reporting banks are:-

-    investment trusts (i.e. banks which are engaged in (vi) above only,

-    banks operating a giro network for securities on behalf of those trading at a stock exchange (i.e. banks which engage in (v) above only), and

-    banks engaged only in guaranteeing business (i.e. banks which engage in (vii) above only).

The number of these banks is small; 82 in all at the end of 1979. In addition some 2,000 small co-operative banks are excluded. All non-reporting banks together do not account for more than 3 per cent of the total volume of banking business.

Table 2.1 provides data on the number of banks and their branches in selected years for various categories of banks.

TABLE 2.1: BANKS AND BANK BRANCHES 1957, 1967 AND 1979

	1957				1967				1979			
	Banks	Branches	Total	Per Cent	Banks	Branches	Total	Per Cent	Banks	Branches	Total	Per Cent
Commercial Banks	364	1917	2281	8.7	322	4017	4339	11.7	252	5891	6143	13.9
Big Banks	8	787	795	3.0	6	2103	2109	5.7	6	3104	3110	7.0
Regional Banks	96	1020	1116	4.2	107	1686	1793	4.8	101	2463	2564	5.8
Branches of Foreign Banks	15	6	21	0.1	20	11	31	0.1	56	47	103	0.2
Private Bankers	245	104	349	1.3	189	217	406	1.1	89	277	366	0.8
Savings Institutions	885	8383	9268	35.2	876	13749	14625	39.5	615	17069	17684	39.9
Central Giro	14	191	205	0.8	14	311	325	0.9	12	317	329	0.7
Savings Banks	871	8192	9063	34.4	862	13433	14300	38.6	603	16752	17355	39.2
Co-operative Banks[a]	11814	2394	14208	54.0	9331	7978	17309	46.7	4453	15166	19619	44.3
Central Institutions	19	89	108	0.4	19	101	120	0.3	10	49	59	0.1
Credit Co-operatives[a]	11795	2305	14100	53.5	9312	7877	17189	46.4	4443	15117	19560	44.2
Universalbanken	13063	12694	25757	97.8	10529	25744	36273	97.9	5320	38126	43446	98.1
Mortgage Banks	44	19	63	0.2	47	23	70	0.2	39	29	68	0.2
Private	25	8	33	0.1	29	12	41	0.1	25	21	46	0.1
Public	19	11	30	0.1	18	11	29	0.1	14	8	22	0.1
Hire Purchase Banks	194	225	419	1.6	195	488	683	1.8	115	503	618[g]	1.4
Banks with Special Functions[b]	16	34	50	0.2	28	45	73	0.2	17	76[h]	93	0.2
Post Office	15	..	15	0	15	..	15	0	15	..	15	0
Building Societies[c]	29	..	29	0	29	..	29	0	29	18	47	0.1
Private[d]	16	..	16	0	16	..	16	0	16	18	34	0.1
Public[d]	13	..	13	0	13	..	13	0	13	..	13	0
Reporting Banks[a]	13361	12972	26333	100	10832	26283	37115	100	5535	37852	44287	100
Reporting Banks[e]	3658	..	..		3689	..	..		3396	..	..	
Investment Funds	5	..	5		10	1	11		34	1	35	
Security Depositors	7	1	8		7	1	8		8	..	..	
Credit Guarantee Association	30	1	31		54	..	54		39	..	39	
ALL BANKS	13403	12974	26377		10903	26285	37188		5616	38783	44369	

Please see Notes following.

50.

NOTES TO TABLE 2.1:

a. Including non-reporting co-operatives.

b   No branches reported as all Post Offices serve as such.

c. No data on branches available for 1957 and 1967..

d   Including those that are legally branches of other public
    banks (10 in 1957; 11 in 1967 and 10 in 1977-1979).

e   Excluding non-reporting co-operatives.

f   In addition there are three banks (with 298 branches) which
    have been classified as regional banks, and another three
    banks with 7 branches which have been classified as private
    bankers.

g   In addition there are four banks with 309 branches which have
    been classified as regional banks, and a further three banks with
    9 branches which have been classified as private bankers.

h   Including (for the first time) 46 branches of the Deutsche
    Verkehrs-Kredit-Bank AG primarily engaged in foreign exchange
    business which had previously not been considered bank
    branches.

Source: Deutsche Bundesbank, Monatsberichte, various issues.
         Bericht (1979), pp. 424-425.

TABLE 2.2: SHARES OF VARIOUS BANKING GROUPS IN TOTAL VOLUME OF BANKING BUSINESS IN SELECTED YEARS, 1957-1979 (PER CENT)

	1950	1957	1960	1967	1970	1977	1978	1979
Commercial Banks	36.7	27.7	24.4	22.1	24.9	24.9	25.1	24.7
Big Banks	19.5	13.8	11.3	9.6	10.2	10.4	10.6	10.5
Regional Banks					10.7	10.9	11.0	10.9
	12.6	11.1	10.4	10.2				
Branches of Foreign Banks					1.5	1.9	1.9	1.8
Private Bankers	4.6	2.8	2.7	2.3	2.5	1.7	1.6	1.5
Savings Institutions	32.1	36.1	35.7	38.1	38.5	38.5	38.2	38.3
Central Giro Inst.	11.6	14.6	13.5	14.9	15.6	16.5	16.4	16.4
Savings Banks	20.5	21.5	22.2	23.2	22.9	22.0	21.8	21.9
Cooperative Banks	10.4	8.5	8.6	10.6	11.5	14.0	14.3	14.6
Central Institutions	3.7	2.9	2.8	3.7	3.8	4.2	4.2	4.1
Credit Cooperatives	6.7	5.6	5.8	6.9	7.7	9.8	10.1	10.5
Credit Cooperatives[a]			(7.6)		(9.6)	(10.9)		
All Universalbanken	79.2	72.3	68.7	70.8	74.9	77.4	77.6	77.6
Mortgage Banks	5.8	11.3	17.2	16.5	13.7	13.0	13.1	13.1
Private Mortgage Banks	2.7	5.5	5.8	6.7	6.6	8.2	8.3	8.2
Public Mortgage Banks	3.1	5.8	11.4	9.8	7.1	4.8	4.8	4.9
Hire Purchase Banks	.7	1.3	1.5	1.0	1.1	1.1	1.1	1.2
Banks with Special Functions	11.4	12.5	10.2	9.6	8.4	6.5	6.2	6.3
Post Office	3.9	2.6	2.4	2.1	1.9	2.0	1.9	1.8

Note:

a including non-reporting ones; the share reported relates to the total volume of business including that of non-reporting credit cooperatives, and thus is not fully comparable.

Sources: Deutsche Bundesbank (1976), p. 254; Monatsbericht 8/1978, p. 15; Monatsbericht, Statistische Beihefte Reihe 1, 10/1979, Tab. 1.

Over a period of more than twenty years, the number
of banks has declined by more than half, while the number of
bank branches has almost tripled. Taking 1967 (the year in
which the cartel-like fixing of interest rates and conditions
was abandoned) as a bench mark, one has the following
average annual growth rates:-

Table A : Average Annual Growth Rates of Banks and Bank
          Branches

Period	Banks	Branches	Total
1957-1967	-2.0	7.3	3.5
1967-1979	-5.5	3.2	1.5
1957-1979	-4.0	10.1	2.4

Source: Table 1.

Thus the rapid extension of the branch networks occurred in
the period before 1967 but continued thereafter, while the
decline in the numbers of banks accelerated after 1967.

Looking at individual groups of banks, it is clear
that the decline in their total number is primarily due to
the disappearance of private bankers, and the enormous
decline in the number of credit co-operatives. In both cases
the main reason for the decline in numbers was mergers.
At the same time, there was a general increase in the branch
networks in virtually all banking groups.

Table 2.2 presents data on the share of the various
banking groups in the total volume of banking business.   It
will be seen, firstly, that the dominant position of
Unviersalbanken in terms of numbers has a counterpart in
their share in the total volume of banking business, even
though their share in business is smaller than their share
in numbers. This share declined in the 1950s and rose again
in the 1960s and 1970s mainly on account of the public
mortgage banks which were used in the 1950s to channel funds
into the housing sector and the building industry. When the
importance of these subsidies declined, the importance of

public mortgage banks within the banking sector declined.
Similar reasons account for the decline in the share of
banks with special functions. Within the Universalbanken
the share of commercial banks has declined, particularly
that of the Big banks. On the other hand, the shares of
the savings institutions and of the co-operative banks
have increased. Their shares are probably somewhat over-
estimated because inter-group bank liabilities play a larger
role in their balance sheets than in any other group of
banks but there is no doubt that they have grown more rapidly
than other groups.

Both Table 2.1 and 2.2 suggest structural changes
within the German banking system which are due to the force
of competition. This is brought out more clearly when one
considers the relationship between the share in total volume
of business and the share in the number of banks including
bank branches. Looking at Universalbanken only, this
relationship was as follows:

Table B: Share in Total Volume of Business Divided by
          Share in Total Number of Banks and Bank Branches

	1957	1967	1978	1979
Commercial Banks	3.20	1.89	1.81	1.78
Big Banks [1]	4.57	1.69	1.51	1.50
Regional Banks	2.57	2.07	2.14	1.95
Private Banks	2.11	2.09	1.90	1.88
Savings Institutions	1.03	.97	.93	.96
Co-operative Banks	.16	.23	.32	.33
Universalbanken	.74	.72	.79	.79

Note: 1. Including branches of foreign banks.

Source: Tables 1 and 2.

The volume of business per bank or bank branch was
much lower for co-operative banks than it was for all
Universalbanken taken together and much higher for commercial
banks. There are obvious structural reasons for this

TABLE 2.3: NUMBER OF MONTHLY REPORTING BANKS AND THEIR CLASSIFICATION BY SIZE (End December 1979)

The banks reporting for the monthly banking statistics are graded as follows according to their volume of business:

BANKING GROUP	Total number of monthly reporting banks (1)	Less than DM 1 million	DM 1 million to less than DM 5 million	DM 5 million to less than DM 10 million	DM 10 million to less than DM 25 million	DM 25 million to less than DM 50 million	DM 50 million to less than DM 100 million	DM 100 million to less than DM 500 million	DM 500 million to less than DM 1 billion	DM 1 billion to less than DM 5 billion	DM 5 billion and over
Commercial banks	250	4	10	10	14	25	26	62	38	49	12
Big banks (2)	6	-	-	-	-	-	-	-	-	1	5
Regional banks and other commercial banks	100	1	2	3	5	8	9	24	14	27	7
Branches of foreign banks	56	-	-	1	1	5	2	22	14	11	-
Private bankers	88	3	8	6	8	12	15	16	10	10	-
Central giro institutions (including Deutsche Girozentrale)	12	-	-	-	-	-	-	-	-	-	12
Savings banks	603	-	-	-	1	9	33	282	165	102	11
Central institutions of credit co-operatives (incl. Deutsche Genossenschaftsbank)	10	-	-	-	-	-	-	-	1	-	9
Credit co-operatives (3)	2,294	(2)	1	4	162	849	688	543	31	14	-
Mortgage banks	39	-	-	-	-	-	3	5	-	10	21
Private	25	-	-	-	-	-	2	1	-	6	16
Public	14	-	-	-	-	-	1	4	-	4	5
Instalment sales financing institutions	125	10	17	4	19	12	12	41	6	5	-
Banks with special functions	17	-	-	1	-	-	1	4	-	7	4
Postal giro and postal savings bank offices	15	-	-	-	-	-	-	-	-	-	-
Building and loan associations	30	-	-	-	-	-	1	3	9	10	7
Private	17	-	-	-	-	-	1	3	5	4	4
Public	13	-	-	-	-	-	-	-	4	6	3
Total 4 excluding building and loan associations	3,365	(16)	(28)	(19)	(196)	(895)	(763)	(937)	(241)	(187)	(69)
including building and loan associations	3,396	(16)	(28)	(19)	(196)	(895)	(764)	(940)	(250)	(197)	(76)

(1) Including banks in liquidation - (2) Deutsche Bank AG, Dresdner Bank AG, Commerzbank AG, and their Berlin subsidiaries - (3) Partial statistics covering, since end - 1973, those credit co-operatives whose total assets on December 31, 1972 amounted to DM 10 million and more, and smaller institutions which on November 30, 1973 were required to render returns; see Table III, 22. Including other banks not organised in the form of a co-operative but affiliated to Bundesverband der Deutschen Volksbanken und Raiffeisenbanken e.V. Up to December 1971 the figures of credit co-operatives (Schulze-Delitzsch) and credit co-operatives (Raiffeisen) were recorded and published separately. -(4) Figures in brackets do not contain postal giro and postal savings bank offices.

Source: Deutsche Bundesbank, Monthly Report June 1980, Table III.24.

observation but what is interesting are the trends through time. In spite of the enormous extension of their branch networks, the Big banks saw a decline in the volume of business per bank branch. That they nevertheless saw fit to extend their branch networks was due to their fear of losing business to the savings institutions and also to the credit co-operatives. Similarly the savings institutions extended their branch networks in the face of a slightly declining volume of business per bank or bank branch. Only the co-operative banks were able to increase the volume of business per bank or bank branch due to the very large number of mergers within their group.

Table 2.3 provides data about the relative size of banks. Co-operative banks tend to be smaller (in terms of the volume of business they handle) than savings institutions. Savings institutions are of about equal size to regional banks if allowance is made for the fact that there are a few rather small regional banks. Big banks, of course, top the list as a group but it should be noted that some of the central institutions of the co-operative banks, and even more so the central giro institutions, are of about equal size.

Commercial Banks

This group includes the Big banks, regional banks, branches of foreign banks and private banks.

(a) Big Banks

There are three Big banks: Deutsche Bank AG, Dresdener Bank AG, and Commerzbank AG. In statistical terms, their number is six because for legal reasons their Berlin subsidiaries are counted separately. Traditionally, the Big banks are the archetype of the commercial bank. Historically they all have their roots in banks which were founded in the middle of the nineteenth century, most of them with the active participation of private bankers. Their share

in the total volume of banking business has been falling
throughout most of the post-war period. It should be noted,
however, that the figures in Table 2.2 overestimate this
decline. All of the Big banks have wholly or partly owned
subsidiaries among the regional banks, private banks, and
(particularly) specialist banks, as well as non-bank
financial intermediaries, so that their share in the total
volume of business would be much larger if these long-term
investments were taken into account. If nevertheless their
collective share in banking business has fallen, this is due
to the rising importance of long-term business vis-a-vis
short-term business.

That all three Big banks are well known internationally
is a reflection of their growing involvement in foreign
business. All three have foreign subsidiaries, and are also
partners in various European or international banking consortia.
In their balance sheets this shows up in their lending to
foreign banks as well as in their holdings of foreign securities
which do not form a large part of their assets but still account
for more than a quarter of all foreign securities held by German
banks. Similarly, their liabilities to foreign banks account
for more than a third of all such debt incurred by German banks
and their liabilities to foreign non-banks for more than a
third, even though both items do not account for a large
proportion of their own liabilities.

Their holdings of domestic securities tend to be small
and reflect very inaccurately their strong involvement in
both placing new issues and trading in existing ones, as
well as their often dominant role in placing consortia.
Traditionally, the three Big banks concentrated on short-term
lending to industry and commerce. In recent years their
long-term lending has increased but not as much as that of
other banking groups. Yet they often act as agents, arranging
loans either from foreign sources (often their own subsidiaries)
or from domestic non-bank financial intermediaries.

In the past the Big banks used to finance a sizeable proportion of their business by sight deposits (which in 1960 accounted for more than a quarter of their total liabilities). In recent years, however, sight deposits have declined, and the Big banks were forced to attract savings deposits (invading the traditional territory of the savings banks) as well as to issue bank bonds on a large scale (thus entering into competition with the Landesbanken-Girozentralen).

Another well-known aspect of the business activities of Big banks is their involvement in non-bank enterprises, particularly in industry, trade and insurance. Many companies have bank directors among the members of their supervisory boards even if the relevant banks do not have a stake in the company and directors of the Big banks tend to have a more than proportional share on such boards compared to other banking groups (see Chapter 5).

Bank involvement in industry also arises from the fact that German company law gives shareholders the right to transfer their voting rights to a bank which will vote as it sees fit unless instructed otherwise. Figures given in Chapter 5 indicate that about 47 per cent of all such share deposits are with Big banks.

(b) Regional Banks

This category includes a rather diverse assortment of banks. Among them is the Bank für Gemeinwirtschaft in Frankfurt which to all intents and purposes is a national bank with more than 240 branches. There is also the Bayerische Hypotheken und Wechselbank and the Bayerische Vereinsbank, both in Munich, both with more than three hundred branches but both mainly confined to Bavaria, although they have both moved into other parts of Germany in recent years. Both share the peculiarity that they are privileged, by tradition, to engage in mortgage business so that they are not fully comparable to other commercial

banks which are not so privileged. Among the regional banks
is also the Berliner Handels-und Frankfurter Bank in Berlin
and Frankfurt, which has grown out of a merger of two
formerly independent institutions one of which had regional
importance only; it has in recent years extended its field
of activity over the whole of the country, notwithstanding
the fact that it has only some thirty branches. There are
also banks which would normally be classified as private
banks were it not for the fact that they are not in the
legal form of sole proprietorships or unlimited or partially
limited partnerships. Among them is the Effektenbank
Warburg AG in Frankfurt which grew out of the fusion of the
Deutsche Effekten & Wechselbank (L.A. Hahn) with the German
side of the business of S.G. Warbury & Comp. in London.
Another example of this kind of regional bank is (or rather
was) I.D. Herstatt KGaA in Cologne. Yet another group of
banks included in this category are the few remaining German
overseas banks such as the Ibero-America Bank AG in Bremen,
or the Deutsch-Sudamerikanische Bank AG and the European
Asian Bank AG, both in Hamburg. Finally, this category
includes foreign banks, i.e. subsidiaries of foreign banks
incorporated under German law, such as the Citibank AG, the
Chase Bank AG and the Bank of Tokio (Deutschland) AG, all in
Frankfurt.

In view of this diversity it is difficult to say much
about common features of their business activity. In most
respects they resemble Big banks but show a wider
range of variation. Many of the regional banks are rather
strong in industrial business; others are stronger in non-
bank deposit business (e.g. the two Bavarian banks mentioned
above). Some of them are specialists in a few kinds of
banking business, mostly dealing on capital markets, and
in placing business but most should be regarded as
Universalbanken with respect to their business range, even
though they may deal with only limited sections of the public.

(c)   Branches of Foreign Banks

The first branch of a foreign bank in Germany (which
is not incorporated under German law) counts as a bank; all
further branches are counted as branches of the first branch.
Foreign banks incorporated under German law are listed as
regional banks. Among those listed as having branches in
Germany are most of the internationally known banks, not
surprisingly in view of the growing use of the Deutschmark
as international currency, and the strong involvement of
German banks on Euro-markets. Apart from a number of branches
of French banks near the German-French border, most of the
branches are situated in one of the German banking centres,
with Frankfurt being the most favoured. Few foreign banks
have more than one branch in Germany.

Their total volume of business is small. Naturally,
their involvement with foreign banks is large and dominates
their balance sheets. Domestic business consisted for a
long time in channelling funds into Germany but more
recently their net position has changed to exporting funds.

(d)   Private Banks

This category includes all commercial banks in the legal
form of a sole proprietorship, unlimited partnership, or
partially limited partnership (Einzelkaufmann, offene Handel-
sgesellschaft (OHG), or Kommanditgesellschaft (KG)). Among
the larger more well-known ones are:

-      Trinkaus & Burkhardt in Dusseldorf

-      Sal. Oppenheim jr. & Cie. in Koln

-      M.M. Warburg-Brinckmann Wirtz & Co in Hamburg

-      Schröder, Münchmeyer, Hengst & Co. in Hamburg (and
       Frankfurt)

-      Merck, Finck & Co in Munich

-      Bankhaus Hermann Lampe KG in Bielefeld

-      Karl Schmidt Bankgeschäft in Hof/Saale

Of these, the first three date back, at least in part, to
the eighteenth century as do a number of the smaller ones
not listed here. Most of them have no branches, some of them
a few. The last of the ones listed above is the exception
with some 90 branches which account for 40 per cent of all
the branches of private bankers.

As Table 2.3 shows, there are great variations in
size among banks listed as private bankers. This is due
primarily to differences in the range of business they
engage in. Some of the smaller private bankers are in effect
engaged only in real estate administration, or the
administration of financial investments and do not actively
seek deposits or other business. On the other hand,
the large size of the Bankhaus Hermann Lampe KG is due
primarily to the fact that this is the house bank of the
Oetker group of companies, one of the country's leading
manufacturers of processed foods.

In spite of this diversity, certain marked features
are discernible. Many of the private bankers have
specialized in discounting bills of exchange. Their
collective share of discounting business is larger than that
of the Big banks, and is half that of the regional banks
even though their total volume of business amounts to only
a fifth of that of regional banks. There is also some
specialization in stock market business; private bankers
typically have a higher share of securities in total assets
than all banks taken together. Moreover, the proportion
of securities held probably underestimates their importance
for the capital market as some firms, and not only the
larger ones, are among the most active in the placing business
Finally, it is well known that some private bankers play a
leading role in foreign exchange business.

Few of the private bankers are equally strong in all
types of banking business. Particularly the smaller ones
have been able to survive only because they have specialized.
Nevertheless they are still Universalbanken. Indeed, that

quality may well have given them the ability to adapt to
changing markets in a system characterized by rapid structural
change and strong competition.

Savings Institutions

Originally founded as public institutions in order to
provide cheap credit particularly to non-businessmen and to
stimulate saving among the lower classes, the oldest savings
banks (Sparkassen) date back to the second half of the
eighteenth century. Since the reorganization of local
administration after the Napoleonic wars most of them are
closely associated with local or regional authorities, though
some (so called freie Sparkassen) are still private
foundations. Thus most Sparkassen are guaranteed by local
authorities in towns or cities (Stadtsparkassen) or in
counties (Kreissparkassen). Because of their public status,
Sparkassen enjoyed tax privileges which in the past gave
them an advantage over other banks. These have been reduced
in recent years but still continue to some extent.[1] Again
because of their public status, there are also certain
restrictions on their business activities. Many Sparkassen[2]
are not allowed to trade in securities, or to invest in
securities other than those issued by local authorities or
other public institutions; similarly, their ability to trade
in inter-bank money markets and in foreign exchange markets
is severely limited. There is also a rule that savings
deposits have to be used for long-term lending, particularly
mortgage lending and lending to their sponsoring local
authority. Nevertheless there is competition between locally
close, or neighbouring Sparkassen, especially in larger towns
and cities where typically a Stadtsparkasse exists next to
a Kreissparkasse.

---

1. Legislation currently (April 1981) before parliament
   would remove the remaining priveleges and, in the
   opinion of savings banks, actually place them at a
   disadvantage.

2. Legislation concerning Sparkassen is a matter for
   the Länder (States) and not the Federation, and
   therefore differs from State to State.

The restrictions under which savings banks operate give importance to their central institutions. There are eleven Landesbanken/Girozentralen on the State level (one for each State except Berlin, and a second one for Baden-Württemberg,[1] and the Deutsche Girozentrale in Frankfurt on the national level. Landesbanken/Girozentralen[2] operate a giro system for cheques and money transfers among Sparkassen, provide those services Sparkassen cannot engage in such as foreign exchange business, and also provide cost-saving centralized services such as computerized book-keeping, centralized safekeeping of securities for customers, etc., which individual Sparkassen would find it difficult to operate. Important though these are, most important of all is the operation of the giro system, and the fact that the Landenbanken/Girozentralen offer an opportunity for investing surplus funds to savings banks, i.e. in effect operate an internal money market. This allows the Landesbanken/Girozentralen to collect all the excess liquidity of the Sparkassen in their region, providing an internal equalization of demand and supply, and to place any excess supply on the money market. It is this mechanism which has given them the strong position on short-term money markets they have enjoyed for so long (see Chapter 8). Moreover, the Landesbanken/Girozentralen co-operate with each other via the Deutsche Girozentrale in the same way.

Another characteristic of the Landesbanken/Girozentralen is the fact that almost all of them operate a mortgage bank as a branch (a relic of their Lankesbanken past); the one which does not has a mortgage bank as a subsidiary.

In view of all this it is not surprising that the Landesbanken/Girozentralen are among the largest and fastest

---

1.   This is an historical relic: Baden/Württemberg started as three independent States after 1945.

2.   The long name derives from the fact that the Girozentralen were merged, in the 1950s and 1960s, with Landesbanken which used to be the housebanks of the formerly independent German states and originally enjoyed the privilege of issuing notes.

growing banks in the country. Moreover, some Sparkassen
are large enough to rival the largest of the regional banks
and even the smallest of the Big banks. In spite of their
restrictions they have for some time operated as
Universalbanken, and they have become competitors of Big
banks and regional banks, especially since they started to
merge into larger units, and to extend their branch networks.

All savings institutions together have a larger volume
of business than all commercial banks taken together. About
two fifths of this is due to the twelve Landesbanken/Giro-
zentralen, the rest ot some 600 Sparkassen and their branches
(with the exception of the Norddeutsche Landesbank/Giro-
zentrale, which has more than three hundred, the Landes-
banken/Girozentralen have few branches). They still enjoy
a more than proportional share in savings deposits, although
their share has fallen over the years. Nevertheless savings
deposits still account for more than two-thirds of the
aggregate liabilities of all Sparkassen. For the Landesbanken/
Girozentralen saving deposits play a minor role. They
finance themselves by issuing bank bonds, by taking in
deposits from other banks (primarily, naturally, from Sparkassen), and by taking in long-term deposits from non-banks.
On the asset side, long-term lending dominates in the
balance sheet of Sparkassen; they also invest heavily in bank
bonds, naturally those issued by institutions of their own
organization. Similarly, Landesbanken/Girozentralen have a
strong position in long-term lending, and also in inter-bank
lending. The strong position of all savings institutions
taken together is reflected by the fact that they hold more
than half of all domestic securities (most of them however
bank bonds issued by the Landesbanken/Girozentralen; Sparkassen have only recently started to issue bank bonds on their
own). But they also hold almost 40 per cent of all foreign
securities held by German banks, receive more than 50 per
cent of all savings deposits, 40 per cent of all sight
deposits, and almost 25 per cent of all time deposits.
Moreover, the Landesbanken/Girozentralen have acquired a
strong position in foreign exchange business, particularly

on short-term Euro-markets, in addition to their traditionally strong position on domestic short-term money markets.

The rapid growth of the savings institutions is primarily due to several factors. Traditionally, they were the recipients of the largest part of all savings deposits. Hence they stood to gain most from the rise in the savings ratio which accompanied the growth process of the German economy since the end of the war. As long as the (compulsory) interest rate cartel was in operation, these savings deposits were a relatively cheap source of money which could be put to good use because of the close co-operation between the various savings institutions. Moreover, the building boom which accompanied the reconstruction period, and continued when affluence came to stay, favoured the long-term business in which they again had a strong tradition. Finally, the rising level of average real income meant that many people began to demand banking services other than the acceptance of savings deposits; because of their nature as Universal-banken, Sparkassen were in a good position to offer these services, and thus to benefit from the rising level of prosperity while at the same time building up a strong position in short-term business. Thus when the compulsory interest rate cartel was abandoned in 1967 the savings institutions were already in a good competitive position vis-a-vis other banks, and commercial banks in particular. They have since been able to compete more actively for funds, and their organizational structure has clearly helped them to hold and improve on their market share. Competition in banking has many aspects, but it is clear that the Big banks would not have felt the need to extend their branch network as much as they did had it not been for the competition of the savings institutions.

Co-operative Banks

Co-operative banks have a structure similar to savings institutions, but have different origins and play a different role within the German banking system. Sparkassen have typically been municipal institutions catering for townsmen,

primarily those in employment. Credit co-operatives
(Kreditgenossenschaften) have been, and to some extent still
are, typically self-help institutions catering for both
agrarian and artisan producers. They have their origins in
two different but related movements, both associated with the
names of the men to whose agitation they owe their existence.

Volksbanken owe their existence to the endeavours of
Hermann Schulze from Delitzch (in Saxony) who propagated
self-help credit co-operatives for artisans in the 1840s when
the beginnings of industrialization threatened their livelihood.
By 1970, there existed more than seven hundred such Volksbanken.
Raiffeisenbanken owe their existence to the attempts of
Friedrich Wilhelm Raiffeisen to help the poor farmers and
peasants of the Eifel region (in the Rhineland) to form
credit co-operatives in the 1840s and 1950s. In many cases
these co-operatives combine the functions of credit
co-operatives with those of trading co-operatives. More than
ten thousand of them qualified as banks in the 1950s. Since
then their number has been reduced to just under eight
thousand in 1970.

In 1971 both branches of the co-operative movement
combined. Since then mergers have reduced the number of
credit co-operatives that qualify as a bank to just below
five thousand; many of the formerly independent co-operatives
have been retained as branches, so that the co-operative
banks have more branches than any other banking group in Germany.
In view of their large number it is not surprising that most of
them are fairly small (some of them are so small that they
are operated by part-time staff). Only some 2,300 are
reporting institutions, and even these are as a rule smaller
than most Sparkassen.

Like the savings institutions, the co-operative banks
are organized on three levels. Besides the local Volksbanken
and Raiffeisenbanken, there exist on a regional level nine
Genossenschaftliche Zentralkassen (two each in Munich and
Hannover, one each in Stuttgart, Kassel, Frankfurt,

Düsseldorf and Saarbrücken), and the Deutsche Genossens-
schaftsbank in Frankfurt on a national level.

The genossenschaftliche Zentralbanken and the Deutsche
Genossenschaftsbank operate a giro system for cheques and
money transfers, offer money market investment opportunities
to their members, and like the Landesbanken/Girozentralen
provide services the local credit co-operatives cannot
provide or find it uneconomic to provide because of their
size. This gives them a comparable position on capital
markets, in foreign exchange business, an on short-term
money markets, although on a smaller scale, because credit
co-operatives did not benefit from the post-war increase
in savings as much as did savings banks.

Again, as in the case of the savings institutions,
co-operative banks compete against each other only on a very
limited scale. They also enjoy certain tax privileges in
consequence of their co-operative status, though these will
be removed by legislation now before parliament. A rule which
restricted lending to their members was lifted in 1974. Since
then they are in effect Universalbanken like Sparkassen, or
commercial banks. Nevertheless most of their lending to non-
banks is still lending to members. Their holdings of securities
has increased, but they are still the nearest German banks
come to pure deposit banking, particularly if it is kept in
mind that much of their security holdings is in the form of
bank bonds issued by their central institutions. Credit
co-operatives cannot issue bank bonds and are therefore
limited by their ability to attract funds. Although this
means that they have the highest proportion of savings
deposits to total liabilities of all banks, this has also
somewhat hampered their growth. Genossenschaftliche
Zentralbanken can issue bank bonds, but do so only on a
moderate scale, so that co-operative banks as a whole are
largely limited to the deposits they can attract. This is
also reflected in their asset structure which is dominated by
short-term lending.

On the whole, the genossenschaftliche Zentralkassen
have behaved much more like central institutions and much
less aggressively than have the Landesbanken-girozentralen.
In consequence, the co-operative banks have not been as much
a force making for competition as have savings institutions.
But partly no doubt because they have built on their own
resources they have grown and have extended their market share,
particularly in periods in which other funds were scarce, or
costly, or both.

Specialist Banks

This category comprises all banks which are
Universalbanken. Bundesbank statistics typically include
under this heading mortgage banks, hire purchase banks, and what
are known as banks with special functions. For the sake of
completeness the Post Office will also be included here.

(a)   Mortgage Banks

Mortgage banks are subject to special legal provisions
(the Hypothekenbankgesetz) which limit their
activities to long-term business, but which also grant them
the so-called Pfandbriefprivileg, i.e. the privilege to issue
Pfandbriefe (mortgage bonds) and Kommunalbriefe (local
authority bonds).[1] Due to special legal provisions, these
are relatively riskless assets which enjoy a particular role
whenever investments have to conform to particular standards
(as e.g. those of savings institutions, or insurance companies
have to).

---

1.   These are special kinds of bank bonds which are secured
      by either mortgages or loans to public authorities.
      Local authority bonds are called "communal bonds" in
      Bundesbank statistics.

Of the 39 mortgage banks, fourteen are public
institutions, ten of them branches of Landesbanken/Girozen-
tralen. Of the 25 private ones most are subsidiaries of
Big banks or regional banks. Four of them specialize in
ship mortgages, the others are predominantly involved in
housing mortgages. Many of the public institutions, by
contrast, specialize in agricultural business.

Due to the restrictions under which they operate,
more than five sixths of all assets of mortgage banks
consist of long-term lending. On the liability side, public
and private institutions differ. Private mortgage banks use
predominantly mortgage bonds, and, increasingly, local
authority bonds, to finance themselves, such that two-thirds
of their liabilities account for almost a third of all bank
bonds. The rest is made up of long-term deposits. Public
mortgage banks, by contrast, issue bank bonds on a much
smaller scale and therefore have a much higher share of
long-term time deposits (which accounts for almost a quarter of
all such deposits). This is of course due to the fact that
public funds and public subsidies are channelled through these
institutions.

(b) Hire Purchase Banks

Hire purchase banks (Teilzahlungskreditinstitute) do not
have a monopoly in this type of business; most commercial
banks will be prepared to finance hire purchase arrangements.
Most hire purchase banks are rather small, the larger ones
are either subsidiaries of commercial banks or have strong
ties with them, as with few exceptions hire purchase banks
are not allowed to accept deposits from non-banks and
therefore depend on inter-bank lending. Some are in effect
the credit departments of durable goods producers, especially
car manufacturers. None of them is permitted to issue bank
bonds; few engage in other business on a scale worth
mentioning.

(c)   Banks with Special Functions

        This category consists of three different groups of
banks.   There are,firstly,some public banks specifically
created to channel public funds (mainly, but not only, public
subsidies) into the economy and then administer them.   Among
them are the Kreditanstalt fur Wiederaufbau AG in Frankfurt
and the Lastenausgleichsbank in Bonn as well as such
institutions as the Bayerische Landesanstalt fur Aufbaufinan-
zierung in Munich which is mentioned elsewhere in this
study (Chapter 6).   The first is now the principal agent for
the administration of German development aid; all those
mentioned provide subsidized loans for small businesses and
may be called development banks.

        Secondly, there are a number of institutions, both
public and private, that specialize in providing subsidized
long-term industrial loans such as the Industrielkreditbank AG
and the Finanzierungs AG, or subsidized long-term agricultural
loans such as the Landwirtschaftliche Rentenbank.   But this
group also includes the house bank of the Federal railways.

        Thirdly, there are two banks which provide export
credit that qualifies for government guarantees; the
Privatdiskont AG in Frankfurt which provides a market for
export and import bills of exchange and plays a role in the
inter-bank money market and the Liquiditäts Konsortialbank AG
which operates the 'lifeboat' arrangements for German banks.

(d)   Post Office Services

        The Post Office operates two banking services.   The
Postscheckdienst operates a giro system for cheques and
money transfers, and the Postsparkasse operates a savings
bank.   Together they attract about two per cent of all banking
business.   As all Post Offices serve as branches, charges
tend to be low.   Together with comparatively long opening
hours, and exemption from postal charges, the Post Office

provides an attractive service particularly for small accounts.
In recent years the Post Office has also started to cash
cheques from other banks.

Other Banks and Financial Institutions

Under this heading we discuss building societies
(which are officially classified as reporting banks),
investment funds and some other institutions which qualify
as banks but are not included in the monthly statistical
reporting to the Deutsche Bundesbank.

(a) Building Societies

Building Societies (Bausparkassen) are better
described as mutual savings and mortgage associations because
they provide a special service which differs somewhat
from that provided by building societies in other countries.
Their sole purpose is to provide second rank mortgages to
those who have saving deposits with them. There are
thirteen public building societies, all but three in effect
branches of Landesbanken Girozentralen. Among the private
building societies are the Bausparkasse Gemeinschaft der
Freunde Wustenroth GmbH, the Bausparkasse Schwäbisch Hall AG
(which is associated with the co-operative banks), and the
Beamtenheimstattenwerk gemeinnützige Bauskparkasse für den
öffentlichen Dienst GmbH. Of the others most have strong
links with either commercial banks or leading insurance
companies.

Both public and private building societies benefited,
and still benefit, from the fact that their deposits (which
cannot be withdrawn except in special circumstances) attract
favourable tax treatment. Mainly because of this, they grew
rapidly in the 1960s and early 1970s. In more recent years,
their growth has slowed down somewhat. Measured in terms of
their aggregate balance sheet, the total volume of their
business is equivalent to about 5 per cent of the total

volume of all bank business.

(b) Investment Funds

Like mortgage banks, investment funds (Kapitalanlage-
sellschaften) are subject to rigid legal provisions. They
are defined as institutions "which invest funds according
to the principle of risk diversification, and which issue
certificates detailing the rights of depositors to their
investments" (Gesetz über Kapitalanlagegesellschaften, Art. 1)
and are restricted to this type of business. There are 34
such institutions, most of them owned by commercial banks.
They all operate open funds either in shares or in bonds or
in both; there are also some real estate funds. After rather
timid beginnings in the 1950s they have developed rapidly
since 1975, but still account for only five per cent of the
holdings of all securities.

(c) Credit Guarantee Associations

Credit guarantee associations (Kreditgarantiegemeinschaften, or Burgschaftsbanken) are banks created mainly by
commercial banks and savings banks, but also by local and
regional chambers of commerce, to offer guarantees for their
members, mainly smaller firms in various branches of industry
and trade, which can be used in lieu of collateral in
obtaining bank loans. Their operation is discussed in some
detail in Chapter 6 below.

(d) Securities Depositories

Securities depositories (Wertpapiersammebanken) are
banks which hold securities and operate a giro system for
securities holdings for their members (mainly banks) in each
of the seven seats of German stock exchanges.

Structural Change and Competition

There are a number of structural changes discernible in the German banking system. Over the last twenty years or so, the commercial banks and the Big banks in particular, have made successful attempts to turn to small scale deposit taking and to attract savings deposits in particular. At the same time, they have offered more long-term lending than they used to, partly via their subsidiaries, and not only to the traditional industrial clients.

On the other hand savings institutions, and to a lesser degree the co-operative banks, have turned to large scale industrial lending, to trading in securities, to issuing and placing business, and to dealing on international markets on a much larger scale than they used to do.

Thus the savings institutions in particular have broken into the traditional territory of the commercial banks, and of the Big banks in particular, while these have extended their business in directions which used to be the realm of the savings institutions. It has been argued above that this is to a large extent the result of the fact that the growth process that the German economy experienced favoured savings institutions more than it did other types of banks, and that this intensified the competitive process which was further stimulated by the decision, in 1967, to abandon the compulsory interest rate and conditions cartel which had operated up to that time. As a result German banks have, under the force of competition, lost some of their formerly distinguishing characteristics.

The force of the competitive process is also evinced by the concentration process the German banking system has experienced, and the enormous extension of the branch networks. Part of this process was no doubt the result of much needed rationalization, particularly within the co-operative banks but also among the savings institutions.

But there is also a clearly discernible trend towards
larger units which in more recent years has been fostered by
the gowing role of the Deutsche Mark as an international
currency and the consequent involvement of German banks in
international markets.

Behind these processes there has been a marked shift
in importance from short-term to long-term business. This
is most obvious in the structure of deposit taking, as shown
by the following comparison of the shares of sight deposits,
of time deposits (for four years and more), and of savings
deposits (including saving bonds) in the toal of all non-bank
deposits for all banks:

Table C: Structure of Non-Bank Deposits with all German
Banks

	1958	1978	1979
Share of sight deposits [1]	23.9	14.4	15.4
Share of time deposits	15.2	13.1	13.9
Share of savings deposits	34.1	51.5	50.4

Source: Deutsche Bundesbank (1976), p. 136-137, and
Monatsberichte 8/1980, Table III.3.

These changes coincide with higher growth rates of
long-term lending than of short-term lending. There are a
number of reasons for this growing importance of long-term
lending. On the one hand, the growth process of the German
economy was based, in part at least, on its export
performance. German firms often attempted aggressively
to expand exports. This required long-term finance in view
of the well-known fact that the credit risk has typically
been shifted from the importer to the exporter. On the
other hand, the industrial investment which supported the
growth process required long-term finance in view of the
scarcity of capital and the rapidity of structural change
within industry. Furthermore, growing affluence and the
official housing policy made for a booming market in

---

1. Sight deposits, less than 1 month; time deposits 1 month
and over.

mortgage credit which benefitted banks as much as it
benefitted non-bank financial intermediaries. Finally, the
growing need for investment in infra-structure, and the
reform policies of the last decade have created a great
demand for long-term credit on the part of public authorities,
and in particular on the part of local authorities.

Traditionally German savers have shown a strong
liquidity preference (though much less so than in the UK) and
this has not been eroded by the fact that they have also become
much more interest rate conscious than they used to be.
This liquidity preference has forced the banking system to
transform relatively short-term liquid savings deposits into
long-term lending to industry, commerce, and the public
authorities. This was achieved partly by the structural
changes described above, but also by issuing bank bonds which
have gained importance particularly in more recent years as
an instrument for the inter-bank transfer of funds without
loss of liquidity as well as an asset which can be used to
tap resources of non-bank financial intermediaties and also,
though to a smaller extent, the public at large. That there
has been a marked shift from mortgage bonds to local
authority bonds is but one indicator of the growing need for
finance on the part of public authorities.

On the money markets the savings institutions and
the co-operative banks are still the main source of supply
but the Big banks are less demanding than they used to be.
Here, too, the "structural equalization" has wrought changes.
Moreover, the increased and still growing involvement of
German banks on international markets has presented problems
for monetary policy at least as much as it has opened up new
opportunities for German non-banks to tap the cheapest
source of credit.

Finally, something needs to be said about the investment
policy of German banks. To a large extend this can be seen
as an attempt to round off the range of services they can

offer their customers and to reap the benfits of scale economies.[1] Moreover, the growing internationalization of banking required large units as an entry requirement. Yet, however good the reasons, the results have given cause for concern. Large units may be more efficient, but they are also more powerful. The concentration process in the banking sector has been a matter for public debate for some years. The Federal Cartel Office has recently made moves to investigate certain aspects of banking policy. The Monopoly Commission investigated the banking industry and argued that more competiton was possible. More recently, the so-called banking structure commission[2] recommended a number of changes, most notably a limitation of bank investments in other banks and in non-banks. This will certainly not be the end of the discussion but what the outcome of the debate will be is still uncertain.

What is certain is that in spite of the concern that has been voiced there can be no doubt that there is still a strong element of competiton in the banking sector. To some extent the market for bank services is still a buyers' market rather than a sellers' market. This is shown not only by the high incidence of advertising and the fact that entry barriers (at least for foreign competitors) seem to be low but also by the fact that there is considerable variation in bank charges across banks, and that there are indications that bank customers attempt to play off one bank against another.[3] After all, one aspect of the extension of the branch networks is that virtually everybody now has the choice between various banks in his vicinity. Thus, while there is concentration and economic power that may give cause for concern, there is also competition which seems to benefit thecustomer and which does not seem to have done much harm to the economy at large.

---

1. See Monopolkommission (1976), para. 70.
2. See Bericht (1979).
3. See Stein (1975), esp. pp. 220-235.

2. FINANCIAL MARKETS

Money Markets

The German money market is an inter-bank market as far as money on call and time deposits are concerned. By contrast, all transactions in money market paper are so heavily dominated by Bundesbank operations that an inter-bank market ceases to exist and trading takes place only between the Bundesbank and individual banks. A very small market for prime acceptances, a special kind of bill of exchange, is the only exception but even this market is under the strong influence of the Bundesbank. As there is, in addition, a high degree of substitutability between money on call and time deposits traded in the inter-bank money market, and the money market paper traded between the Bundesbank and the banks, both markets are strongly affected by whatever open market operation the Bundesbank conducts. (See Section 3 below and Chapter 8).

Only some 200 banks in Germany trade regularly on the inter-bank money market. As explained above, both the savings institutions and the co-operative banks operate an internal money market so that even large savings banks or credit co-operatives do not trade on the inter-bank money market. But the savings institutions' central giro institutions are very active traders on that market, as are (though to a lesser degree) the central institution of the credit co-operatives. Similarly, many private bankers and quite a few regional banks rarely participate, while others are active traders. Information about the size of the market is not available but it is said to be considerable. Indeed, in recent years the market has expanded as a consequence of the growing internationalization of all the money markets in the major European currencies as well as the Euro-currency markets.

By contrast, the money-paper market is very much a domestic market. Sales to foreigners need Bundesbank

permission which is regularly denied. The main assets traded
are short-term Treasury bonds.   They do not carry a repurchase
obligation ahead of their maturity date but, nevertheless,
there is no secondary market in them analagous to the
Treasury bill market in London. This is largely due to the
way in which the Bundesbank operates its rediscount and
lombard facilities, described in Section 3 below.

Security Markets

Security markets do not play the important role in the
German financial system they play in other financial systems
including that of the UK. The reason most frequently advanced
for this relative unimportance is that the German security
markets are narrow: the flow of funds to industry and commerce
is channelled predominantly via bank lending and only to a small
degree via the security markets. While this is true, some
qualifications need to be made. Considered in an
international context, the German market for new security
issues is substantial, especially if one considers not only
bonds and shares, but includes also borrowers' notes
(Schuldscheine).[1] Moreover, the growth of the public debt
in recent years has increased the flow of funds through the
market for new issues. Yet, for reasons to be discussed
below, a large part of the new issues are held for most of the
period up to their maturity by their first buyer. Thus
secondary markets are narrow; there is in fact much less trade
in bonds and shares outstanding than one would expect from
the volume of new issues or the amount of securities outstanding.

Another feature of German securities markets is that
they are dominated by banks. Not only do banks issue a
sizeable amount of securities, especially bonds, they also
hold considerable amounts of them. Moreover, there are few

1.   That this should be done has been argued by Richebächer
     (1968) p. 36-37. The OECD does so in their regular financial
     statistics on this basis of estimates provided by the
     Bundesbank, but the Bundesbank does not provide this information
     in its own monthly or annual reports.

transactions in securities that are not handled by banks.
Often they also 'make' the market, particularly in those
instances in which a security is not traded on the stock
exchange. Table 2.4 presents some data on the amount of
securities outstanding at the end of 1979. As the data
relates to nominal values, the relative weight of shares is
underestimated. At prices current at the end of 1979, the
total value of shares would have nearly DM312 bn, rather
less than two-thirds of the total value of bonds.[1]
Borrowers' notes outstanding amount to more than 40 per cent
of the amount of shares outstanding valued at current prices.
Table 2.4 also shows that the major issues and holders differ
considerably for bonds, shares and borrowers' notes and these
are discussed separately in the following paragraphs.

The bond market is by far the largest part of the
security market[2]. Table 2.5 shows the amount of bonds
outstanding. The major reason for the rapid growth has been
the growth of public debt. Public bond issues have increased
more rapidly in the 1970s than bonds issued by other borrowers.
But public issues do not indicate the full extent of the use
of the bond market for the public purses. Traditionally
German local authorities rarely issue bonds, but rely on bank
loans, especially from savings banks. Similarly, Länder do
not use the bond market much, but equally use bank loans. A
large part of these bank loans is financed by issuing bank
bonds known as "local authority bonds" (or "communal bonds")
because bank loans to local authorities (and other public
bodies) are used as collateral for these bonds, thus endowing
them with a higher degree of security (which enables, e.g.
insurance companies to invest in them). Hence in order to
gauge the extent of the public use of the bond market, the
amount of local authority bonds should be added to the amount
of bonds issued by public authorities because they represent
indirect borrowing on the bond market by public authorities.

---

1. It should be noted however that this is a fairly recent
   development. Up to the early 1970s the amount of shares
   outstanding at current prices was about equal to the
   amount of bonds outstanding.

2. Bonds (anleihen) here include convertibles (Wandelanleihen
   and Optionsanleihen) as well as Treasury notes
   (Kassenobligationen).

TABLE 2.4: SECURITIES OUTSTANDING[a] AT END OF 1979 (Mill. DM)

Issuers / Holders	Bonds Issued by				Total Domestic Bonds	Foreign DM Bonds	Total Bonds	Shares	Borrowers Notes
	Government	Public Enterprises	Private Enterprises	Banks					
Central Bank	1056	1045	-----	4	2105	-----	2105	-----	-----
Banks	31089	7200	657	173488	212434	6440	218874	6301	.
Insurance Companies	5742	1426	900	50882	58950	365	59315	1935	107997
Investment Funds	3246	1369	536	21759	26910	284	27194	3075	.
Government	2660	241	29	9050	11980	17	11997	6140	.
Firms	4467	790	529	21646	27432	522	27954	13394	.
Households[b]	44555	6402	2031	57772	110760	2852	113612	13926	.
Rest of World	11414	2702	245	8602	22963	52969	75932	4939	.
Unknown[c]	-----	710	902	29378	30990	6671	37661	35281	29785
Total	104229	21885	5829	372581	504524	70120	574644	84991	137782

Notes: a At nominal values; only securities denominated in DM.
        b Only amounts held by banks for private household sector
        c Either in private holdings outside the banking system, or held abroad, or by non-reporting banks.

Source: OECD Financial Statistics, Suppl. 13D (1980), Table A 162/01.

TABLE 2.5: DOMESTIC BONDS OUTSTANDING AT END OF YEAR

	Total	Of which					DM Bonds Issued by Foreign Institution:
		Bank Bonds (Total)	Mortgage Bonds	Local Authority Bonds	Industrial Bonds	Public Bonds	
	(Mill. DM)	%	%	%	%	%	(Mill. DM)
1955	14841	66.9	41.6	19.6	13.0	19.8	-----
1960	43076	63.4	34.7	23.0	11.9	18.4	514
1965	95961	71.2	35.6	23.1	7.2	21.7	2966
1970	158005	74.5	30.6	32.1	4.9	20.5	19371
1975	316863	75.7	23.7	34.4	2.8	21.5	35941
1979	503648	73.9	19.4	35.6	1.2	25.0	70120

Source: Deutsche Bundesbank, Monatsberichte, various issues.
          Statistisches Jahrbuch, various years.

These two kinds of bonds are the only ones which increased their share in the total amount of bonds in the 1970s.

Even excluding local authority bonds, bank bonds form the largest part of all bonds outstanding. To some extent, they constitute the counterpart to, and financing instrument of, the large (and increasing) amount of long-term bank loans. This is true for mortgage bonds as well as for the bonds issued by banks with special functions (see above), and the growing amount of other bank bonds.

Industrial bonds[1] form a small and dwindling part of the total amount of bonds outstanding. During most of the 1970s redemptions have exceeded new issues. This is primarily a reflection of the high cost of this way of borrowing funds for industry and commerce compared with other means, especially borrowers' notes (Schuldschein loans). (See Chapter 4.)

Finally, the use of the German bond market by foreign issuers has grown rapidly in the 1960s; in the 1970s the share of foreign issues has stabilized at about 12 per cent of domestic issues. Domestic non-banks (predominantly households) buy a large amount of new issues, but typically reduce their purchases whenever the yield rises and bond prices fall. On the whole, domestic banks counteract these cycles in their purchases which on average are about as large as those of domestic non-banks. Bundesbank operations in the bond market are often substantial, and certainly add to the instability of demand, as does foreign demand. Indeed, bonds have often been the vehicle for the massive inflows of foreign funds which the German economy experienced in the 1960s and 1970s.

By comparison with the relatively large market for new issues, the secondary market for outstanding bonds is small (see Table 2.6). It is well known that a large proportion of domestic non-banks do not sell their bonds without necessity nor do bank holdings of bonds vary

---

1.   "Industrial"here stands for all non-financed enterprises.

TABLE 2.6: STOCK EXCHANGE TURNOVER[a]
(Mill. DM)

	Domestic Bonds	Domestic Shares	Foreign Bonds	Foreign Shares	Total
1963	1517	5539	154		7210
1964	2534	6645	351		9530
1965	2592	4523	276		7391
1966	2196	4545	491		7233
1967	4508	7639	627		12775
1968[b]	5381	14994	1455		21829
1969	6308	19542	2707		28559
1970	6730	12194	2805		19727
1971	6287	15700	3244	964	26177
1972	10131	22132	6410	1672	40301
1973	13498	18978	4467	1239	38182
1974	11325	13211	2825	941	28303
1975	30796	27466	4615	2256	65134
1976	27770	24919	5752	2747	61190
1977	35518	27615	8807	2596	74537
1978	37553	34127	10990	4388	87059
1979	29995	25663	8500	4173	68334

Notes: a All German stock exchanges except Berlin.
       b Before July 1968 banks were not obliged to transact
          all security business on the stock exchange.

Source: Börsen-und Wirtschaftshandbuch 1970 and 1979.

substantially. For banks, bonds are not just an asset in
which to invest liquid funds, they are just as much an
instrument with which to transfer funds from one bank to
another. Savings banks and credit co-operatives, it is true,
hold much of their liquid reserves in the form of bonds
because (as shown above) they do not use the money market.
But other banks use bank bonds in particular as an alternative
to direct lending which has the advantage of not being
subject to the rules applying to bank loans (see below). To
a considerable extent, therefore, the bond market is an
inter-bank market.

The fact that the bond market is to a large extent an
inter-bank market has in the last few years led to an enormous
extension of the telephone trade between banks, so much so
indeed that the turnover on the telephone market for bonds
is now considerably larger than the turnover on the stock
exchange market. A large part of this trading involves sales
with repurchase arrangements at prices which are different
from current market prices, so that the telephone trade is
not entirely comparable to trading on the stock exchange.
This is not the only reason why the bond market is dominated
by banks. Banks are not only important issuers as well as
buyers and holders of bonds; they also act as issuing houses,
as buying and selling agents, and as dealers on their own
account who play an important role as marginal buyers and
sellers. In this latter capacity they have a strong influence
on the price of bonds, and thus on yields.

It should be noted, finally, that the absence of large
institutional buyers and the comparatively small size of
German non-bank financial intermediaries as well as the
legal restrictions under which they operate accounts both
for the role played by banks in the bond market, and for its
instability. In the 1960s indeed, the social security funds
acted as stabilizing institutional buyers but the difficulties
in which they have found themselves in recent years because
of the recession and the social policies pursued by the
federal government, have turned them from buyers to sellers

of bonds. Moreover, because there are no large institutional buyers it is necessary to "retail" new issues. This is yet another reason for the dominant role played by banks in the bond market.

In spite of the fact that the market for new bond issues is larger than is often allowed for, it is not very robust. This is perhaps best shown by the fact that the eleven banks which are most strongly involved in issuing and placing new bonds have formed a consortium (Zentraler Kapitalmarktausschuss) which attempts to provide an orderly market by recommending the conditions (terms, yield, etc.) for new issues, and by applying the Indian fiel principle: a new issue should be put onto the market only after the previous one has been wholly taken up. This consortium can only use moral suasion, but in spite of this lack of formal sanction this consortium has been successful in preventing a glut of new issues at any one time. Although this consortium is a private affair there is co-operation and indeed mutual consultation with an interministerial committee (Ausschuss fur Kreditfragen der öffentlichen Hand) which attempts to co-ordinate the issue of bonds by public authorities and other public agencies.

In terms of the current value of all shares outstanding the share market was until recently of about equal size as the bond market. The large increase of the public debt in recent years has, however, made the bond market larger by a considerable margin. Foreign equities account for a substantial part of share market business; in recent years they attracted at least a quarter, and often a third, of all funds invested in equities. Among buyers, domestic non-banks predominate. Households form a large part of them, but so do non-financial firms and also some non-bank financial intermediaries. Demand by non-banks varies again with the level of share prices but not quite as markedly as in the case of bonds. Foreign buyers from a larger part of demand in the share market than they do in the bond market, and a somewhat more stable one, too. Banks buy far fewer shares than bonds, and indeed have been net sellers in some years.

But in accordance with their role as issuing houses for shares
they are prepared to act as buyers if the public at large is
unwilling or unable to buy, as in 1976-1977.

As in the case of the bond market, the secondary market
in shares is considerably smaller than the market in new
shares (see Table 2.6). Again it seems that the main reason
for this is the fact that a substantial part of all shares
outstanding is held by non-financial firms as long-term
investment or as means of domination. Casual empiricism also
suggests that households are often slow in adapting share
portfolios, although this seems to be less true today than it
was twenty years ago. There is very little inter-bank
trading in shares on a regular basis.

The absence of large institutional investors and the
narrowness especially of the secondary market means that the
banks dominate the share market as they dominate the bond
market. Again they act as issuing houses, as retailers,
as buying and selling agents, and as buyers on their own
account, not to mention their role as advisors to investors
as well as to borrowers. In contrast to the situation on
the bond market, however, their direct involvement is much
smaller, and therefore their influence on share prices smaller
than their influence on bond prices.

The banks also dominate the market for share options
which is a small market on the fringe of the share market.
Centred in Frankfurt, it has grown since its inception in
1970 (previously all trading in futures was banned), but
still does not amount to much: less than a dozen banks trade
regularly on the market, contracting a few hundred transactions
per day in the less than 50 shares that are admitted to
option trading.

Technically borrowers' notes (Schuldscheine) do not
qualify as securities, which is one of the reasons for their
popularity. But they are an instrument which allows banks to

mobilize a part of their long-term loans by selling them to
insurance companies and other investors. There is not however,
a formalized market for borrowers' notes, nor are they
traded competitively; indeed, they are rarely traded at all.
The bank which sold them will normally arrange for a transfer
from one investor to another, and will in some cases enter into
repurchase arrangements. Yet there is no open market:
transactions are conducted within a relatively small group of
clients and business partners. Buyers are largely, though by
no means wholly, insurance companies.

Because borrowers' notes are technically issued against
a bank loan, banking statistics do not record them separately,
so that no data are available about the total amount of
borrowers' notes outstanding, or about the amounts issued
from year to year. Such statistical information as we have is
contained in the OECD figures in Table 2.4. It is known,
however, that the federal government has repeatedly made use
of this instrument; most of the loans from non-banks other
than social security institutions are said to take this form.
While this is not a large part of the public debt it would add
another 7.6 billion DM in 1975 and 12.6 billion DM in 1979 to
the (unknown) total amount of such debts outstanding.

In recent years borrowers' notes have increasingly
replaced bonds as long-term debt instruments. One reason
for this is that interest earned on bonds held by foreigners
is subject to the 25 per cent witholding tax introduced in
1964, while borrowers' notes are not. Borrowers' notes are
therefore an attractive instrument for foreign investment in
DM, and have frequently been issued for this purpose. That
even the federal government did so earlier this year (1980)
by selling borrowers' notes to Swiss banks has understandably
caused some raised eyebrows.

It hardly needs to be added that this is another
'market' which is dominated by banks: they advise the issuer,
take new issues into their portfolios,sell them to investors,
and arrange for repurchases and renewed sales if necessary.

Stock Exchanges

There are seven stock exchanges in Germany; in Berlin, Bremen, Düsseldorf, Frankfurt, Hannover, Munich and Stuttgart. They are public institutions subject to special legal provisions (the Börsengesetz), but otherwise self-governing. Thus the Land in which they are situated appoints official brokers (amtliche Kursmakler), who are public officials while the stock exchanges themselves admit free brokers (freie Makler) as well as traders (mostly bank representatives or partners of non-financial companies). Official brokers have the task of fixing the price of those securities which are officially admitted to be traded on the stock exchange. They collect all offers to buy or sell and fix the so-called unit price (Einheitskurs) such that turnover is maximized. They are not allowed to trade on their own account except when this is technically necessary to balance demand and supply. Free Brokers handle securities which are admitted to be regularly (but not officially) traded on the stock exchange (geregelter Freiverkehr), theycan trade on their own account. Like official brokers, they usually look after a particular group of securities, and fix unit prices. All business on the stock exchange has to go through the hands of one of these two groups of brokers. The only exception is a small group of shares which are admitted to continuous trading (fortlaufende Notierung) in larger lots.

There are strict conditions for the listing of securities to be traded on the stock exchange. Indeed, the strictness of conditions is the reason why a distinction is made between admittance to "official" trading, and to "regular" trading, conditions for the latter being slightly less onerous. Every stock exchange is independent, and has its own admittance procedure. By no means all securities are traded on all stock exchanges: it is quite common that they are traded on only one or two. Nevertheless there are few securities that are not traded in either Frankfurt or Düsseldorf. Indeed, more than 70% of all security trading on stock exchanges is concentrated on those two; by comparison, all the others are insignificant. Despite this concentration, the business of German stock exchanges is small by international standards.

There is a security depository (Wertpapiersammelbank or
Kassenverein) attached to each stock exchange which operates
a giro system for securities, so that it is normally unnecessary
to transfer the securities themselves from one holder to
another. Indeed, for legal reasons, most of the foreign
securities traded on German stock exchanges are in fact
certificates representing foreign securities owned by the
Deutscher Auslandskassenverein in Frankfurt. The operation of
the stock exchanges is discussed in more detail in Chapter 8.

3.   THE DEUTSCHE BUNDESBANK

Introduction

     There are two features which set the Deutsche Bundesbank,
the West German central bank, apart from other central banks.
Firstly, the Bundesbank is a banking system of its own with a
branch in every major town or city. Secondly, it is arguably
the most independent central bank in any western country.

     The Deutsche Bundesbank was created in 1957 by
restructuring the central banking system which had been
instituted after the end of the Second World War by the Allied
Powers. Although much more centralized than its predecessor,
the Bundesbank still shows some marked federal features. Thus
it has a main branch in each of the Länder which make up the
federation; these Landeszentralbanken act as head offices for
more than 200 branch offices. The Bundesbank therefore has
a presence in every town which may be said to be a regional
centre for industry, commerce or banking.

     The federal structure is also discernible in the way
the Bundesbank is governed. It is headed by a council (Zentralbankrat) which consists of its board of directors and of
the presidents of the eleven Landeszentralbanken. The board
of directors (which consists of the president and the vice-
president of the Bundesbank, and at the most six, and at the

time of writing four, directors) is essentially chosen by
the federal government. The presidents of the Landeszentralbanken, on the other hand, are basically chosen by the
governments of the various Länder. There is thus a strong
Länder presence in the higher decision making body of the
Bundesbank which meets once a fortnight to consider the
state of the economy and to decide (by simple majority voting)
on measures of monetary policy. The board of directors
usually meets twice a week, conducts the day-to-day business
and implements the decisions of the Zentralbankrat. All
members of the Zentralbankrat are elected for an eight year
term; to minimize political influences, appointments are
staggered. Reappointments are possible and customary. Indeed
there have been few political appointments.

The independence of the Bundesbank stems from two
facts. On the one hand, it is a public law company whose
tasks are explicitly defined in its statutes (the
Bundesbankgesetz)[1] - "to regulate the circulation of money
and the supply of credit ... with the aim of safeguarding the
currency". Of course, the Bundesbank "is obliged to support
the general economic policy of the federal government" - but
"without neglecting its tasks".[2] Thus the Bundesbank is
given a specific task to perform, which is generally interpreted
as keeping down the rate of inflation.[3] As this could bring
it into opposition with the federal government the statutes
explicitly stipulate that "in the execution of its tasks ...
(the Bundesbank) is independent of orders from the federal
government".[4] This is the second element of the Bundesbank's
independent status - it cannot be given orders. Cabinet

---

1. For the text, see Müller and Consbruch (1977). For an
   English version, see Deutsche Bundesbank Instruments
   of Monetary Policy in the Federal Republic of
   Germany (Frankfurt, 1971)

2. The quotations are taken from Art. 3 and Art. 12 of
   the Bundesbankgesetz.

3. It should be noted that apart from this (macroeconomic)
   task the Bundesbank is also charged with a more
   microeconomic one, i.e. to help to preserve an efficient
   banking and payments system.

4. Art. 12 Bundesbankgestz.

ministers may participate in meetings of the Zentralbankrat
(and have on occasions done so), but have no vote. They can
ask for a two week moratorium on any decisions taken, but
(as far as is known) no use has ever been made of this
provision. The Bundesbank's independence is further
emphasized by another rule which stipulates that the president
of the Bundesbank shall be consulted when the federal
government considers matters of monetary policy.[1] This has
frequently happened, and it is well known that the Bundesbank
has on occasions been a major influence on federal government
policy decisions. Indeed, although there have been instances
when the Bundesbank deemed it necessary to counteract federal
government policy, co-operation has been the rule. Yet it
should be noted that even when there was co-operation it was
often the Bundesbank which called the tune, based on its
image of independent experts.

The Bundesbank's independent status is further
emphasized by its membership in a number of institutions with
either consultative or policy-making character, such as the
so-called concerted action (konzertierte Aktion), the inter-
governmental business cycle committee (Konjunkturrat), the
interministerial fiscal planning committee (Finanzplanungsrat),
the interministerial public debt committee (Ausschuss fur
Kreditfragen der öffentlichen Handel) and the federal debt
consortium (Bundesanleihekonsortium).

There are three aspects of the activities of the
Bundesbank which should be discussed briefly before the
Bundesbank's policy instruments are analysed in detail.

First, the large branch network of the Bundesbank and
the fact that every bank has an account[2] with at least one
branch implies that the Bundesbank provides a giro network
for all German banks which can (and is) used for credit
transfers as well as a clearing house for cheques and other

---

1.   Art. 13 Bundesbankgesetz.

2.   Non-reporting credit co-operatives do not: but they are
      required to have one with their central co-operative
      institution, which have in turn to hold one with the
      Bundesbank.

inter-bank debts. It will be seen below that its discount
facility in effect also provides a clearing system for bills
of exchange. There is no need, therefore, for private
clearing houses.

Second, as central bank, the Bundesbank controls the
issue of notes. However, for historical reasons, coins are
issued by the federal government and put into circulation
by the Bundesbank. Coins therefore do not appear in the
balance sheet. At one time, there were limitations on the
amount of notes and coins that could be issued but these no
longer exist.

Third, the Bundesbank is the banker of both the
federal and the Land governments. All public authorities
other than local ones are obliged to deposit all their liquid
funds with the Bundesbank; they can hold deposits with other
banks only after permission to do so has been obtained from
the Bundesbank. This provision has on occasions been used
to ease a liquidity shortage; by asking public authorities
to deposit funds with other banks (frequently the Kreditanstalt fur Wiederaufbau, but also the former Landesbanken),
the Bundesbank in effect provided funds for the inter-bank
money market. As the public authorities' banker, the
Bundesbank also issues their debt, i.e. acts as agent for
the sale of Treasury bills, Treasury bonds, Treasury notes,
etc. It is, however, not the sole agent, and public
authorities are free to acquire funds through other channels.
In practice, Treasury paper as well as (public) bonds are
issued through the Bundesbank except that the Länder use their
own former Landesbanken (now merged with the Girozentralen).

The Bundesbank may also give loans to public authorities
(except local ones, but including the Federal Railways and the
Federal Post Office) at its current discount rate, but it need
not do so, and is in any case obliged to keep the total of
all such loans to less than 10 billion DM.[1] All public

---

1.   Treasury bills are to be counted against this quota;
        which is one reason why they are no longer issued.

authorities have therfore taken up loans from other banks
as well as from financial intermediaries or other non-banks
such as insurance companies, often against borrowers' notes.
Thus the Bundesbank has very little control over public
borrowing, but need not satisfy the demand of public
authorities for funds either. As it also has no control
over the use of funds deposited with it, fiscal policy is
altogether outside the realm of the Bundesbank.

There are a number of instruments the Bundesbank can
use to conduct monetary policy: it can vary minimum reserve
requirements, can alter discount and lombard facilities, and
can conduct open market policies. In addition, the Bundesbank
has developed an array of instruments designed to cope with
the problem which has beset German monetary policy since the
late 1950s - the influx of foreign funds. These are discussed
in the following paragraphs.

Minimum Reserve Requirements

Variations of minimum reserve requirements are one of
the most powerful policy instruments the Bundesbank can
wield. The reason is simple - they affect all banks, albeit
differently, and there is nothing banks can do to escape
their effects.

All banks are required to hold minimum reserves on
their Bundesbank account.[1] There are some minor exceptions
of which the most important are building societies and
security depositories.

The amount a bank is required to hold as minimum reserve
is calculated[2] as a particular proportion of all deposits

---

1.   Non-reporting credit co-operatives are allowed to hold
      their minimum reserves on a special account with their
      genossenschaftliche Zentralkasse; which in turn has to
      hold the requisite amount on its own Bundesbank account.

2.   What follows is based on the Bundesbank ordinance on
      minimum reserve requirements (Anweisung uber Mindest-
      reserven) which is printed in the Annual report. See
      also Deutsche Bundesbank Monatsbericht 3/1977 pp 21-24, and
      Dickertmann and Siedenberg (1979).

whose term is below four years by non-banks, by banks which are
themselves exempt from the minimum reserve requirement, and
by foreign banks, minus the amount of cash at hand.[1]
Reserve ratios vary for different kinds of deposits as well
as with the size of deposits. Sight deposits (terms of less
than a month) attract the highest ratio, time deposits (terms
of one month or more, but less than four years) a somewhat
lower ratio, and savings deposits the lowest. For each
category, the ratio rises with the amount of deposits held.
There are three intervals (see Table 2.7, where they are called
"stages on the progressive scale") which are constructed in
such a way that the average reserve ratio for each type of
deposit is a continuously rising function of the level of
deposits held. There have also been marginal reserve ratios
at times, mainly, but not only, on non-domestic deposits.

The Bundesbank Act provides for maximum ratios which
cannot be exceeded; actual ratios have been well below
maximum ones, except for savings deposits. As the maximum
ratios are averages, this does not prevent the Bundesbank
from fixing ratios for non-domestic deposits which are much
higher. Similarly marginal ratios have for a time been set
as high as 100 per cent (provided the average does not exceed
the statutory maximum).

The minimum reserves a bank is required to hold are
calculated as monthly averages but there is an interval of
a fortnight between requirements and actual holdings. The
amounts required to be held in each month are calculated on
the average of all deposits at the end of the day between
the 16th of the previous month and the 15th of the current
month[2] (for non-workdays, the amounts of the previous work-

---

1. Changes were made in the system in July 1977 and Table
   2.7 shows ratios that have been in force since that date.
2. Alternatively, banks may calculate the average from
   deposits on the 23rd and last day of the previous month
   and the 7th and 15th day of the current month - provided
   the Bundesbank does not suspect that this is used to
   lower reserve requirements.

days are used), while actual holdings are calculated as the average of the balances at the end of the day on all days of the current month.[1] Thus banks know on the 16th of each month how large their reserve requirements for the month are, and can use the remainder of the month to adjust their holdings so that they fulfil them. This has various consequences. On the one hand, there is less need to hold precautionary excess reserves, and so excess reserves have been rather small. On the other hand, banks may find themselves in urgent need of funds towards the end of the month. This imparts a strong seasonality on the money market which typically causes rates to rise towards the end of the month. Further, banks can use their holdings on their Bundesbank account as working balances as well as minimum reserve requirement holdings. This compensates somewhat for the fact that minimum reserve requirements do not attract interest. Finally, the Bundesbank may be forced to create central bank money against its wishes. If banks have been somewhat careless in fulfilling their minimum reserve requirements in the first half of a month, their attempts to acquire central bank money may put the Bundesbank in a position in which it has the choice between pushing some banks to the brink of illiquidity, or creating the required amounts of central bank money. After some bad experiences in 1973 and 1974, when the Bundesbank attempted to "wipe out" any liquidity reserves the banking system had, and succeeded in driving some firms perilously close to the wall, it has generally chosen to allow the necessary creation of central bank money. The repeated use of very short-term money market operations (for between four and ten days) indicates this. The form chosen for such operations - purchases of money market paper or securities with fixed repurchase agreements attached - demonstrates however that the Bundesbank tries to minimize

---

1.   In the case of cash at hand the average for the end of the last two days of the previous twelve months can be subsituted for actual holdings on the end of the last two days of the current month.

TABLE 2.7: RESERVE RATIOS. MARCH 1977 – JUNE 1980

% of liabilities subject to reserve requirements

	Liabilities subject to reserve requirements to residents								
	Sight liabilities			Time liabilities			Savings deposits		
	Stage on the progressive scale (1)			Stage on the progressive scale (1)			Scale on the progressive scale (1)		
Applicable from	1	2	3	1	2	3	1	2	3
	DM 10 mn and under	DM 100 mn and under, but more than DM 10 mn	more than DM 100 mn	DM 10 mn and under	DM 100 mn and under, but more than DM 10 mn	more than DM 100 mn	DM 100 mn and under	DM 100 mn and under, but more than DM 10 mn	more than DM 100 mn
1977 –									
March 1(2)	9.35	12.7	14.9	6.6	8.8	10.45	6.15	6.4	6.6
June 1	8.9	12.05	14.15	6.3	8.4	9.95	5.85	6.06	6.3
Sep. 1	8	10.85	12.75	5.65	7.55	8.95	5.3	5.45	5.65
1976 –									
Jan. 1	8	10.85	12.75	5.65	7.55	8.95	5.3	5.45	5.65
March 1	8.65	11.7	13.75	6.1	6.15	9.65	5.7	5.9	6.1
June 1	8.05	10.9	12.8	5.7	7.55	9	5.3	5.5	5.7
Nov. 1	8.75	11.85	13.95	6.2	8.25	9.8	5.8	6	6.2
1979 –									
Feb. 1	9.2	12.45	14.65	6.5	8.65	10.3	6.05	6.3	6.5
1980 –									

than DM 100 million; reserve class 4: less than DM 10 million – 2. From January 1, 1969 to June 30, 1972 the ratio for all savings deposits with banks in reserve class 4 in Bank Places was equal to the reserve ratio for time liabilities; from July 1, 1972 to October 31, 1973 this applied only to residents' savings deposits. From November 1 to December 31, 1973 the reserve ratio for these savings deposits was 9% – 3. The ratio of stage 1 on the progressive scale applies to the first DM 10 million of liabilities subject to reserve requirements, the ratio of stage 2 to the next DM 90 million and the ratio of stage 3 to liabilities exceeding DM 100 million – 4. From March 1, 1977 to February 28, 1978 the following discounts were in force for liabilities to residents in places withou a Bundesbank office: 1 percentage point for sight liabilities, 0.5 percentage point for savings deposits – a "Bank Places" are places in which there is an office of the Deutsche Bundesbank.

Liabilities subject to reserve requirements to non-residents

Liabilities subject to reserve requirements				Growth of liabilities			Explanatory notes on the growth reserve regulations	Applicable from
Sight liabilities	Time liabilities	Savings Deposits		Sight liabilities	Time liabilities	Savings deposits		
14.9	10.45	6.6						1977 March 1
14.15	9.95	6.3		no special ratios				June 1
12.75	8.95	5.65						Sep. 1
20	15	10			80		Additional reserve ratio for growth over the average level during the period from September 16 to December 15, 1977.	1978 Jan. 1
20	15	10			80			March 1
12.8	9	5.7						June 1
13.95	9.8	6.2		no special ratios				Nov. 1
14.65	10.3	6.5						1979 Feb. 1
13.45	9.45	6						1980 May 1

subject

Notes: (1) Printed Note 3
(2) Printed Note 4

Other notes should be disregarded.

Source: Deutsche Bundesbank, Monthly Report, June 1980, Table IV.I.

such short-term deviations from more long-term policy objectives.[1]

If a bank does not fulfil its obligations to hold the required minimum reserve it has to pay a penal interest rate (the current Lombard rate plus 3 per cent) on the difference for 30 days. The penal rate is high enough to ensure compliance in the great majority of cases.

Variations of minimum reserve ratios is a frequently used policy instrument: typically they are changed two to three times a year. Such variations change the level of interest rates, and affect the ability of banks to increase their lending. That they are effective is on the whole undisputed. What has been criticized is that minimum reserve ratios are at odds with a monetarist conception of controlling the money supply because they do not directly affect either the money supply or the amount of central bank money outstanding. While this is true it is doubtful whether the Bundesbank actually follows monetarist policies.[2] Another aspect which has been criticized, and justly so, is that the structure of reserve ratios favours banks with a high share of savings deposits and thus distorts competition between different banking groups. Such differences can be substantial, and suggest that the rapid growth of the savings banks has been favoured by this preferential treatment given to saving deposits.

Discount and Lombard facilities

As part of the role as lender of last resort, the Bundesbank offers both discount and Lombard facilities to banks. Traditionally, variations in the rates and conditions applying to such transactions have been among the major policy instruments of most central banks. In the 1950's the

---

1. See, e.g. the argument in the Annual Report of the *Deutsche Bundesbank* for 1975, Part I, Section 2(b).

2. For a similar argument, see Caesar (1976).

Bundesbank made much use of them. After full convertability
of the DM had been achieved, however, foreign exchange
transactions became much more important to most banks as a
source of central bank money, and variations in discount
and Lombard rates and conditions lost somewhat in
importance. The Bundesbank continued to use them as a
policy instrument, but used them cautiously. Only after the
obligation to buy all foreign currency offered had ended
with the demise of the Bretton Woods system in 1973 has this
policy instrument regained its former importance.
The emergence of the European Monetary System has again
threatened its role, but so far has not seriously impaired
it in the way the pre-1973 system of fixed exchange rates
did.

The discount facility is offered only to banks, and
applies only to bills of exchange which satisfy certain
criteria. They must have not less than five days and no
more than three months to maturity, must be based on
commercial rather than purely financial transactions, and
must carry the binding signature of three firms of undisputed
standing.[1] Bills of exchange which have their origins in
hire purchase transactions or which grew out of interim
financing arrangements of construction projects are
acceptable under certain conditions. So are bills
originating in export or import business; in some cases
they will even be given preferential treatment (i.e. will
be bought outside the so-called rediscount quotas - see
below). This applies, e.g., to bills which are used to
finance business with under-developed countries, or with
the German Democratic Republic. A particular category by
themselves are prime acceptances, i.e., import or export
bills in round amounts of 5,000 DM with a nominal value of
between 100,000 and 1,000,000 DM, because they will be
treated as money market paper if offered by the

---

1. This is judged by the local Bundesbank branch, and
   has to be demonstrated by the bank offering them for
   purchase by their balance sheets and profit-and-loss
   accounts. These reports and accounts are one of the
   major sources of intelligence about the economy for
   the Bundesbank.

Privatdiskont AG (which makes a market for them); if offered
by any other bank they will be treated like any other bill of
exchange.

The discount facility is, however, only available up
to a definite limit. These so-called "rediscount quotas"
are fixed individually for each bank and revised annually.
Account is taken in their determination of the bank's
capital resources, the structure of its business, and the
volume of bills of exchange it customarily discounts.[1]
Although fixed individually, rediscount quotas are uniformly
increased or decreased by the Bundesbank. Individual quotas
are known only to the banks concerned but changes in the
aggregate for all banks form part of the Bundesbank's measure
of "free liquid reserves", and are published regularly.
Banks have rarely made full use of their rediscount quotas.
Throughout the 1950s and 1960s rediscount quotas were never
used by more than 50 per cent (except possibly for very
short periods). In the 1970s the utilization rate was
higher, yet only during 1973-1974 and again in 1979, was it
higher than 80 per cent.

Still more frequent than changes in rediscount quotas
are variations of the discount rate - the rate at which
the Bundesbank discounts bills within the limit of available
rediscount quotas (see Table 2.8).

Like the discount facility, the lombard facility is
open only to banks. Basically it provides banks with an
additional source of central bank money by offering securities
as collateral so they can acquire loans from the Bundesbank.
Requests for such loans will not, however, be granted
automatically. Bundesbank regulations stipulate that the
loans be given only when this is necessary to relieve a
temporary shortage of liquidity, and when it is in keeping
with the general trend of monetary policy. Between 1970
and 1973 a general credit line (20 per cent of the relevant

---

1. For details see Deutsche Bundesbank Monatsbericht
   4/1975 pp 21-27, and Ch. II of the second part of the
   Bundesbank's annual report.

TABLE 2.8: DISCOUNT AND LOMBARD RATES OF THE DEUTSCHE BUNDESBANK AND SPECIAL INTEREST CHARGED FOR FAILURE TO MEET MINIMUM RESERVE REQUIREMENTS

Applicable from	Discount rate 1 % p.a.	Lombard rate % p.a.	Special rate of interest for failure to meet minimum reserve requirements % p.a. over lombard rate	Applicable from	Discount rate 1 % p.a.	Lombard rate % p.a.	Special rate of interest for failure to meet minimum reserve requirements % p.a. over lombard rate
1948 July 1	5	6	1	1959 March 21	3	4	3
Dec. 1	5	6	3	April 18	4	5	3
1949 May 27	4½	5½	3	June 20	5	6	3
July 14	4	5	3	Sep. 11	6	7½	3
1950 Oct. 27	6	7	3	Dec. 5	6	9	3
Nov. 1	6	7	1				
1951 Jan. 1	6	7	3	1970 March 9	7½	9½	3
				July 16	7	9	3
				Nov. 18	6½	8	3
1952 May 29	5	6	3	Dec. 3	6	7½	3
Aug. 21	4½	5½	3	1971 April 1	5	6½	3
1953 Jan. 8	4	5	3	Oct. 14	4½	5½	3
June 11	3½	4½	3	Dec. 23	4	5	3
				1972 Feb. 25	3	4	3
				Oct. 9	2½	5	3

Date				
1957 Jan. 11	4½	5½		3
Sep. 19	4	5		3
1958 Jan. 17	3½	4½		3
June 27	3	4		3
1959 Jan. 10	2¾	3¾		3
Sep. 4	3	4		3
Oct. 23	4	5		3
1960 June 3	5	6		3
Nov. 11	4	5		3
1961 Jan. 20	3½	4½		3
May 5	3	4	2	3
1965 Jan. 22	3½	4½		3
Aug. 13	4	5		3
1966 May 27	5	6½		3
1967 Jan. 6	4½	5½		3
Feb. 17	4	5		3
April 14	3½	4½		3
May 12	3	4		3
Aug. 11	3	3½		3
1974 Oct. 25	6½	8½		3
Dec. 20	6	6		3
1975 Feb. 7	5½	7½		3
March 7	5	6½		3
April 25	5	6		3
May 23	4½	5½		3
Aug. 15	4	5		3
Sep. 12	3½	4½		3
1977 July 15	3½	4		3
Dec. 15	3	3½		3
1979 Jan. 19	3	4		3
March 30	4	5		3
June 1	4	5½		
July 13	5	6		3
Nov. 1	6	7		3
1980 Feb. 29	7	6½		3
May 2	7½	9½		3

1. This is also the rate for cash advances. Until May 1956 lower rates likewise applied to foreign bills and expert drafts; fixed special rates were charged for certain credits which had been granted to the Reconstruction Loan Corporation and which ran out at the end of 1958 (for details see footnotes to the same table in the Report of the Deutsche Bundesbank for the Year 1961, page 91) - 2. An allowance of ¾% per annum was granted to banks in respect of the lombard loans taken between December 10, 1964 and December 31, 1964 - 3. Banks have not in principle been granted lombard loans at the lombard rate from June 1, 1973 up to and including July 3, 1974.

Source: Deutsche Bundesbank, Monthly Report, June 1980, Table V.I.

rediscount quota) was applied, more strict limits were used
between September 1979 and February 1980. In practice,
however, most banks seem to be able to get lombard loans
(at a price) if they can offer the right collateral.

Securities acceptable for lombard operations include
bills the Bundesbank would be prepared to (re)discount;
Treasury bill ans Treasury bonds with less than one year to
maturity, bonds issued by public authorities and other bonds
with a remaining term to maturity of less than four years.[1]

The lombard rate is higher than the discount rate,
usually by 1/2 to 2 percentage points. This is a reflection
of the role of lombard loans as a short term instrument for
for the acquisition of central bank money.[2] Yet the spread
between discount and lombard rate also plays another role.
In normal times, money market rates for three-month loans
will not be below the discount rate because most banks have
both unused rediscount facilities and bills they can offer
for (re)discount. Nor will it be above the lombard rate
because the lombard facility (if available) would be a
cheaper source of funds. If, however, monetary policy
is restrictive, and rediscount quotas fully used, money market
rates may easily stand above the lombard rate (as they did
in 1973-74, and again in recent months). Thus, by calibrating
the spread between the discount and the lombard rate, the
availability of lombard loans, and the size of rediscount
quotas the Bundesbank can (and does in fact) influence the
(short end of the) interest rate structure. This is the
reason why the Bundesbank has chosen to give banks ample

1.   That they can be used for lombard operations explains
      why such bonds (called Kurzläufer, or short-distance
      runners) are so popular with some banks, particularly
      savings banks and credit co-operatives (which
      frequently have no other means of acquiring central
      bank money in view of the fact that their statutes do
      not permit them to operate on the inter-bank money market'

2.   Note that a lombard loan can be had for as short a
      period as a day: whereas bills offered for (re)discount
      may not have less than five days to maturity, so that
      "discount loans" cannot behad for less than five days.

rediscount quotas for most of the period under review. For
the same reason, variations in rediscount quotas, or the
discount and lombard rate,have a signalling effect on the
economy at large as well as for the financial sector -
quite apart from the fact that the discount rate serves, as
it were, as a peg in relation to which many other interest rates
are set by banks.

It goes without saying that changes in redsicount
quotas do not affect the money supply directly. But if monetary
policy is restrictive, and rediscount quotas almost fully
used, their reduction will force banks to rearrange their
assets if they wish to acquire central bank money. This may
well bring about a change in the money supply, but this is
by no means certain. Hence variations of rediscount quotas
and (a fortiori) in discount and lombard rates are in the first
instance policy instruments which affect the level of
interest rates and the cost of central bank money in
particular.

Open Market Operations

Open market operations by the Bundesbank do not play
the predominant role they play in other countries, although
its traditional restriction to trade in short-term assets
with banks has long been transcended: since 1967 the Bundesbank
uses long-term assets as well as short-term assets, and
since 1971 these assets are also regularly sold to non-banks.
In spite of this broad scope the nature of the German security
market places severe restrictions on open market operations.

Indeed the lack of short-term paper which could have
been used for open market operations in a period of prudent
fiscal policies and persistent budget surpluses proved to be
so restrictive that a particular asset (Mobilisierungs-und
Liquiditätspapiere) has had to be created whose sole purpose is
to provide the Bundesbank with material for open market
operations (see Chapter 8).

TABLE 2.9: CHANGES IN CENTRAL BANK MONEY[a] AND IN BANKS' FREE LIABILITY RESERVES[b] DUE TO MONETARY POLICY ACTIONS (Bill. DM)

	1972	1973	1974	1975	1976	1977	1978	1979
Changes in								
Net Foreign Position	+16.9	+27.2	-2.8	-2.1	+8.3	+8.4	+20.3	-5.2
Net Deposits of Public Authorities (increase: -)	+3.0	-1.1	-3.0	+1.7	+3.7	+5.0	-2.1	+4.0
Minimum Reserve Requirements (increase: -)	-11.0	+6.4	+12.7	+7.2	-4.6	+8.1	-1.8	-3.2
Rediscount Quotas	-3.6	-11.9	+4.5	+4.5	+0.7	+6.5	+4.4	+5.1
Open Market Policies	-2.1	-6.3	-1.5	+11.6	-8.6	-0.7	-3.6	+2.7
Swap Operations								-2.4
Lombard Loans	0.0	+1.1	+2.0	-2.0	+6.5	-6.5	+1.0	+2.2
Other Factors	-0.2	-0.1	-4.6	-1.1	-5.6	-3.5	-3.8	-5.1
Changes in Central Bank Money and Banks' Free Liquidity Reserves	+3.0	+2.5	+7.4	+19.9	+0.3	+17.3	+14.3	-1.9
in Central Bank Money	+10.4	+6.9	+5.8	+9.5	+7.9	+10.9	+14.1	+7.8
in Banks' Free Liquidity Reserves	-7.5	-4.4	+1.6	+10.4	-7.6	+6.3	+0.2	-9.7
Stock of Banks' Free Liquidity Reserves at end of year	7.3	3.0	4.5	14.9	7.3	13.6	13.8	4.1

Notes: a   Bundesbank definition: Notes and coin circulating plus minimum reserve requirements on domestic deposits.

b   Excess reserves plus money market paper redeemable on demand plus unused rediscount quotas.

Source: Deutsche Bundesbank, Monatsbericht, 8/1980, Table I.3.

Another consequence of the nature of security markets for the conduct of open market policies is that open market operations are to a large extent conducted by issuing and selling new assets rather than by buying and selling existing assets. Of course, the fact that the discount and lombard facilities can be used to increase the amount of central bank money avaiable makes it possible to concentrate open market operations on the selling of new assets (and thus the reduction of central bank money available) and at the same time increases the importance of the market for new issues vis-a-vis the secondary market for existing issues. The preponderance of operations in new assets is further helped by the fact that the Bundesbank determines the prices at which it buys back short-term assets before maturity, and finally by the fact that since 1974 the Bundesbank has not as a rule issued to banks short-term assets which are redeemable on demand. Further details of these operations and of their effect on short-term money markets are given in Chapter 8.

In most of its open-market operations, the Bundesbank sets the price at which it will sell the various kinds of paper in which it deals, hence open market operations are used primarily to influence interest rates. However, open market operations do have an effect on the amount of central bank money in the economy, particularly when they involve the sale of assets which cannot be redeemed on demand. Such assets can of course be used to obtain central bank money via the lombard facility but use of the lombard facility is at the discretion of the Bundesbank and not automatic. Hence the sale of such assets does not create a stock of assets which can be converted into central bank money at short notice by the banking system. The effect on the amount of central bank money is of course the prime consideration when the Bundesbank offers to buy bills or securities for short periods.

Table 2.9 shows that the effects of open market operations on the money supply can be substantial.

Policies Which Influence Capital Flows

Insofar as the exchange rate of the DM is fixed, the determination of the rate is the prerogative of the federal government rather than the Bundesbank. Up to 1973, therefore, the Bundesbank was generally faced with the obligation to buy any amount of foreign currency offered. This obligation ceased with the freeing of exchange rates in March 1973 but since the creation of the European Monetary System in March 1979 the Bundesbank again has the obligation to buy any amount of the member states' currencies. For most of the 1960s and 1970s such involuntary purchase were the prime source of liquidity in the German financial system. To deal effectively with this often enormous and sometimes overwhelming influx of foreign funds the Bundesbank relied in addition to policy instruments already discussed, on an array of measures which were specifically designed to influence capital flows.

One of these instruments was differential minimum reserve requirements for domestic and for non-domestic deposits, and especially differential marginal rates. These have already been discussed above. What remains to be said here is that for a period in the early 1960s banks could deduct their lending abroad from their foreign deposits when calculating minimum reserve requirements, so that in effect their net foreign position was relevant to their minimum reserves. This so-called "compensation privilege" was discontinued, however, when it was found that it was misused.

Another instrument was a restriction on interest payments, in particular the so-called "witholding tax" which is levied on all interest payments on domestic securities held by foreigners. This regulation is still in force, and one reason why domestic security holdings are not particularly attractive to foreigners.[1]

---

1.   Securities issued by foreigners are exempt, even those denominated in DM. Foreign holdingsof DM - securities tend therefore to be concentrated on securities issued by foreigners - so much so indeed that the domestic security market is more or less sealed off from the market in foreign securities denominated by DM.

Yet another instrument was the cash deposit (Bardepot) scheme which was in operation from 1972 to 1974. This scheme required non-banks to deposit a certain fraction of any loan taken up abroad with the Bundesbank (without interest). For most of the period the fraction (fixed by the Bundesbank)[1] stood at 50 per cent so that the effect of the scheme was to increase the effective cost of borrowing abroad rather than inhibiting it (for that the sale would have to be at the legally permitted maximum of 100 per cent). The scheme was discounted after borrowing abroad had decreased considerably following the floating of exchange rates in March 1973.

By far the most frequently used instrument in this area were sway operations, i.e. the concomitant spot sale and forward purchase (or spot purchase and forward sale) of a foreign currency at a swap rate which induced banks to take up the Bundesbank offer. Such swap operations (involving spot sales and forward purchases in dollars) were much used between 1958 and 1971, but proved prone to misuse and were therefore often combined with a stipulation to invest the proceeds in US Treasury Bills. Basically, therefore, they amounted to a transfer into private (banking) ownership of part of the Bundesbank's reserve holdings in US dollars. They were again used in 1979 but this time not in order to stimulate capital exports but as a means to influence domestic liquidity; essentially, US dollar holdings served the same purpose as domestic security holdings serve as far as open market operations are concerned. This is shown by the fact that the Bundesbank not only used both spot/ forward purchase and spot purchase/forward sale swap operations, but also sold for fixed periods part of its own holdings of US treasury paper with a repurchase clause attached. Thus swap operations involved not only US dollar holdings but also (the right to) US money market paper.

---

1. Like the witholding tax, this scheme required an act of parliament and is therefore not really a Bundesbank policy instrument. Yet the act gave the Bundesbank the right to fix the relevant rates - and that is what matters here.

This seems an interesting and promising extension of open market operations in domestic assets.

In addition to such swap operations the Bundesbank has also intervened directly in both the spot and the forward markets for the US $ and other currencies.

It is generally agreed that none of the instruments used to influence capital flows is as effective as are the instruments used to influence domestic liquidity. The main reason for this comparative inefficiency is the fact that policies which are designed to effect the relative profitability of assets cannot really affect speculative holdings: Holders of DM denomiated assets who speculate on appreciation of the DM will not be deterred by a low, or even zero, rate of interest on their holdings.

Monetary Policy

The following paragraphs give a brief account of the ways in which the Bundesbank has pursued its monetary policy and how this affects the flow of funds to industry and commerce. Further discussion of monetary policy and of its relationship to inflation in both Britain and Germany is contained in Chapter 9.

There is no question that the Bundesbank cannot directly control the money supply as usually defined[1] and no such attempt is in fact made. Until the earl 1970s the Bundesbank aimed at controlling bank liquidity and (although this was never stressed as much) the level of interest rates.[2]

---

1.   The Bundesbank uses three concepts in their regular reportings: Ml (= notes and coins in circulation plus sight deposits);
     M2 (= Ml plus time deposits with less than four years to maturity); and
     M3 (= Ms plus savings deposits).

2.   See Irmler (1972) and Schlesinger (1977).

In 1973/74, amid much publicity, a shift to another policy
target was announced: the "new monetary policy" aims at
controlling the amount of "central bank money".

   "Central bank money" is defined by the Bundesbank as
notes and currency in circulation plus the minimum reserve
requirements banks have to hold on their domestic liabilities,
calculated on the basis of the reserve ratios in operation
in January 1974. As all those (sight, time and savings)
deposits which are subject to minimum reserve requirements
are also included in M3, "central bank money" as defined by
the Bundesbank can be viewed as a weighted form of M3, the
(constant) weights being given by the January 1974 reserve
ratios. This aggregate thus differs from more conventional
definitions of central bank money, or the so-called monetary
base. In particular, deposits held by public authorities
with the Bundesbank are not included as public authorities
do not need to hold minimum reserves. Like M3, the amount
of "central bank money" in the economy cannot be controlled
directly by the Bundesbank. This is indeed admitted by the
Bundesbank[1] which argues that "central bank money" measures
not the supply of central bank money but the realized
demand for central bank money: it indicates to what extent
the financial system and the non-banking sectors of the
economy have made use of the supply of central bank money made
available by the Bundesbank either voluntarily or involuntarily.
Nevertheless the Bundesbank treats this aggregate as a
target variable, and for   a number of years has announced at the
end of a year a target growth rate for "central bank money"
for the coming year. As Table 2.10 shows, the growth of
"central bank money" has rarely been kept within the limits
announced by the Bundesbank which tends to treat the announced
growth rate as a prediction rather than as a target, but
nevertheless justifies particular policy actions by reference
to the announced growth rate, i.e. acts as if it were a
target, but is prepared to let it go when the need arises.

---

1.   See Deutsche Bundesbank Monatsbericht 7/1974 pp 14-23.
     For a critique of the use of this aggregate, and of its
     alleged properties, see Neumann (1975) and Courakis (1980).
     Bockelmann (1980) offers some points in defence.

TABLE 2.10: CENTRAL BANK MONEY GROWTH: TARGETS AND OUTCOMES

Year	Nature of Target[a]	Target %	Outcome (JV) %	Outcome (JD) %
1975	JV	8.0	9.8	7.8
1976	JD	8.0	8.3	9.2
1977	JD	8.0	10.0	9.0
1978	JD	8.0	11.8	11.4
1979	JDiv	6.0-9.0	6.3	9.1
1980	JDiv	5.0-8.0		

NOTE: a Targets were defined as follows:

JV growth rate between December of one year and December of year for which growth rate is announced

JD average of growth rates for all ends of months during the year for which target growth rate is announced

JDiv average of growth rates for all months in the last quarter of the preceeding year compared with all months in the last quarter of the year for which target growth growth rate is announced

SOURCE: Deutsche Bundesbank, Geschäftsberichte, various years

However the margin of error has been much smaller than that
of the Bank of England in relation to its £M3 target.

The amount of "central bank money" will change when
non-banks change their sight deposits into time or savings
deposits, as happened increasingly in the 1970s, particularly
in years which saw high interest rates such as 1973/74 or
1979/80. Hence there is no definite, or even strong,
relationship between M1, M2 or M3 on the one hand, and
"central bank money" on the other hand. M3 tends to move
in the same direction as "central bank money" but that is
about all (see Table 2.11).

In practice, therefore, and without admitting as much,
the Bundesbank still treats bank liquidity (or more accurately,
banks' free liquidity reserves) as a major policy target.
This magnitude is defined as excess reserves plus money market
paper redeemable on demand held by banks, plus unused
rediscount facilities, plus unused lombard facilities which
have been announced to banks. Of these components, the
second is zero since (in 1974) the Bundesbank ceased to make
money market paper which is redeemable on demand (or which the
Bundesbank stands to buy back at any time) available to banks.
Similarly, the last component is zero since 1974 as banks
cannot rely on an automatic granting of lombard facilities.
Hence in practice banks' free liquidity reserve comprises
excess reserves and unused rediscount facilities: i.e. those
amounts of central bank money which banks have at their
disposal or which they can create even against the wishes of
the Bundesbank. This is therefore a measure of the banking
system's capacity to increase the amount of central bank
money at their disposal over and above the amount of "central
bank money" they hold already. In a sense, therefore, this
is a supply oriented measure, which can be controlled very well
by the Bundesbank. Indeed, in 1973 the Bundesbank announced
their intention to reduce banks' free liquidity reserves to
an "operationally required minimum" and succeeded in doing so:
as Table 2.11 shows, banks' free liquidity reserves were very
low in 1973 and 1974. Similarly the tightening of monetary

TABLE 2.11: MONETARY DEVELOPMENTS, 1973-1979
(Changes during the period indicated[a])

	1973	1974	1975	1976	1977	1978	1979
Central Bank Money and Banks' Free Liquidity Reserves (Billion DM)[b]							
Bundesbank Net Foreign Position[c]	+27.2	-2.8	-2.1	+8.3	+8.4	-20.3	-5.2
Public Authorities' Deposits (-)	-1.1	-3.0	+1.7	+3.7	+5.0	-2.1	+4.0
Minimum Reserve Requirements (-)	-6.4	+12.7	+7.2	-4.6	+8.1	-1.8	-3.2
Rediscount Quotas	-11.9	+4.5	+4.5	+0.7	+6.5	+4.4	+5.1
Open Market Operations[d]	-6.3	-1.5	+11.6	-8.6	-0.7	-3.6	+0.3
Lombard Loans	+1.1	+2.0	-2.0	+6.5	-6.5	+1.0	+2.2
Other Factors	-0.1	-4.6	-1.1	-5.6	-3.5	-3.8	-5.1
Central Bank Money and Banks' Free Liquidity Reserves	+2.5	+7.4	+19.9	+0.3	+17.3	+14.3	-1.9
Central Bank Money[e]	+6.9	+5.8	+9.5	+7.9	+10.9	+4.1[m]	+7.8
Banks' Free Liquidity Reserves[f]	-4.4	+1.6	+10.4	-7.6	+6.3	+0.2	-9.7
Stock of Banks' Free Liquidity Reserves at end of year	3.0	4.5	14.9	7.3	13.6	13.8	4.1
Stock of Lombard Loans at end of year	0.8	2.8	0.8	7.3	0.8	1.8	3.9
Important Monetary Indicators (%)							
Central Bank Money[b,g]	+7.3	+6.3	+9.8	+8.3	+10.0	+11.8[m]	+5.3
(average during year)	+10.6	+6.1	+7.8	+9.2	+9.0	+11.4[m]	+9.1
Bank (and Bundesbank) Lending to Domestic Non-Banks	+9.8	+7.9	+10.4	+10.1	+9.4	+11.5	+11.5
M1 (=Notes+Coins+Sight Deposits)	+1.3	+11.1	+14.3	+5.0	+11.7	+14.2	+3.8
M2 (=M1+time deposits up to 4 ys)	+13.1	+4.7	-0.1	+7.1	+11.1	+12.9	+7.9
M3 (=M2+savings deposits)	+8.4	+8.3	+8.7	+8.6	+11.0	+10.8	+5.7
Money Stock and Its Components (bill. DM)							
M3 (= 1 + 2 - 3 - 4 - 5)	+34.0	+35.2	+38.4	+41.0	+58.9	+64.8	+39.2
1 Bank Lending[h]	+67.5	+59.8	+85.5	+91.2	+94.2	+125.4	+139.0
2 Net Foreign Assets[h]	+23.5	+13.2	+16.8	+8.3	+10.1	+7.1	-21.8
3 Long-term Deposits	+45.6	+34.5	+61.3	+59.1	+42.9	+54.8	+75.8
4 Public Authorities' Deposits with Bundesbank	+4.2	+0.4	+1.4	-10.2	-0.8	+2.5	-1.7
5 Other Factors	+7.2	+2.9	+1.2	+9.6	+3.3	+10.4	+3.8

NOTES: (a) calculated on averages of end of month stocks. (b) calculated on averages of daily stocks during December. (c) Excluding swap operations. (d) Including (in 1979) swap operations and operations involving repurchase arrangements. (e) Excluding, since March 1978, cash at hand. (f) Including (up to May 1973) unused lombard facilities. (g) Calculated on the basis of reserve ratios in operation in January 1974. (h) Including Bundesbank. (m) Corrected for the change in the definition of central bank money (see Note e).

SOURCE: Deutsche Bundesbank, Geschäftsbericht 1979, p. 21.

policy in early 1979 resulted in an enormous decrease of
banks' free liquidity reserves (from more than 13 billion DM
at the end of 1978 to less than 3 billion DM in the second
half of 1979).

The main instrument used to affect banks' free
liquidity reserves are changes in rediscount quotas. As
argued above, these have been used frequently and have
contributed strongly to changes in this aggregate. But on
such changes work better when monetary policy is
meant to be restrictive: increasing rediscount quotas does
not ensure that banks expand their use of the discount
facility, especially as (as explained above) rediscount quotas
tend to be ample in any case. The same is true for changes
in reserve ratios: while their increase is bound to restrict
the banking system, a lowering of reserve ratios does not
necessarily lead to an increase in bank lending. The third
instrument used to influence banks' free liquidity reserves
are open market policies. However, the way in which they are
conducted implies that their effect is on interest rates as
much as on quantities, so that controlling banks' free
liquidity reserves is invariably intertwined with changes in
interest rates. Indeed, the Bundesbank has always attempted
to influence interest rates as much as it attempted to
influence banks' free liquidity reserves.

The main reason for the attention given to interest
rates is the openness of the German economy. Ever since
the Deutsche Mark was freely convertible (i.e. since 1959,
and to a varying extent even earlier) the inflow of foreign
exchange has created problems for the Bundesbank, no matter
whether the inflow was the consequence of the persistent
balance of trade surplus, or of capital flows. As long as
the exchange rate was fixed, the Bundesbank could only attempt
to sterilize the creation of central bank money it could
not prevent. Since March 1973, of course, exchange rates
are no longer fixed, so that in theory changes in the net
foreign position of the Bundesbank should no longer lead to
involuntary increases in central bank money. However, there
have been frequent interventions in foreign exchange markets

in consequence of international agreement (both formal and informal). While on the whole it can be argued that such interventions have been both stable and neutral[1], this has certainly not been the case since 1978/79. Since the coming into operation of the European Monetary System in March 1979 there is of course also the obligation to intervene in foreign exchange markets in order to hold the exchange rate of the DM constant in relation to the other currencies involved, so that to this extent there is again the necessity to create (or destroy) central bank money.

Changes in the Bundesbank's net foreign position are therefore still (or again) an important, and, sometimes, the dominating source of liquidity for the German financial system (see Table 2.11), and the Bundesbank was repeatedly forced to use domestic monetary policy in the first place to sterilize the influx of foreign funds. The situation as described is exacerbated by the growing use of the DM as a reserve currency.

As explained above, the German money market is sheltered from the consequences of such capital flows, but the capital market is not. Nor are normal credit markets on which non-banks take up loans. This permits the Bundesbank to conduct open market operations on the money markets without much (direct) interference from foreign exchange markets, and is probably one reason why its use of monetary policies for sterilisation purposes have been so successful both before and after the shift to flexible or managed exchange rates.[2] But at the same time the existence of these capital flows tends to

---

1.   See Lehment (1980), where it is also shown that the Bundesbank's net foreign positon can also change without any action on the part of the Bundesbank because of interventions by the Federal Reserve System in the foreign exchange market which use Deutsche Mark lent to them by the Bundesbank: and which are repaid by Deutsche Mark not acquired on foreign exchange markets.

2.   See Willms (1971), Branson, Halttunen and Masson (1977), Herring and Marston (1977) and Lehment (1980).

induce changes in interest rate levels which potentially
interfere with Bundesbank actions. This is probably the
main reason why the Bundesbank is still concerned with
interest rates. A good case can be made for the argument
that before the change to flexible exchange rates the level
of interest rates in Germany was lower than it would have
been had the Bundesbank fixed its discount rate as high as
it should have been for purely domestic reasons because it
feared the consequences for international capital flows.
There is also some evidence that the difference between the
Bundesbank discount rate and the prime deposit rate has
narrowed since 1973/74, and also that the difference between
the Bundesbank discount rate and the Euro-Dollar rate has
narrowed. Both these trends indicate that the Bundesbank
no longer sees it necessary to hold the level of interest
rates lower than it would otherwise have been. But it would
be wrong to assume that the Bundesbank is no longer concerned
with interest rates: on the contrary, almost every commentary
the Bundesbank publishes shows that the level of interest
rates is of as much concern to them as is the amount of
"central bank money" and banks' free liquidity reserves.
Indeed it can be argued that interest rates have become more
important for them since most of the policies introduced in
the 1960s to deal with capital flows have been dismantled,
and the Bundesbank has only those left which work via price
incentives. Precisely because the Bundesbank rarely pursued
only a quantity goal or only an interest rate goal, its
measures are usually a mixture of operations designed to
affect both quantities and interest rates.

Turning now to the effect of monetary policies on the
flow of funds to industry and commerce, two aspects should
be singled out. First, few if any of the Bundesbank's
policy instruments involve quantity restrictions which affect
non-banks directly. In particular, there have been no
limitations to bank lending. Non-banks therefore could
always get the funds they wanted provided they were prepared
to pay the price. In fact, from the point of view of
non-banks, monetary policy affects primarily the rate of

interest at which funds can be invested or obtained as loans.
Obviously loans at acceptable rates were hard to come by at
times but the competition between banks which was discussed
above does seem to work in favour of non-banks by keeping
lending rates as low as is possible in view of the stance
on monetary policy.

A second aspect plays a role in this context. All
financial markets in Germany have felt increasingly the
influence of international developments. Even before 1973
most German financial markets were open to international
competition; since the change to flexible exchange rates this
trend has accelerated. What was before 1973 an attempt by
either banks or non-banks to escape the influence of the
Bundesbank and its policy actions has more and more become
a search for the cheapest source of funds. For large firms,
lending abroad has become a genuine alternative to lending
from domestic banks. Even not so large firms have at times
been told by their domestic banks to look beyond the borders:
and have often been given help to do so. German monetary
policy has therefore only limited relevance to those firms
who are able to borrow abroad and does not seem to have
obstructed significantly the flow of funds from the banking
system (or the savers as the ultimate source) to industry
and commerce.

4.   RETROSPECT AND PROSPECT

The discussion of the structure and (to some extent)
performance of the West German financial system on the
preceeding pages necessarily emphasized the situation in
the 1960s and 1970s. By way of conclusion it should be
observed that the 1980s may well bring changes which deeply
affect the West German financial system.

It is unlikely that the Gessler commission report on
the structure of banking industry will bring far-reaching
changes but changed economic circumstances may well affect
the banking sector far more than any proposal by that

commission. The outlook for continued economic growth is
much bleaker in 1980 than it was in 1970, and certainly much
less confident than in 1960. The recent turnaround in the
balance of trade, ending the almost proverbial persistence
of balance of trade surplusses, is only the latest indication
that the German engine of growth has slowed down. Export
performance is not what it was and has shown an almost
continued decline over a number of years. One reason, but
not the only one, is a continued, and seemingly inevitable,
rise in labour costs, which together with the appreciation
of the exchange rate seems to have reduced the competitiveness
of German products in international markets. Productivity
is still increasing, but did not rise enough in value terms
to prevent an increase in costs which affects not only export
industries, and which is generally thought to be the reason
for the high level of foreign investment by German firms in
recent years.   There is no doubt that the profitability of
German industry has declined, and that investment is not as
high as it was in the past. While one may be guardedly
optimistic about a return of the savings ratio to the high
level achieved in the early 1970s, there is some concern
about both the rate of investment in domestic assets,
and the rate of innovation . Both are considered by many to
be below what they should be for continued growth.

All this has obvious consequences for the banking
system. A recent analysis by the Bundesbank of bank
profitability has shown that profit rates have declined
considerably in recent years, and especially in 1978 and 1979.
Obviously many banks were caught out by the rise in interest
rates in 1979 and 1980: that they allowed themselves to be
caught out so badly seems to indicate that in their quest
for expansion they accepted lower profit margins than they
should have done. Viewed in a different perspective,
competition has obviously been so strong that many banks
were prepared to lend at fixed rates which did not allow for
a rising level of interest rates. At the same time, savers
have become much more interest-conscious, and have switched
away from savings accounts with low yield to forms of

investment which yield higher rates, thus robbing many
banks of their traditional sources of funds, and at the same
time further reducing bank profit margins. This is one
reason (the other being increased operating costs, especially
labour costs) why some banks opened a discussion of a topic
which in the past was kept well below the counter: the
structure of bank fees. The introduction of waht was termed
'cost-related' bank fees by a number of banks shows that the
pressure of competition is still strong, but may also herald
a period in which expansion at almost any price gives way
to lower growth rates and more selective policies in both
lending and deposit business. How this will affect the
structure of the German banking sector it is too early to say.

German banks are unlikely to be under severe liquidity
pressures; most of them have a large branch network which
generates funds, and additional funds can be obtained via the
discount and lombard facilities from the Bundesbank, at least
in the short term. Nevertheless banks have in recent years
been more dependent on the Bundesbank for central bank money
than they had become accustomed to be. The floating of
exchange rates in March 1973 has affected their main source
of liquidity, and has moreover greatly added to its variability.
This has created a higher level of uncertainty for them than
they had to cope with in earlier years, and has certainly
induced them to hold more precautionary excess reserves with
the Bundesbank than previously.[1] In addition, the monetary
policies pursued by the Bundesbank affect bank liquidity
much more since banks' free liquidity reserves have been
reduced by Bundesbank action. Thus directly as well as
indirectly, banks are now probably more affected by Bundesbank
policy actions than they were in the 1960s or even the early
1970s. The fact that use of the lombard facility has greatly
increased since the mid-1970s, and shows greater variability,
is an index for this. One can only surmise what the future
will bring, but it seems unlikely that Bundesbank policies
will change drastically; thus one may expect banks to have

---

1.   See Richter and Teigen (1980)

to live with the higher level of uncertainty which is the
result of the variability of floating exchange rates, and
the monetary policies used to contain their influence on
the domestic economy.

On the whole, the attempt of the Bundesbank at "fine
tuning" the supply of central bank money has not worked
badly. Presumably this is one reason why the German rate of
inflation is still lower than those of her major trading
partners. But will the Bundesbank be able to continue its
(relative) success? Again this is difficult to say, but one
fact seems to be certain: with the turnaround of the balance
of trade, balance of payments considerations will play
a larger role in the making of monetary policy than they
did in the mid-1970s. It seems likely that the level and
structure of interest rates will once more be susceptible
to non-domestic influences, and that the Bundesbank will have
to set its key interest rates not only with the stance of
domestic monetary policy in mind, but also with a view to the
financing of the balance of payments deficit. Again, this
may well affect the performance of the banking system, and
in particular its channelling of funds from savers to
investors in ways which it is too early to predict.

Finally, the high level of interest rates particularly
in 1979 and 1980 has pushed up particularly bond yields, and
induced non-banks to invest considerable sums in the bond
market. Probably this is more a cyclical phenomenon than a
change in long-term trends.

But the fact that bank liquidity has been reduced
has already led to a structure of interest rates which is
characterized by money market rates being higher than bond
yields. If this is to continue, one may well expect that
banks will invest less in the bond market, and correspondingly
that non-banks will invest more. This will be true particularly
if bond yields stay ahead of the rate of inflation (as they
have done so far), offering a better protection against
depreciation than more conventional forms of savings. It

should be kept in mind, however, that households have reacted
sharply in the past when bond prices fell heavily, and that
they may well do so again. With the average yield on shares
well below the rate of inflation, the share market looks
less than promising. The trend towards less use of the
capital market, and more use of direct lending from banks,
is therefore likely to continue.

The prospect, therefore, is mixed: if there is
confidence, it should be based on the fact that the forces of
competiton are still strong in the German financial sector,
and that this gives rise to the expectation that German banks
will be able to adapt to the changed economic circumstances
of the 1980s.

CHAPTER 3:   THE SUPPLY OF SAVINGS

By E. Victor Morgan

1.   INTRODUCTION

The main concern of this Chapter is to examine the
role of the banks in encouraging and mobilising savings,
particularly household savings. Section 2 considers trends
in the volume of saving, in total and by households, in the
two countries; Section 3 looks at household savings in
more detail, including the effects of official policies and
the ways in which savings are held; and Section 4 examines
the attitudes of the banks, and the kinds of savings
instruments that they provide.

In discussing these matters, differences in definition
and structure must be kept in mind. The differences between
the two banking systems have been described in Chapters 1
and 2. There are also important differences in the
statistical treatment of saving and investment. The three
major ones are:-

(a)   The UK figures include non-corporate business in
      the personal (household) sector, whereas the German
      ones do not.

(b)   Housebuilding for owner-occupation is also included
      in the personal sector in the UK but not in Germany.

(c)   Pension rights are financed on a "pay-as-you-go"
      basis in Germany to a greater extent than in the UK.
      Where German pensions are funded it is generally
      by "balance-sheet funding" whereby firms record
      liabilities in their balance-sheets but do not
      establish separate funds.

The effect of these differences is discussed in an
Appendix to this Chapter. Broadly speaking they lead to an
under-statement in Germany, relative to the UK, of
household saving and of the ratio of saving to disposable
income (generally called "the savings ratio"). In
estimating the sector's net acquisition of financial
assets (NAFA) this under-statement is largely offset by the

fact that the German conventions make it unnecessary to deduct
investment expenditures by non-corporate businesses and in
housing from total household saving, as is done in the UK.

2.   THE VOLUME OF SAVINGS

Tables 3.1 and 3.2 show the volume of total saving and
of household saving in the UK and Germany since 1960. The
UK figures are exclusive and the German ones inclusive of
capital transfers. This makes no difference to total saving
(since transfers for the whole economy must sum to zero), but
it is important for the household sector. In the UK net
capital transfers for the personal sector are insignificant,
but for Germany the treatment of housing explained in the
Appendix leads to large negative transfers. In 1978 these
amounted to a net DM25 bn.

Many observers of the two economies have drawn
attention to the relatively low level of saving (as a
proportion of national income) in the UK compared with
Germany. The Tables confirm this, especially when it is
remembered that the German figures are probably under-stated
for reasons mentioned above and in Appendix 3.A. However,
there seems to have been a significant narrowing of the gap
during the past decade.

Though the proportion of national income saved has
remained higher in Germany, the direction of change has been
very similar in the two countries. Both countries experienced
very low saving in the early post-war years (largely because
households were rebuilding stocks of consumer durables) and
both enjoyed a substantial recovery in the 1950's although
this went further in Germany than in the UK. From 1960 to
the early 1970's there were cyclical fluctuations with no
clear trend, and there was a sharp decline in both countries
during the seventies, which started rather earlier in the UK.
It is too soon to tell whether the slight upturn towards the
end of the decade was a change of trend or only a cyclical
fluctuation.

TABLE 3.1: SAVINGS IN THE UK, 1960-1979

Year	1 National Income £bn.	2 Saving £bn.	3 2 as % of 1	4 Household Savings £bn.	5 4 as % of 1	6 4 as % of 2	7 Savings Ratio
1960	20.8	2.9	13.6	0.9	4.5	32.6	7.0
1961	22.3	3.0	13.4	1.3	5.7	42.3	8.9
1962	23.3	2.7	11.8	1.0	4.5	38.3	7.9
1963	24.8	2.9	11.9	1.0	4.1	34.2	7.5
1964	26.9	3.8	14.0	1.2	4.5	32.4	8.0
1965	28.8	4.4	15.2	1.5	5.2	34.3	8.7
1966	30.4	4.1	13.5	1.7	5.7	41.8	9.0
1967	32.0	3.9	12.2	1.6	5.1	41.5	8.4
1968	34.3	4.5	13.4	1.4	4.0	30.4	7.5
1969	36.2	6.1	16.9	1.6	4.4	26.2	8.1
1970	39.6	6.8	17.2	2.2	5.6	32.4	9.3
1971	44.8	6.2	13.8	1.8	4.0	29.0	7.6
1972	49.8	6.5	13.1	2.9	5.8	44.6	9.7
1973	58.5	8.6	14.7	4.1	7.0	47.7	11.7
1974	67.2	5.9	8.8	5.7	8.5	96.6	13.5
1975	83.6	5.8	6.9	6.4	7.6	92.8	12.7
1976	99.2	8.3	9.4	6.6	6.7	79.5	11.8
1977	110.3	10.5	9.5	6.4	5.8	61.0	10.5
1978	126.4	12.2	9.7	9.7	7.7	79.5	12.4
1979	141.8	13.8	9.7	13.0	9.2	94.2	13.8

NOTE: Money values are at current prices. Saving is net of depreciation and stock appreciation but includes tax and dividend reserves.

Source: National Income and Expenditure, 1980 Edition.

TABLE 3.2: SAVINGS IN GERMANY, 1960-1979

Year	1 National Income DM bn.	2 Total Saving DM bn.	3 as % of 1	4 Household Savings DM bn (1)	5 as % of 1	6 as % of 2	7 Savings Ratio
1960	279.6	62.9	22.5	16.0	5.7	25.4	9.2
1961	304.2	65.1	21.4	18.9	6.2	29.1	9.3
1962	329.0	65.8	20.0	19.2	5.8	29.1	9.4
1963	346.8	65.2	18.8	22.8	6.6	31.9	10.6
1964	381.2	78.9	20.7	28.3	7.4	35.8	11.8
1965	415.5	80.2	19.3	34.2	8.2	42.6	12.8
1966	430.7	81.6	18.6	33.7	7.8	41.3	12.3
1967	443.9	72.8	16.4	31.8	7.2	43.6	11.7
1968	482.7	89.3	18.5	38.0	7.9	42.5	13.0
1969	540.2	104.8	19.4	44.9	8.3	42.7	13.6
1970	610.3	123.9	20.3	53.9	8.8	43.5	14.6
1971	649.5	127.3	19.6	59.7	9.2	46.9	14.4
1972	742.2	133.6	18.0	70.1	9.4	52.5	15.5
1973	781.1	148.4	19.0	72.6	9.3	48.9	14.9
1974	879.9	139.9	15.9	85.1	9.7	60.8	16.1
1975	911.4	103.9	11.4	96.8	10.6	93.1	16.5
1976	995.3	128.4	12.9	86.2	8.7	67.1	14.6
1977	1,066.4	132.2	12.4	85.3	8.0	64.5	13.7
1978	1,148.8	141.0	12.3	88.3	7.7	57.5	13.8
1979	1,245.7	189.6	15.2	98.7	7.9	52.1	14.3

Source: Deutsche Bundesbank, Zahlenübersichten und methodische Erläuterungen zur gesamtwirtschaftlichen Finanzierungsrechnung der Deutschen Bundesbank 1960 bis 1977. and Monatsberichte, May 1979.

(1) Including capital transfers.

NOTE: The savings ratio shown by the Bundesbank is about one percentage point higher than that of the Statistisches Bundesamt because the former includes pension rights secured by "balance sheet funding" and the latter does not.

This fall in the proportion of total income saved has been partly due to a fall in corporate saving associated with declining profitability, and partly to the emergence of large deficits (negative saving) in the public sector. Both these tendencies have operated more strongly in the UK than in Germany. Household saving has risen greatly in both countries over the past two decades, though there has been an interesting difference in the timing of the change.

Column 5 of Tables 3.1 and 3.2 shows household saving as a proportion of national income. In 1960 the savings of German households amounted to 5.7 per cent of national income, compared with 4.5 per cent in the UK, a considerably smaller gap than that for total saving. From 1960 to 1972, however, the German figure rose by two-thirds, while that for the UK fluctuated from year-to-year but with little sign of a rising trend. The savings of German households continued to rise until 1975, when they amounted to 10.6 per cent of national income, but then fell. In the UK there was a big rise from 1972 to 1974, a fall to 1977 and a renewed rise in 1978 and 1979. As a result the relative position of the two countries has been reversed. In 1978 household saving in both countries amounted to 7.7 per cent of national income, but in 1979 the UK percentage was 9.2 against 7.9 for Germany.

These changes obviously imply an increase in the proportion of household savings in total saving, and this is shown in Column 6. Household savings have consistently formed a rather larger proportion of the total in the UK, though this is explained by the treatment of housing and non-corporate business discussed above. Far more significant, however, is the rise in that proportion of both countries over the past 20 years. Over the five years 1960-1964, household savings in the UK averaged 36 per cent of all savings; for the five years 1975-1979 the average was 81 per cent. The corresponding figures for Germany were 32 per cent and 67 per cent.

To obtain the sector's net acquisition of financial assets, the UK savings figures have to be adjusted for capital transfers and for investment expenditure (see Appendix). Table 3.3 shows net acquisition of financial assets by households in absolute amounts and as a proportion of national income. The same differences between the two countries are apparent; Germany began the period with a higher ratio than the UK; the German ratio showed a strong upward trend in the sixties and early-1970's when no such trend was apparent in the UK. The UK ratio rose by more than the German in the early 1970's and fell more sharply in 1975-77. Over the five years 1960-1964 UK households acquired net financial assets amounting to 2.1 per cent of national income compared to 6.3 per cent for German households. The corresponding figures for 1974-78 were 6.0 per cent and 9.0 per cent.

This rise in household savings, relative to corporate and public saving is of great importance for banks and other financial institutions. Public and corporate saving largely by-passes the financial system; funds are channelled directly to the finance of investment with, at most, only a short sojourn with a financial institution on the way. It is household savings that are the main "raw material" of banks and other financial institutions, and it is the mobilisation of these savings and the distribution of them to borrowers that are their major functions.

The final Column of Tables 3.1 and 3.2 shows what is generally called "the savings ratio", i.e. the ratio of saving by the household sector to its disposable (after tax) income. The growth paths of disposable income tends to follow closely that of national income, but the two may diverge because of changes in the shares in national income of retained corporate profits and of personal taxation, net of government payments to households. Such changes would be reflected in divergent growth rates between Columns 5 and 7.

TABLE 3.3: NET ACQUISITION OF FINANCIAL ASSETS BY HOUSEHOLD SECTOR, 1960-1978

Year	UK £m.	UK Per Cent of National Income	GERMANY DMbn.	GERMANY Per Cent of National Income
1960	342	1.6	15.97	5.7
1961	658	2.9	18.92	6.2
1962	565	1.6	19.17	5.8
1963	487	2.0	22.82	6.5
1964	597	2.2	28.25	7.4
1965	953	3.3	34.19	8.2
1966	1,101	3.6	33.72	7.7
1967	869	2.7	31.76	7.2
1968	526	1.5	37.95	7.9
1969	755	2.1	44.76	8.3
1970	1,461	3.7	53.91	8.8
1971	459	1.0	59.68	8.5
1972	1,286	2.9	70.10	9.4
1973	2,865	4.9	72.63	8.8
1974	012	7.5	85.13	9.7
1975	5,642	6.7	96.76	10.6
1976	5,656	5.7	86.24	8.7
1977	4,877	4.4	85.29	8.1
1978	8,198	6.5	88.28	7.7
1979	11,050	7.8	98.65	

Source: National Income and Expenditure, 1980 Edition and Deutsche Bundesbank. As Table 3.2

The ratios in Column 5 are consistently lower than these in Column 7, because part of national income accrues to the government and to the corporate sector, but the growth rates of the two columns are strikingly similar for both countries. This implies that explanations for the rise in household savings must be sought almost wholly in the increase in the proportion of disposable income that is saved, and only to a

very small extent in changes in the share of national income
that accrues to households. The reasons for the rise in the
savings ratio, and the part played in it by the banks, are
the main topics of the next two sections.

3.   HOUSEHOLD SAVING

This Section considers three aspects of household
saving; official policies for its encouragement; some
other possible explanations for the changes described in
Section 2; and the main types of asset in which household
savings are held.

Government Policies

Both British and German governments have adopted
policies designed to encourage household saving, though in
very different ways. Such policies are relevant here both
for their effects on the total amount of household saving
and for their influence on the relative positions of banks
and other institutions in competition for savings. A full
discussion would be outside the scope of this study, but
the following paragraphs summarise the main features.

In the UK interest and dividend income is subject to
an "investment income surcharge" if its amount exceeds a
certain threshold. The threshold was £1,000 until 1977 but
has subsequently been raised to £5,000; the surcharge
rate is currently 15 per cent. Incentives to saving are
almost wholly in exemptions either from ordinary income
tax, investment income surcharge, or capital gains tax.
They operate in four main fields:-

> "National savings".
> Other government securities.
> Life assurance and pension funds, and
> Building Societies.

"National savings" include deposits with the National
Savings Bank (formerly the Post Office Savings Bank),
National Savings Certificates, National Savings Bonds,
Premium Bonds and the "Save-as-you-earn" scheme operated
by the Department of National Savings.   The National
Savings Bank pays interest (currently at 5 per cent) on
"ordinary account" deposits, which are withdrawable at
short notice, and the first £70 of interest is tax free.
Interest on Savings Certificates and under the SAYE scheme
is paid in the form of "bonuses" which are added to the
repayment value and these are tax free, as are the prizes
on premium bonds.

Government securities held for more than a year are
free of capital gains tax, and the value of this concession
is enhanced by the existence of a number of "low coupon"
stocks selling well below their redemption value.   For
example, at the time of writing a £100 unit of 3 per cent
Exchequer stock 1981 is selling for £92.12.   The yield to
redemption[1] is approximately 10.8 per cent, but the personal
holder takes only about 3.25 per cent of this in taxed
income and the rest in untaxed capital gain.   This has
obvious attractions for wealthy individuals, particularly
those liable to the investment income surcharge.

Until 1976 tax payers with life or endowment assurance
policies were able to claim remission of income tax at half
the standard rate on premiums paid up to a maximum of £1,500.
Since 1976 the administration has been transferred to the
companies, who are entitled to give the insured a rebate of
17.5 per cent on premiums and claim this from the Revenue.
Employees' contributions to pension schemes (provided they
comply with certain Inland Revenue rules) are deductable
from income i.e. they get relief from tax at the full
marginal rate payable by the person concerned.   The income
and capital gains of pension funds are free of income-tax
and capital gains tax.   Pension payments are taxed as

---

1.   Allowing for the difference between the buying price
      of £92.12 and the redemption price of £100.

"earned income" (i.e. they are not liable to the investment income surcharge) and a lump sum up to 1½ times final year's pay may be taken tax free on retirement. Self-employed persons can pay contributions to approved schemes operated by insurance companies, and secure similar tax reliefs.

Interest payments on loans of up to £25,000 for the purchase or improvement of the borrowers' main residence can be offset against income, thus gaining remission of tax at the full marginal rate. Interest on other loans has not been deductible since 1974. This concession therefore affects the building societies in two ways. It increases the interest rate that is consistent with any given demand for loans and it encourages borrowing from them rather than from other institutions, e.g. by taking the maximum available mortgage on the house and buying the car out of savings, rather than putting more savings into the house and buying the car on hire-purchase.

Building societies pay interest to depositors net of income-tax at the standard rate. Tax is collected by payments by the societies at a "composite rate" designed to secure the same revenue as would have accrued if it had been collected from individual depositors. However, since some depositors are not tax-payers, the composite rate is well below the standard one; at the time of writing it is 21 per cent against a standard rate of 30 per cent. The current rate recommended by the Building Societies' Association is 10.5 per cent, which is worth 15 per cent to the tax-paying depositor but costs the societies only 13.3 per cent. This is not a subsidy from the exchequer but a subsidy from depositors with incomes below the tax exemption limit to those with incomes above. It does, however, give the societies a competitive edge over other institutions in attracting savings from tax-payers. The societies also benefit from paying corporation tax at only 30 per cent compared with the general level of 52 per cent.

It is impossible to say how much effect these various incentives have on the total amount of household saving. They cannot explain the rapid rise in the savings ratio during the seventies since most of them have been in operation, with only minor changes, during the whole period we are considering. They do, however, give savers strong reasons for holding their wealth in some assets rather than others; four types of discrimination are particularly significant:-

> The encouragement of long-term investment through institutions rather than the direct personal ownership of securities.
>
> The preferential treatment of government securities.
>
> The favourable treatment of the building societies, and
>
> Discrimination against the banks, since the acquisition of bank deposits does not qualify a saver for any of the privileges described above.

Government incentives for saving in Germany[1] were originally in the form of tax exemptions but the scope of these was reduced in 1959, and the emphasis has switched to the payment of premiums on schemes for regular saving. The following payments are still deductible from income:-

> Premiums on life assurance policies and also for insurance against accident, ill-health and civil liability.
>
> Social security contributions, including those paid by the employer.
>
> Contractual savings through a building society, provided that no savings premium is claimed.

There are limits to the amount of deductions depending on the size of the family. The maximum total for a single person is currently DM 2,100 and for a married couple with two children, DM 5,400.

---

[1] The following paragraphs describe the system at the time of writing, in the Autumn of 1980. Legislation was introduced in November 1980 to reduce the premiums on saving for house purchase, and other contractual saving premiums and remove most of the tax incentives to saving.

There are three premium schemes; saving for house purchase ((Wohnungsbauprämien); contractual saving (Sparprämien); and Arbeitnehmer-Sparzulagen (investment premium), workers' saving schemes.

Premiums on saving for house purchase were introduced in 1952. They are paid on contractual savings schemes running for a minimum of seven years and designed to lead to the purchase of a house or flat in Germany, though premiums may be retained at the end of seven years even if no such purchase is made. Premiums are paid annually on the sum saved during the previous year. Normal rates range from 25 per cent to 35 per cent according to the size of family, with higher rates for low income families. There is a maximum premium of DM 400 in any year, and premiums are only payable provided that:-

> Deposits have not been financed by borrowing elsewhere.

> No tax deduction or other subsidy has been claimed, and

> No other savings premiums have been claimed.

Premiums on contractual saving were introduced in 1959, and operate through the banking system. There are three types of scheme involving respectively:-

> The deposit of a single lump sum.

> A contract to make regular deposits of a stated sum at weekly, monthly or quarterly intervals, and

> A contract to deposit all benefits accruing under an "investment premium" scheme (see below).

In all three cases no withdrawals may be made from the account until the end of the contract period (between six and seven years according to the date of the first deposit). Premiums are not payable if a deposit has been financed by borrowing but payment can be made by the deposit of a wide variety of securities as well as in cash. It is thus possible, subject to the limit on total amounts, to switch

past savings from a non-premium to a premium category,
though only by foregoing the opportunity of drawing upon
them before the end of the contract period. In such cases
the premium is a compensation for sacrificing liquidity
rather than an incentive to new savings.

The annual premium is at a rate of 14 per cent of
the sum deposited during the year plus 2 per cent for each
child, with a maximum deposit qualifying for premium of
DM 800 for a single person and DM 1,600 for a married couple.
There is also a limit on taxable income of DM 24,000 per
annum for a single person and DM 48,000 for a married couple
plus DM 1,800 for each child. Banks normally make no charge
for the management of these accounts, though a fee is
charged on securities deposited.

"Investment premium" schemes were introduced in 1961
and modified in 1965 and 1970. Schemes are normally the
result of collective agreements, though individual contracts
are possible. If an employer agrees to contribute to an
approved contractual savings scheme to which an employee is
a party, such contributions up to a maximum of DM 624 a year
qualify for premium. The premium rate is 30 per cent of the
employer's contribution (or 40 per cent if the employee has
more than 2 children) and the premium is payable in addition
to any other to which the employee may be entitled. Approved
schemes comprise the various premium schemes described above
and a number of others including:-

Premiums on endowment and deferred annuity policies.

Repayment of loans for house purchase or improvement.

Repayment of credits granted by an employer, and

Payments for the purchase of shares under an
employee shareholder scheme.

There are the same limits on taxable income as for
Sparprämien schemes.

A very high proportion of the German population
derives some kind of benefit from these schemes. About 16
million employees benefit from "investment premiums";

over 90 per cent of German households have one or more
savings account and about half have accounts which qualify
for premiums; over 35 per cent of households have
contractual savings with building societies, a large majority
of which qualify for premiums.

The proportion of savings which attract subsidy is
considerably less than the proportion of households that
benefit, both because of the limits on the amounts that
qualify and because holders are not willing to "lock-up" the
whole of their savings for the periods that are necessary
to attract premiums. There are considerable difficulties in
estimating the proportion of all savings that are subsidised.
The evidence is reviewed in detail in one of our supplementary
papers[1] where the conclusion is reached that between 40 and
50 per cent of all savings benefit either from premiums or
tax concessions.

An even more difficult question is how far these
incentives have added to the total amount of savings. It is
possible to attract premiums in a number of ways that do not
involve new saving, e.g. by depositing securities acquired
by past saving or inheritance; by re-depositing sums "freed"
by maturing contractual arrangements; and by making deposits
in contractual schemes or paying insurance premiums by
running down other assets. It has been argued that savers
are only willing to "lock-up" their assets in the way
necessary to attract premiums when they have accumulated
enough to satisfy their desire for liquidity, so that sums
deposited in premium accounts represent either savings made
in the past or that would have been made anyway. This view
derives some support from the fact that there is no close
relationship in time between changes in total saving and
changes in amounts qualifying for premium. Statistical
estimates can only be made on rather arbitrary assumptions.

1.   The Promotion of Savings in Germany by
      K.H. Hennings.

Again the evidence is reviewed in more detail in our supplementary paper, where it is concluded that, on the most optimistic assumptions, no more than 10 to 15 per cent of saving can be attributed to the effect of incentives, while on pessimistic assumptions the effect appears neglegible.

Whatever the effect on total saving, there can be little doubt that the incentives have influenced the pattern of asset formation and, hence, the structure of the financial system. Here, the big difference between the UK and Germany is in the prominent part played by contractual saving through the banks in the German system.

Reasons for differences in saving

We are thus left with the problem of explaining the differences in household saving behaviour revealed by Tables 3.1 and 3.2; the disparity between the high and rising savings ratio in Germany and the lower and fairly stable one in the UK in the 1960's and early-1970's; and the contrast between the fall in the German ratio and the sharp rise in that of the UK since 1973. The possible role of the banks will be discussed in the next section; here we note briefly some other possible explanations that have been offered.

The experience of the 1960's may be a consequence of differences in the growth rate of income between the two countries; if changes in consumer spending habits tend to lag behind changes in real income, then the rapid rise in real income in Germany at this time could explain both the rise in the savings ratio and the gap between the two countries; the fall in the ratio in Germany in the mid-seventies could be related, by the same reasoning, to the decline in the growth rate of real income, but this kind of explanation can obviously not apply to the rise in the UK ratio.

A possible explanation of the difference between the two ratios is the higher proportion of self-employed (who tend to save more than employees) in Germany. However, this cannot explain the rise in the German ratio since the proportion of self-employed was falling. Any attempt to explain the rise by this kind of demographic change would have to assume that the effect of a falling proportion of self-employed was more than offset by other changes such as the rise in the number of "white collar" relative to "blue collar" workers, but this is not very convincing.

Another and more plausible hypothesis with regard to the rise in the German ratio depends on changes in the pattern of consumer spending. Rising real income tends to be associated with rising expenditures on house purchase and on the acquisition of relatively expensive consumer durables. Such expenditures may be financed either by borrowing or by "saving up" and there is evidence that the proportion of "saving up" is higher in Germany than in most other industrial countries. Consumer credit is less developed than in the USA and the UK and there is still fairly widespread prejudice against using it. Moreover, German building societies encourage "saving up" far more than their British opposite members. The typical German contract relates to a stipulated total amount of finance, and requires that the borrower should save 40 per cent of this sum with the society before the remaining 60 per cent is advanced. The results of a number of opinion surveys, mostly conducted by the savings banks, confirm the importance of "saving up" as a motive.

These hypotheses are not mutually exclusive and, together, they are consistent with the behaviour of the German ratio and the differences between the UK and Germany in the sixties. They do not, however, offer any clue to the rise in the UK ratio after 1973. This rise took place during a period of low growth and high inflation. One possible explanation is that the growth of uncertainty about the future associated with rising unemployment and gloomy economic forecasts may have encouraged saving for the traditional "rainy day".

The only other plausible explanations that have been offered relate to the effects of inflation on the real wealth of the personal sector. The Wilson Committee notes that between 1957 and 1972 the net wealth of the personal sector rose more than fourfold while the price level less than doubled. By contrast, between 1972 and 1977 net wealth rose by 70 per cent but the price level more than doubled so that real wealth fell by a sixth.[1] If consumption is influenced to a substantial extent by real net worth as well as income, the decline in real wealth could explain the rise in savings.

A similar argument has been put forward in relation to liquid assets (money and "near money" assets such as building society deposits). Since these are fixed in value in terms of the unit of account, they are much more vulnerable than total wealth to inflation. There is a good deal of empirical evidence that consumers tend to maintain their real holding of liquid assets as a fairly stable proportion of real income. Hence if the real value of such assets is reduced by inflation, consumers may be expected to increase their saving in order to re-build their asset stocks.

How savings are held

We now turn to a rather different aspect of consumer behaviour, the way in which financial assets are held. Tables 3.4 and 3.5 show financial balance-sheets for the household sector in the two countries for 1967, 1972, 1977 and 1978. The comparison has not been taken back beyond

---

1.   Wilson Committee Report. Cmnd. 7937. paragraph 216.

TABLE 3.4: FINANCIAL ASSETS AND LIABILITIES OF UK PERSONAL SECTOR, 1967, 1972, 1977 and 1978

£bn.

	1967	1972	1977	1978
ASSETS				
Cash and bank deposits	10.5	16.2	28.0	32.2
National savings	8.3	9.8	13.6	15.7
Building society shares and deposits	6.9	14.2	31.7	36.6
Other liquid assets	0.7	0.7	0.6	0.6
ALL LIQUID ASSETS	26.4	40.9	73.9	85.1
British government securities	3.9	3.9	10.5	8.8
Listed UK ordinary shares	17.8	31.7	23.1	23.2
Other stocks and shares	11.2	16.5	19.5	21.1
ALL STOCKS AND SHARES	32.9	52.1	53.1	53.1
Loans and debtors	5.2	5.5	8.8	9.7
Equity in life assurance and pension funds	16.2	28.1	51.6	59.6
ALL FINANCIAL ASSETS	80.7	126.6	187.4	207.5
LIABILITIES				
Loans for house purchase	8.4	15.9	33.2	38.6
Other debts	7.3	11.8	16.8	19.5
ALL LIABILITIES	15.7	27.7	50.0	58.1
NET FINANCIAL WORTH	65.0	98.9	137.4	149.4

Source: Report of Wilson Committee
Cmd. 7937. Appendix, Table 10.2.

1967 because of discontinuities in some of the British statistics. Table 3.6 presents some of this information in a different way by showing the shares of various asset types in total (gross) financial asset holdings. Definitions are not always precisely comparable, but a number of important differences between the two countries emerge quite clearly.

The most striking difference from the point of view of this study is the relative position of bank deposits. In

TABLE 3.5: FINANCIAL ASSETS AND LIABILITIES OF GERMAN HOUSEHOLDS, 1967, 1972, 1977 and 1978

				DM bn	
	1967	1972	1977	1978	1979
ASSETS					
Long-term[1]					
Deposits with banks:-					
Time deposits	1.0	1.9	4.5 ⎫	87.4	119.2
Savings bonds and certificates	0.2	10.5	51.6 ⎭		
Savings deposits	142.4	264.7	440.7	470.6	484.4
Deposits with building societies	27.7	52.1	86.6	94.0	101.7
Payments to insurance companies	55.7	100.4	177.8	201.2	224.0
Fixed interest securities[2]	24.7	57.9	134.8	138.7	170.5
Shares[2]	43.7	59.2	66.7	30.9	30.4
Equity in pension funds [3]	25.7	40.2	72.5	81.6	90.2
ALL LONG-TERM ASSETS	321.1	586.9	1,035.2	1,104.4	1,220.4
LIQUID ASSETS					
Cash and night deposits	40.7	65.8	100.9 ⎫	114.2 ⎫	119.8
Time deposits	2.5	13.1	18.3 ⎭	⎭	
ALL LIQUID ASSETS	43.2	78.9	119.2	114.2	119.3
ALL FINANCIAL ASSETS	364.3	665.8	1,154.4	1,218.4	1,340.3
LIABILITIES					
Bank credit	15.6	43.0	80.2	96.3	115.1
Other liabilities	3.6	6.5	8.9	9.2	10.1
ALL LIABILITIES	19.2	49.5	89.1	105.3	125.2
NET FINANCIAL WORTH	345.1	616.3	1,065.3		

NOTES: 1. Over four years
2. At market value
3. Value of pension rights in "balance sheet funded" schemes.

Source: Deutsche Bundesbank. As Table 3.2.

TABLE 3.6: SHARES IN GROSS FINANCIAL ASSETS OF HOUSEHOLD SECTOR. UK AND GERMANY, 1967 AND 1977

Per cent

Category of Asset	UK		GERMANY	
	1967	1977	1967	1977
Bank deposits:-				
- Short-term[1]	13.0	14.9	11.9	10.3
- Long-term			39.4	43.9
Building society deposits	8.5	19.5	7.6	7.5
Stocks and shares	40.8	28.3	18.8	17.5
Life assurance	20.1	27.5	15.3	15.4
Pension rights			7.0	6.3

NOTE: 1. Includes cash.

Source: Tables 3.4 and 3.5.

the UK they form less than 15 per cent of all holdings
of financial assets; in Germany more than 50 per cent.
In both countries, the proportion has increased slightly
over the past decade. Part, though only a small part, of
this difference is accounted for by the exclusion of savings
banks from the UK banking figures (see Chapter 1). However,
bank deposits in Germany are very different from those in
the UK. As shown in Chapter 1, the vast majority of the
"retail" deposits that would be held by the personal sector
can be withdrawn on demand or at seven days notice, while
even the "wholesale" deposits, that are held to some extent
by wealthy individuals, have typical maturities of only a
few months. By contrast, about 80 per cent of German
deposits are in savings accounts, certificates or bonds
that are classed as "long-term" (over four years). Reasons
for this difference are discussed in the next section.

A counterpart of the greater importance of the banks
in Germany is the smaller role of the building societies.
Their deposits form about 7.5 per cent of all household
financial assets and they grew over the decade at the same
rate as total financial asset holdings and rather more slowly
than bank deposits. In the UK, building society deposits
grew by 359 per cent over the decade, (compared with 166
per cent for bank deposits) and increased their share in
total household financial assets from 8.5 per cent to 19.5
per cent. Building society deposits, like bank deposits,
are much more liquid in the UK than in Germany. Most German
deposits are subject to the contractual arrangements already
described. In the UK the societies attract some term
deposits for a year or more but the amounts are small in
proportion to their totals.

A consequence of these features is that the household
sector in Britain is very much more liquid than in Germany.
Allowing for savings bank deposits (not shown separately in
the tables) about 35 per cent of the financial assets of
UK households are encashable either on demand or at only a
few days notice. Only about 10 per cent of financial assets

are classified as short-term deposits in Germany, though
notice on some deposits classed as long-term may be
waived (see below).

The value of holdings of stocks and shares fluctuates
not only with purchases and sales, but also with market
prices. In Germany the share of these securities in total
financial assets fell slightly over the decade from 18.8
per cent to 17.5 per cent. On a historic cost valuation
there was a slight rise, with a decline in the relative
importance of equities rather more than offset by a rise
in fixed interest securities. In the UK, holdings of
securities are considerably more important than in Germany,
but their share in total financial assets has fallen sharply
from nearly 43 per cent in 1967 to 28 per cent in 1977.
Individuals have been steady sellers of ordinary shares,
largely because of the tax position described above, and
these sales have not been fully offset by increased
purchases of government stocks.

Life assurance and pension rights formed a smaller
proportion of all assets in the UK in 1967 (20.1 per cent
against 22.3 per cent) but the position was reversed
during the decade as a result of very rapid growth in the
UK. This rapid growth was partly attributable to the tax
advantages described above, but it also reflected the
effect of high inflation in the "topping up" of funded
pension schemes to keep them actuarially solvent.

A final point that can be made before leaving these
tables concerns the relative size of financial asset
holdings. Taking an exchange rate of DM 4 to £1, German
households had gross holdings of £288 bn. of financial
assets in 1967 against £167 bn. for the UK. The corresponding
per capita figures would be approximately £4,700 and £3,000.
German households also have a lower ratio of debts to gross
financial assets than the UK. This is partly, but not
wholly, because of the different treatment of housing.
Consumer debt, other than for house purchase, in the UK was

9 per cent of the sector's financial assets in both 1967 and
1977; in Germany it was only 6 per cent in 1967, though it
had grown to 7.7 per cent in 1977. This is a reflection of
German attitudes towards consumer credit described earlier.

Because the value of the stock of some assets is
affected by price changes as well as net acquisitions, a
comparison of balance sheets does not always give an
accurate impression of how new savings are allocated.
Table 3.7, therefore, shows net acquisitions in the main
asset categories for the average of the three years
1975-1977. More detailed figures are given annually from
1960 in Appendix Tables 3A1 and 3A2. Again the disparity
between the two countries with regard to the relative
importance of banks and building societies comes out very
strongly. Increases in bank deposits accounted for no less
than 64 per cent of NAFA in Germany against only 16 per
cent in the UK, while building societies accounted for 83
per cent in the UK but only 7 per cent in Germany. The
difference in the scale of life assurance and pension
provision between the two countries also comes out more
strongly than in the balance sheet figures. This is largely
because of the high rate of inflation in the UK in 1975-1977
which both raised current contributions to pension schemes
and also created the need for "topping-up" already
mentioned.

Looking at the figures for the past two decades in
the Appendix Tables, the position in Germany has been
relatively stable. The main changes have been the rise in
popularity of bank savings bonds and certificates, which
were first introduced in the sixties and accounted for
over 22 per cent of the increase in the sector's holding of
all bank liabilities in 1977; a slight decline in the
market share of building societies and a moderate increase
in that of insurance companies.

TABLE 3.7: NET ACQUISITIONS OF FINANCIAL ASSETS BY HOUSEHOLDS.
ANNUAL AVERAGE 1975-1977

Category	UK £bn.	UK Per cent of NAFA	GERMANY DMbn.	GERMANY Per cent of NAFA
Bank deposits:-				
- Short-term			3.0	4
- Long-term	0.9	16	45.4	60
Building society deposits	4.5	83	5.7	7
Stocks and shares:-				
- Fixed interest[1]	1.4	26	11.1	15
- Other[2]	-1.5	-27	0.8	1
Life assurance[3]			14.5	19
Pension rights	5.4	100	5.7	7
Other (net)[4]	-5.3	-98	-10.4	-14
NAFA	5.4		75.9	

NOTES: 1. For UK British government securities and long-term local authority debt. Acquisitions of company and other fixed interest securities are not shown separately but were almost certainly negligible.

2. For UK "company and overseas securities" see also Note 1.

3. For Germany "payments to insurance companies".

4. For Germany liabilities incurred. The UK figure includes other items, some of which were positive.

Source: National Income and Expenditure, 1979 Edition, and Deutsche Bundesbank. As Table 3.2.

In the UK, changes have been more dramatic mainly because of the big increase in household saving and NAFA in recent years. During most of the 1960's "contractual saving" through life assurance and pension funds exceeded household NAFA so that net acquisitions of all other assets taken together were negative. In 1975-1977, despite the effect of inflation on the growth of pension funds, this "contractual saving" accounted for only 60 per cent of NAFA, against 64 per cent for bank and building society deposits together. The main beneficiaries from this rise in the volume of "free" savings have been the building societies and, to a lesser extent the banks and government securities. The personal sector was a net seller of government securities in the 1960's and is now a substantial net purchaser.

These changes have at least two very important consequences for the banking system. Firstly, they have greatly increased the volume of funds that are the subject of competition both between banks themselves and between banks and other financial institutions. Secondly, given the highly liquid character of UK deposits, there is a problem of how the vastly increased flow of personal saving can be channelled to meet the needs of industry, commerce and government without generating an inflationary increase in the money stock. These matters will be discussed in later Chapters. Meanwhile, we turn to a brief account of savings vehicles provided by banks in the two countries and of their respective attitudes towards savers.

4.   THE BANKS AND HOUSEHOLD SAVING

The vast majority of household deposits in the UK are held as "retail deposits" through the national branch networks of the London Clearing Banks (LCBs) and their affiliates in Scotland and Northern Ireland. The National Giro, the Co-operative Bank and the Yorkshire Bank (owned

144.

by a group of London Clearing Banks) also take retail
deposits but their total is less than 6 per cent of that of
the LCB's. As shown in Chapter 1, the merchant banks and
overseas banks have not entered into the retail banking
business; the only significant exception to this is
Citibank and its share is still extremely small. The
Clearing Banks and other banks will accept "wholesale"
deposits from individuals but the sums involved (until
recently £10.000 or more) are too large to be of interest
to the great majority of savers.

The London Clearing Banks told the Wilson Committee
that personal deposits accounted for 64 per cent of all
their deposits by UK residents,[1] the corresponding figure
for sterling retail deposits is not given but it must be
considerably higher.

Virtually all retail deposits are held on either
"current account" or "deposit account". Current accounts
are payable on demand and can be transferred by cheque,
standing order or direct debit. No interest is paid on
current accounts, though charges are waived for customers
who keep a sufficient credit balance. One leading bank
states that 70 per cent of its current accounts are kept
free of charge.[2] Where an account is overdrawn or does not
keep a sufficient credit balance charges vary with the
number of entries and the amount of the balance, but they
are not uniform between banks and are not widely publicised.
For example, the leaflet mentioned above states that the
cost of a current account, "depends on the extent to which
it is used and the balance you keep in it" and advises
prospective customers, "to find out what your charges are
likely to be, ask your branch manager". There has been a

1. The London Clearing Banks, evidence to Wilson
   Committee. Committee of London Clearing Bankers,
   London 1978.
2. "The Many Ways you can Bank on Lloyds" Promotional
   leaflet displayed on branch counters.

tendency for banks to increase the proportion of the cost of operating accounts that is covered by charges but, even so, the LCBs told the Wilson Committee that the costs not recovered were equivalent to interest at 7 per cent on all current account balances.[1]

Deposit accounts are subject to 7 days' notice but in fact can be withdrawn on demand, though only at the branch at which the account is held. No charges are made and interest is paid at rates related to "base rate". Base rate is usually, though not invariably, equal to the Bank of England's Minimum Lending Rate (MLR). Deposit rates have varied from 1.5 per cent to 4.5 per cent below base rate. Prior to 1971 the banks agreed on a uniform deposit rate. The agreement was dissolved as part of the monetary changes of that year but the LCB's told the Wilson Committee that:- "Although there have been divergences from time to time.... competitive pressures since 1972 have tended to result in uniformity".[2] Deposit rates are usually displayed in branches, but otherwise are not widely advertised. Higher rates are obtainable on deposits of substantial sums for periods longer than seven days. Until recently a minimum deposit of £10,000 was required, but some banks have now reduced their limits.

Some LCBs offer "savings accounts". These are similar to a deposit account except that the holder has a "pass book" in which deposits and withdrawals are recorded, and which entitles him to withdraw limited amounts from branches other than that at which the account is held. The amounts involved are very small and minimal publicity is given to the facility. A very recent development is the introduction by Citibank of a North American style savings account earning interest and giving chequing facilities.

---

1.   The London Clearing Banks, p.47.

2.   Ibid. p.48.

Among institutions competing with the banks for household savings but not included in the UK definition, the Trustee Savings Banks now offer four different types of account:-

Cheque accounts, similar to bank current accounts.

Savings accounts earning interest (currently 4 per cent), withdrawable on demand and carrying limited money transmission by standing order or direct debit but not by cheque.

Investment accounts, paying a higher rate of interest but with notice of withdrawal (7 days to a month) and with no money transmission.

Term accounts, fixed rate deposits for sums of £1,000 or more and for terms of six months to five years.

The building societies receive most of their resources in the form of "shares" which as shown in Chapter 1, are very similar to the deposits of other institutions. Some notice of withdrawal is required but is often waived and in practice sums of up to £100 can generally be withdrawn on demand and larger amounts in a matter of a few days. From this point of view building society shares are very close substitutes for deposit accounts with banks. As already noted, interest is paid net of tax; rates are recommended from time to time by the Building Societies' Association, though not all societies adhere to the recommended rates. Rates vary with the supply and demand for funds. The grossed-up rate averages several percentage points above the LCB deposit rate.

The range of options offered to the saver by German banks are considerably wider than in the UK. Sight deposits are the counterpart of current accounts in the UK but with several differences. Interest is normally paid at 0.5 per cent on credit balances over DM 800 and 1 per cent on balances over DM 1,000. Cheques can be drawn against sight deposits, but are less widely used than in most developed countries. The most common form of payment is the Giro system, pioneered by the savings banks but now operated by

all banks; standing orders and direct debits are also common.
Charges are usually DM 2.50 per annum plus DM 0.25 for
each entry per month from the 8th onwards, but proposals
have recently been put forward by some banks for substantial
increases. The banks also gain from the widespread practice
of debiting items to the paying account several days before
they are credited to the payee. About 40 per cent of sight
deposit accounts are linked with overdraft agreements.
Interest on these is normally 4 to 5 percentage points above
the Bundesbank discount rate with a commission of 0.25 per
cent of credit actually used per month.

Time deposits are not widely used (see Table 3A2)
largely because they have been supplanted by subsidised
savings deposits. Fixed rates are usually offered for
periods of up to four years. Some banks also take deposits
for periods of five to eight years subject to four years
notice of withdrawal and carrying interest at 1 percentage
point above the current rate for four year saving's deposits.

Savings deposits are either at "legal term" or
"agreed term". The former require three months notice of
withdrawal, in the latter notice is subject to agreement
with a minimum of 6 months. However, up to DM 2,000 of
"legal term" deposits per month may be withdrawn without
notice, and banks may waive the notice on both types of
account. Thus, although there is no strict equivalent of
the British deposit account short-term savings deposits
are in practice almost as liquid. Deposits and withdrawals
are entered in a pass-book as in the UK. Withdrawals from
accounts held with savings banks can be made, on presentation
of the pass-book and proof of identity, at any savings bank
branch in Germany or Austria. Other banks normally allow
withdrawals only at their own branches. Postal savings
accounts can be withdrawn at any post office.

The various subsidy arrangements described earlier
apply to savings deposits for periods of six to seven years,
but banks also offer other incentives on agreed term
deposits for long periods. A typical rate structure at the
time of writing (May 1980) would be:

	Per cent Per Annum	
Three months	5	
Twelve months	6	
Two years	6.25	
Four years	7	
Six/seven years	6	(plus subsidy)

Banks also offer bonuses to holders in connection with
various contractual savings schemes of their own, i.e.
independent of the state schemes already supplied. For
example, at the time of writing one bank was offering a
bonus of 3 per cent of the total sum saved to customers
agreeing to deposit a minimum of DM 50 a month for four
years. Another had a scheme involving regular deposits
for five years but not withdrawable for seven years from the
date of the first deposit, a bonus of 10 per cent of the
total sum deposited was payable on withdrawal after 7 years,
rising by annual increments of 5 per cent to 25 per cent
after 10 years.

A different type of incentive scheme applies to
short-term as well as longer-term deposits. Savers agree to
deposit multiples of DM 10 per month. Of each DM 10
deposited DM 8 is treated as a normal savings account and
DM 2 paid into a lottery with prizes ranging from DM 5 to
DM 10,000.

Savings certificates of deposit (Sparbriefe or
Sparkassenbriefe if issued by a savings bank) were first
introduced in 1967 and have grown rapidly in amount partly
because they are free of restrictions on sale to foreigners
that have been imposed from time to time on other
securities in order to control capital inflows. The
issuing bank sells certificates in multiples of DM 100 to
persons named on the document and with periods of four to
ten years to maturity. They may be sold at their full face
value, in which case interest is paid, usually at six
monthly intervals. Alternatively they may be sold at a
discount and repaid at face value, no interest being paid

in the meantime. Certificates are not traded in any
organised market but can be sold; issuing banks are normally
willing to try to arrange a sale (in return for a small
commission) or to take certificates as collateral for a
loan. Interest rates vary from bank to bank but are about
the same as those on bonds of similar maturity and about
1.5 percentage points above these on four year savings
deposits.

Savings bonds are issued only by savings banks which
began issuing in 1971. They are somewhat longer term
(up to twelve years) than savings CD's and are issued in
larger amounts (minimum DM 1,000). They are issued in
three forms; sold and repaid at face value with periodic
interest payments; sold at a discount and paid at face value
with no interest payments; and sold at face value with
interest (compounded) paid with the principal on maturity.
They are not listed on stock exchanges but can be bought
and sold, and issuing banks undertake to re-purchase after
four years at prices related to market interest rates at the
time.

Mortgage bonds are issued only by mortgage banks and
against actual mortgages held by the banks and certified
by a public official. They are the least liquid of bank
liabilities with maturities of up to 20 or even 30 years.
Other banks issue bank bonds, normally with a life of six
to fifteen years.

Savings banks and co-operative banks were originally
more prominent than commercial banks in developing small
savings media but, as shown in Chapter 2, the commercial
banks now operate actively in the household savings field
just as the savings institutions have moved into
commercial lending. Banks are competing for saving with
one another, with building societies and with various
types of notes, certificates and bonds issued by the
federal government, the Länder and local authorities.

These differences between the UK and Germany in the
range of savings media offered are accompanied by
differences in attitudes towards promotion. As already
noted, UK banks do not give much publicity either to the
interest rates that they pay on deposit accounts or to the
value of the free services that they provide for current
account holders. They attract deposits by the size of
their branch networks and they have added to the convenience
of current accounts by issuing bankers' cards (guaranteeing
payment of cheques up to £50) and by installing cash
dispensing machines, enabling customers to obtain cash when
the bank is closed. They have made considerable efforts to
attract students by opening branches on or adjacent to
university and college campuses and by favourable terms for
keeping accounts, but attempts to encourage the payment of
wages into bank accounts have been less than strenuous.
Advertising is limited in amount and is usually in fairly
general terms; when it is specific it tends to be aimed
more at the business customer than at the saver.

The high interest rates prevailing during 1980 have
led to some increase in competition for personal savings.
The clearing banks now offer rates above those on normal
deposit accounts for longer-term deposits of less than
£10,000, though without much publicity. One large non-
clearer has recently advertised a rate of 15 per cent on
deposits of £1,000 or more at 21 days notice together with
free personal accident insurance, but this is the only scheme
of its kind that has so far come to our notice.

Until recently, savings banks in Britain were
severely restricted in their activities by law and such
promotion as was done was through the government sponsored
National Savings Movement. Now that the Trustee Savings
Banks have gained more independence they are becoming more
active in seeking deposits, e.g. by the development of
savings accounts and the acceptance of term deposits in

relatively small amounts. Building societies have, as already noted, made some attempts to attract longer term deposits, and they advertise their rates more extensively than do the banks.

The German attitude appears to be more positive. German banks, particularly savings banks, have undertaken a considerable amount of market research into motives for saving and consumer preference between savings media. Banks give wider publicity than their UK opposite number to the terms associated with different savings instruments, and they have been very active, especially during the fifties and early sixties in developing arrangements for payment of wages into bank accounts. Examples of incentive bonus schemes initiated by individual banks have already been quoted. Another field of activity almost wholly ignored by UK banks, is the encouragement of families to save on behalf of their children and of saving by children themselves; for example German parents who announce the birth of a child in the press are likely to get invitations to open a savings account for it, and a gift of 5DM if they do.

The reasons for these differences are a matter of speculation. The oligopolistic structure of the British banking system encourages a belief that competition for deposits only reduces profits and so fosters collusion. This attitude is also given some justification by the relationship between bank liabilities and the money stock. Prior to the growth of "secondary banking" in the 1960's and 1970's, clearing bank deposits formed almost the entire money stock (apart from notes and coin), and virtually all bank liabilities (apart from shareholders' funds) were classed as money. In such circumstances effective control over the money supply inevitably restricts the growth of bank lending and so limits the gain, to the system as a whole, from competition for deposits. The growth of secondary banking means that a significant part of the money stock is now held outside the clearing banks; hence clearers

find it worthwhile to compete, and do compete, with non-
clearers for deposits, but such competition operates only at
the wholesale level. Banks could attain greater freedom if
they developed longer-term liabilities that were not classed as
money, but so far they have shown no tendency to do this.

Another inhibiting factor was the quantitative
restrictions on lending that were frequently used by the
Bank of England in the 1950's and 1960's. These restrictions
tended to bear more heavily on the clearing banks than others
and they effectively imposed quotas on each individual
institution. The most profitable ways of expanding lending
were thus cut off, and the incentive to compete for
loanable funds was correspondingly diminished. Finally,
the tax treatment of savings outlined above discriminates
strongly against UK banks.

Whatever the reasons for the differences between the
two banking systems, there is no doubt that German households
are much more deeply involved with the banks than British.
One aspect of this involvement has already been demonstrated
in figures for the relative importance of the two systems
in mobilising savings (Tables 3.4 and 3.7). The picture in
terms of number of households is more difficult to present
because of the very different role of the savings banks in
the two systems. In the UK about 53 per cent of the
population aged 15 and over hold accounts with a bank, 25
per cent with the National Savings Bank and 13 per cent
with a Trustee Savings Bank. There is, of course,
considerable overlap between these categories, and about 25
per cent of the adult population have no account with either
a bank or savings bank. In Germany there are about 37
million sight accounts with banks of all kinds, about 0.8
per head of the population over 15, and 1.5 per household
and well over 90 per cent of all households (though not
necessarily individuals) hold savings accounts.

A student of these matters writing ten years ago would have been tempted to ascribe at least part of the difference between household savings ratios in Britain and Germany to differences in their banking systems, but this hypothesis would be hard to defend now. The fall in the German savings ratio since 1975 has not been associated with any decline in the role or activity of the banks. The large rise in the UK ratio has been accompanied by a rise in acquisitions of bank deposits, but the rise has been much smaller for banks than for building societies, and there have been no significant changes in bank attitudes or policies towards the household saver.

In view of this, it seems improbable that differences between the two systems have had much effect on the total supply of saving. What is certain, however, is that the German system has persuaded savers to forego liquidity to a much greater extent than the British and so has developed a capacity to transmit a large volume of funds from savers to borrowers without generating an inflationary expansion of the money supply.

APPENDIX 3.A: DEFINITIONS OF SAVING

Saving can be defined either gross (i.e. including depreciation and stock appreciation) or net of these items. The gross figure has to be compared with gross fixed capital formation plus the increase in the value of stocks, (gross investment). The net figure has to be compared with net fixed capital formation plus the value of physical increases in stocks (net investment). Figures according to both definitions are readily available for the UK but for Germany the figures are normally presented on a net basis. Moreover, the net figures are more relevant to financial transactions. For these reasons all savings figures used here are on a net basis.

In principle the relationships between income, saving and the acquisition of financial assets can be set out in three simple equations:-

1.   Saving = income - consumption.

2.   Saving ± capital transfers - investment = net acquisition of financial assets (NAFA).

3.   NAFA = gross acquisition of financial assets (GAFA) - net borrowing.

The application of these principles to the different sectors of the economy involves some awkward questions of definition. There are a number of differences between the two countries, of which three are of major significance. These involve the treatment of:-

1.   Non corporate business,

2.   Housing, and

3.   Pension rights.

Non-corporate business

In the UK non-corporate business is included in the personal (household) sector. This implies that retained

profits of unincorporated businesses are treated as part of
personal saving, and capital formation as investment by the
personal sector. In Germany all business activity is
excluded from the household sector. Saving is estimated
directly from financial transactions and is equal to:

> Gross acquisition of financial assets less
> Increase in consumer borrowing plus Capital
> transfers to other sectors less Capital
> transfers from other sectors.

Income figures include income from self-employment so
retained profits of non-corporate business are:-

> Income
> less Consumption
> less Saving

The effect of this on the absolute level of savings is to
reduce German recorded saving, relative to British, by the
amount of retained profits. The estimate of retained
profits, being a residual, is subject to wide margins of
error; it has fluctuated considerably from year-to-year
but its relationship to other savings has shown a strong
downward trend. For much of the fifties and early
sixties the two were roughly equal but in 1973-1976
retained profits were actually negative.

In calculating the savings ratio the UK statistics
include retained profits (after tax) in both disposable
income and in saving; the German statistics exclude them
from both. Thus, so long as retained profits are positive,
the German convention produces a lower savings ratio than
the British one. This can be illustrated by reference to
the following German figures for 1978.

	DM bn.
Disposable income	822.4
Retained profits	12.2
Saving excluding retained profits	102.3
Savings ratio	$\frac{102.3}{822.4} \times 100 = 12.4\%$

Using the British convention, the DM 12.2 bn. of retained
profits would have been added both to numerator and

denominator, giving a ratio of $\frac{114.5}{836.6}$ x 100 = 13.7%.

In calculating NAFA, the British convention takes
saving including retained profits and deducts capital
formation. Under the German convention retained profits
are excluded from saving, but there is no deduction for
capital formation (since this comes into the business
sector). The British convention thus tends to understate
NAFA (relative to the German one) if capital formation in
non-corporate business exceeds retained profits and vice
versa.

Housing

In the UK expenditure on housebuilding by the
personal sector is regarded as part of the sector's capital
formation and is treated in the same way as that outlined
above for capital formation by non-corporate business. In
Germany housebuilding is regarded as a sub-sector of the
business sector. In practice only that part of building on
behalf of private households that is financed through building
societies (Bausparkassen) gets counted. This building is
recorded as expenditure by the housing sub-sector and has its
counterpart in a transfer to the sub-sector from the building
societies. That transfer, in turn, has its counterpart in
another transfer (comprising deposits in building society
accounts and repayments of loans) from the household sector
to building societies. So far as this part of housebuilding
is concerned, there is thus no difference between the two
conventions in the amount of household saving recorded, in
savings ratios, or in NAFA.

The situation is quite different with personal sector
building financed by other means. Here, the expenditure is
treated as consumption rather than capital formation under
the German convention so there is an under-statement, relative
to Britain, both of the absolute amount of saving and of the

savings ratio. However, higher saving that would be recorded
under the British convention would be balanced by expenditure
on capital formation, so there is no difference between the
two conventions in recorded NAFA.

Pension rights

In the UK most occupational pension schemes are
funded and the surplus (i.e. contributions plus investment
income less pensions paid and expenses) of funds is treated
as personal saving. Some unfunded schemes in the public
sector also generate small surpluses of contributions over
payments, and these too are included in personal saving
with a counterpart in an increase in government liabilities.

In Germany most pensions are unfunded or subject to
"balance sheet funding", whereby a firm makes provision for
future pension liabilities in its balance sheet but does
not establish any separate fund. In the Statistisches
Bundesamt figures the accumulation of these pension rights
is not treated as household saving, but it is in the
Bundesbank flow of funds accounts. This, together with some
minor differences, raises the savings ratio recorded by the
Bundesbank about 1 percentage point above that of the
Statistisches Bundesamt.

APPENDIX 3.B:

FINANCIAL TRANSACTIONS OF HOUSEHOLDS
ANNUAL STATISTICS

TABLE 3B.1: HOUSEHOLD TRANSACTIONS IN MAIN CATEGORIES OF FINANCIAL ASSETS, UK, 1961-1979

£mn

ASSETS/LIABILITIES	1961	1962[a]	1963	1964	1965	1966	1967	1968	1969	1970
ASSETS ACQUIRED:										
Notes and coin	49	3	42	71	136	143	63	-90	70	113
British government securities	-58[b]	-32[b]	-226	-86	-69	-21	-217	-246	76	-200
National savings securities	211[b]	240[b]	116	144	-68	-127	12	-6	-119	-20
Local authority debt:										
- short-term	40	-3	35	56	71	48	-25	31	58	-104
- long-term	201	292	174	67	218	184	190	124	182	8
Deposits with banking sector	189	301	366	458	512	250	740	682	308	822
Deposits with savings banks										
- ordinary department	n.a.	n.a.	71	66	43	-74	-58	-81	-101	-25
- "investment" and "special investment" departments	n.a.	n.a.	133	149	102	167	168	168	111	165
Deposits with building societies	209	372	490	501	657	726	1090	762	890	1484
Funds of life assurance and superannuation schemes	869	934	1142	1213	1215	1230	1359	1502	1500	1719
Unit trust units	7	34	60	77	59	105	84	258	186	89
Company and overseas securities	-306	-396	-497	-544	-668	-463	-558	-689	-481	-827
Other identified transactions	24	16	19	7	48	27	11	37	-98	-46
Total	1435	1761	1925	2179	2256	2195	2859	2452	2582	3178
LIABILITIES INCURRED:										
Bank lending	61	221	90	134	-34	-60	138	38	-77	59
Loans for house purchase	369	414	573	755	708	761	979	981	858	1245
Other credit from retailers and financial institutions	1	7	70	144	98	-94	-2	42	9	71
Unidentified items	346	554	705	549	531	487	875	865	1055	341
Total	776	1196	1438	1582	1303	1094	1990	1926	1827	1716

ASSETS ACQUIRED:

Notes and coin	115	240	231	353	408	307	485	601	509
British government securities	434	-11	742	604	1006	1754	804	270	2393
National savings securities	282	306	-20	-140	263	485	1127	1315	1175
Local authority debt									
- short-term	-10	30	133	-182	-264	70	-341	-144	319
- long-term	-196	-114	223	959	33	175	321	-1	-209
Deposits with banking sector	953	1767	3381	2973	990	1321	562	3238	6367
Deposits with savings banks									
- ordinary department	92	157	127	129	160	107	163	210	-113
- "investment" and "special investment" departments	241	354	162	62	211	201	606	583	867
Deposits with building societies	1961	2139	2188	1969	4161	3301	5932	4849	5832
Funds of life assurance and superannuation schemes	2115	2955	3412	3695	4450	5568	6138	7333	9320
Unit trust units	47	203	162	31	100	79	25	117	-35
Company and overseas securities	-1265	-1267	-2120	-974	-1042	-1547	-1851	-1289	-1875
Other identified transactions	18	-21	-300	-377	-84	-234	57	-122	-662
Total	4787	6738	8321	9102	10392	11587	14028	16960	23888

LIABILITIES INCURRED:

Bank lending	576	1999	1027	24	-472	519	1164	1597	2649
Loans for house purchase	1823	2784	2831	2370	3648	3872	4285	5390	6368
Other credit from retailers and financial institutions	203	272	243	12	83	236	350	563	746
Unidentified items	1726	470	1355	1708	1488	1304	3352	1242	3075
Total	4328	5525	5456	4090	4744	5931	9151	8792	12858
NET ACQUISITION OF NET ASSETS	459	1213	2865	5012	5648	5656	4877	8168	11050

NOTES: a   Break-in series

b   Includes deposits with savings banks

Source: CSO Financial Statistics and National Income and Expenditure.

TABLE 3B.2: FINANCIAL ASSETS (GROSS) AND LIABILITIES OF PRIVATE HOUSEHOLDS WEST GERMANY (CHANGE OVER PREVIOUS YEAR)

in millions DM

	1961	1962	1963	1964	1965	1966	1967	1968	1969
I FINANCIAL ASSETS (GROSS)									
1. Long Term									
(a) Deposits with banks	7.0	8.8	11.3	13.0	16.8	16.8	17.6	22.4	22.6
aa) Time deposits	0	0.1	0.1	0	0.1	0	0.1	0	0.2
ab) Saving DCs*(1)	-	-	-	-	-	-	0.2	1.5	1.8
ac) Saving deposits	6.8	8.8	11.5	12.9	16.7	16.8	17.4	20.8	20.6
(b) Deposits with building societies	1.9	1.7	2.1	2.1	3.5	4.5	2.7	2.5	3.9
(c) Payments to insurance companies**	3.4	3.9	4.0	4.8	4.9	5.7	6.2	6.9	7.5
(d) Holdings of fixed-interest securities	1.3	2.4	3.0	4.6	4.4	2.4	2.5	2.6	7.2
(e) Holdings of shares	1.3	0.7	0.1	0.6	1.8	0.9	1.4	2.2	3.5
(f) Claims against Firm-owned Pension Schemes (2)	1.5	1.7	1.6	1.2	2.2	2.3	1.5	1.6	1.6
(g) TOTAL	16.4	19.2	22.3	26.5	33.5	32.5	31.9	37.3	46.2
2. Short Term									
(a) Cash and sight deposits	3.0	1.9	2.0	2.8	3.0	2.5	1.8	3.5	4.2
(b) Time deposits(3)	0.1	0.2	0.1	0.2	0.2	0.1	0.1	0.1	0.8
(c) TOTAL	3.2	2.0	2.1	3.0	3.2	2.6	1.9	3.7	4.9
Total of financial assets	19.5	21.3	24.4	29.5	36.7	35.1	33.9	40.9	51.1
Memoranda Items:									
Fixed interest securities at current prices	1.2	2.3	3.0	4.3	2.9	2.0	3.3	2.6	5.5
Shares at current prices	1.2	-5.4	1.9	1.4	-0.4	-1.8	9.4	7.0	10.2
II LIABILITIES									
1. Bank credits	1.1	1.9	1.2	1.1	1.7	0.6	1.1	3.0	4.9
2. Other liabilities	0.3	0.3	0.2	0.2	0.2	0.0	0.3	0.3	0.2
TOTAL LIABILITIES	1.3	2.3	1.4	1.3	1.9	0.6	1.5	3.2	5.0

I FINANCIAL ASSETS (GROSS)

1. Long Term

(a) Deposits with banks	23.0	30.3	35.3	21.2	37.1	74.8	45.7	40.9
aa) Time deposits	0.3	0.2	0.2	0.3	0.2	0.3	0.8	1.0
ab) Saving DSC*(1)	1.5	2.0	3.5	5.3	4.9	8.6	10.0	12.3
ac) Savings deposits	21.2	28.0	31.7	15.6	31.9	66.0	34.9	27.6
(b) Deposits with building societies	5.5	5.4	7.1	8.8	5.7	6.9	6.6	6.5
(c) Payments to insurance companies **	8.4	10.3	11.6	12.9	12.3	16.5	16.9	18.8
(d) Holdings of fixed-interest securities	10.8	7.7	11.0	11.7	12.5	8.9	18.9	12.4
(e) Holdings of shares	0.4	1.2	-0.2	1.7	0.5	2.0	0.5	1.4
(f) Claims against Firm-owned Pension Schemes(2)	3.6	3.5	4.2	4.9	7.1	6.9	5.7	6.9
(g) TOTAL	51.7	58.2	69.2	61.2	75.2	116.0	95.1	86.9

2. Short Term

(a) Cash and sight deposits	2.6	7.0	7.8	1.8	6.9	9.2	5.6	11.6
(b) Time deposits(3)	4.1	1.8	3.8	16.3	5.3	-19.1	-0.1	2.8
(c) TOTAL	6.7	8.8	11.6	18.0	12.3	-9.9	5.5	14.4
Total of financial assets	58.4	67.0	80.8	79.2	87.4	106.1	100.7	101.3

Memoranda Items:

Fixed interest securities at current prices	8.9	7.6	8.6	8.5	11.6	12.5	24.4	19.9
Shares at current prices	-7.4	3.4	2.3	-1.5	-1.5	9.3	-3.3	4.5

II LIABILITIES

1. Bank credits	3.8	6.5	9.2	4.1	0.2	6.9	13.5	13.5
2. Other liabilities	0.3	1.1	1.0	0.9	0.6	0.1	0.2	0.6
TOTAL LIABILITIES	4.2	7.5	10.2	5.1	0.8	7.0	13.7	13.2

III NET ASSETS (I - II)

III NET ASSETS (I - II)	54.2	59.5	70.6	74.1	66.7	99.0	87.0	88.1

NOTES: 1. Since 1970 including bearer bonds. 2. Including other assets. 3. Since 1973 including Federal Treasury notes

* Variously translated as "savings bonds" and "saving CDs"

** i.e., payments on insurance policies (insurance companies are not licensed to take deposits; any deposits private households may have with insurance companies would be listed as "other assets" I 1f).

Source: Deutsche Bundesbank

CHAPTER 4:   THE SUPPLY OF FUNDS
FOR INDUSTRY AND COMMERCE
By E. Victor Morgan

1.   INTRODUCTION

The role of British and German banks in providing funds
for industry and commerce is influenced by differences in the
structure of the two economies, while the statistical
evidence is affected by differences in coverage. These
matters are discussed briefly in Section 2. Section 3
presents balance sheet data, and Section 4 summarises the
available statistics on sources and uses of funds. Section
5 deals more specifically with the role of the banks,
including comments on some important differences in types
of bank loan.

2.   COVERAGE AND SOURCES

The relevant UK statistics relate to "industrial and
commercial companies". The sector includes both public and
private companies[1] but excludes all non-corporate business
which is treated as part of the personal sector (see
Chapter 3). Virtually all housing is excluded, since it
comes into either the personal or local authority sectors.
Also excluded is most nationalised industry. Industries
that are classed as "public corporations" (including coal,
gas, electricity, posts and telecommunications, rail and
some road and air transport, shipbuilding, aerospace and
the British National Oil Corporation) are treated as part of
the public sector, and their finances are discussed in
Chapter 7. Some companies that are publicly owned are,
however, not public corporations and are in the company
sector. These include British Leyland and Rolls Royce.

---

1.   "Public companies" are companies that are entitled to
     issue share to the general public whereas private
     companies can have only restricted share ownership.

The business sector in Germany is much more broadly
defined. As shown in the Appendix to Chapter 3, it includes
all non-corporate business and housing. The public sector
is much smaller than in the UK; only the Post Office and
the railways have a status similar to that of UK public
corporations.

Non-corporate business is much more important in
Germany than in the UK. The share of non-corporate business
in Germany is discussed in detail in a supplementary
paper.[1] Turnover statistics derived from VAT returns show
the following percentages for 1976:

Sole traders	19.7
Partnerships	34.2
Shareholders' companies (AG & KGaA)	20.8
Limited liability companies (GmbH)	18.0
Co-operatives and other companies	7.2

Non-corporate business accounted for nearly 54 per cent of
total turnover.

Turnover figures are not available for the UK but
some idea of the relative positions can be gained from
shares in capital stock. The figure most closely comparable
with the German business sector would be the total of the
personal sector; industrial and commercial companies; and
public corporations. The shares of these three in their
total net capital stock at the end of 1976 were:

	Percentage of three sector total	
Personal	31	
Industrial and commercial companies	43	
Public corporations	26	[2]

---

1.   "The Share of Non-corporate Firms in the German
     Business Sector", by K.H. Hennings.

2.   National Income and Expenditure, 1979 Edition,
     Table 11-11.

For Germany the balance value of fixed assets in the "enterprise sector" was distributed as follows:

	Percentage
Corporations	41
Unincorporated partnerships	28
Single proprietorships	31 [1]

Non-corporate business included 59 per cent of the sectors' total fixed assets compared to only 31 per cent in the UK. These figures are compiled by very different methods in the two countries but the differences should not greatly affect the distribution of assets between corporate and non-corporate owners.

Private companies (GmbH) are more important relative to public companies in Germany than in the UK. The turnover figures already quoted show that private companies with 18 per cent of total turnover are almost as important as public companies (20.8 per cent). Finally, the degree of concentration in British industry is generally higher than in Germany.

These differences affect the role of the banks in at least three ways. Non-corporate business has very limited sources of external finance apart from the banking system, so the greater size of this sector in Germany tends to enhance the importance of the banks and the need for their services. A similar effect is produced by the small part played by public corporations in Germany, since these bodies in the UK make only limited use of the banks and derive most of their external finance from the central government. Thirdly, very large firms can, to some extent, act as their own financial intermediary, using surpluses generated in one "profit centre" to finance deficits incurred by another. The smaller part played by giant firms in the German economy leaves less scope than in the UK for this kind of by-passing of the financial system.

---

1. Deutsche Bundesbank. Jahresabschlusse der Unternehmen in der Bundesrepublik Deutschland, 1969-1976, p.11.

A further difference between the two countries, which might work in the opposite direction, is in the ability of private firms to borrow and lend abroad. In Germany, during most of the period of our study, there were no restrictions on such transactions - in the UK they were severely restricted by exchange controls until these were abolished in October 1979.

3.   BALANCE-SHEET DATA

Balance-sheet data present a lot of problems of interpretation but they provide some relevant information that is not available elsewhere. The obligation to publish balance-sheets in Germany is confined to public companies (AG) and about 130 large undertakings that operate as private companies (GmbH) or are unincorporated. These are analysed by the Statistisches Bundesamt but cover only a small part (probably less than 30 per cent by turnover) of the whole sector. A much broader sample is obtained by the Deutsche Bundesbank as a by-product of its rediscount operations. The rediscount privilege is given only to the paper of approved enterprises, and firms seeking approval must submit balance-sheets. The Bank receives over 48,000 balance-sheets, which it grosses-up to provide estimates for the whole sector. However, the sample is still not wholly representative; small non-corporate firms (who would be unlikely to get approval) tend to be under-represented and so do activities where bills of exchange are not widely used (e.g. services). There are also differences between the Bundesbank and Statistisches Bundesamt figures in the way in which items are classified, and in the amount of "netting-out".

Table 4.1 shows data from both sources, with the Bundesbank categories re-arranged as far as possible to fit the Statistisches Bundesamt classification. Fixed capital, long-term financial assets and cash are more important in the balance-sheets of public companies than of private

TABLE 4-1: BALANCE-SHEET SUMMARY – GERMAN ENTERPRISES, 1976. (Percentage of balance-sheet total)

	STATISTISCHES BUNDESAMT SAMPLE			DEUTSCHE BUNDESBANK SAMPLE			
	AG	GmbH	Non-corporate Firms	Corporate Firms	Partnerships	Single Traders	ALL FIRMS
Firms in sample	1563	95	35	8900	24500	14100	48400
ASSETS:							
Fixed assets	36.3	27.9	25.4	40.1	27.7	30.9	36.2
Financial assets (long-term)	13.6	8.1	11.0	11.2	4.8	2.4	7.7
Long-term assets	49.9	36.0	36.4	51.3	32.5	33.3	43.9
Stock	19.1	25.6	28.6	17.5	25.4	25.8	20.8
Debtors	22.6	28.0	27.5	26.0	34.7	26.4	28.9
Trade debts	10.1	–	–	13.4	21.0	19.0	16.2
Other	12.5	–	–	12.6	13.7	7.4	12.7
Cash and sight departments	7.4	8.7	7.0	4.2	4.6	3.3	4.1
Short-term assets	49.1	62.3	63.1	47.7	64.7	55.5	53.8
Other assets	0.3	0.3	0.4	1.1	2.8	3.3	2.2
TOTAL ASSETS	100.0	100.0	100.0	100.0	100.0	100.0	100.0
LIABILITIES:							
Capital	15.5	19.6	23.7	25.4	19.9	19.7	23.2
Reserves	12.4	7.2					
Special reserves	2.7	1.3	1.0				
Provisions	17.9	19.7	17.5	16.5	9.0	4.3	11.8
of which:							
Pensions	9.1	9.0	11.8	–	–	–	–
Other	9.9	10.7	7.7	–	–	–	–
Loans	49.4	46.9	54.5	46.1	68.5	74.2	57.0
Long-term	20.8	12.1	14.0	16.4	21.7	18.5	18.9
Short-term	28.6	34.8	40.5	29.7	46.8	55.8	38.0
Profits	2.0	5.2	0.9	12.0	2.6	1.8	8.1
Other liabilities	0.2	0.2	0.5				
TOTAL LIABILITIES	100.0	100.0	100.0	100.0	100.0	100.0	100.0

Sources: Statistisches Jahrbuch 1979, pp. 122-123, and 126.
Deutsche Bundesbank, Jahresabschlusse (1976), pp. 4 and 11.

companies, and more important for the corporate sector as
a whole than for non-corporate business. On the other hand,
stocks, and trade and other debtors loom larger in the
balance-sheets of non-corporate business. As would be
expected, shareholders' interests (in the form of capital
and reserves) are a larger part of the balance-sheet total
for public companies than for either private companies or
non-corporate business, while the non-corporate sector makes
considerably more use of loans, particularly short-term
loans, mainly from the banks.

The only source of similar data in the UK is the
analysis carried out by the Central Statistical Office (CSO)
and published in Business Monitor. The 1976 figures, shown
in Table 4.2, relate to a sample of 1,479 companies in
manufacturing and distribution which had net assets of over
£5 million or gross trading profits of over £500,000 in 1973.
In comparing Tables 4.1 and 4.2 we need to bear in mind not
only the differences in coverage already mentioned but also
at least two other points. Firstly, German balance-sheets
value assets at historic cost, whereas a number of UK
companies have re-valued fixed assets from time-to-time to
take account of inflation. The extent of under-valuation in
Germany is estimated at between 15 and 20 per cent. This
may not, however, be greater than in the UK. Not all
British companies have re-valued and few, if any, do so
every year; hence the British figures only partially reflect
inflation, which has been much higher in Britain than in
Germany.

Secondly, assets which are leased or rented do not
appear in the balance-sheet. Though we do not have any
comprehensive statistics we believe that leasing is more
common in Britain than in Germany.

TABLE 4.2: BALANCE-SHEET SUMMARY, UK COMPANIES IN MANUFACTURING AND DISTRIBUTION. (BUSINESS MONITOR SAMPLE), 1976
Percentages of balance-sheet total

ASSETS:		
Fixed assets:		37.2
Current assets:		
– Stocks	28.4	
– Trade debtors	24.0	
– Cash	5.8	
– Other	4.6	
– Total		62.8
TOTAL		100.0
LIABILITIES:		
Current liabilities:		
– Trade creditors	25.7	
– Bank loans	10.0	
– Other[1]	6.1	
– Total		41.8
Deferred taxation		8.2
Long-term loans		9.6
Minority interests in subsidiaries		2.2
Shareholders interest:		
– Ordinary shares	10.3	
– Preference	0.6	
– Reserves	27.3	
– Total		38.2
TOTAL		100.0

NOTE: 1. Including tax and dividend reserves.

Source: Business Monitor, M3, Table 1.

On the assets side of the balance-sheet, fixed capital
in the UK figures forms a similar percentage to that of
the German corporate sector, though larger than for the non-
corporate sectors. Holdings of cash (mainly bank deposits)
are broadly similar but other financial assets play a larger
part in German corporate balance-sheets. Trade debtors are
more important in the UK.

On the liabilities side, shareholders' interests are
much more important in the UK with over 38 per cent of the
balance-sheet total, compared with 30.6 per cent (AG) and
26.8 per cent (GmbH) on the Statistisches Bundesamt figures
and only 25.4 per cent for the Corporate sector as a whole
shown by the Bundesbank. Trade creditors figure more
prominently in the UK. German corporate firms finance about
10 per cent of their balance-sheet total by pension
provisions (see Chapter 3) for which there is no counterpart
in the UK. Finally, German industry, as is well known, has
a far higher proportion of loans. UK companies had 10 per
cent of their liabilities in long-term loans, mainly
debentures issued through the capital market, and a further
10 per cent in short-term loans, mainly from banks. Loans
formed between 45 and 50 per cent of balance-sheet totals
for German corporate sector, and even more for non-corporate
business. Short-term loans made up about two-thirds of the
total but, as will be shown later, a large part of long-term
lending as well as almost all short-term, comes from the
banks.

4.   FLOWS OF FUNDS

Tables 4.3 and 4.4 show the relative importance of
internal and external sources of funds for the two countries.
The UK figures are for the company sector, as defined above.
The German ones, from the Bundesbank's flow of funds
accounts, relate to the business sector, excluding housing.
There is considerable year-to-year variation in both
countries, but during most of the period covered, the UK

TABLE 4.3: SOURCES AND USES OF FUNDS: SUMMARY - UK

| | PERCENTAGES OF TOTAL | | | | |
| | SOURCES | | USES | | |
Year	Internal	External	Fixed Capital Gross	Stocks[1]	Other[2]
1963	68.5	31.5	51.4	8.2	40.4
1964	67.1	32.9	52.1	18.9	29.0
1965	70.5	29.4	58.7	16.0	25.3
1966	70.3	29.7	67.3	13.5	19.2
1967	72.3	27.7	62.4	6.8	30.8
1968	68.4	31.6	51.7	16.9	31.4
1969	69.0	31.0	52.5	18.4	29.1
1970	62.7	37.3	53.0	20.5	26.5
1971	70.4	29.6	48.6	11.4	40.0
1972	57.8	42.2	37.0	9.4	53.6
1973	55.1	44.9	31.7	23.1	45.2
1974	54.9	45.1	39.5	39.3	21.2
1975	73.6	26.4	50.3	18.5	31.5
1976	68.5	31.5	43.2	30.1	26.7
1977	71.9	28.1	46.9	26.2	26.9
1978	73.6	26.4	51.6	18.1	30.3
1979	73.7	26.3	43.4	30.2	26.4

1. Increase in book value of stocks.

2. Including unidentified items and accruals adjustment.

Source: Financial Statistics.

TABLE 4.4: SOURCES AND USES OF FUNDS: SUMMARY - GERMANY

| | PERCENTAGES OF TOTAL | | | |
| | SOURCES | | USES | |
Year	Internal	External	Fixed Capital	Other
1963	64.9	35.1	86.6	13.4
1964	63.7	36.3	86.3	13.7
1965	60.1	39.9	85.8	14.1
1966	67.2	32.7	88.7	11.3
1967	72.9	27.1	75.0	22.3
1968	69.2	30.8	79.8	20.1
1969	57.0	43.0	81.7	18.3
1970	55.9	44.1	82.0	18.0
1971	53.3	46.7	79.0	21.0
1972	54.4	46.6	76.4	23.6
1973	59.1	40.9	83.6	16.4
1974	57.8	42.2	77.6	22.4
1975	68.9	31.1	77.7	22.3
1976	65.7	34.3	75.7	24.3
1977	66.6	33.4	77.1	22.9
1978	75.7	24.3	75.7	24.3
1979	71.5	28.5	81.1	18.9

Source: Deutsche Bundesbank, Zahlenübersichten und methodische
Erläuterungen zur gesamtwirtschaftlichen Finanzierungsrechnung
der Deutschen Bundesbank, 1960 bis 1979.

has the higher proportion of internal financing. The internal financing ratio tends to fall, in both countries, in years of abnormally high fixed capital formation and also in years where there is a large increase in the value of stocks (either because of physical increases or rising prices).

The high UK ratio is somewhat surprising in view of the fact that the German figures include a large non-corporate sector. One reason may be the relatively large use of external finance on the part of the German non-corporate business (Table 4.1). Other contributing factors may have been the low level of investment in the UK industry, and the reluctance to borrow engendered by high and variable inflation rates and rates of interest.

There is no clear evidence of trend in either countries. UK companies went through a period of heavy dependence on outside finance in 1972-74, mainly because of the large demands on funds made by stock appreciation at a time of rapidly rising inflation, but the internal financing ratio for 1975-79 was not greatly different from that of the sixties. German enterprises had an abnormally low proportion of internal financing from 1969 to 1972, but the average of the seventies did not differ greatly from that of the sixties.

Though the proportions of internal and external financing do not seem to be changing much, the absolute amounts involved have increased as a result of both rising real expenditure and of inflation. The latter has, of course, been much more marked in the UK than in Germany. The total amount of external finance raised by German non-financial enterprises rose from DM21.9 bn. in 1963 to DM63 bn. in 1977. Over the same period external funds raised by UK industrial and commercial companies rose from £1.17 bn. to £5.80 bn.

Tables 4.3 and 4.4 also show the allocation of funds
between gross domestic fixed capital formation, increases in
the book value of stocks and acquisition of other assets
(domestic, financial and overseas). Fixed capital naturally
accounts for the major part of expenditure in both countries,
but the proportion is markedly lower in the UK than in
Germany, while UK companies tend to spend more on stocks
(not shown separately in the German table) and on financial
assets. The larger role of stocks in the UK figures is
partly a result of the higher UK inflation rate. At the
beginning of our period UK companies employed a much higher
proportion of their total funds in the acquisition of
financial assets, but this has changed considerably. UK
acquisitions rose very sharply in 1971-73, at a time of very
expansionist monetary policy, but have since fallen sharply.
The German figure has shown large year-to-year fluctuations
but about a rising trend.

Sources and uses accounts in the UK normally show
internal funds including depreciation, and expenditures
including gross fixed capital formation and the increase in
the book value of stocks (i.e. the product of changes in
physical volume and in prices). In Germany, stocks are
valued at historic cost but internal funds include
depreciation and expenditure includes gross fixed capital
formation. These conventions were followed in Tables 4.3
and 4.4, but they can give a misleading impression of the
role of external finance, and hence of the importance of
banks and other financial institutions. Any business that
is to maintain the real value of its assets must provide for
depreciation and stock appreciation out of internal funds.
Hence, if we want to measure the contribution of the
financial system to providing funds for investment, it is
often more helpful to use net figures.

In Tables 4.5 and 4.6, saving is shown net of
depreciation and (in the UK) stock appreciation. Similarly,
German capital formation is shown net of depreciation of fixed
capital, and includes only the value of physical additions

TABLE 4.5: SAVING, NET CAPITAL FORMATION AND NAFA OF INDUSTRIAL AND COMMERCIAL COMPANIES - UK,

£bn.

Year	Saving[1]	Capital Transfers	Net Capital Formation[2]	NAFA
1963	1.46	0.01	-1.12	0.35
1964	1.71	0.01	-1.88	+0.16
1965	1.56	0.02	-1.74	-0.16
1966	1.14	0.02	-1.42	-0.28
1967	1.00	0.23	-1.24	-0.01
1968	1.15	0.43	-1.63	-0.05
1969	1.36	0.57	-1.95	-0.02
1970	1.07	0.48	-2.09	-0.54
1971	1.62	0.55	-1.46	0.71
1972	2.46	0.38	-1.57	1.26
1973	3.20	0.35	-3.61	-0.06
1974	0.27	0.33	-4.13	-3.52
1975	1.23	0.40	-0.99	0.64
1976	2.96	0.36	-3.35	-0.03
1977	4.18	0.25	-4.89	-0.47
1978	4.84	0.37	-4.85	0.35
1979	2.53	0.32	-6.21	-3.37

1. After providing for depreciation and stock appreciation but including additions to tax and dividend resources.

2. Gross fixed capital formation less depreciation plus value of physical increase in stocks.

Source: National Income and Expenditure, Tables 5.6 and 13.1.

TABLE 4.6: SAVING, NET CAPITAL FORMATION AND NAFA, ENTERPRISES, EXCLUDING HOUSING - GERMANY.

DM bn.

Year	Saving	Capital Transfers (net)	Net Capital Formation	NAFA
1963	11.68	2.18	-27.38	-13.51
1964	15.09	2.02	-33.66	-16.56
1965	15.60	2.42	-39.89	-21.88
1966	13.04	2.50	-32.16	-16.61
1967	13.11	2.48	-17.10	-1.52
1968	18.25	2.45	-30.10	-9.39
1969	13.92	4.80	-45.84	-27.12
1970	18.32	5.81	-59.28	-35.14
1971	10.85	6.02	-52.95	-36.07
1972	9.15	6.96	-48.35	-32.25
1973	6.42	8.32	-49.92	-35.18
1974	-5.76	10.36	-33.00	-28.41
1975	-2.45	10.09	-19.58	-11.93
1976	10.74	14.45	-43.12	-17.94
1977	12.22	14.43	-46.46	-19.82
1978	37.76	15.52	-53.29	-
1979	44.37	18.18	-86.35	-23.81

Source: Deutsche Bundesbank. As Table 4.4.

to stocks. The acquisition of financial assets is also shown
net (i.e. deducting acquisitions from gross liabilities
incurred).

Net capital formation is naturally much smaller than
gross and also much more subject to cyclical variation. The
main point of interest in the present context is the
relationship between net capital formation and NAFA. After
a small surplus in 1963, the UK company sector had small or
marginal financial deficits in each of the six years to
1969. The deficit averaged 7 per cent of net capital
formation over this period.

In the following ten years, however, the company
sector has swung frequently between moderate surpluses and
deficits which were very large in 1974 and 1979. Over this
later period, the net financial deficit averaged 15 per
cent of net capital formation and in the peak years of 1974
and 1979 the percentages were 85 per cent and 54 per cent
respectively. The UK company sector has become more
dependent on external finance than is apparent from the
sources and uses statistics.

German enterprises have had a financial deficit throughout the period, except for 1978, though only a small one in
1967. Apart from these two years and 1979, the deficit was
never less than 30 per cent of net capital formation. The
proportion rose from about 50 per cent in the early sixties
to a peak of 86 per cent in 1974 and then fell back to 42
per cent in 1976 and 43 per cent in 1977.

One further point should be made in relation to the
degree of dependence of industry on external finance.
Renting offices, shops or factory buildings and the leasing
of plant and equipment are alternatives to purchase. Assets
rented or leased are "off-balance-sheet"; they do not appear
in the accounts of the companies concerned, and so are not
included in the sector statistics. Equipment leasing has

grown very rapidly in the UK during the seventies and it
is estimated that in 1979 it accounted for 11 per cent of
all investment in plant and machinery. Our UK figures thus
understate the increase in the degree of dependence on
external finance. In Germany, leasing accounted for 2.1
per cent of gross fixed investment (other than dwellings)
in 1971 and 4.3 per cent in 1978. In the UK leasing
grew from very modest beginnings in the early seventies
to 6.2 per cent of all non-housing fixed investment in 1978.
To that extent, comparison of the figures in Tables 4.5 and
4.6 understates the relative importance of external
finance in the UK.

So far, this discussion has dealt with external
finance in general rather than specifically with the banking
system. In both countries the banks are the predominant
suppliers of external finance to industrial and commercial
enterprises, but they are by no means the only ones. In
order to put the role of the banking system in perspective,
Tables 4.7 and 4.8 show the main types of assets acquired
and liabilities incurred. There are some differences in
classification between the two countries that are apparent
in the Tables, but several points of interest emerge.

First, a substantial part of bank lending is matched,
for the sector as a whole, by acquisitions of cash and bank
deposits. The majority of these are short-term - current
accounts in the UK and sight deposits in Germany, but time
deposits in Germany and longer-term, "wholesale" deposits
in the UK are becoming increasingly important. Any
enterprise has to have some working balances so that even
those that are in debt to banks may have a credit balance in
a current account. The greater prevalence of the overdraft
system in the UK probably means that this situation occurs
less often than in Germany, but we have no statistical
information on this. More important is the fact that, at
any point in time, some firms are likely to be in financial

TABLE 4.8: FINANCIAL TRANSACTIONS OF GERMAN ENTERPRISES (EXCLUDING HOUSING)

DM bn.

	1963	1964	1965	1966	1967	1968	1969	1970	1971	1972	1973	1974	1975	1976	1977	1978	1979
FINANCIAL ASSETS ACQUIRED:																	
Bank deposits	3.79	4.86	5.46	3.66	10.74	12.83	10.65	15.79	18.95	25.08	14.59	3.53	16.79	17.63	25.17	33.43	15.94
Funds with insurance companies	0.46	0.38	0.64	0.60	0.73	0.81	0.92	0.98	1.74	2.06	2.63	1.45	1.16	0.73	0.82	1.53	1.82
Bonds	0.42	0.49	0.48	0.42	0.07	1.60	0.88	-0.01	0.13	0.86	0.78	0.07	2.01	4.85	3.00	2.10	5.30
Shares	0.06	0.61	1.69	0.87	1.03	0.21	2.10	2.74	3.01	0.13	1.48	2.98	3.12	2.34	1.07	2.27	5.87
Other: Domestic	0.75	0.34	0.62	0.44	1.13	0.38	0.43	0.36	0.48	0.91	0.42	0.84	0.10	0.33	0.78	0.19	0.16
Foreign	2.89	3.39	3.13	2.76	4.94	1.98	5.09	4.24	5.31	5.49	3.68	23.39	7.19	17.68	12.40	11.49	17.51
TOTAL	8.38	10.07	12.02	8.75	18.65	17.82	20.06	24.11	29.63	34.54	23.58	32.27	30.38	43.55	43.23	50.92	46.60
FINANCIAL LIABILITIES INCURRED:																	
Bank credit	10.22	12.67	15.70	12.99	9.60	14.83	36.15	30.12	37.21	46.77	27.17	28.29	12.06	32.71	30.88	33.53	52.66
Sale of money market paper	0.36	0.34	0.40	-	-0.54	-0.08	1.13	-0.24	-0.58	0.62	-1.23	0.67	0.15	-0.14	-0.93	0.30	0.70
Loans from insurance companies	1.33	1.18	1.43	1.02	1.26	1.22	1.62	1.37	2.82	3.34	2.63	2.64	2.59	2.65	2.87	2.88	3.60
Issue of bonds	1.87	1.59	0.92	-0.55	1.66	1.00	0.27	1.43	3.72	3.31	1.22	1.82	0.85	0.36	0.93	-0.48	-2.66
Issue of shares	1.15	1.92	3.67	2.31	1.73	2.51	2.10	2.79	4.24	2.41	2.33	2.25	4.08	4.37	2.95	3.57	3.80
Other: Domestic	2.99	2.41	2.60	1.86	3.10	2.88	0.20	4.19	4.36	6.80	11.12	13.23	11.24	10.09	7.69	7.51	6.90
Foreign	3.97	6.54	9.15	7.73	3.36	4.83	5.69	19.57	13.92	3.55	15.52	11.76	13.05	11.45	18.67	3.61	5.39
TOTAL	21.89	26.63	33.90	25.36	20.17	27.22	47.16	59.25	65.70	66.79	58.76	60.67	42.31	61.49	63.05	50.92	70.41
NAFA	-13.51	-16.56	-21.88	-16.61	-1.52	-9.40	-27.10	-35.14	-36.07	-32.25	-35.18	-28.40	-11.93	-17.94	-19.82	-	-23.81

Source: Deutsche Bundesbank. As Table 4.4.

TABLE 4.7: FINANCIAL TRANSACTIONS OF UK INDUSTRIAL AND COMMERCIAL COMPANIES

	1963	1964	1965	1966	1967	1968	1969	1970	1971	1972	1973	1974	1975	1976	1977	1978	1979
ASSETS ACQUIRED:																	
Notes, coin and bank deposits	308	108	186	10	383	460	-138	329	1077	2294	2504	93	1378	2071	2560	2554	562
Export and other credit given	165	167	85	136	66	-6	76	160	118	322	595	1011	412	1417	622	1130	1792
Other liquid assets[1]	95	-30	-182	-105	71	-50	-67	-144	127	100	156	52	354	341	352	250	265
Subsidiaries and trade investments	209	353	382	233	339	335	259	251	338	783	903	367	365	837	686	761	1054
Overseas[2]	201	239	282	198	185	192	301	344	431	216	990	825	210	629	696	1768	3508
Other (including unidentified items)[3]	559	469	333	358	31	639	1322	933	672	2020	1819	1046	1550	644	520	-290	-2953
TOTAL	1537	1306	1086	830	1075	1570	1753	1873	2763	5735	6967	3394	4269	5939	5436	6173	4228
LIABILITIES INCURRED:																	
Bank credit	537	752	497	187	333	569	664	1126	732	2988	4504	4411	477	2397	2969	2900	4913
Other loans and mortgages	96	142	180	104	58	205	188	372	164	155	816	110	466	500	139	218	240
Import and other credit received	38	33	3	-4	-24	34	118	128	169	397	596	693	250	852	517	527	1441
Domestic new issues:																	
- Fixed interest securities	212	254	345	451	350	183	335	159	215	290	51	-56	202	42	-67	-71	-22
- Ordinary shares	123	158	63	124	65	303	210	83	231	334	143	126	1050	785	729	837	906
Overseas[4]	168	111	153	212	288	315	257	546	541	309	921	1634	1181	1393	1614	1411	117
TOTAL	1174	1450	1241	1074	1070	1609	1772	2414	2052	4473	7031	6918	3626	5969	5901	5822	7595
NAFA	363	-144	-155	-244	5	-39	-19	-541	711	1262	-64	-3524	643	-30	-465	351	-3367

NOTES:

1. Includes UK government securities.
2. Investment in overseas securities and intra-company investment by UK companies overseas.
3. Residual, including unidentified items and accruals adjustments.
4. New issues overseas, overseas investment in UK company securities and intra-company investment in UK by overseas companies.
5. Intra-company investment overseas, incoming and outgoing, excludes unremitted profits.

Source: Financial Statistics.

surplus and building up their bank deposits, while others
are in financial deficit and increasing their borrowing.
Thus, a significant part of banking activity in both
countries consists of channelling funds from firms in
temporary deficit to those in temporary surplus.

The ratio of deposits acquired to borrowing is shown
in Table 4.9. In both countries there are very large
variations from year-to-year. In years when business is
subject to strong financial pressures additions to deposits
are small or even negative while borrowing tends to be
large. Such periods are, however, quickly followed by
periods where the ratio is abnormally high as liquidity is
restored. These variations are considerably greater in the
UK than in Germany, as would be expected in view of the
violent changes in monetary and fiscal policies that have
affected the UK company sector. Apart from these short-run
variations there does not seem to be any significant
difference in the ratio between the two countries. There is
a slight upward trend in both, possibly related to the growing
tendency already noted to hold time and wholesale deposits.

The second largest item in both countries is
transactions abroad. These include export credit given and
import credit received; the acquisition of foreign securities;
and inward and outward investment by companies in foreign
branches and subsidiaries. For the UK, import and export
credit are shown along with domestic trade credit in
Table 4.7. Credit given has generally, though not always,
exceeded credit given. There have been large year-to-year
fluctuations partly due to "leads and lags" at times when
exchange rates were expected to change. Other overseas
transactions have undergone marked changes. In 1963-65
outward investment (assets acquired) exceeded inward
investment (liabilities incurred) by nearly £100 m. a year.
In later years inward investment was usually the larger and
for 1974-77, the gap averaged nearly £850 m. Foreign

TABLE 4.9: RATIOS OF INCREASE IN CASH HOLDINGS TO BANK BORROWERS.

Per Cent

Year	Germany	U.K.
1963	37	57
1964	38	14
1965	35	37
1966	28	5
1967	112	115
1968	87	53
1969	29	-[1]
1970	52	29
1971	51	147
1972	54	77
1973	54	56
1974	12	2
1975	139	296
1976	54	64
1977	81	87
1978	100	88
1979	30	11

1. Bank balances reduced by £138m.

Source: Tables 4.7 and 4.8

transactions thus swung from making a significant net demand on domestic finance to making a significant contribution to it. In 1978 and more particularly in 1979, with the strengthening of sterling and the removal of exchange controls outward investment rose strongly, while inward investment fell back reversing this swing. The very sharp fall in inward investment in 1979 is partly due to the high level of unremitted profits of overseas subsidiaries. The rise of inward investment during the seventies was mainly due to North Sea oil.

In Germany the much broader definition of the enterprise sector means that domestic trade credit is largely netted out. Import and export credit is included in foreign transactions in Table 4.8. The complete Tables published by the Bundesbank give separate figures which show a strong upward movement both in export credit given and in import credit received, large year-to-year fluctuations, and a tendency for credit received to exceed credit given by an increasing margin. Other foreign transactions also show very large fluctuations related closely to speculative movements into and out of the DM.

The most important domestic source of finance outside the banks, both in the UK and Germany, is the issue of securities on the long-term capital market, but in both countries the relative importance of such issues has been declining. In Germany, issues of bonds and shares together were smaller in 1977-79 than they had been in 1963-65, but their share in total borrowing declined from 13.5 per cent to 4.4 per cent. In the UK the absolute amount of new issues increased but failed to keep up with inflation and their share in total company borrowing fell from 29.9 per cent in 1963-65 to 12.0 per cent in 1977-79. In the UK the market for fixed interest securities has practically dried up as a result of the high nominal interest rates associated with inflation. This process occurred later in Germany but in both countries repayments exceeded new issues in 1978 and 1979.

Table 4.10 shows bank lending for both countries as ratios of net capital formation, total sources of funds; total borrowing, and total domestic borrowing. All four ratios show considerable year-to-year fluctuation, as would be expected from what has gone before, all four show the German banking system usually having the higher ratio, but the gap has narrowed very much during the seventies as UK companies made increasing use of their bankers to help finance massive stock appreciation.

TABLE 4.10: BORROWING RATIOS – UK AND GERMANY

INCREASE IN BANK LOANS AS PERCENTAGE OF:

	Net Capital Formation		Total Sources of Funds		Total Borrowing		Total Domestic Borrowing	
	U.K.	Germany	U.K.	Germany	U.K.	Germany	U.K.	Germany
1963		37.3	14.4	16.4	45.7	46.7	53.4	57.0
1964		37.6	17.0	17.2	51.9	47.6	56.2	63.1
1965		39.3	11.8	18.5	40.0	46.3	45.7	63.4
1966	13.0	40.4	5.2	16.8	17.4	51.2	21.7	73.7
1967	26.3	56.1	8.7	12.9	31.1	47.6	42.6	57.0
1968	34.6	49.3	11.2	16.8	35.4	54.5	44.0	66.2
1969	34.0	78.9	11.6	33.0	37.5	76.7	50.5	87.2
1970	53.5	50.8	17.8	22.4	46.6	50.8	60.3	75.9
1971	45.6	50.3	10.6	26.4	35.7	56.6	48.4	71.9
1972	186.2	96.7	30.0	31.9	66.8	70.0	71.7	74.0
1973	122.9	54.4	31.2	18.9	64.0	46.2	73.7	62.8
1974	104.6	85.7	22.9	19.7	63.8	46.6	83.5	57.8
1975	51.6	61.6	4.0	8.8	13.2	28.5	19.3	41.2
1976	74.8	75.8	14.2	10.4	39.6	53.2	52.0	65.4
1977	60.9	66.5	16.2	16.3	51.0	49.0	68.6	69.6
1978	58.0	62.9	14.8	16.0	49.7	65.8	65.4	76.4

Source: Tables 4.5, 4.7 and 4.8.

These differences are clearly linked to the relatively small corporate sector of the German economy, the relatively small number of listed companies, and the limitations of the long-term capital market, though the direction of cause and effect is by no means clear.

5.   BANK LENDING

Types of loan

Table 4.11 shows the structure of bank lending to domestic firms and private persons in Germany by term and type of credit instrument. Short-term lending (less than one year) formed only 23 per cent of the total, and long-term lending (over four years) accounted for two-thirds. "Book credits and loans", discussed in more detail below, accounted for over 91 per cent of all lending, and bills of exchange for 4.5 per cent. The remaining 4 per cent, "loans on trust" were loans provided out of public funds but administered by the banks.

Table 4.12 shows the term structure of credit to business firms and self-employed persons since 1968. The Table excludes loans to the private sector for non-business purposes and loans related to housing, which account for approximately half the total lending of Table 4.11. Short-term loans are more important for the business sector than for the rest of the private sector, but their proportion has been falling steadily and in 1979 they accounted for only 37 per cent. Medium-term lending increased its share in the total in the early seventies but has since declined. By contrast, the share of long-term lending has grown from about 46 per cent in the late sixties to around 54 per cent in the late seventies.

TABLE 4.11: STRUCTURE OF BANK LENDING TO DOMESTIC FIRMS AND PRIVATE PERSONS[1]
(AT END OF 1979)

	Book Credits and Loans		Bills Discounted		Loans on Trust		TOTAL	
	DM bn.	Per Cent	DM bn.	Per Cent	DM bn.	Per Cent	DM bn.	Per Cent
Short-term	194.5ol	19.0	41.771	4.1	-	-	236.272	23.1
Medium-term	1o5.360	10.3	4.324	0.4	0.966	0.1	11o.650	1o.8
Long-term	634.514	62.1	-	-	40.581	4.0	675.095	66.1
TOTAL	934.375	91.4	46.095	4.5	41.547	4.1	1022.017	1oo.o

NOTE: 1. Excluding Treasury Notes, Securities and Equalization Claims.

Source: Deutsche Bundesbank, Monatsbericht Mai 1980, Table III.4.

TABLE 4.12: TERM STRUCTURE OF GERMAN BANK LENDING TO DOMESTIC FIRMS
AND SELF-EMPLOYED PERSONS

Per Cent

Year	SHORT-TERM	MEDIUM-TERM	LONG-TERM	
			Mortgages	Other
1968	42.0	11.6	9.9	36.5
1969	43.8	11.0	9.7	35.5
1970	42.5	12.2	9.5	35.8
1971	41.9	13.3	9.6	35.3
1972	41.6	13.2	9.8	35.4
1973	40.6	13.0	10.3	36.1
1974	41.0	13.0	10.6	35.4
1975	37.4	11.5	11.6	39.5
1976	37.1	10.7	11.5	40.8
1977	36.4	9.8	11.1	42.7
1978	35.8	9.4	11.9	43.0
1979	37.3	9.4	11.6	41.7

Source: Deutsche Bundesbank, Monatsbericht.
May 1980 Table III.19a and corresponding tables in earlier
issues.

The term "book credits and loans" covers a variety
of instruments. A large part of short-term lending is by
means of overdrafts. As in the UK the customer is allowed
to overdraw his account up to an agreed limit, and payments
into the account reduce the debit balance. An alternative
arrangement is for a customer to open a line of credit for
an agreed amount repayable over an agreed term; he then
keeps his current account in credit by having the sums
required credited to his current account and debited to
loan account.

Mortgages account for about a fifth of long-term
borrowing, and a substantial part of the rest is in
"Schuldscheindarlehen", sometimes translated as "borrowers
notes", though we prefer "loan certificates". These were
first issued by public authorities in return for bank loans,
mainly from savings banks, but they became increasingly
important for industrial financing from the early 1960's.
They are informal documents and can embody a variety of
terms and conditions to fit the circumstances of particular
transactions; this makes it difficult to define them and
the Bundesbank does not show them as a separate category in
its statistics. There is, therefore, no reliable figure for
amounts outstanding.

The sums involved are always large, normally DM1m. or
more. Loans are for at least four years but often up to ten
or fifteen years. Interest is fixed and repayment may be
either at the end of the term or in accordance with a
schedule of instalments specified in the certificate;
early repayment is normally precluded. Loans are commonly
secured on land or property, and contracts may also impose
an obligation to maintain specified accounting ratios.
Certificates normally empower the original lender to cede
his rights to a third party but do not allow further transfers.

This has prevented the development of a secondary
market in Schuldscheindarlehen, but banks frequently sell
them to insurance companies or building societies. In

some cases banks will also take back and re-sell certificates from institutions that want to dispose of them.

From the point-of-view of the borrower, loan certificates have the advantages of flexibility, informality, and low costs of issue. For the lender they offer a secure cash flow over a known period of time (since early repayment is not allowed). Moreover, since they are not marketable, holders show them in their balance-sheets at par, and are thus spared the embarrassment of having to show capital losses in times of rising interest rates. Against these advantages have to be set the lack of liquidity due to the absence of an organised market, and the need to satisfy supervisory authorities. We were informed in interviews that supervisory authorities for the insurance industry have recently adopted a more restrictive attitude towards Schuldscheindarlehen, and that this has led to some decline in the popularity of the instrument. The alternative is a straightforward term loan; these are normally secured, and are obtainable for periods up to 15 years.

Until recently German bank lending was normally at a fixed rate of interest but the increased volatility of rates in recent years has brought a change in 'banks' attitudes. Many loans are now made at rates subject to review at intervals of three or six months, and it is also common for customers to be offered a choice between a higher fixed rate and an (initially) lower one that is subject to review.

Statistics on term structure and types of lending in the UK are very sparse but a qualitative picture, with a few figures, has emerged from evidence to the Wilson Committee. Twenty years ago, almost all bank lending in the UK was by overdraft, and the overdraft is still very widely used, though there has been a very rapid growth of other types of lending in the past decade.

The original concept of the overdraft was a temporary facility for the financing of working capital. The need for such finance varies with seasonal and other influences and overdrafts were regarded as "in and out", with accounts being sometimes overdrawn and sometimes in credit. However, the Committee of London Clearing Bankers told the Wilson Committee that, "it is quite usual for some accounts to operate permanently in overdraft, though with the overdrawn balance fluctuating from day-to-day" and that "in many cases they (overdrafts) cover all a customer's financing needs including the purchase of fixed assets". Formally, overdrafts are repayable on demand but, "it is not the practice of the clearing banks to call in overdrafts from customers who conduct their business in a proper manner, indeed the normal practice is to renew facilities for business customers from year-to-year.[1]

The overdraft has the advantages for the borrower that it is possible to negotiate a facility very quickly (on the spot for small sums and in a matter of a few days for larger ones) and that interest is only charged on the daily debit balance. Its disadvantage is the right of the bank to require repayment on demand, even though this is not normally exercised. From the point-of-view of the banks, the system involves considerable uncertainty about the extent of the demands that will be made on them, particularly as only about half of the total amount of agreed overdraft limits is in use at any one time. This means that the banks have to keep relatively large amounts of low yielding liquid assets as a safeguard against a sudden increase in the use of overdraft facilities, and also creates difficulties for them in times of restrictive monetary policy.

An alternative form of short- and medium-term lending is the loan account. The customer borrows a fixed sum which is technically repayable on demand but in practice

---

1. *The London Clearing Banks* Evidence, Committee of London Clearing Bankers, 1978, p.99.

repayment is spread according to an agreed schedule over a period of years. The difference between this and contractual term lending, described below, is that the bank retains the legal right to recall a loan on demand and that both parties are spared the trouble and expense of formal contracts. The method is mainly used where small firms are borrowing small sums.

Contractual medium-term lending has grown very rapidly during the past decade. The latest figure is that given to the Wilson Committee for November 1977 when this type of lending accounted for 42 per cent of all advances by the clearing banks and their subsidiaries to UK residents other than persons. Inclusion of special export finance schemes (classified as lending to the overseas sector) would have brought the figure up to 50 per cent. No figures are available for banks outside the clearing bank groups, but it is known that their proportion of term lending is higher than that of the clearing banks. The proportion for the system as a whole, not counting export schemes, is probably around 50 per cent.

UK banks do not have a category of "long-term" lending and medium-term is defined as over two years. The Wilson Committee states that, "The term of the loan is usually five to seven years, though periods of up to twelve years or even longer are becoming more common".[1] UK medium-term lending would thus correspond to German long-term and part of medium-term. Allowing for these differences, it appears that this type of lending is still a larger proportion of all bank lending in Germany, but that the gap has substantially narrowed.

Contractual term lending is undertaken by individual banks and, in the case of very large sums, by 'ad hoc' syndicates. The agreement between borrower and lender is a formal contract which sets out the timing of drawings and repayments, and "covenants" that the borrower agrees to observe. Failure to comply with conditions laid down in

1. Report Cmnd. 7937, paragraph 801.

covenants renders the loan liable to repayment on demand, though banks would not usually insist on this except in very bad cases. The terms of covenants vary considerably with the size and purpose of loans and with the standing of the borrower. They commonly include a "negative pledge", prohibiting the borrower from creating any new charges on the firm's assets, entering into new financial commitments above a specified limit, and borrowing from any other bank. On the positive side, covenants normally seek to ensure solvency, financial stability and adequacy of cash flow. The common test of solvency is the ratio of current assets to current liabilities, and banks regard a 1:1 ratio as a minimum. Where some current assets are not readily saleable, a "quick assets" ratio may be used. Gearing (the ratio of fixed charge securities to equity capital) is sometimes used as a test of financial stability but a debt equity ratio is more common and again, 1:1 tends to be regarded as a minimum. The definition of debt may present problems, e.g. commitments in relation to leased assets and other "off-balance sheet" items and contracts usually specify detailed definitions. Borrowers are normally required to provide cash flow projections and, if there is any doubt of the adequacy of cash flow, covenants may impose restrictions on dividend payments. There is always an obligation to supply the bank with financial information, which may extend to management accounts as well as published figures.

In contrast with Germany very little British term lending is at fixed interest. The most common terms are a fixed margin over "London Inter-Bank Offered Rate" (LIBOR) averaged over three, six or twelve months. An alternative, usually at the borrowers' choice, is a fixed margin above the lending bank's base rate.

There is very little evidence as to how much lending, either short- or medium-term, is secured, though the clearing banks told the Wilson Committee that, "Much bank lending is unsecured, and where security is taken the banks are not unduly restrictive",[1] and the report states that, "the majority of lending (by value) is unsecured".[2]

Bills of exchange account for between 4 and 5 per cent of bank lending to the private sector in both countries, but there are significant differences between them. The Bank of England will re-discount only bills bearing the signatures of two "good names", one of which must be a bank on the Bank of England's list; inclusion in the list is at the discretion of the Bank and is still regarded as a valuable privilege. These bills, known as "bank bills" sell at the finest rates, but banks and discount houses also discount other bills, known as "trade bills". The Bundesbank will re-discount only bills originating in a commercial transaction (as distinct from finance bills) and bearing three "good" signatures. However, the Bundesbank's list of good names is much wider than that of the Bank of England, and includes industrial and commercial firms whose accounts are approved. As mentioned earlier, the Bundesbank processes some 48,000 accounts for this purpose. German banks take mainly bills re-discountable at the Bundesbank, but will discount other bills at higher rates.

Despite these more generous re-discount facilities, the bill of exchange has been declining in importance in Germany over the past twenty years. In Britain the movement has been the other way. In the late fifties and early sixties bill finance had fallen to a very low ebb, but there has since been a recovery. Part of the reason for this is that bills, subject to certain qualifications described in Chapter 1, are classed as "reserve assets" for the purpose of the reserve asset ratio that UK banks are required to maintain. Besides discounting bills themselves, UK banks accept them on behalf of customers. These acceptances do not count as liabilities of the banks for control purposes, but they can be sold in the London

---

1. The London Clearing Banks, p.98
2. Wilson Committee Report, Cmnd. 7937. p.398.

discount market either to discount houses or to outside
holders. They thus form an alternative source of credit,
in which the banks do not actually lend but act as
guarantors. Normally, the volume of bank acceptances is
small but it tends to rise sharply when bank lending is
restricted; the most notable example was during the
operation of the "corset" (see Chapter 1) between 1978 and
1980, when the amount of bank acceptances held outside the
banking system rose by about £3 bn.

Cost of borrowing

The cost of bank borrowing obviously varies in both
countries with the general level of interest rates. In
recent years interest rates have been much higher in the
UK than in Germany but, if allowance is made for inflation,
real rates have often been lower. Both countries, however,
have established practices that link the cost of borrowing
to certain key rates.

In the UK, overdraft charges used to be "x per cent
above Bank rate" and the minimum value for "x" was fixed by
a cartel agreement. In 1971 this agreement was abandoned
and each bank fixed its own "base rate". These rates are
fixed by each bank independently but competition ensures a
high degree of uniformity, and base rates move closely in
line with the Bank of England's minimum lending rate (MLR),
formerly known as Bank rate. The amount by which a charge
exceeds base rate is negotiated with individual borrowers
and may range from one per cent for a large "blue chip"
company to 2 or 3 per cent for a medium-sized company and
as much as 5 per cent for a small one. There has been a
tendency for margins to increase in recent years to meet
rising costs. Interest is charged on the daily debit
balance outstanding. Sometimes higher rates are charged on
the "hard core" element of an overdraft (i.e. the minimum
debit balance which is in fact, though not in form, a medium-
term loan). No other charges are normally made.

As already noted, most contractual term lending is at variable rates linked either to base rate or LIBOR. The clearing banks told the Wilson Committee that a typical margin over LIBOR would be 0.75 to 1.5 per cent. By contrast with overdraft rates, competition has tended to narrow margins on contractual term lending.

Germany had an interest rate cartel which was enforced by law, but this was abandoned in 1967. Rates are quoted, as in Britain, in terms of a number of percentage points above a base, in this case the Bundesbank's discount rate. There are, however, variations in the way interest charges are calculated; commitment fees are charged (again with considerable variety) for arranging lines of credit, and penal rates may be charged where indebtedness rises above an agreed limit. In addition, costs are affected by charges for handling an account (related to the number of transactions) and by the practice of charging debit items to an account almost immediately while delaying credit items for up to four days. When allowance is made for all these things the effective margin over discount rate may vary from zero to six per cent. These differences in practice between the two countries make precise comparisons impossible but, if the central bank rediscount rate is taken as a base, the absolute margins in percentage points seem to be similar in the two countries. Since the central bank rate has in recent years generally been higher in the UK, the proportionate margin is rather lower.

Lending by type of bank

Table 4.13 shows German bank lending at the end of 1979 analysed by type of bank. The figures confirm the variety and lack of concentration of the German system described in Chapter 2. The commercial banks provide nearly half of all short-term credit, but less than a third of all bank finance. Within this group the regional banks have, in aggregate, a slightly larger market share than the

TABLE 4.13: GERMAN BANK LENDING TO DOMESTIC FIRMS AND SELF-EMPLOYED
PERSONS BY TYPE OF BANK, END-1979.
(Percentages of totals)

Type of Bank	TYPE OF LENDING				
	Total	Short-Term	Medium-Term	Long-Term Mortgage	Other
COMMERCIAL BANKS:					
- Big banks	13.1	17.8	16.7	1.4	11.2
- Regional banks	13.7	19.3	14.6	15.5	8.3
- Foreign banks	1.6	3.8	0.9	-	0.3
- Private banks	2.4	5.3	2.5	0.1	0.5
Total	30.8	46.2	34.7	17.0	20.3
SAVINGS BANKS:					
- Central institutions	13.8	7.0	14.2	18.8	18.1
- Others	21.1	22.8	16.3	24.9	19.8
Total	34.9	29.8	30.5	43.7	37.9
CO-OPERATIVES:					
- Central institutions	2.6	3.4	4.4	0.2	2.2
- Others	14.6	17.8	16.1	6.2	13.7
Total	17.2	21.2	20.5	6.4	15.9
MORTGAGE BANKS:					
- Private	6.2	0.1	1.6	30.4	6.2
- Public	1.4	0.1	0.4	2.0	2.8
Total	7.6	0.2	2.0	32.4	8.8
Other Banks[1]	9.7	2.6	12.4	0.4	17.2
TOTAL	100.0	100.0	100.0	100.0	100.0

NOTE: 1.   Hire-purchase banks, banks with special functions and
postal giro.

Source: Deutsche Bundesbank: Beihefte Reihe 1, May 1980, Table 6.

"big banks". The savings banks have over a third of the total market, 37 per cent of long-term lending other than mortgages, and nearly 44 per cent of mortgage loans. Co-operative banks provide about 17 per cent of all lending but over a fifth of short-term credit. The specialised mortgage banks have nearly a third of the mortgage market but, as one would expect, are relatively weak elsewhere. Foreign banks provide less than 2 per cent of all bank finance, most of it short-term.

Table 4.14 presents a similar analysis for UK banks though, for reasons explained in Chapter 1, the classification is very different. Again, the figures illustrate relationships described in earlier Chapters, particularly the greater concentration of the UK system and the absence of institutions corresponding to the German regional banks, savings banks and co-operative banks. The London Clearing Banks, dominated by the "big-four" have nearly 55 per cent of the market, not counting their subsidiaries and associates included in other categories. By contrast, the three "big banks" in Germany have only 13 per cent of the market. The Scottish and Northern Ireland banks (the nearest thing to the German regional banks) have about 9 per cent of the market and other UK banks, mainly London based, about 20 per cent. Foreign banks play a much more important part in the domestic banking system of the UK with about 16 per cent of all lending to the private sector, compared to less than 2 per cent in Germany. [1]

Lending criteria

Evidence on lending criteria is sparse and difficult to interpret in both countries. We have supplemented published information with a number of interviews but we found that this was a subject on which bankers were reluctant to talk except in very general terms.

---

1. This figure refers only to branches of foreign banks not incorporated under German law. See Chapter 2.

TABLE 4.14: UK BANK LENDING TO PRIVATE SECTOR BY TYPE OF BANK,
END-1979.
(Percentages of totals)

Type of Bank	Advances	Bills	TOTAL
London clearing banks	54.6	47.5	54.3
Scottish clearing banks	6.8	5.1	6.8
Northern Ireland banks	2.1	1.4	2.1
Accepting Houses	3.7	9.9	3.9
Other UK banks	16.8	17.5	16.8
American banks	9.2	8.5	9.2
Japanese banks	0.6	–	0.6
Other overseas banks	5.4	8.5	5.5
Consortium banks	0.8	1.5	0.8
TOTAL	100.0	100.0	100.0

Source: Bank of England, Quarterly Bulletin, June 1980, Table 3.2.

In the UK clearing banks (the only part of the system
with a wide branch network) lending decisions are taken by
branch managers in respect of small loans, by area
management in the case of larger sums and by head office in
the case of very large transactions.

Written evidence by the American Banks' Association
of London to the Wilson Committee caused some controversy
by contrasting the "going concern" and the "gone concern"
or "liquidation" approach. The former stresses the ability
of a firm to generate a cash flow adequate to provide for
payment of interest and repayment of principal, while the
latter concentrates more on the break-up value of assets.
The American banks claimed that they adopted a going concern
approach and suggested that UK banks tended to use a

liquidation approach. However, oral evidence both from banks
and customers gave no support to this suggestion and the
Committee concluded that, "it seems there are no marked
differences...... between American and UK banks when the
same type of lending is under consideration".[1]

UK banks have sometimes been criticised for over-caution
in their lending criteria. The Wilson Committee found that
some small firms had difficulty in complying with banks'
requirements (see Chapter 6) but that, "there is little
indication that for medium- and large-sized firms that there
has been any real difficulty in this area".[2]

Lending decisions are made more on general evidence
and the judgement of bank managements than on highly
specialised knowledge or formal techniques. Some banks told
us in interviews that they had appointed specialist
advisers on certain industries but the practice is recent,
and the numbers are still small. Some banks also told us
that they were experimenting with formal techniques of risk
assessment, but that these were still in the "pilot" stage
and were not part of the regular lending decision process.
There is a tendency, however, for banks to review the
performance of borrowers in greater detail and at more
frequent intervals than in the past. Critics of these
informal methods could argue that they lead to some good
risks being turned down and some bad ones accepted, and that
they tend to produce an inefficient pattern of charges in
which good risks pay for bad ones. Defenders of current
methods can point to their flexibility and to the lack of
clear evidence that greater formality would improve
performance.

In Germany as in the UK, decisions on small loans are
made at branch manager level, but our impression is that the
extent of such delegation is rather more limited. For

---

1.   Wilson Committee Report, Cmnd. 7937, paragraph 527.
2.   Ibid. paragraph 526.

medium-sized and larger loans German procedures are rather different.

The point of contact between customer and bank is the Kundenberater (or customer adviser) who advises firms about suitable size, terms and conditions of a loan, informs them of the information that the bank will require, and helps them to prepare an application. The Kundenberater has no authority to make decisions, though he may be asked for an opinion. The application then goes to the credit department for scrutiny and report and, finally, to a committee of management for decision.

Three criteria seem to be important: "security", "standing", and "bank strategy". German banks are more insistent than their UK opposite numbers on security, and unsecured loans are granted only in special circumstances. It was pointed out to us in interviews that the declining ratio of equity to debt had increased the need to take security, and it was admitted that some firms had difficulty in meeting requirements. The preferred security is a mortgage on land and/or buildings. Marketable financial assets are accepted (though for substantially less than their full market value) as are marketable commodities, but stocks and work in progress (apart from marketable commodities), plant and machinery, and trade debtors are rarely accepted, except for short-term loans. It has also become common to require a "negative pledge".

Guarantees of various kinds play an important role. Public guarantees are common in export/import trade, for new firms and for firms in special development areas. Small firms have the help of credit guarantee associations (see Chapter 6). Non-corporate firms may also rely, as in the UK, on personal guarantees of their members or on mortgages on property owned by them or their families outside the business.

The "standing" of a firm includes its overall financial strength, profitability, liquidity, cash flow, gearing and other financial commitments. All these are assessed not only in isolation but in relation to industry, area and national averages. In this type of comparison the commercial banks have the services of their own intelligence departments, while savings banks and co-operatives can draw on similar facilities from their central organisations. Banks also use credit rating agencies for information about smaller companies and non-corporate firms. The presence of a banker on a supervisory board may help the bank concerned to assess the risks involved and so facilitate a loan, but we were told that this is not normally of great importance.

"Strategy" relates to the way in which a particular loan fits in with the overall objectives of a bank. These normally include a desired "mix" of loans giving a spread of risks across different industries and, in the case of banks operating nationwide, different areas, and also a spread of loan sizes and maturity dates. A loan which helps a bank move towards a desired pattern will obviously be more acceptable than one that does not.

The manner in which these three factors are assessed, and their relative importance vary from bank to bank and from loan to loan, and banks may find themselves obliged to accept transactions that fall short of their ideal both by competition among themselves and by the bargaining power of some large firms. It is impossible to quantify the extent to which this happens, but the impression gained from interviews was that banks were more willing to compromise on matters of standing or strategy than on security.

CHAPTER 5: BANKS AND INDUSTRIAL MANAGEMENT
By Graham Bannock

1.   INTRODUCTION

There are several important differences between UK and German banks in the relationships with their corporate industrial and commercial customers. As shown in Chapter 2, the big commercial banks, most of the regional banks, and the central institutions of the savings banks and co-operative banks are "universal". They not only provide the lending and foreign exchange services normally expected of commercial banks in any country, but they also offer advice on long-term financial strategy, arrange new issues both of fixed interest securities and equities, and play an important role in secondary securities markets. They also provide, either directly or through subsidiaries, facilities for leasing of buildings and equipment, and factoring, and they have interests in investment companies. Large German companies (with a capital of DM 500m. or more) may have dealings with a number of banks and we were told in interviews of some very large firms that dealt with up to thirty. Except for a few large firms, however, it is usual for German companies to have a "house-bank", on which it relies for all the services mentioned above.

In the UK, the clearing banks have been moving towards "universality" by forming or acquiring merchant banking, hire-purchase, leasing and factoring subsidiaries, but most companies still go to one or more banks for "ordinary" banking services, and to a different bank for matters of corporate financial strategy, new issues, mergers and takeovers. Most of this type of business is still in the hands of members of the Accepting Houses Committee and a few other merchant banks who are not members of that select group, but are members of the Issuing Houses Association. Some of the functions related to new issues that would be handled by German banks are also performed by stockbrokers (see Chapter 8).

German banks have much more potential influence over companies than do their UK counterparts, both through direct ownership of shares and through proxy votes in respect of shares deposited by customers.

In both countries there are a substantial number of directors who serve on the boards both of banks and of industrial and commercial companies, but this superficial resemblance conceals important differences in functions.

These differences tend to be viewed differently in the two countries, partly because neither side seems to know much about the other. UK critics of their own system tend to stress the benefits that German firms get from a close relationship with their house-bank, and even put this forward as a factor in the superior performance of German industry. Their opposite numbers in Germany tend to stress possible conflicts of interest between banker and customer and to blame the banking system for the relatively weak state of the German long-term capital market.

In Section 2 of this Chapter we examine the facts about bank shareholding and voting rights in the two countries, and in Section 3 we bring together similar factual information about directorships. It has not been easy to establish the facts, but it is far more difficult to assess what lies behind them - how voting rights and the power and influence of directors are actually used, and what effect they have on company performance. We have tried to do this from interviews as well as published sources, and our conclusions are summarised in Section 4.

2.   SHARE HOLDINGS AND VOTING RIGHTS

Germany

The German supervisory authorities set maximum values for bank holdings of equities in relation to their own

capital (see Chapter 10). The 1968 guidelines of the
Federal Banking Supervisory office state that the balance
sheets of banks should distinguish equity shareholdings
from holdings of other securities where they account for
over 25 per cent of the nominal capital of the company
concerned and where the bank intends to retain the shares
in the long-term. A code of practice on this subject
published by the Institute of Accounting in 1977 was heavily
criticised by the Monopolies Commission. The accounting
practices of banks as they affect disclosure of shareholdings
remain far from uniform and are the subject of continuing
controversy. Some banks specify shareholdings of over 10 per
cent, others only those over 25 per cent.

Table 5.1 derived from the Bundesbank statistics shows
that the proportion of quoted ordinary shares held by banks
has averaged about 7.5 per cent in the 1970's with no clear
trend upwards or downwards. According to the
Konzentrationsenquete, in the early-1960's the banks owned
3.2 per cent of non-bank quoted share capital. Because these
figures are based upon the analysis of balance sheets they
probably exclude all holdings below 10 per cent and some
shareholdings between 10 and 25 per cent. They therefore
understate the importance of bank equity holdings. The
difference between these figures and those of the Bundesbank
is explained by these holdings, and by shares in one bank
held by another.

The Gessler Commission[1] carried out a survey of bank
shareholdings in non-banks which covered all shareholdings
of 10 per cent and more by 336 banks. Table 5.2 shows that
all six of the major banks had shareholdings which accounted
for 41 per cent of the total. Only 37 per cent of regional
banks and 28 per cent of private banks had holdings that
came within the scope of the survey, but their combined
holdings came to over 25 per cent of the total. A further
25 per cent was held by the central institutions of the

---

1.   Bericht der Studienkommission: Grundsatzfragen der
      Kreditwirtschaft, (Schriftenreihe des Bundesministeriums
      der Finanzen Heft 28) Bonn: Stollfuss Verlag, 1979
      (Gessler Kommission)

TABLE 5.1: NOMINAL VALUE OF HOLDINGS OF QUOTED SHARES BY DOMESTIC BANKS IN GERMANY AND THEIR PERCENTAGE OF TOTAL ISSUES, 1971-1978

	1971	1972	1973	1974	1975	1976	1977	1978
Nominal value (million DM)	4,300	4,900	5,100	5,400	5,500	5,700	6,100	6,200
Per cent of total shares	7.3	7.8	7.8	7.9	7.5	7.5	7.6	7.5

NOTE: Domestic issues only, includes Bundesbank.

Source: U. Immenga: Beteiligungen von Banken in anderen Wirtschaftszweigen 1978 and from 1977 compiled from the monthly reports of the Central Bank.

TABLE 5.2: BANK SHAREHOLDINGS IN NON-BANKS ACCORDING TO TYPE OF BANK. GERMANY, 1974

	Number of Institutions in survey	Number of Institutions with holdings	Holdings in non-banks		Per Cent of Total
			Number	Nominal-value (DM million)	
Major banks	6	6	87	1,489.4	41.0
Regional banks	112	41	211	740.5	20.4
Private banks	123	35	101	188.7	5.2
Savings banks: Central institutions	12	12	135	901.8	24.8
Other	53	25	62	72.6	2.0
Co-operative banks Central institutions	12	11	45	158.8	4.4
Other banks	18	8	21	80.5	2.2
	336	138	662	3,631.8	100.0

NOTE: Holdings are all shares of 10 per cent or more, regardless of where shown in balance sheet.

Source: Gessler Kommission op.cit.

savings and co-operative banks. Table 5.3 shows that over
half of all bank shareholdings are in the hands of 5 banks
while over three quarters are held by 10 banks.

The size of these shareholdings relative to the issued
capital of the companies concerned can be seen in Table 5.4.
It can be seen that most holdings are relatively large:
over 90 per cent are over 25 per cent. It should be
remembered that only holdings over 10 per cent were included
in the survey and it is also relevant that a holding of 25
per cent or more of the nominal capital of a company by
another freed the holder from double taxation (that is from
the payment of taxation on dividends received) though recent
tax reforms ensure that double taxation is avoided regardless
of the size of holding. Moreover German company law requires
a 75 per cent majority for a number of decisions, so that a
shareholder with over 25 per cent has a power of veto.

Only limited information is available about the size
of companies in which banks have substantial holdings, but
they seem to be in the medium to large rather than very large
range. The Monopolies Commission has analysed holdings in
the largest hundred German companies, by turnover, with the
following results.

Proportion of Equity:	Number of Bank Holdings		
	1972	1975	1977
Less than 25 per cent	4	4	4
25 - 50 per cent	25	28	32

There were no bank holdings of more than 50 per cent. Other
research by Hein and Floter shows that the companies where
the banks do have holdings are not amongst the 20 largest
(except for Daimler Benz and Gütehoffnungshütte). Almost
three quarters of the number of bank holdings were, in
fact, in the lower half of the "Top 100" companies.

TABLE 5.3: SHAREHOLDINGS OF INDIVIDUAL BANKS IN NON-BANKS – ARRANGED ACCORDING TO SIZE
(NOMINAL VALUES) IN GROUPS OF 5, GERMANY, 1974

	(1) Holdings in non-banks (DM Millions)	(2) Cumulative (DM Millions)	Column 2 as per cent of total holdings
1– 5	1,936.7	1,936.7	53.3
6–10	817.3	2,754.0	75.8
11–15	372.8	3,126.8	86.1
16–20	89.7	3,216.5	88.6
21–25	122.2	3,338.7	91.9
26–30	32.0	3,370.7	92.8
Remaining banks	261.1	3,631.8	100.0
	3,631.8	3,631.8	100.0

Source: Gessler Kommission, op.cit.

TABLE 5.4: CLASSIFICATION OF BANK SHAREHOLDINGS IN NON-BANKS ACCORDING TO PROPORTION OF EQUITY CAPITAL. GERMANY, 1974

Per cent of equity	HOLDINGS IN NON-BANKS		
	Number	Nominal Value (DM million)	Per Cent of Total
10 - under 25%	174	298.6	8.2
25 - 50% inclusive	285	2,558.7	70.5
Over 50 - under 75%	50	265.6	7.3
75 - under 100%	54	153.6	4.2
100%	99	355.3	9.8
TOTAL	662	3,631.8	100.0

Source: Gessler Kommission, op.cit.

Table 5.5 shows the percentage of the equity capital of quoted companies owned by the banks by economic sectors. Only in construction and brewing do bank shareholdings reach 10 per cent or more of the total. However, the broad categories conceal a greater concentration of ownership within some sub-sectors, particularly, according to Hein and Floter, in certain parts of retail distribution (department stores) and in the cement industry.

All these figures relate to quoted companies only, the banks also have shareholdings in unquoted companies but there appears to be no information available on these. Banks are also important shareholders in investment trusts which have holdings in industrial shares and these are not included in the data reviewed here.

In addition to their own shareholdings which give them voting rights at company meetings, the banks can represent customers who have deposited shares with them (Depotstimmrecht). The assignment of proxies in this way is common practice in Germany. Before 1965, the banks were able to exercise voting rights for shares deposited with them if no other instructions were given by the customer. With the Share Law reform in 1965, banks could only exercise voting rights where they were explicitly given a proxy to do so. These proxies are limited to 15 months and may be revoked at any time. The bank also is required to ask the customer for instructions on how to vote and put forward its own suggestions (for example, that the vote should be for the management's proposals). But very few shareholders (2-3 per cent it is estimated) in fact make any use of this opportunity to instruct the bank on how to vote. Where no instructions are given the bank is entitled to use the voting rights in accordance with its own recommendations. The general view is that the change in the law has had no significant effect upon the freedom of the banks to use the voting rights on the shares deposited with them.

TABLE 5.5: BANK SHAREHOLDINGS IN NON-BANKS AS A PERCENTAGE OF ISSUED
CAPITAL BY ECONOMIC SECTOR, GERMANY, 1974

Sector	(1) Number of Cases	(2) Nominal Value of Shareholding (DM millions)	(3) Capital End-1974	(4) Column (2) as % of (3)
Agriculture	2	0.6	201.1	0.3
Power, water mining	9	165.9	18,101.3	0.9
Chemical industry and mineral oil	2	5.4	18,987.8	0
Non-metallic minerals, ceramics and glass	15	99.3	2,758.2	3.6
Steel, mechanical and vehicle engineering	21	476.0	15,925.0	3.0
Leather and Textiles, and Clothing	18	130.8	2,347.2	5.6
Brewing and malting	34	212.4	896.2	23.7
Other manufacturing	44	240.1	25,521.1	0.9
Construction	24	126.6	1,266.7	10.0
Distribution	28	393.9	9,425.2	4.2
Transport and telecommunications	19	120.7	4,217.1	2.9
Insurance	13	70.9	2,145.9	3.3
Land and housing	125	158.6	6,321.8	2.5
Holding companies (excluding investment trusts)	148	1,141.3	12,881.8	8.9
Other services	155	242.8	6,514.4	3.7
Not listed	5	46.6	-	-
TOTAL	662	3,631.8	127,510.8	2.8

NOTE: Holdings are 10 per cent and over.

Source: Gessler Kommission, op.cit.

Table 5.6 shows that the proportion of all quoted shares deposited with the banks has been declining slowly but still in 1976 exceeded half of the total. Together with their direct holdings the banks command nearly 60 per cent of voting rights.

Table 5.7 shows the distribution of deposited securities by type of bank. The "big three" together with their Berlin affiliates have 47.5 per cent of the total, other commercial banks 29 per cent and savings banks and co-operative banks 22 per cent.

Banks are also able to take over the voting rights of other shareholders including other banks by mutual agreement. These are called Leihstimmen - loaned votes. Under the new law, transfer of voting rights between banks in this way is no longer permitted where the bank making the transfer has a branch in the town where the shareholders meeting takes place. In effect this rules out transfer by the large commercial banks, with branches in all the major towns, but means that they can continue to represent other banks. The representation of voting rights by the banks for other banks and other third parties accounted for about a third of all voting rights controlled by 172 banks in a Gessler Commission survey.

This survey classified voting rights acquired by direct ownership, deposit and borrowing according to the proportion of companies' equity that they represented, and the results are shown in Table 5.8. In nearly 90 per cent of all cases, voting rights amounted to less than 5 per cent of equity, and in only 4.3 per cent of cases did rights exceed 25 per cent. This dispersion means that the power of individual banks is much less than would appear from the high proportion of voting rights controlled by the banking system as a whole.

The Monopolies Commission found that despite the concentration of share representation among the larger banks, in 1974 single banks controlled more than 50 per cent of the

TABLE 5.6: NOMINAL VALUE OF QUOTED SHARES DEPOSITED WITH AND DIRECTLY HELD BY THE BANKS WITH
PERCENTAGES OF TOTALS, GERMANY, 1963-76

DM bn - and per cent end-year

	1963	1964	1965	1966	1967	1968	1969	1970	1971	1972	1973	1974	1975	1976
Total shares DM bn.	38.0	40.5	44.1	46.7	48.3	50.3	52.9	54.5	56.5	62.5	65.1	68.5	73.8	76.3
of which: - In deposit with the banks (including Central Bank) DM bn.	21.0	22.1	23.6	25.5	25.7	26.7	28.2	29.2	29.4	30.7	32.5	34.1	36.5	38.7
- Per cent of total	55.2	54.7	53.6	54.6	53.1	53.2	53.3	53.6	50.1	49.1	49.9	49.8	49.5	50.7
- Direct holdings of banks DM bn.	1.8	2.0	2.2	2.3	2.4	2.8	3.2	3.6	4.3	4.9	5.1	5.4	5.5	5.7
- Per cent of total	4.7	5.0	5.0	5.0	5.0	5.5	6.0	6.5	7.3	7.8	7.8	7.9	7.5	7.5
Total share capital represented by banks DM bn.	22.8	24.1	25.8	27.8	28.1	29.5	31.4	32.8	33.7	35.6	37.6	39.5	42.0	44.4
Per cent of total	59.9	59.7	58.6	59.6	58.1	58.7	59.3	60.1	57.4	56.9	57.7	57.7	57.0	58.2

NOTE: 1963-70 direct shareholdings are estimated. Holdings of insurance shares are excluded throughout.

Source: U. Immenga op.cit.

TABLE 5.7   NOMINAL VALUE OF CUSTOMERS' DEPOSITS OF DOMESTIC QUOTED
SHARES WITH THE BANKS BY TYPE OF BANK, GERMANY. END-1977

Bank Group	Nominal Value (Mill.DM)	Per Cent of Total
Commercial banks	28,882	76.4
Major banks	17,943	47.5
Regional banks	8,118	21.5
Branches of foreign banks	110	0.3
Private banks	2,711	7.1
Savings banks		
Central institutions[1]	3,394	9.0
Other	3,629	9.6
Co-operative sector		
Central institutions[2]	228	0.6
Other	925	2.5
Other banks[3]	738	1.9
	37,796	100.0

NOTES: 1.   Including Deutsche Girozentrale.

2.   Including Deutsche Genossenschafts Bank.

3.   Instalment banks, banks with special functions, Post
Office savings and giro banks and capital investment
companies, insurance shares are excluded.

Source: Gessler Kommission, op.cit.

TABLE 5.8: NUMBERS OF SHARE VOTING RIGHTS CONTROLLED BY BANKS BY PERCENTAGE OF EQUITY CAPITAL REPRESENTED, FRG, 1977

Numbers of holdings and per cent

Size of Voting Rights Representation	Own Holdings		Customers Holdings		Third Party Holdings	
	Number	Per Cent	Number	Per Cent	Number	Per Cent
< 5%	400	64.2	5,825	93.6	3,430	96.6
5% < 10%	25	4.0	186	3.0	56	1.6
15% < 25%	41	6.6	104	1.7	37	1.0
25% < 50%	97	15.6	65	1.0	20	0.6
50% < 75%	33	5.3	29	0.5	3	0.1
75% < 100%	24	3.8	15	0.2	5	0.1
100%	3	0.5	2	–	–	–
TOTAL	623	100.0	6,226	100.0	3,551	100.0

Source: Gessler Kommission Survey of 172 banks.

voting rights (taking direct holdings and deposits together)
in only 136 quoted companies, out of the total of 2,036, or
7.3 per cent.[1] One bank controlled more than 25 per cent of
the voting rights in 300 cases or 14.5 per cent of the
total.

Even with proxies, the Gessler Commission was not able
to find a single instance where one bank was able to
exercise control over more than 50 per cent of the capital
in 1974/5 of any of the 74 large companies accounting for
84 per cent of stock market equity capitalisation, although
there were many cases where a bank had exercised control of
over 25 per cent. In many cases where a bank has large
shareholdings their power is muted by the existence of large
shareholdings in other hands, including other banks.

United Kingdom

Data on beneficial shareholdings in UK quoted companies
(that is those held by the banks on their own behalf) is
available from a study by the Department of Industry[2] and
amounted to £322 million at market values at the end of 1975.
Of this total, shareholdings in financial companies were
£213 million and in non-financial companies £109 million.
This represented, in total, only 0.7 per cent of market
capitalisation in 1975 though about twice as much in the
1960's. (Table 5.9)

It can be estimated from the Unit Trust Yearbook[3] that
unit trusts managed by the banks, or their investment

---

1. The majority rested in:
   - 56 cases (37.6 per cent) on the bank's direct holdings
   - 63 cases (42.3 per cent) on deposited shareholdings
   - 12 cases (7.4 per cent) on third party representation
   - 18 cases (12.0 per cent) in a combination of these
     three.

2. M.J. Errit and J.D.C. Alexander, Ownership of Company
   Shares: A New Survey, Department of Industry.
   Reported in Economic Trends, September 1977.

3. The Unit Trust Yearbook, Furidex Ltd., 1979.

TABLE 5.9: BENEFICIAL EQUITY SHAREHOLDINGS BY UK BANKS IN DOMESTIC FINANCIAL AND NON-FINANCIAL QUOTED COMPANIES AS A PERCENTAGE OF TOTAL MARKET VALUE OF SUCH SHARES, 1963, 1969 and 1975

	1975	1969	1963
Financial	2.2		
		n.a.	n.a.
Non-Financial	0.3		
TOTAL	0.7	1.7	1.3

Source: M.J. Errit and J.C.D. Alexander, op.cit.

TABLE 5.10   REGISTERED HOLDINGS OF UK COMPANY EQUITIES BY UK
BANKS HELD ON OTHERS' BEHALF AT 31ST DECEMBER
1975 BY CATEGORY OF BENEFICIAL OWNER

£m

	Market Value
Pension funds	3,972
Persons (UK)	2,270
Listed investment trust companies	1,798
Unit trusts as trustees	1,441
Insurance companies	1,234
Overseas holders other than persons	827
Public sector other than local authorities	467
Non-profit making bodies serving persons	241
Persons (overseas)	215
Industrial and commercial companies	211
Other financial companies	152
Stock brokers and jobbers	116
TOTAL	12,944

Source: M.J. Erritt and J.C.D. Alexander, op.cit.

management subsidiaries held, very approximately, UK quoted
shares to the market value of £770 million at the end of
1975, roughly £650 million in non-financial and £120 million
in financial companies, or 1.9 and 1.2 per cent respectively
of market capitalisation.

The Department of Industry survey also gives information
on registered holdings of equities by the banks held on
others' behalf, including shares held through nominees. The
total of these holdings of £12,944 million is very much
larger than the beneficial or unit trust holdings of the
banks. Table 5.10 lists these holdings by owner-category.

These figures include substantial amounts which are
effectively managed by the beneficial owners, using a bank
merely as a nominee. However, a large part of the holdings
on behalf of persons, charities, investment and unit trusts,
insurance companies and pension funds are likely to be
effectively managed by banks or their investment subsidiaries.
The accepting houses are the most active banking group in
fund management, and the Wilson Report says of them:

> "At the end of 1976 the accepting houses had over
> £7.5 billion of funds under management on behalf of
> pension funds, insurance companies, investment and
> unit trusts, charities and individuals. About half
> of the funds were invested in UK equities and
> amounted to some 9 per cent of the market at that
> time".[1]

Unfortunately the report does not give similar figures for
other banking groups. The £12.9bn. of Table 5.10 represented
about 29 per cent of the total market value of UK equities
at the time. If they had all been managed by the banks, they
would have controlled over 31 per cent of all voting rights
made up as follows:

---

1.   Wilson Committee Report, Cmnd. 7937, p. 414.

	Per Cent of Voting Rights
Direct ownership	0.7
Own unit trusts	1.7
Held on behalf of others	29.0
	31.4

This represents a maximum figure. We have no information of the value of nominee holdings that are managed by their beneficial owners, but it would be surprising if those managed by banks exceeded 25 per cent of all voting rights. This compares with 51 per cent for Germany, 7.5 per cent from direct ownership and 49.5 per cent from deposited shares.

3.   BANKERS ON COMPANY BOARDS

In discussing this question it is necessary to bear in mind the difference in board structure between the two countries. Large German companies have a "management board", with functions similar to those of the board of a UK company, and a "supervisory board", and bank representatives normally sit only on supervisory boards. Supervisory boards comprise equal numbers of employees of which at least one quarter must be union representatives and shareholders' representatives with the Chairman, appointed by the shareholders, having a casting vote. Prior to 1976 employees (with a few exceptions) elected one third of the members of supervisory boards. In practice the 1976 amendment to the law has led to the enlargement of supervisory boards and it seems to be common knowledge that the extension of co-determination has made management boards more reticent and less informative. The role of unofficial groups of owner and management representatives on the supervisory board, including bankers, may possibly have increased in these circumstances although as we argue below the potential influence of the banks on management is little exercised. It is common for a retiring chief executive to become Chairman of the supervisory board. The supervisory board appoints the management board, though on the recommendation of the chief executive, and no management board member may be removed

without the Chairman's approval. Apart from this the main
function of the supervisory board is to monitor the performance
of the company with reference to the interests both of
shareholders and employees. Boards usually receive
quarterly reports from the chief executive, who attends
meetings but does not have a vote. They are also entitled
to access to accounts at any time, and must approve the
annual accounts. Besides these general powers conferred by
law, some companies have written additional powers into their
articles of association, e.g. the approval of large
investment projects.

A Gessler Commission survey of 336 German banks showed
that they had representatives on the boards of 665 out of
2,036 quoted companies, with 232 boards having more than one
banker member. The results of this survey, analysed by
sector, are shown in Table 5.11. It appears that bank
representation is most common in chemicals, metals, engineering
and construction, and least common in agriculture, distribution
and services.

Bank representation on the board might be expected to
be linked with voting rights, but a substantial proportion of
bank directorships, especially in the smaller quoted companies,
are not associated with bank shareholdings or proxy voting
rights. The Gessler Commission found that in 69 per cent of
the quoted companies with bank directors, the bank had either
no shareholding or one of less than 10 per cent while more
than half of the board positions were in companies where no
voting rights or less than 10 per cent of voting rights were
in the hands of the banks.

In the largest companies the role of the banks on the
board is much greater than the average. Out of 66 large
quoted companies (excluding banks) examined by the Gessler
Commission, 59 had bank representatives on the board, 51 had
more than one bank representative and of the 74 largest
companies (including 8 banks) the bank provided the chairman

TABLE 5.11: QUOTED COMPANIES WITH ONE AND MORE THAN ONE BANK REPRESENTATIVE ON THE BOARD BY ECONOMIC SECTOR, FRG, END-1974

Sector	Number of Companies in Sector	Companies with Bank Representatives on Board		Companies with more than one Bank Representative on the Board		
		Number	Per cent of (1)	Number	Per Cent of (1)	Per cent of (2)
	(1)	(2)	(3)	(4)	(5)	(6)
A	8	1	13	1	1	1
B	148	36	24	12	8	33
C1	75	37	49	10	13	27
C2	25	11	44	3	12	27
C3	77	31	40	11	14	35
C4	62	29	47	13	21	45
C5	145	68	47	29	20	43
C6	88	46	82	13	15	28
C7	55	22	40	4	7	18
C8	107	49	46	17	16	35
C9	178	64	36	27	15	42
D	46	30	65	8	17	27
E	144	38	26	16	11	42
F	125	26	21	6	5	23
G	233	55	24	19	8	35
H	520	122	23	44	8	36
Key to sectors on page	2,036	665	33	232	11	35

Source: Gessler Kommission Survey of 336 Banks.

KEY TO ECONOMIC SECTORS

A	Agriculture, forestry, animal husbandry, fisheries.
B	Power and water supply, mining.
C1	Chemicals (including coking by-products) and oils.
C2	Plastics, rubber and asbestos manufacture.
C3	Production and processing of non-metallic minerals, fine ceramics and glass.
C4	Iron and non-ferrous metals, foundries and steel reduction.
C5	Steel construction, engineering and vehicle building.
C6	Electrical engineering, precision engineering and optics, production of iron goods, sheet metal and hardware, musical instruments, sporting apparatus, toys and jewellery.
C7	Wood, paper and printing.
C8	Leather, textile and clothing.
C9	Food, drink and tobacco.
D	Construction.
E	Distribution
F	Transport and communications
G	Financial services (excluding banks and holding companies) and insurance.
H	Service industry (without investment companies).

Source: Grundsatzfragen der Kreditwirtschaft
Schriftenreihe des Bundesministeriums der Finanzen.

in 32 cases (Table 5.12) and accounted for 18 per cent of the total number of supervisory board members. For larger quoted companies there is also a much closer association between bank directorships and the proportion of voting rights controlled by the banks. (Table 5.13)

Both in the largest companies and in quoted companies as a group the six large banks are of major importance: according to another analysis by the Gessler Commission they provided over half of all bank directorships in quoted

TABLE 5.12: BOARD POSITIONS HELD BY BANK REPRESENTATIVES IN 74 LARGE QUOTED COMPANIES, FRG, 1974-75

	SUPERVISORY BOARD POSTS						CHAIRMAN OF THE BOARD					
	In Total		In Other Banks		In non-banks		In Total		In Other Banks		In non-banks	
	Number	Per Cent	Number	Per Cent	Number	Per Cent	Number	Per Cent	Number	Per Cent	Number	Per Cent
Deutsche Bank	54	30	2	9	52	33	18	48	1	20	17	53
Dresdner Bank	28	15	3	14	25	16	6	16	-	-	6	19
Commerzbank	19	11	2	9	17	11	1	3	1	1	1	3
3 Big regionals	15	8	3	14	12	7	4	11	2	40	2	6
Savings banks(1)	14	7	3	14	11	6	2	6	1	20	1	3
Co-operatives	1	1	-	-	1	1	-	-	-	-	-	-
Other[2]	51	28	9	40	42	26	6	16	1	20	5	16
TOTAL	182	100	22	100	160	100	37	100	5	100	32	100
Large banks together	101	56	7	32	94	60	25	67	1	20	24	75
Large banks and 3 big regionals[3]	116	64	10	46	106	67	29	78	3	60	26	81

NOTES: 1. Including central institutions

2. Includes investment companies

3. Bayer. Vereinsbank; Bayer. Hypotheken u. Wechselbank; Bank für Gemeinwirtschaft.

Source: Gessler Kommission.

TABLE 5.13: NUMBER OF CASES OF BANK REPRESENTATION ON THE BOARDS OF 74 LARGE QUOTED COMPANIES IN RELATION TO THE PERCENTAGE OF VOTING RIGHTS (PROXIES AND OWN HOLDINGS) CONTROLLED BY THE BANK, GERMANY, 1974-75

Share of Voting rights:	Over 50 per cent	25-50 per cent	Over 10 to 25 per cent	Under 10 per cent
Number of bank board members:				
1	3	3	1	1
2 or more	38	12	5	4
of which chairmen	30	6	0	1

NOTE: The number of board positions held by the banks was 182 or 17.8 per cent of the total, see Table 5.12

Source: Gessler Kommission.

companies. In the 74 largest companies the six largest
banks provided 67 per cent of the bank directorships and 81
per cent of the board chairman. (Table 5.13)

United Kingdom

EAG could trace no previous attempt to quantify the
number of directors common to banks and industrial companies
in the UK. Although involving considerable labour, however,
the materials for such an exercise are readily available in
the Directory of Directors which lists the board memberships
of 45,000 directors of UK companies with a paid-up capital
of £50,000 or more. We first identified all directors of
UK banks, quoted and unquoted, from the Bank of England
listings of reporting banks and then noted where they were
directors of UK quoted non-financial companies listed in the
daily Financial Times Share Information page. Bank board
members on the board of subsidiaries of quoted industrial
and commercial companies were only counted (and only counted
once) where there was no bank director on the board of the
parent company. This lengthy exercise was repeated for 1970
and 1979 and the results are summarised in Tables 5.14 and
5.15.

In 1979 over 17 per cent of UK domestic quoted industrial
and commercial companies had directors who were also directors
of UK banks and nearly 7 per cent had two or more bank board
members. In fact, there were 422 bank directors who also
held board positions on quoted companies, 208 of them, or
nearly half, were directors of the London or Scottish
Clearing Banks. There were also many bank directors on the
boards of larger unquoted companies; from the same source
we calculated that there were 417 such directorships in 1970
and 471 in 1979, again approximately half of them were
directors of the Clearing Banks.

At first sight these results are surprising. We have
seen that there are bank directors on 33 per cent of quoted

TABLE 5.14: NUMBER OF QUOTED UK INDUSTRIAL AND COMMERCIAL COMPANIES[1]
HAVING ONE OR MORE DIRECTORS WHO ARE ALSO DIRECTORS OF
UK BANKS, AND NUMBER OF BANK DIRECTORS HOLDING SUCH
POSITIONS, 1970 AND 1979

	1970	1979
One or more bank directors on the board	257	254
Two or more bank directors on the board	79	101
Total number of bank directors with seats on boards of quoted companies	421	422

NOTES: 1. On at least one of their subsidiaries

2. List of quoted companies from Financial Times Daily Share
Information List excluding Land, Property, Trusts, Finance
Banking, Insurance, Shipping, Canadians and Americans.

Sources: Director of Directors, 1970, 1979.

Who Owns Whom, 1970, 1979.

TABLE 5.15: NUMBER OF QUOTED UK INDUSTRIAL AND COMMERCIAL COMPANIES HAVING ONE OR MORE DIRECTORS WHO ARE ALSO DIRECTORS OF UK BANKS, BY SECTOR, 1970 AND 1979.

Sector	1970			1979		
	Number of Companies with Bank Director(s)	Total Companies in Sector	Per Cent	Number of Companies with Bank Director(s)	Total Companies in Sector	Per Cent
Industrials (miscellaneous)	58	418	13.9	73	402	18.2
Engineering and machine tools	49	266	18.4	52	217	24.0
Electricals	13	80	16.5	11	72	15.3
Food, groceries, etc.	12	85	14.1	18	62	29.0
Building industry, timber and roads	26	199	13.1	19	126	15.1
Leisure[1]	7	11	63.6	10	29	34.5
Hotels and caterers	3	30	10.0	2	20	10.0
Chemicals and plastics	10	34	29.4	5	41	12.2
Motors, aircraft trades	11	91	12.1	10	63	15.9
Teas	4	49	8.2	1	12	8.3
Beers, wines and spirits	11	31	35.5	7	31	22.6
Oil	4	24	16.7	10	32	31.3
Textiles	11	85	12.9	8	74	10.8
Drapery and stores	9	114	7.9	8	102	7.8
Newspapers, publishers	9	19	47.4	6	24	25.0
Paper, printing, advertising	7	43	16.3	7	38	18.4
Tobacco	3	8	37.5	4	5	80.0
Steels	1	6	16.7		Not Shown	
Rubber	4	37	10.8		Not Shown	
Shoes	2	27	7.4		Not Shown	
Mines	3	109	2.8	3	112	2.7
TOTAL	257	1,697	15.1	254	1,462	17.4

NOTE: 1. In 1970 some of the companies in the leisure sector were included in miscellaneous industrials.

Source: See Table 5.14.

companies in Germany, less than twice the proportion in the
UK and a much smaller difference than is suggested by the
very different proportions of share capital or voting rights
controlled by the banks in the two countries. In fact,
however, it is clear that interlocking directorships between
banks and quoted companies in the UK and Germany are different
in nature. In Germany, full-time board members of industrial
and commercial companies are sometimes appointed as part-time
members of bank boards, but the general flow is in the
opposite direction, practicing bankers who are full-time
directors or senior executives of their banks are appointed
as shareholders' representatives on the supervisory boards
of industrial and commercial companies. All supervisory
board members are, of course, part-time and, since boards
usually meet only once a quarter, the commitment is not very
onerous. The initiative for such appointments may come either
from a bank or from the management of the company concerned;
there is no means of knowing which, but the large number of
directorships not associated with large voting rights
suggests that the latter must be common. We were told that
bankers were welcome on boards not only for financial advice
but also for advice on executive recruitment. A representative
of one large firm interviewed referred to the "bank network"
for recruiting senior executives, and said that access to this
was often a reason for inviting a banker to join the board.

In the UK it is rare for full-time bankers to serve as
part-time directors of industrial and commercial companies.
It is much more common for banks to invite full-time directors
of other companies to become part-time members of their
boards. In our interviews with UK banks we were informed
that this was regarded as one way in which banks could keep
themselves informed of developments in industry and commerce.
This kind of appointment is one important source of
interlocking directorships. Another is the practice, common
both among banks and other companies, of appointing
distinguished public figures (often titled) as part-time
board members. Such people often hold a number of directorships, and are likely to appear on the boards of both banks

and industrial companies;   their contribution to both is
their name and their general experience of business and
public life.

4.   BANKS' INFLUENCE ON MANAGEMENT

German banks clearly are in a position to exert some
influence on industrial and commercial companies, particularly
the larger quoted companies. Their direct holdings of equity
capital, the proxies they exercise on behalf of their
customers, their board membership and, of course, their role
as providers of loan capital together give the banks
considerable potential influence over management.

There is, however, no evidence that this influence is
commonly exerted to alter either the policy or the day-to-day
management of profitable companies, nor is there any evidence
that the potential for influence has been extended
significantly in recent years. The conclusions of the
Gessler Commission and our own interviews among banks and
German companies support the view that the influence of
German banks over the management of German industry,
especially as compared with their UK counterparts, has been
exaggerated.

Large direct shareholdings by German banks are a small
proportion of the 2,000 quoted companies in existence, and
are not common among the biggest companies. Moreover, they
do not seem to have been acquired with the object of exerting
control or influence. Some of the biggest derive from
rescue operations carried out by the banks in the nineteen-
thirties, while others are the result of underwriting new
issues on behalf of customers. Shares deposited with banks
are widely dispersed so that, in the great majority of cases,
no single bank controls more than 5 per cent of a company's
voting rights (see Table 5.8 above). Bankers sit on the
boards of only a third of quoted non-financial companies

though board membership is much more heavily concentrated than share ownership among the largest companies.

Our interviewees both among German banks and their clients were unanimous in asserting that banks do not interfere with the management of successful companies. What they do is to support management, whether it be through their representative on the supervisory board or at shareholders meetings through their control of voting rights. One respondent, a director of a major German industrial company, told us unequivocally that the house-bank would be expected to advise its clients to buy shares in his company and to advise them to vote with management at shareholders meetings. A house-bank which did not show solidarity with management in this way would soon cease to be the company's house-bank.

As noted already supervisory boards play no part in the day-to-day management of their companies. We found some differences of opinion as to the part they played in longer-term strategy, which probably reflects differences in policy between companies and in personalities. Some of those interviewed gave the impression that management reported to the supervisory board only in very general terms and that the board neither had nor sought information relevant to long-run strategic planning. On the other hand, we were told that some companies have voluntarily written into their articles a requirement that their supervisory board should approve major investment projects and that in some companies supervisory boards exert considerable influence on long-term strategy. This is supported by a representative of a leading German bank, who is quoted as saying:

> "the Board which was a Supervisory organ has become
> an advisory one. Evolving insight into the
> purpose of control is no longer to detect mistakes
> made... rather today control is understood to begin
> at decision making level in order to avoid mistakes
> from the very beginning"[1].

---

1. M. Hein and H. Flöter Macht der Banken - Folgerungen aus der bisherigen Diskussion. WSI. Mitteilungen 7/1975

This lack of involvement by banks in the day-to-day
management of industry and commerce is confirmed by the
Wilson Committee who state that:

> "Those members of the Committee who visited Germany
> and France were assured that in neither country did
> the banks seek to interfere in the day-to-day
> management decisions of their customers, with the
> exception of those relating to the services they
> provide. Indeed, in most cases they did not have
> the technical expertise to do otherwise.[1]"

There is no doubt, as shown in other parts of this
report, bank lending plays a larger part in the finance of
German companies than of UK; that German banks do more long-
term lending, though here the gap has narrowed considerably;
that German banks provide services in financial advice
and raising of capital on securities markets, for which UK
companies rely largely on merchant banks and stockbrokers. In
consequence, German banks generally have a closer relationship
with their customers than do their UK counterparts. However,
these differences can be explained partly by the historical
evolution of the two systems, and partly by the relative
weakness of the German capital market, to which the policies
of the banks may have contributed.

We have found no evidence that large UK companies are less
well serviced, in relation to their needs, than are German
companies. We have shown in Chapter 4 that the cost of bank
finance, in relation to the central bank's discount rate, is
no higher in the UK than in Germany. The wider use of overdrafts gives greater flexibility to UK customers and UK banks
provide more unsecured loans. (Theoretically lack of security
gives the bank a bigger stake in the success of a company
and hence gives British banks a greater incentive to interfere
in management than their German counterparts). Neither the
Wilson Committee nor the NEDO survey of industrial finance
found any evidence that the operations of UK industry were

---

[1]   Wilson Committee Report, Cmnd. 7937, p. 249.

hampered by lack of bank support and our own interviews produced no complaints on this score. Indeed, the criticisms mentioned at the beginning of this Chapter have come almost entirely from academics, trade unionists and politicians, not from industry.

When a German company gets into difficulties then the house-bank is likely to become more closely involved in management and, where it is a shareholder, may seek representation on the Management Board. It would be quite exceptional for the bank to call in its loans and 'walk away'. The house-bank (or banks) will regard its duty as being to organise a rescue operation. There have been many cases of intervention by banks of this kind, two recent examples being the assistance provided to AEG Telefunken and Klöckner-Werke. There have been cases, which have attracted a lot of attention, where UK banks have withdrawn overdraft facilities from companies in trouble, or called in contractual term loans where the conditions of a covenant have not been met, leaving the company to be rescued by another bank or a government agency or to go into liquidation. However, such cases have been few, and British banks which we interviewed assured us that they make strenuous efforts to avoid them.

To some extent the differences between the UK and German systems reflect different degrees of specialisation. The clearing banks put their case on this to the Wilson Committee as follows:

> '.... beyond a point, a bank's involvement in the affairs of individual companies must run the risk - now widely recognised in Germany - of creating conflicts of interest. The clearing banks do not have an unlimited supply of managerial expertise; to provide greater assistance to their customers would require the further recruitment of highly qualified personnel which would directly increase the cost of bank services....the banks must stress that the role of banker is different from the role of proprietor or manager, and that it is dangerous to confuse them'[1].

---

1. Committee of London Clearing Bankers, <u>The London Clearing Banks</u>. Evidence to the Wilson Committee, London, 1977.

The multiple role of German banks as lenders, shareholders; financial advisers to companies, investment advisers or trustees for personal customers, underwriters, and operators in securities markets, can create a number of conflicts of interest. Banks may find themselves under pressure, as noted above, to recommend the shares of a customer company to other clients even though such a purchase might not be in their best interests; such conflicts could be intensified when a bank is underwriting a new issue or if it wishes to sell securities from its own portfolio.

Possibly more important in the present context, a bank which is lending large sums on profitable terms to a successful company has little incentive, in its role as financial adviser, to encourage that company to go to the capital market. As one large company put it in an interview, the banks tend "to hang on to the goodies". We have noted in Chapter 4 the low ratio of shareholders' funds to total liabilities in Germany compared to the UK. Both this and the small size of the primary market in company securities are linked by some German critics to this kind of conflict of interest within the banking system.

For these and other reasons the majority of the Gessler Commission recommended that bank shareholdings in the equity of any one company should not exceed 25 per cent plus one share. A large minority of the Commission, however, proposed a limit of 10 per cent. It seems quite likely that forth-coming legislation will adopt the lower figure while allowing the banks up to 10 years to divest themselves of the excess. Banks will also be allowed additional short-term holdings of perhaps up to 5 per cent. However, the banks are arguing that a 10 per cent holding would not give them the necessary power at shareholders meetings to block changes in the articles of association (the minimum holding for this under German company law is 25 per cent plus one share) and that

this, in turn, would inhibit them from committing large
amounts of their funds to rescue operations. However, the
draft bill now under consideration proposes no further changes
to the laws affecting Depotstimmrecht so that where the banks
hold proxies they would in some cases still have the necessary
power to block changes.

To sum up, the differences between the two systems
that we have identified here and elsewhere in this report
are not primarily matters of business management. We
believe that alleged differences in the influence exerted
by banks over management are based on misunderstanding of
how the German system actually works. There is no doubt
that German banks have greater potential for influencing
management than do their UK counterparts, though even this
potential power is less than would appear from a cursory
examination of the statistics. We have found no evidence,
however, that banks seek to exercise this power or, in most
cases, that they have the technical capacity to do so. With
the possible exception of rescue operations, we do not
believe that differences between the two countries in the
degree in which banks are involved with management are
significant. We have no evidence that larger UK companies have
suffered from their rather more "arm's length" relationship
with their bankers, and we do not believe that differences
in this respect can have had any bearing on differences in
economic performance.

CHAPTER 6: FINANCE FOR SMALL FIRMS

By Graham Bannock

1.   INTRODUCTION

In the UK there are fewer small businesses and they
account for a much smaller proportion of output and employment
than in Germany. It has been estimated that 'Using comparable
definitions there might well be over 40 per cent more small
businesses in Germany than in the UK, even allowing for
differences in population'.[1] Precise comparisons cannot be
made because of major differences in the coverage of the
available statistics but, in manufacturing for example,
establishments with fewer than 200 employees accounted for
31 per cent of employment in Germany and 23 per cent in the
UK in 1976. These German statistics however exclude
Manufacturing Handwerk; if these 'craft' establishments are
included, then over 54 per cent of employment in German
manufacturing is in establishments with less than 200
employees.[2]

The major structural difference in the role of small
business between the two countries in also shown in the
national accounts: income from self employment is very much
larger in relation to employment income in Germany than it
is in the UK (Table 6.1). Although satisfactory statistics by
size of firm are not available for both countries it is also
clear that a larger proportion of business activity in Germany

---

1.

The Smaller Business in Britain and Germany, Graham
Bannock for the Anglo-German Foundation, Wilton House,
1976.

2.

Handwerk refers to firms whose proprietors are
registered as members of statutorily recognised
professional bodies which (in manufacturing) cover such
skills as toolmaking and baking. Some of these firms
would in Britain be classified to the distributive
trades and some to manufacturing. The exclusion of
Handwerk would therefore understate the relative
importance of small firms in Germany as compared to
Britain. See Bannock, Smaller Business in Britain and
Germany, op. cit.

236.

TABLE 6.1: INCOME FROM EMPLOYMENT AND SELF EMPLOYMENT AS A PERCENTAGE OF THE NATIONAL INCOME UK AND GERMANY, 1976

	UK		GERMANY	
	£m	%	DM billions	%
Income from employment	78,233	71.3	626.3	62.5
Income from self employment	12,005	10.9	187.4	18.7
National Income	109,791	100.0	1,002.4	100.0

Source: National Accounts of OECD Countries 1960 - 1977, OECD, 1979.

is accounted for by unincorporated enterprises. In fact
there are less than 200,000 companies in total in Germany
compared with over 500,000 active companies registered in the
UK. Other indicators of this difference in the role of non-
corporate business have been discussed in Chapter 4.

The causes of this difference in the role of small
business in the two countries (which can also be seen in
comparisons between the UK and other European countries) are
not fully understood.[1] However, small businesses are
everywhere largely precluded,for well known reasons, from
raising finance on the Stock Exchange and depend heavily,
as far as institutional sources of finance are concerned, upon
the banks. We should expect, therefore, that the greater
importance of small business in Germany would be reflected
in a relatively greater provison of bank finance for small
firms. We shall see in this chapter that this is in fact so
and that there is also evidence that public policy, as well
as structural and institutional differences in the banking
systems, affect the relative provision of bank finance for
small firms in the two countries.

2.   THE VOLUME OF LENDING TO SMALL FIRMS

The volume of lending to the Mittelstand

In neither the UK nor Germany are there statistics on
bank advances by size of borrower. Following a 'recommendation' by the Federal Government in 1969, the bank associations
now publish end year totals of business loans outstanding
which do not exceed a DM1 million commitment to any single
firm. The data exclude agriculture, fishing and forestry,
mining, the utilities and financial services and for this
reason do not cover all small firms. By contrast, although

---

1.   It is only partly the result of a larger agricultural
        sector in Germany. See also The Economics of Small
        Firms, Graham Bannock, Blackwell, 1981.

intended to reflect lending to small business (referred to as
the "Mittelstand" in Germany) it is clear that some businesses
which could not be counted as small will have bank borrowings
within the DM lm. limit. The data are also not on an
enterprise basis (so that some of the firms covered will be
subsidiaries of large firms) and exclude mortgage loans on
real property. Moreover the data refer to total loan
commitments by individual banks to individual firms,and some
firms will have borrowings from more than one bank. These
and other technical limitations of the data are clear from
the notes to the Tables which follow and in a translation of
the recommendations included in Appendix 1.

Table 6.2 shows that loans to the Mittelstand, so
defined, by the three main types of bank (the Commercial
Banks, Savings Banks and Giro Centres and the Co-operative
Banks), which account for the vast majority, approached DM 150
billion in 1979 or some 30 per cent of total bank advances to
all incorporated and unincorporated businesses. The data
suggest that the share of the Mittelstand in total bank
lending has declined, but it should be remembered that with a
fixed cut-off limit in terms of size of loan, inflation
alone could explain this.

Table 6.3 gives a breakdown of advances to the Mittelstand
by sector. This shows, as would be expected, that these
advances account for a higher proportion of total advances in
the sectors where small businesses predominate (construction,
the distributive trades and services) though the largest
sub-total of lending to the Mittelstand is, in fact, in
manufacturing where capital requirements are generally
larger than in the other sectors. The capital intensive
nature of manufacture and the effects of inflation are
probably the principal reasons why the share of manufacturing
in total lending to the Mittelstand fell so heavily between
1970 and 1978 (Table 6.4). The share of small establishments in
manufacturing employment changed little over this period,
although in Germany as in other advanced countries there
has also been some shift in employment and investment away

TABLE 6.2:   BANK LENDING TO THE MITTELSTAND AS A PERCENTAGE OF TOTAL
BANK LENDING TO BUSINESSES, GERMANY, 1970-1978

DM Billion and Per Cent

Year	Total bank advances to businesses[1]	Bank advances to the Mittelstand			Bank advances to the Mittelstand as % of total bank advances to businesses	
		(1) Total	(2) 3 main types of bank	Per cent (2)of(1) %	Total %	3 main types of bank %
1970	216.7	95.6	78.7	82.3	44.1	36.3
1971	252.7	104.2	86.4	82.9	41.2	34.2
1972	297.3	119.6	98.7	82.5	40.2	33.2
1973	324.3	125.7	104.4	83.1	38.8	32.2
1974	345.9	133.3	109.9	82.4	38.5	31.8
1975	352.6	116.2	113.5	97.7	33.0	32.2
1976	380.5	130.7	127.0	97.2	34.3	33.4
1977	406.2	122.2	118.7	97.1	30.1	29.2
1978	436.9	132.9	129.3	97.3	30.4	29.6
1979	488.1	151.3	146.4	96.8	31.0	30.0

Notes: 1.   Domestic companies only including advances to the self
employed, excluding mortgage loans on industrial land.
Mortgage loans to companies and the self employed were
DM55.1 billion in 1978 or 11 per cent of total advances
(9 per cent in 1970).

Source: Monatsberichte der Deutschen Bundesbank

2.   Excluding mortgage loans on industrial land. These loans are
however included only for co-operative banks prior to 1977.
See Table 4.

Source: Col. 1 Bundesministerium für Wirtschaft. Unpublished
data collected on the basis of government recommendations
of 1969.

Col. 2 compiled by EAG from the annual reports of the
Private Commercial Bank, Savings and Giro Bank Associations
and unpublished data from the Association of Raiffeisen
and Volksbanks.

TABLE 6.3: BANK LENDING TO ALL BUSINESSES AND TO THE MITTELSTAND BY
SECTOR, GERMANY, 1979

DM billion and Per Cent

	Total Bank Advances to Businesses[1]	Total Bank Advances to the Mittelstand	Per Cent
Manufacturing	144.0	43.4	30.1
Construction	25.1	13.6	54.2
Distributive trades	94.4	38.4	42.5
Transport and communications	52.0	9.0	17.3
Services	97.2	42.0	43.2
Other[2]	75.4	n.a.	n.a.
TOTAL	488.1	146.4	30.0

NOTES:
1. Including advances to the self employed.

2. Agriculture, forestry and fishing, financial services
(non-bank), mining, public utilities.

3. Excluding lending to small and medium size firms in the
sectors listed in Note 2. Figures relate to the 3 main
types of bank only.

Sources: Bundesministerium für Wirtschaft for data on Mittelstand.
Total bank advances from Monatshefte der Deutschenbundesbank.

TABLE 6.4: BANK LENDING TO THE MITTELSTAND BY TYPE OF BANK AND BY SECTOR, GERMANY, 1970 AND 1979

DM Billion and Per Cent

	Commercial Banks		Savings Banks and Giro Centres		Co-operative Banks		Total 3 Main Types of Bank	
	1970	1979	1970	1979	1970	1979	1970	1979
Manufacturing DMbn.	11.7	14.4	8.9	13.8	7.5	15.2	28.1	43.4
Per Cent	48.0	32.0	35.3	26.4	37.7	31.0	40.4	29.6
Construction DMbn.	1.3	2.3	3.1	5.2	2.0	6.1	6.4	13.6
Per Cent	5.3	5.1	12.3	9.9	10.1	12.4	9.2	9.3
Distributive Trades DMbn.	6.6	12.3	6.1	14.1	6.4	12.0	19.1	38.4
Per Cent	27.0	27.3	24.2	27.0	32.2	24.4	27.5	26.2
Transport and Communications DMbn.	1.1	2.0	2.6	4.8	0.5	2.2	4.2	9.0
Per Cent	4.5	4.4	10.3	9.2	2.5	4.5	6.0	6.1
Services DMbn.	3.7	14.0	4.5	14.4	3.5	13.6	11.7	42.0
Per Cent	15.2	31.1	17.9	27.5	17.6	27.7	16.8	28.7
TOTAL DMbn.	24.4	45.0	25.2	52.3	19.9	49.1	69.5	146.4
Per Cent	100.0	100.0	100.0	100.0	100.0	100.0	100.0	100.0

NOTE: For 1970, available data for the Co-operative banks have been adjusted by deducting estimates of the value of mortgage loans in the following proportions: Manufacturing, Construction and Transport, 30 per cent; Distributive Trades 28 per cent and Services 40 per cent.

Source: See notes to Table 6.2.

from manufacturing and towards other sectors.[1] Except in
distribution, where the share of small firms in employment
has probably been declining, the share of lending to the
Mittelstand accounted for by other non-manufacturing
activities has increased.

The volume of bank lending to small firms in the UK

We have been able to trace three published estimates
of bank lending to small firms in Britain. The banks do not
regularly publish any data, even of advances by size of loan.
The Committee of Inquiry on Small Firms estimated on the
basis of a sample inquiry amongst firms that in 1968 total
advances to manufacturing firms employing less than 200
persons 'were of the order of £250 million, about 10 per cent
of advances to the total manufacturing sector'.[2]

EAG, in a study carried out for the Association of
Independent Business, put the total of bank lending to
incorporated and unincorporated small enterprises (including
agriculture, forestry and fishing, mining and quarrying,
financial and other services) 'at around £2,500 million as
at May 1977'. This was 13 per cent of total bank advances or
21 per cent if lending to the financial, personal and public
sectors was excluded.[3]

---

1. The assessment of changes in the share of small firms
    in output and employment in Germany is obscured by a
    break in the statistical series from 1977 onwards and,
    as compared with the UK, by differences in the coverage
    of the statistics. See Bannock, op.cit., and for a
    discussion of more recent trends. The Promotion of
    Small Business, Graham Bannock, Vol. 2, EAG, forthcoming.

2. Report of the Committee of Inquiry on Small Firms,
    HMSO, 1971.

3. Small Firms and the Clearing Banks, A.I.B. 1978. The
    estimate which was qualified as having a margin of
    error of ± 20 per cent was based upon sample surveys of
    balance sheet data, estimates of the capital stock of
    the small firm sector and information supplied in
    interviews with the banks.

One bank, Barclays, has published a few details of the
results of a sample survey of lending by one-third of its
branches in the UK.[1] This indicated that 52 per cent of
business advances were made to businesses with a turnover of
less than £2 millions and which employed fewer than 200
people. No attempt was made to exclude subsidiaries of
larger firms so that because of this and because of the much
higher cut-off limit outside manufacturing we should expect
the volume of lending, according to the Barclays survey, to be
very much higher than the EAG estimate. In fact, 52 per cent
of 1977 UK bank business advances from Table 6.5 (excluding
financial, persons and government) gives a figure of £11,625m.,
over four times the EAG estimate.

The volume of lending: Comparisons

Given the lack of comparable data it is not possible
to go very far in comparing bank lending to small business in
the two countries. At the end of 1978, UK bank advances to
all businesses can be estimated at £38 billion.[2] This
compares with total bank advances to businesses in Germany
of DM 437 billion or about £115 billion at then current
exchange rates. However, Germany has 10 per cent more
population and well over twice the Gross National
Product (at current exchange rates). Increasing UK business
advances by 88 per cent to allow for the lower level of GDP

---

1.   British Banks and Small Businesses, T.H. Bevan in
      The Banks and Small Businesses, The Institute of
      Bankers, September, 1978.

2.   This includes non-sterling advances to UK residents
      and is made up of loans to: non-bank financial
      institutions, £5,592 millions, industrial and
      commercial companies, £28,402 millions, and loans to
      the personal sector minus loans to persons, households
      and individual trusts (i.e. uninocrporated business and
      non-profit making institutions), £4,336 millions.
      Source: Financial Statistics, HMSO. These figures
      differ in timing and coverage from those given in
      Table 6.5 because they cover the private sector and
      relate to December.

TABLE 6.5: TOTAL ADVANCES TO UK RESIDENTS BY BANKS IN THE
        UK, 1977-1979

	£ million		
	1977[1]	1978[1]	1979[1]
Manufacturing	9,366	10,648	12,932
Construction	1,578	1,703	1,975
Distributive trades	3,930	4,784	3,930
Transport and Communications	1,580	1,606	1,751
Other services	4,411	3,601	4,562
Sub total	20,865	22,342	26,884
Financial	6,986	7,428	7,822
Agriculture, forestry and fishing	1,512	1,945	2,592
Mining and Quarrying	1,402	1,356	1,243
Public Utilities, central and local government	4,002	3,663	3,504
Persons[2]	4,761	5,848	7,522
	38,104	42,582	49,567

NOTES: 1.   November

          2.   Lending to persons for house purchase was
                £1,471m. in 1977, £1,715m. in 1978 and £2,293m. in 1979.

Sources: Financial Statistics, Central Statistical Office, HMSO,
          various issues.

per head would bring them to £71bn. compared with £115bn. in
Germany. This difference is to be explained both by the greater
capital intensiveness of the German economy and the greater role
of the stock exchange in the provision of business finance in
Britain. The second of these explanations does not apply to
a comparison of bank advances to small firms so that even if
we take the Barclays estimate as being more appropriate for
this purpose, bank lending to small business is relatively
much lower in Britain than in Germany: in a ratio of at
least 26:40 £ billions even after allowing for differences
in GNP and population.[1] While these comparisons involve
"heroic" assumptions the crude comparison is even more
striking: total bank advances to the Mittelstand according
to the German statistics significantly exceed total UK bank
advances to business <u>and</u> the public sector taken together.

3.   DIFFERENCES IN BANKING STRUCTURE AND THEIR IMPLICATIONS

The sources of bank lending to the Mittelstand

    Table 6.6 shows how the share of lending to the
Mittelstand compares with the share of total business advances
by each of the three main types of bank. It can be seen that
there is a significant degree of specialisation in small
lending between the categories of bank.

    The commercial banks, a heterogeneous group which

1.

    UK bank advances less to public utilities, central and
    local government, agriculture forestry and fishing,
    mining and quarrying, financial and less loans to persons
    for house purchase (to bring them roughly into line
    with the coverage of the Mittelstand data) amounted
    to £26,475 millions in 1978. If we take 52 per cent
    of this figure and gross it up by 88 per cent to
    allow for the difference in GNP per head, we arrive
    at a figure of £26 billions. Lending to the
    Mittelstand was £40 billions at current exchange
    rates. The ratio of lending to small and medium
    sized firms calculated in this way is lower than the
    ratio of total bank advances, but greater than that
    of the relative sizes of the small firm sector in the
    two countries.

TABLE 6.6: BANK LENDING BY THE THREE MAIN TYPES OF BANKS TO DOMESTIC
BUSINESSES IN TOTAL, AND TO THE MITTELSTAND, 1979. GERMANY

	Total Bank Advances to Businesses 1979[1]		Bank Advances to to Mittelstand 1979[2]	
	DM Billion	%	DM Billion	%
Commercial Banks [3]	197.0	40.9	45.0	30.7
Savings and Giro Banks	191.0	39.6	52.3	35.7
Cooperative Banks	94.1	19.5	49.1	33.5
Total [4]	482.1	100.0	146.4	100.0

NOTES: 1 Includes mortgage lending

2 Excludes mortgage lending

3 Includes Banks with Special Functions

4 Excludes lending by Mortgage and Hire Purchase Banks
and the Postal Giro System

Source: Total Bank Lending, Deutsche Bundesbank Beihefte Reihe 1,
May 1980, Table 6. Remaining Data, see Notes to Table 2.

includes the Big 3, the regional and other commercial banks
as well as branches of foreign banks and the private banks,
has the largest share of total advances, but the smallest
share of advances to the Mittelstand. The share of the
commercial banks in lending to the Mittelstand fell between
1970 and 1978, that of the savings banks fell slightly and
that of the co-operative banks increased. (Table 6.7)

Table 6.8 shows that the role of the commercial banks
in advances to the Handwerk sector is relatively smaller still.
The savings banks have by far the largest share and they seem
to have been increasing it mainly at the expense of the
co-operative banks. Overall, advances to Handwerk have been
increasing as a percentage of total loans of up to one million
DM as inflation has increased the capital requirements of these
small firms.

It is to be expected that smaller banks with more
limited resources would be more likely to concentrate upon
lending to smaller firms and that this tendency would be
strongly reinforced by geographical factors. Small banks
inevitably tend to be more deeply rooted in the community
in which their directors are located. We have seen (in
Chapter 2.) that the savings banks are obliged, by law, to
restrict their activities to the local authority area in
which they are located while the co-operative banks were
limited to lending to their own members until 1974. We
have also seen that the credit co-operatives were originally
self-help institutions for farmers and artisans and thus
were founded to assist small business. They have continued
to perform this role while the savings banks, whose original
emphasis was upon employed townspeople, have become
involved in the development of small businesses in urban
areas.

Table 6.9, in conjunction with the earlier Tables,
suggests that lending to small business is, in fact, size

TABLE 6.7: PERCENTAGE OF TOTAL LENDING TO THE MITTELSTAND
BY EACH OF THE THREE MAIN TYPES OF BANK, GERMANY 1970 and 1978

	1970	1978
Commercial Banks	35.1	30.7
Savings and Giro Banks	36.3	35.7
Co-operative Banks	28.6	33.5
TOTAL	100.0	100.0

SOURCE: See notes to Table 6.4

TABLE 6.8: BANK LENDING TO HANDWERK BY TYPE OF BANK AND TOTAL
LENDING TO MITTELSTAND, GERMANY 1970 and 1978

	DM Billions and Per Cent			
	1970 DM m	Per Cent	1978 DM m	Per Cent
Commercial Banks	1.2	12.5	3.0	12.1
Savings and Giro Banks	4.4	45.8	14.2	57.3
Co-operative Banks	4.0	41.7	7.6	30.6
Total advances to Handwerk	9.6	100.0	24.8	100.0
Total advances to Mittelstand	69.5		129.3	
Per Cent Handwerk of total		13.8		19.2

SOURCE: See notes to Table 6.2. Mortgage loans by the Co-operative
banks have been excluded on an estimated basis in both
1970 and 1978 using a similar method to that described in
note to Table 4.

TABLE 6.9: NUMBER OF BANKS, BANK BRANCHES AND PERCENTAGE OF BANKS WITH A
            TURNOVER OF LESS THAN DM 1 BILLION, THREE MAIN TYPES OF BANKS,
            GERMANY, 1978

	Number of Banks	Number of Branches [1]	Percent. of Banks with volume of business of less than DM 1 Billion[2]
All Commercial Banks	255	5840	77
Big Banks	6	3068	–
Regional Banks	104	2451	71
Private Banks	92	278	91
Savings and Giro Banks	623	16893	84
Co-operative Banks	4614	14892	99

NOTES: 1 All banks.

         2 Reporting banks only.

Source: Bericht, 1979, Monatsbericht, 11/1979.

related and related to the geographical density of banks and
their branches. Were our figures of lending to the Mittelstand
broken down in more detail it seems probable that these
relationships would emerge more clearly. For example, lumping
together lending by the regional and private banks with that
of the Big 3 probably conceals an even smaller involvement by
the largest banks in lending to smaller business. Both private
banks and branches of foreign banks are highly unlikely to lend
much to small firms. Some of the regional banks are clearly
heavily involved in small business lending (for example, the
Bank für Gemeinwirtschaft and the two Bavarian banks, the
Bayerische Vereinsbank and the Bayerische Hypotheken-und
Wechselbank) but most of the others are probably not. Handwerk
firms mainly employ 9 or fewer persons and the smaller share of
the commercial banks in lending to Handwerk (Table 6.8) shows
that their lending is concentrated at the upper end of the scale
of advances to the Mittelstand. At the same time, were advances
to agriculture, forestry and fishing included in the Mittelstand
data, then the role of the co-operatives, which have a major
role in lending to farmers, would be seen to be correspondingly
greater.

The sources of bank lending to small business in the UK

It is not possible to break down any of the estimates of
bank lending to small firms by type of bank in the UK. There
can, however, be no doubt that the vast majority of
bank lending to small firms will be accounted
for by the London and Scottish clearing banks and their
subsidiaries. This group consists of six banking enterprises
which, with their subsidiaries, account for about 60 per
cent of total sterling advances to residents. Of the remaining
banks, most are overseas banks whose industrial and commercial
lending is probably heavily concentrated upon large firms,
particularly subsidiaries of foreign companies, and non-retail
banks. The merchant banks are heavily involved in the
provision of finance for larger unquoted companies, but their
total term lending to small businesses cannot be very large.

It is clear that bank lending to small business is concentrated amongst fewer and very much larger institutions in the UK than in Germany. Whilst in Germany the Big 3 account for less than 30 per cent of lending to the Mittelstand, it would be surprising if the four London clearing banks and their subsidiaries accounted for less than twice that proportion. The contrast, however, is much more dramatic at the other end of the scale: whilst there are several thousand independent banks in Germany most of which make advances to small business, in the UK there are only a few hundred, very few of which are concerned with lending to small business.[1] We also find that the density of bank branches is lower in the UK than in the FRG. The retail banks in the UK (the London and Scottish clearing banks, the Northern Ireland banks, the Yorkshire Bank - these two groups are owned by the former groups - and the Co-operative Bank) have, according to the Wilson Report, about 13,000 branches. The three main types of bank in Germany have some 38,000 branches.

Although the overall population density is similar in the two countries, in Germany it is more dispersed and we might on these grounds expect a somewhat higher density of branches per square mile there. However it is clear that the principal reason for the difference lies in the large number of co-operative and savings bank branches which account for over 80 per cent of the total number of commercial bank branches. The Big 3 German banks have a much smaller branch network than their counterparts in Britain (Table 6.10).

4.   CREDIT GUARANTEES

In addition to structural differences (both in banking and among the banks' industrial and commercial customers) a number of other factors could contribute to the greater

---

1.   There are legal restrictions on lending by savings banks in the UK. See Chapter 1.

TABLE 6.10: NUMBER OF SQUARE MILES PER BANK BRANCH, BY TYPE OF BANK,
UK AND GERMANY, 1978

UK		GERMANY 1	
London and Scottish Clearing Banks	7.7	Commercial Banks Big 3	15.7 31.2
Trustee Savings Banks	53.5	Savings Banks	5.5
(Building Societies	19.1)	Co-operative Banks	4.9

Note 1:   Includes banks and bank branches

Source: EAG calculations. Sources: Land Area and Population,
Whittakers Almanac, 1977
Number of branches: Great Britain, Report of the Committee
to Review the Functioning of Financial Institutions,
HMSO 1980 (The Wilson Report) Germany: Bericht, 1979,
Monatsbericht 11/1979.

volume of bank lending to small businesses in the FRG
compared with the UK. We have selected two of these
factors for further examination in this study, both of them
reflecting important differences in public policy towards
small business. The first, credit guarantees, is discussed
in this section and the second, state subsidised bank lending,
in the following section.

Organisation and finance

Credit guarantees for medium and long term bank loans are available from credit guarantee associations (Kreditgarantiegemeinschaften (CGA)). These are private limited companies (GmbH) established by the business community as mutual assistance organisations from the early 1950s onwards. The CGAs were established for the express purpose of assisting small firms which were unable to obtain bank loans through lack of adequate collateral. Chambers of commerce, trade associations, banks, insurance companies and other private sector organisations contributed the initial capital and are represented on the board. It is of interest that it was the smaller banks, particularly the co-operative and savings banks, which took the initiative rather than the large banks.

All the eleven Länder have at least one CGA and most have several. Rhineland Pfalz for example has four: one a public institution which deals with guarantees (Länderburg-schaft) for large companies and is heavily politicised, most of its activities are concerned with 'lame ducks'; one for hotels and catering, manufacturing and certain services; one for the distributive trades and one for Handwerk (crafts). The structure and operation of the CGAs varies according to their purpose and from one place to another, the following description therefore is a generalised one.

The CGA's capital is invested and the proceeds are added to the guarantee fund. These funds are supplemented by loans and grants from the Länder and by loans from the ERP Guarantee Programme through the Kreditanstalt für Wiederaufbau (KfW).[1]

---

1. The role of the KfW and the ERP (European Recovery Programme) is described briefly below.

These ERP loans, which are made on a 25 year basis at below
market rates of interest, account for between one-third and
one-half of the total guarantee funds. The interest rate is
normally 5.5 per cent but for a newly formed CGA (where ERP
funds are part of the initial capital) it is only 1/8 per
cent per annum. Federal Government assistance of this kind
to the CGAs is important but does not involve heavy public
expenditure; the ERP loans totalled DM42.5m (£11.2m) by the
end of 1978 and commitments in 1978 were DM5.2 m (£1.4m).

Public sector regulation and support

The CGAs are classified as banks and are subject to
regulation in the same way as other banks. They are allowed
to guarantee only up to about 18 times the amount of their
guarantee fund. They are also required to take security and
to guarantee only up to 80 per cent of any loan. The maximum
period of the loan guaranteed is 12 years (23 years for buildings).
In 1976 the maximum individual guarantee available varied from
DM150,000 (£39,000) for the self employed to DM650,000 (£171,000)
for manufacturing but these limits have since been raised:
for manufacturing, for example, it is now DM 1 million.

The Federal Government and the Länder provide counter-
guarantees under which they meet a proportion of any
deficiencies borne by the CGAs. Originally the counter-
guarantee ratio was 80 per cent. It is reviewed at 5 yearly
intervals in the light of the financial situation of the CGAs
and has been progressively reduced to 60 per cent of which
the Federal Government bears three-fifths and the appropriate
Länder two-fifths.[1] The ERP special Funds also share in
meeting deficiencies at a fixed rate for most CGAs of 12.5
per cent of the total deficiency. Since 60 per cent of the

---

1. A further reduction in the counter-guarantee ratio
    planned for the end of 1978 did not take place because
    of a deterioration in the financial position of the
    CGAs following an exceptional number of insolvencies in
    1977.

deficiencies are met by the Federal and Länder Governments and 12.5 per cent by the ERP funds, the CGAs only have to bear 27.5 per cent.

Method of operation

Normally the request for a credit guarantee will come from the bank considering an application for a loan and where adequate security is not available, that is where the bank would reject an application wholly, or more usually partly, for that reason. The CGA then asks the local chamber of commerce or chamber of crafts to carry out a credit assessment on the potential borrower. Each chamber has one or more persons specialising in credit assessment. This will involve:

i.   Visiting the borrower and collecting financial and
     other information on his business;

ii. Consulting the borrower's trade association for an
     opinion on the outlook for the trade in the area in
     question;

iii. Taking the view of a local business "expert".

On receipt of a report and recommendation from the chamber, the board of the CGA will decide whether or not to guarantee the loan. In the vast majority of cases the board will follow the chamber's advice. The board usually meet every 4-6 weeks and the whole process from application by the bank to the issue of the guarantee takes, on average, about 3 months according to one chamber of commerce but other reports put it at much longer than this. Guarantees are available not only for loans for fixed investment, but for working capital, re-financing and acquisitions.

The borrower pays an initial fee of about DM 100 and, if his application is accepted, a further fee of between ½ and one per cent of the guaranteed amount, and twice a year he pays a running commission of between ¼ and ⅛ per cent on the reducing balance of the guaranteed amount. The interest rate charged by the bank could be subsidised by the Länder or the government under various and separate schemes, which are discussed later on, but in principle it will be at the market rate, that is the interest rate will be the same for the guaranteed loan as it would be for a normal bank loan. The CGA will require security but it is prepared to accept a lower quality of collateral than the bank, for example, a second mortgage, stock and work in progress. As mentioned, the CGA will only guarantee up to 80 per cent of the loan, the bank must accept the remainder. A typical loan package would be:

DM200,000	Fully secured bank loan
DM 80,000	CGA guaranteed bank loan
DM 20,000	Partly or unsecured bank loan
DM300,000	

Scale

Table 6.11 shows the amounts of new guarantee commitments each year since 1960 as reported by the central CGAs. The data cover only manufacturing, distribution and Handwerk, but other guarantee bodies (hotels and catering, horticulture) are said to account for only a very small proportion of the total.[1] Since their inception the CGAs had made 58,800 guarantees to the end of 1978, totalling DM3.4 billion (£890 million) against loans totalling DM4.6 billion (£1.2 billion) i.e., the average guarantee was for 74 per cent of the loan. Guarantees outstanding were DM1.2 billion (£316 million). In 1978, 3,200 guarantees were given with a total value of DM300 million (£79 million) or an average of DM94,000 (£25,000) per guarantee.[2] The median guarantee would be lower than this

---

1. ERP and other funds are used to provide guarantees for loans to persons in the professions. This large programme is administered by the Lastenausgleichsbank which in 1976 had guarantee commitments of DM 443 million for the professions which are not included in any of the other figures quoted in this chapter.

2. Kreditanstalt für Wiederaufbau, Annual Report, 1978.

258.

TABLE 6.11: NEW GUARANTEE ACCEPTANCES BY CREDIT GUARANTEE ASSOCIATIONS
FOR MANUFACTURING, DISTRIBUTION AND HANDWERK,
GERMANY, 1960-1978

DM million

	Manufacturing	Distribution	Handwerk	Total
1960	n.a.	n.a.	22.11	n.a.
1961	n.a.	n.a.	27.04	n.a.
1962	n.a.	19.26	37.30	n.a.
1963	n.a.	23.40	45.28	n.a.
1964	23.73	28.51	54.52	106.76
1965	16.76	39.29	64.29	120.34
1966	12.50	31.37	55.24	99.11
1967	16.40	32.42	47.48	96.30
1968	26.28	35.49	63.40	125.17
1969	39.62	44.32	74.36	158.30
1970	48.50	37.71	76.31	162.61
1971	48.20	50.46	81.03	179.69
1972	62.01	57.39	90.42	209.82
1973	40.24	44.52	65.35	150.11
1974	52.47	40.41	68.62	161.50
1975	88.35	80.16	110.06	278.57
1976	n.a.	80.90	123.11	n.a.
1977	n.a.	88.54	126.50	n.a.
1978	n.a.	108.69	159.80	n.a.

SOURCE: Staatliche Massnahmen zur Verringerung der Finanzierungsprobleme
kleiner u.mittlerer Unterneehmen.
G. Kann, Institut fur Mittelstandsforschung
Updated from the annual reports of the Kreditgarantie-gemeinschaft

however: almost half of the guarantees are made for the Handwerk sector where the average loan is only about one-third of that for manufacturing enterprises.

Loss experience

There had been 1,100 guarantee deficiencies from the inception of the CGAs to the end of 1978 to a total of DM31m. (£816,000). We presume these figures are net of recoveries against collateral i.e. they represent deficiency payments by the CGAs to the banks, although only about one-quarter will have actually been borne by the CGAs because of the counter-guarantees given by the public sector. This represents 1.9 per cent of the total number of guarantees and 1.1 per cent of the total value of guarantees made. Annual data are not readily available but we understand that prior to the 1974-5 recession the loss experience was very low indeed. In Handwerk half of all losses in 20 years were incurred in 1974-5.

Conclusion

At DM 300 million, guarantee commitments by the CGAs in 1978 backed advances of about DM 400 million, roughly 0.3 per cent of total advances to the Mittelstand in that year. The total amount of credit made possible by the availability of credit guarantees is, therefore, very small in relation to total bank advances in Germany. It should be noted that this comparison understates the importance of guarantees for very small firms. We estimate that the proportion of bank advances to Handwerk subject to guarantees from CGAs was more than twice the average for all sectors.

The number of new guarantee commitments for Handwerk has varied with the economic cycle and has shown little increase over the long term. The rejection rate, however, has tended to increase (Table 6.13). 10-15 per cent of applications have

TABLE 6.12: NUMBER OF GUARANTEE ACCEPTANCES BY CREDIT GUARANTEE ASSOCIATIONS FOR HANDWERK, DISTRIBUTION AND MANUFACTURING, GUARANTEE AMOUNTS AND PER CENT OF APPLICATIONS REJECTED, GERMANY, 1975

	Number of Acceptances	Guarantee Amount DM millions	Average value of guarantee DM thousands	Total Loan Amount DM millions	% of total loan Guaranteed	% of all Applications Rejected
Handwerk	1454	110.06	75.7	144.99	75.9	12.8
Distribution	830	80.16	96.6	104.90	76.4	18.9
Manufacturing	394	88.35	224.2	132.81	66.5	25.5

SOURCE: See Table 6.11

TABLE 6.13: NUMBER OF GUARANTEE COMMITMENTS ACCEPTED AND PER CENT OF
APPLICATIONS REJECTED BY CREDIT GUARANTEE ASSOCIATIONS
FOR HANDWERK, 1960-1978

| | Number of Acceptances | Rejection Ratios | |
		Per Cent of total by number	Per Cent of total by value
1960	1298		
1961	1695		
1962	1728		
1963	1958		
1964	2143	6.2	8.4
1965	2311	5.8	7.1
1966	1762	8.4	9.1
1967	1434	8.4	10.1
1968	1792	9.9	12.7
1969	1763	7.0	8.4
1970	1515	8.6	10.3
1971	1444	8.1	9.6
1972	1448	8.1	10.5
1973	965	11.8	13.1
1974	1033	12.8	18.5
1975	1454	12.8	20.9
1976	1498	15.0	20.0
1977	1545	12.2	11.9
1978	1826	10.2	14.7

SOURCE: See Table 6.11

been rejected in recent years but this, we understand, relates
only to applications passed to the CGA boards for approval;
about 40 per cent of borrowers referred by the banks to the
CGA are rejected before reaching the boards so that the
overall rejection rate is over 50 per cent. The slow growth
of credit guarantees actually committed does not, in general,
appear to result from an insufficiency of guarantee funds.
We were told that most CGAs are well within their guarantee
commitment limits. The German credit guarantee mechanism
has been the subject of growing criticism in recent years.
Businessmen claim that the CGAs are bureaucratic and over-
cautious and, according to one small firm representative body,
many will not consider CGA guaranteed loans for fear of loss
of independence. Others complain that since the CGAs
require security, the basic problem that the borrower with
good prospects but no collateral cannot obtain funds remains
unsolved. The CGA's willingness to take risks is only
marginally greater than that of the banks 'who take no risks
at all'. These critics look with envy at the SBA credit
guarantee system in the United States. The Federal
Government would have liked to eliminate its counter
guarantees by now but has been unable to do so partly
because of the upsurge of defaults since the 1974-5 recession
and partly because the Länder are, in any event, reluctant
to assume sole responsibility.

Despite these criticisms, it is generally agreed that
the CGAs' guarantees have directly made possible a substantial
volume of lending which would otherwise not have taken place:
it is not the necessity for credit guarantees which is
questioned but the effectiveness of the present system. It
also seems probable that the low loss rate experienced by
the CGAs, at least until recently, has encouraged the banks
to be somewhat more flexible in their lending policies than
they otherwise would be.

It would not be true to say that institutional credit
guarantees for bank lending to small firms are completely

unknown in the UK. The Agricultural Mortgage Corporation, with government support has since 1964 provided guarantees for medium term bank lending to farmers and the Scottish and Welsh Development Agencies have powers to guarantee bank loans which, we are told, they have used to a small extent in support of small firms. Both the NEDC Committee on Finance for Industry (Roll Committee) and Wilson Committee have recommended a publicly underwritten loan guarantee scheme for which small firm representative bodies in Britain have been calling for ten years or more.[1] These recommendations have been hesitant and, given the lack of enthusiasm on the part of both the banks and the government, have not yet been implemented.[2]

Although the availability of credit guarantees in the FRG can only directly explain a small part of the difference between the volume of lending to small firms in Germany and Britain, nothing in the German experience suggests that the introduction of similar facilities in the UK could be anything but of benefit to the development of small business.

5.   SUBSIDISATION OF BANK LENDING BY THE PUBLIC SECTOR

Federal government measures

The Federal and Länder governments in Germany have not limited their attempts to encourage bank lending to small firms to the support of the credit guarantee associations. The Federal Government made loans on favourable terms from

---

[1] See The Financing of Small Firms, Interim Report of the Committee to Review the Functioning of Financial Institutions, HMSO March 1979.

[2] For a fuller discussion of the scope for a credit guarantee system for the UK and the form it might take see Bannock, The Promotion of Small Business, op.cit.

ERP funds to small and medium sized firms totalling DM 1.3
billion in 1978 (Table 6.14). These loans which are made at
well below market rates of interest and at fixed rates
are normally intended to provide medium and long term finance
of up to 10 years (15 years for buildings). They are made
through the commercial banking system and administered by
the Kreditanstalt für Wiederaufbau (KfW) and the Lastenausgleichsbank (LAB).[1] Both these state banks also provide loans
for small firms from their own resources financed by capital
market borrowings. These supplementary loans now substantially
exceed those from ERP funds. In all cases borrowers may
apply through any commercial bank which, if the loan is
granted, assumes full liability and will secure the loan
in the normal way (or refer the borrower to a CGA). The
lending bank is remunerated from a part of the interest
charged to the borrower. Table 6.14 shows that total lending
under these programmes is substantial in money terms, amounting
to DM 5 billions in 1978, although that represented only 3 per
cent of total bank advances to the Mittelstand.

Länder government measures

The Länder, as well as the Federal government, also
subsidise bank lending through the commercial banks.
Länder aid is generally administered through public banks
(Spezialbanken) such as the Landeskreditbank Baden
Württemberg, Bayerische Landesanstalt für Aufbaufinanz-
ierung and the Hessische Landesentwicklungs-und Treuhand-
gesellschaft. The general conditions for the loans and
their administration are similar to those for the Federal

1.
The LAB is a Federal government owned bank set up in
1950 to help refugees and war victims by means of loans
and other financial aid which is now involved in a
wide range of government social projects including
finance for small firms. The KfW is owned 80 per cent
by the Bund and 20 per cent by the Länder and was
formed in 1948 to finance the reconstruction of the
German economy through medium and long term credit.
It has since acquired other functions, including the
provision of finance and assistance for developing
countries.

TABLE 6.14:   FEDERAL GOVERNMENT LOANS TO SMALL AND MEDIUM
SIZED FIRMS AND THE PROFESSIONS, GERMANY, 1975-1978

DM millions

	ERP Special Fund	KfW	LAB	Total
1975	682.9	1451.5	24.2	2158.6
1976	675.9	1475.3	30.6	2181.8
1977	884.5	2023.2	124.4	3032.1
1978	1296.5	3582.2	82.2	4960.9
1979	1804.6	3708.9	87.9	5601.4

SOURCE: Leistung in Zahlen, 1979

programme described above. The administrating public banks
finance the loans by borrowing on the capital market and
receive subsidies from the Länder to allow them to on-lend
at below market rates. However, the public banks also have
their own programmes in the same way as the KfW and the LAB
have them at Federal level.

No-one seems to have attempted to assess the total
volume of bank lending to small firms which is subsidised
by the Länder but from some examples we can give it is
clearly substantial. In 1976 the Free State of Bavaria
subsidised new bank advances to small firms totalling
DM152.8 million and the state bank provided from its
own resources loans totalling a further DM69.6 million.
Schleswig-Holstein subsidised new bank advances to small
firms to a total of DM65.3 million in 1976 at an interest
rate subsidy of 3.5 per cent. In the same year in Baden
Würtemburg the Landeskreditbank accepted 2,455 loan
applications for amounts totalling DM276.7 million. In
Hessen the corresponding total was DM28.7 million.[1]

Länder assistance to small and medium sized firms,
which also includes the provision of counter-guarantees to
the CGAs, investment grants and other financial aid, varies
considerably in scale with the policies of the state
authorities and the scale of their resources and problems.
If we take the total of subsidised bank lending by the four
Länder given in the previous paragraph and gross it up in
line with their share in the FRG's GNP, we arrive at a
total of DM1.3 billion for new subsidised lending to small
firms by the Länder in 1976.[2] In terms of advances
outstanding therefore, subsidised bank lending by the Länder
could be approaching one per cent of total advances to the
Mittelstand.

---

1.   These examples are taken from G. Kann, op.cit.
2.   This is a very rough estimate indeed since it is clear
       that there is little correlation between the scale
       of activity in this respect and share of GNP.

6.   CONCLUSION

There are in fact, no programmes for the provision of
subsidised bank lending to small firms in the UK. Both the
Scottish and Welsh Development Agencies and the Council for
Industry in Rural Areas make subsidised loans to small firms
and low interest loans are also available under the Industry
Acts but none of these loans are available on application
through the banking system and they are available to a much
narrower range of small businesses than German subsidised
loans. Moreover, subsidised lending of this kind is available
on a very small scale in the UK; it is very doubtful if
lending by specialised state agencies was more than £3.5
million in 1979 while lending under the Industry Acts is, to
judge from the sizes of individual loans, predominantly to
large firms. The vast majority of subsidised lending in the
UK is made to large firms.

In Germany perhaps about 4 per cent of bank advances to
the Mittelstand enjoy subsidies from the Bund or Länder
governments. In absolute terms this represents a large sum of
money, although it only goes a little way, in itself, to
explaining the apparently large differences in the volume of
bank lending to small businesses in the two countries. It
seems quite possible, however, that the state subsidy scheme
and the support for credit guarantee have encouraged the banks
to lend more on their own account than they otherwise would have
done. Of course it is impossible to say how much bank lending
would have taken place in Germany in the absence of state
assistance. A critic might argue that the much larger volume
of bank lending in Germany to small businesses simply reflects
the greater role of small business in that country, that is to
say, it is an effect rather than a cause. This seems
implausible: we are convinced from our study that the
differences in the structure of the banking system in the two
countries, as well as state efforts to stimulate bank lending,
have played a major role in channelling more resources into
small firms in Germany than in the UK, though other factors
are undoubtedly at work.

For the sake of comprehensiveness we should add that we have not attempted to compare banking practices, lending criteria, and commercial interest rate policy towards small business borrowers in the two countries in detail. However, these are discussed in general terms in Chapter 4.

In both countries bank executives are vague about the lending criteria which they apply. These clearly ultimately depend upon the banker's judgement of the individuals involved, the strength of the business and the quality of the available security. Similar kinds of lending facilities are available from the banks in both countries though the overdraft system is less flexible in Germany than in Britain. In Germany it seems that the banks normally make a charge for the unutilised portion of an overdraft facility which is never done in Britain. So attractive is the British overdraft system that it is frequently used by small firms to finance fixed assets for which long-term loans would be more appropriate. The British banks have in recent years introduced term loans in various forms specially suited to the needs of small firms including the option of fixed or variable interest rates, moratoria on capital repayments and other features. No figures are available but the banks say that term loans account for an increasing proportion of lending to small firms.

In our judgement, such differences as there are in attitudes towards lending to small firms and in actual banking practices in the two countries are attributable more to differences in the structure of the banking system (and the scope of public sector encouragement) than in the formal lending criteria or the nature of the lending facilities available. We consulted small firm representative bodies in both countries. Whilst the two bodies in Germany had no criticisms at all to make of the banks, four out of five similar bodies in Britain were highly critical of the U.K. banks for their tendency to assess small business borrowers in terms of break-up value rather than as going concerns.

In both the UK and Germany, the commercial banks are
involved in other institutions including own subsidiaries
providing equity and loan capital for small business.
Examples in Germany are the Deutsche Wagnisfinanzierungs-
gesellschaft formed in 1975 by several banks and the Federal
government to provide risk capital for technology based
companies and the Kapitalbeteiligungsgesellschaften which
take equity shares in companies. In the UK in addition to
the Industrial and Commercial Finance Corporations, which is
owned by the clearing banks, virtually all the major banks
now have subsidiaries with special interests in the provision
of risk finance for small firms.[1]

1. These and other aspects of the Clearing Banks'
   services for small business are described in
   The Banks and Small Firms, Banking Information Service,
   July 1980.

APPENDIX 1

Federal Ministry for Economics   18th December, 1969

Recommendations for recording lending to small and middle-sized firms

1. The purpose of these recommendations

The aim is a uniform collection of statistics, in order to make comparison of lending to the 'Mittelstand' easier.
All main bank associations agreed to these recommendations.

Categorisation according to size of borrower would be very desirable, but the recommendations limit themselves to figures which are readily available, i.e. in keeping with existing obligations to the central bank, in order to avoid an unnecessary increase of the work load for the banks and their associations.

2. Details of the recommendations

The necessary figures should be taken from the statistics which are prepared every quarter for the central bank, as follows:

2.1 Categorisation by sector of lending not secured by mortgage, i.e.

- to manufacturing
- to building
- to distribution
- to transport and communications
- to services (including the professions)
- lending to Handwerk which is included in the above should also be shown separately as a total.

A further breakdown under these headings would be desirable (e.g. under distribution into wholesale and retail, etc.)

What does not belong to lending to the Mittelstand is thus:
- agriculture and forestry, animal husbandry and fishing
- power and water supply and mining

- financing institutes (without credit institutes) and
  insurance
- employed and other private persons
- non-profit based organisations

All house building credit not secured by mortgage
appearing in the statistics for the central bank should not
be included in the figures for lending to the Mittelstand,
but does not need to be shown separately due to the amount
of work involved.

2.2 Loans against real property

i.e. credit secured on industrial land and ships but not
on land for housing and agricultural land and other land.

2.3 Date for survey

End of each year.

2.4 Amount of credit

It is recommended that a loan or loans of up to one
million DM to single firms (i.e. total credit commitment
of a firm not to exceed one million DM) should be counted
as lending to the Mittelstand. Other criteria are not
practicable due to the amount of work involved.

2.5 Period to maturity

The loans should also be shown in periods to maturity:
- short term (up to and including one year)
- middle term (over one and under four years)
- long term (four years and over)

2.6 Publication

It is recommended that this statistic should be published
in the annual reports of the bank associations.

CHAPTER 7:   THE FINANCE OF THE PUBLIC SECTOR
AND ITS MONETARY IMPLICATIONS
By Richard L. Harrington

1.   INTRODUCTION

Since the second-world war there has been substantial growth in the size and functions of government. This has been true for all developed economies and today the combined expenditure of all levels of government in such countries usually amounts to between 40 and 50 per cent of GNP. This covers current expenditure on goods and services, capital expenditure, subsidies and transfer payments. Much of this expenditure is covered by taxes of one sort or another but in most countries there is still a significant amount which has to be met by borrowing. Government borrowing will usually have monetary implications: whether the authorities borrow from the banks or from the non-bank public will clearly be important and so will be the type and maturity of assets issued. In virtually all countries certain government assets are eligible for re-discount at the central bank and thus provide excellent liquidity for banks: in addition, in those countries where the banks are obliged to hold part of their assets in nominated liquid assets, it is invariably government assets which comprise all or most of the eligible assets. It is necessary then in order to understand any modern financial system to look at the organisation of government and how it is financed.

But as well as the government sector, there are in most countries today a number of public enterprises and utilities, frequently in need of large amounts of capital, and whose borrowing can also have important monetary consequences. This may be because (as in the UK) it is confounded with government borrowing proper: or because (as in Germany) it gives rise to assets eligible for re-discount at the central bank. However, there are definitional problems as the division between public and private enterprise is blurred; there being enterprises which are partly public and partly privately-owned, as well

as enterprises which, whilst being wholly publicly-owned, are
run as private companies without any privileged borrowing
facilities. In what follows we shall only be concerned with
public enterprise insofar as its finance is likely to have
particular importance for the monetary system. Thus we shall
have to take account of the large UK public corporations,
whose borrowing needs are largely met by the government, and
the two Federal public enterprises of Germany: the federal
Post Office (Bundespost) and the federal Railways (Bundesbahn)
whose borrowing can give rise to re-discountable assets. We
shall ignore the various limited liability companies, partially
owned by the government, such as British Petroleum in the UK
and Veba in Germany. Also we shall ignore the various public
utilities and housing associations in Germany which are owned
by local authorities but which are run as private companies.

The public sector in the UK and Germany

If one puts on one side the public corporations and
looks at the size of general government (national, regional
and local government plus social security funds) then the two
countries appear remarkably similar. In the three years
1975-77 total expenditure by general government in Germany
averaged 47.4 per cent of GNP at market prices; in the UK
46.0 per cent. The composition of this spending differed
somewhat: expenditure on goods and services in Germany
amounted to 20.3 per cent of GNP on average whereas the
corresponding UK figure was 25.2 per cent. Government
transfer payments - largely social security payments - were
much higher in Germany. In both countries government
expenditure both in absolute terms and as a proportion of
national expenditure has been on a rising trend during the
last two decades.

In Table 7.1 we show the main categories of public
expenditure in the UK and Germany for calendar years 1975-77.
The amounts spent per category are shown both in absolute
amounts and as percentages of GNP. There are some differences

TABLE 7.1: PUBLIC EXPENDITURE IN THE UK AND GERMANY, 1975-1977 (ANNUAL AVERAGES)

	UK		Germany	
	Amount (£m)	Per cent of GNP	Amount (DM bn)	Per cent of GNP
Total public expenditure of which:	57,310	46.0	535,345	47.4
Defence	6,090	4.9	33,452	3.0
Social security	12,688	10.2	249,847	22.1
Health, sport, leisure	6,406	5.2	22,687	2.0
Education and science	7,678	6.2	62,014	4.9
Housing and environment	7,093	5.7	20,899	1.9
Transport and communications	2,739	2.2	23,722	2.1
Economic support	3,103	2.5	14,857	1.3
Law and order	1,669	1.4	16,218	1.4

NOTES: GNP is GNP at market prices. Health in the UK is largely financed by direct government payments, in Germany it is largely financed by payments of persons who are re-imbursed by the social security system. This accounts for a part of the large discrepancy between the amounts recorded as spent on social security in both countries.

Source: UK, National Income and Expenditure (Blue book) 1980; Germany, Statistiches Jahrbuch 1980

of classification between the two countries so the figures
should be regarded as showing no more than orders of
magnitude.

The structure of the public authorities differs
significantly between the two countries. In the UK
government is divided between central government and the local
authorities with the former administering the separate
national insurance fund. The local authorities are comprised
of county councils and district councils and (in the large
conurbations) metropolitan counties and metropolitan
boroughs. There is a provisional government in Northern
Ireland. In recent years the spending of central government
(including national insurance) has accounted for between two-
thirds and three-quarters of all government expenditure. The
share of revenue of the central authorities has been higher
still as the local authorities with a single property tax
(rates) as their only important direct source of revenue are
dependent on central government grants for over half their
funds. Current expenditure by local authorities is dominated
by spending on education which consumes about one half of all
current expenditure; other important items in the budget are
personal social services, law and order and upkeep of roads.
Capital expenditure is largely devoted to housing, education
and roads.

In recent years both central and local government have
been in financial deficit and in need of borrowed funds.
This was not always the case: central government has a long
period of surpluses before moving, in the mid-1970's, into
substantial deficit. The local authorities, who are
traditionally in deficit, have seen their need to borrow
fluctuate widely in recent years: it rose sharply in the
early 1970's but fell again thereafter. Part of this
borrowing is carried out in their own name and part is met
through the Public Works Loan Board which means that the
borrowing is done on their behalf by the central government.

In Germany the public authorities comprise the federal government, the Länder (state) governments and the local authorities: there are also many independent social security funds. The Länder number eleven of which eight are regions and three are self-governing city-states (Bremen, Hamburg and West Berlin). The four largest states between them account for over 70 per cent of federal GNP.

In recent years expenditure by the Länder has been slightly greater than expenditure by the federal government, whose expenditure in turn has slightly exceeded that of the local authorities. There is considerable overlap of responsibilities as only a small number of areas are specifically reserved by the Constitution for one tier of government. Defence and foreign affairs are, for obvious reasons, the prerogative of the Federal government. The main responsibilities of the Länder are education, health and welfare, law and order, and the oversight of local government. The local authorities, of which there are county councils (Kreise), boroughs (Gemeinden) and county-boroughs (Stadtkreise) are chiefly concerned with education, public utilities, public housing and social services.

The finance of the different levels of government is met partly by each having its own tax revenue and partly by each having a prescribed share of the produce of certain taxes levied nationally. Thus the Federal government receives the total product of excise taxes on petrol, tobacco and spirits and a share of the taxation of income, corporate profits and value added: the Länder receive the total product of taxes on beer, property and motor vehicles and a share of the taxation of income, corporate profits and value added: the local authorities receive the total product of local taxes on land and buildings and wages paid together with a large share of the trade tax and a small share of income tax. The shares in the divided taxes are re-negotiated from time-to-time. In addition to the sharing of taxation the Federal government makes grants to the Länder who in turn make grants to local authorities.

All three levels of government are normally in financial deficit and all borrow money in their own name. New borrowing by both central and state governments rose sharply in the early 1970's, reached a peak in 1975 but has since fallen back. New borrowing by local authorities was high in the early 1970's but it too has fallen back after 1975.

The many social security funds have their own budgets and are financed largely by the regular contributions of employees and employers and in some cases of the self-employed. Social security is highly developed in Germany and almost the whole of the workforce contributes to one or more funds. In addition the Federal government makes grants to the social security funds. For most of the 1960's and 1970's the funds collectively were in surplus but in recent years, in spite of increased contributions, they have incurred deficits and have had to run down their assets.

Finally, there are two other funds which are federally administered but whose budgets are kept separate from that of the Federal government. They are the Equalization of Burdens Fund (concerned with compensation for war damage and with re-settlement of displaced persons) and the ERP special fund (concerned with economic development and taking its initials from the post-war European Recovery Programme from which it stems). Both of these funds borrow from time to time but in recent years the sums involved have been small.

The fact of Germany being a federal state with large and important state governments has led many English-speaking observers to conclude that an active fiscal policy was not possible and that this was the reason for the supposed primacy of monetary policy. This view is out of date: Germany does have an active fiscal policy. It is worth pausing to look at the relationship between Federal and Länder governments.

Much Federal legislation involves the Länder directly in that it is they who will have to implement it. Further, new legislation cannot be enacted if it has substantial opposition among the Länder as the upper house of the bicameral Federal legislature is composed of the appointed delegates of the Länder. A majority of these delegates can reject Federal legislation. The consequence of this is that all important legislation is subject to consultation between Federal and Länder governments before it is presented to Parliament. There are regular meetings between Federal and Länder ministers and between ministers of different Länder. The result is that in most things Germany does have national policies, although they are policies which are shaped by the continuing dialogue between Federal and Länder authorities rather than being imposed from the centre.

This de-facto co-ordination of government was made explicit as far as macroeconomic policy goes in the Stabilization Law of 1967 (Gesetz zur Förderung der Stabilität and des Wachstums). By this law both Federal and Länder governments are required to concern themselves with the state of the national economy when framing policies on expenditure and taxation. Länder governments have the additional responsibility of seeing that the policies of the local authorities are also influenced by macroeconomic considerations. The 1967 Law also provided for a national advisory council on anti-cyclical policy consisting of members of Federal and Länder governments and representatives of the associations of local authorities.

It is still possible for the different branches of government to pursue contradictory policies in the event of significant differences of opinion as to what is required. However, this has not happened so far and since 1967 the main changes in anti-cyclical policy have involved all levels of government. Examples are when in 1969 both the Federal and the Länder governments agreed to sterilize some of their tax revenue in special accounts at the Bundesbank and in 1973 when all three levels of government agreed on deferring expenditure and limiting borrowing. After the quadrupling

of world oil prices at the end of 1973 policy was reversed –
again collaboratively – and public expenditure and public
borrowing rose.

2.   PUBLIC-SECTOR BORROWING

     The sums borrowed by government in total as well as by
the different levels of government are shown for the UK and
for Germany in Tables 7.2 and 7.3 respectively. The tables
also give figures of borrowing by the UK public corporations
and by the only two such national bodies in the Federal
Republic.

     If we look first at total borrowing by and on behalf of
general government (i.e. excluding those sums raised by the
UK government for on-lending to the nationalized industries)
we can see that for both countries the period covered falls
neatly into two sub-periods. In the first, covering the
1960's and early 1970's,borrowing is generally modest and,
when expressed as a percentage of GNP, is lower in the UK
than in Germany; averaging as low as 0.4 per cent of GNP in
the former and 1.3 per cent of GNP in the latter over the
twelve years to 1972. In the second sub-period from 1973
onwards things are very different: the borrowing requirement
increases sharply in both countries and becomes, in
percentage terms, greater in the UK than in Germany. In the
seven years to 1979 borrowing on behalf of government
averages no less than 4.9 per cent of GNP in the former and
3.5 per cent in the latter. In both countries borrowing
reaches a peak in 1975 as a consequence of policies to combat
the recession engendered by the earlier rises in oil prices
but falls subsequently.

     In neither country is this borrowing wholly centralised.
In Germany each authority is responsible for its own
borrowing; in the UK local authorities borrow partly via the
intermediary of the central government and partly direct from

TABLE 7.2: BORROWING BY GENERAL GOVERNMENT AND BY THE PUBLIC CORPORATIONS : UK

(£ million)

	Central government borrowing on own behalf (i)	Local authorities (ii)	Borrowing on behalf of general government		Public corporations (v)
			Total (iii)	Per cent of GNP (iv)	
1961	- 288	477	189	0.7	515
1962	- 522	567	45	0.2	502
1963	- 246	615	369	1.2	475
1964	- 314	732	418	1.2	572
1965	- 509	1,033	524	1.5	684
1966	- 845	960	115	0.3	849
1967	- 406	1,123	717	1.8	1,146
1968	- 926	1,140	214	0.5	1,081
1969	-2,345	1,159	-1,186	-2.5	741
1970	-2,246	1,238	-1,008	-2.0	1,004
1971	-1,245	1,413	168	0.3	1,235
1972	- 352	1,397	1,035	1.6	1,015
1973	573	2,365	2,938	4.0	1,253
1974	1,519	3,437	4,956	5.9	1,477
1975	5,017	2,818	7,835	7.4	2,649
1976	4,695	1,615	6,310	5.0	2,817
1977	2,607	1,592	4,199	2.9	1,796
1978	6,171	1,021	7,192	4.4	1,139
1979	6,560	2,287	8,847	4.7	3,717

NOTES: Central government borrowing on own behalf excludes borrowing by the central government on behalf of the local authorities and the public corporations. Column (iii) which is the sum of columns (i) and (ii) excludes borrowing by the central government on behalf of the public corporations. It is therefore not the same as the 'general-government borrowing requirement' which includes such borrowing. The sum of columns (iii) and (v) equals the public-sector borrowing requirement. GNP is GNP at market prices.

Source: National Income and Expenditure (Blue book) 1980 and earlier years; Economic Trends Annual Supplement 1980 and earlier years.

TABLE 7.3: BORROWING BY GENERAL GOVERNMENT AND BY TWO PUBLIC CORPORATIONS : GERMANY

(DM million)

	Federal government and federal special funds (i)	Länder (ii)	Local authorities (iii)	Social Security[1] (iv)	Borrowing on behalf of general government[1] Total (v)	Per cent of GNP (vi)	Bundesbahn and Bundespost (vii)
1961	3,583	- 792	1,636	- 4,200	227	0.1	2,204
1962	1,615	- 501	2,263	- 2,035	1,342	0.4	3,143
1963	4,326	- 73	2,618	- 2,154	4,717	1.2	3,380
1964	2,336	962	3,578	- 2,387	4,489	1.1	3,369
1965	2,337	3,110	4,580	- 2,344	7,683	1.7	1,982
1966	3,010	3,927	3,621	- 1,860	7,698	1.6	1,201
1967	8,898	3,860	2,521	3,067	18,346	3.7	1,247
1968	4,771	2,151	2,200	1,944	11,066	2.1	1,433
1969	- 961	- 568	2,477	379	1,327	0.2	2,084
1970	2,714	2,015	3,632	- 3,090	5,271	0.8	5,012
1971	2,371	5,251	7,632	- 4,636	10,618	1.4	7,895
1972	4,549	3,426	8,057	- 5,506	10,526	1.3	6,392
1973	5,805	2,499	7,019	- 6,279	8,044	0.9	4,793
1974	10,532	7,861	6,475	- 1,855	23,013	2.3	7,113
1975	37,093	19,678	8,036	4,757	69,564	6.7	2,613
1976	20,105	14,804	5,419	5,747	46,075	4.1	1,582
1977	21,028	7,778	3,515	9,870	42,191	3.5	- 540
1978	26,785	12,556	3,355	5,391	48,087	3.7	-2,890
1979	26,091	13,761	3,706	2,385	45,943	3.3	-2,448

[1] The figures cover the main pension funds and the unemployment insurance funds. These two funds account for approximately half of all German social security payments.

NOTES: GNP is GNP at market prices.

Sources: Deutsche Bundesbank : Monthly Report and Deutsches Geld-und Bankwesen in Zahlen 1876-1975

the market. The breakdown of borrowing for general government
is therefore relevant.

When we look at this breakdown for the UK it is
immediately apparent that the move into heavy and persistent
deficit in the 1970's is due entirely to the altered
performance of central government. Borrowing by the local
authorities (who are responsible for over 70 per cent of
government capital formation) rose in the three years 1973-75,
but subsequently fell to levels which, in real terms, were
below what was common in the 1960's. Central government on
the other hand has moved from a position of regular, and at
times, large surplus to one of sustained and usually large
deficit.

When we look at the breakdown of borrowing by the
different levels of government in Germany the changes are
less spectacular than in the UK. Both Federal and Länder
governments contributed to the rise in the borrowing
requirement in the mid-1970's that we have already noted.
And in both cases although borrowing has since declined it
has remained at levels that are high by the standards of
earlier years. The local authorities (responsible for about
66 per cent of government capital formation) saw their
borrowing requirements at high levels in the early 1970's
but, as occurred in the UK, these have subsequently fallen
to below the real levels of the 1960's.

The social security funds have alternated between
periods of surplus and periods of deficit. In the 1970's
the swing from large surpluses in the early years of the
decade to even larger deficits in the later years are
particularly sharp. Some increases in rates of contribution
had reduced the deficit by 1979.

Tables 7.2 and 7.3 also include figures of borrowing
by the public corporations in the UK and by the Bundesbahn
and Bundespost in Germany. Borrowing by the UK public
corporations is mostly done on their behalf by central

government: there is some small direct bank borrowing and
(at times of balance-of-payments difficulty) some officially-
inspired foreign currency borrowing. Funds raised for the
corporations by the government add directly to the borrowing
needs of the central government and give rise to exactly the
same range of assets as does government borrowing on its own
behalf. Thus in the UK it is natural to add the borrowing
needs of the public corporations to those of general
government and talk about the public sector borrowing
requirement.

New borrowing by the corporations exceeded that of
general government throughout the 1960's but since 1972 this
has no longer been the case. Borrowing fell (in real terms)
between 1971 and 1974 but was high in 1975 and 1976 and,
after falling back for two years,was again high in 1979.

In Germany there is no meaningful concept of a public
sector borrowing requirement: the line between public and
private sectors is very blurred; most publicly-owned
institutions do not belong to the Federal government;
borrowing for such institutions is decentralised and is often
carried out as if the institutions were privately-owned.
With the two federally-owned corporations, the Bundesbahn and
the Bundespost, each is responsible for its own borrowing but
the assets issued are similar to those issued by Federal and
Länder governments and afford similar liquidity to banks.
Some assets such as Treasury bonds and (prior to 1974)
Treasury bills may be re-discounted by the Bundesbank and in
addition the Bundesbank makes occasional direct loans. Hence
the borrowing requirement of these two corporations is of
potential importance for monetary policy.

Their combined borrowings were positive in all years
up to 1976 since when the large surpluses of the Bundespost
have outweighed the continuing deficits of the Bundesbahn.
The latter had modest deficits in most years during the
1960's but had to borrow more substantially in the 1970's;
the sum involved rising to over three billion DM in 1975 and

in 1976. The Bundespost, whose need to borrow was
traditionally greater, also saw its deficit rising in the
early 1970's. However, first the waiving by the Federal
government of its right to certain payments, then growing
profits from telecommunication business, have led to surpluses
in all years since 1975.

The deficits, regularly incurred by the Bundesbahn and
Bundespost, when combined usually amounted to less than one
per cent of GNP. Borrowing by the UK public corporations
has been proportionately much greater. We have already seen
that the differences in borrowing on behalf of general
government have not, in the main, been large; but in the UK
the addition of the borrowing needs of the public corporations
- met for the most part by central government borrowing on
their behalf - has meant that the mainly centrally managed
'public sector borrowing requirement' has been, relative to
GNP, much greater than in Germany. Until the early 1970's the
sums were kept down by the continuing surplus of central
government on its own transactions, which surplus partially
offset the deficits of local government and the public
corporations. But the move into heavy deficit by the central
government itself led to the need for borrowing on an
unprecedented scale, at least in peace-time. This in turn
usually meant either a rapid increase in the money supply
or periodically very high rates of interest. In Germany,
borrowing was both less and less centralised.

Before we look at how this borrowing was financed there
is one aspect of German finance which should be mentioned:
the amounts borrowed by the different authorities do not
always coincide with their respective financial deficits.
The authorities hold bank balances with the Bundesbank and/or
private banks; in some cases these are large and subject to
large variations. An example of this that we have already
mentioned was the building up by Federal and Länder
governments of special deposits at the Bundesbank in the
early 1970's and the subsequent running down of these after

1974. In this Chapter figures of borrowing relate to actual
borrowing after allowing for changes in cash balances.

3.   METHODS AND SOURCES OF BORROWING

The most significant difference between the two
countries is that in the UK the authorities, taking one year
with another, rely only modestly on the banking system as a
source of funds whereas in Germany the authorities rely very
heavily on the banking system. In the case of the local
authorities the reliance is almost total, in the case of the
Länder it is not much less so. This is something we shall
discuss in detail, but first it will be convenient to take a
brief look at the organization of public borrowing and the
assets issued in the two countries.

In the UK public borrowing is, as we have seen, highly
centralised: central government raises in its own name
most of the funds required by the public corporations and about
one half of the funds required by local government. The
result is that in recent years over three-quarters of all
public borrowing has been undertaken by central government.
It has been achieved in four main ways.

A modest contribution was made by the sale of non-
marketable debt. Of the several assets coming within this
classification the most important, in terms of funds raised,
is the savings certificate: a medium-term asset of which
new issues are made at regular intervals. Current issues
have a five-year maturity. Ordinary savings certificates bear
a fixed rate of interest but a special retirement issue which
is sold in restricted amounts to those over age 60 is index-
linked. A scheme for regular saving which is open to all
also offers index-linking within a prescribed maximum amount
saved. The ordinary department of the National Savings Bank
(operated through the Post Office) usually yields a small net
investment as does the sale of premium bonds (where prizes
drawn in a monthly lottery are a substitute for interest).

The total investment in national savings has grown
very slowly over the years. However, new terms announced in
1980 for the retirement-issue savings certificate and the
regular saving scheme have been taken by many as indicating
a more aggressive approach to selling national savings in
the future.

In the UK the central government automatically receives
the credit in respect of increases in the holding of coin and
bank notes. In normal circumstances this is a regular but
small contribution to government finance: in the inflationary
years of the 1970's it has increased greatly and in the six
years to 1979 averaged nearly £900m. per annum.

Sales of national savings and the counterpart to
increased holdings of currency have in recent years each
provided a useful but passive contribution to government
finance. The main means by which the government has actively
sought to raise funds has been through the sale of government
bonds. These bonds are, apart from three exceptions, fixed
interest stocks and are sold initially through an offer for
sale at a fixed price or by tender and then, day-by-day, with
the Bank of England offering unsold stock in the market, (see
Chapter 8). New issues are made frequently with the terms
depending on prevailing market conditions. Maturities are
varied to try to appeal to the different sections of the
market and range from 5 years for new short-term stocks to 25
years or longer for new long-term stocks.

The residual borrowing requirement is met on a week-to-
week basis by the sale of Treasury bills: these have a
maturity of 91 days and are sold at a discount set by the
market. Treasury bills and government stocks with one year
or less to maturity are reserve assets for the banks and a
large proportion of the amount outstanding is held by the
banking sector.

That part of local authority borrowing not met by
central government is financed in a variety of ways. The

most important of these is the selling of short-term debt
to banks and other financial institutions as well as, on
the lesser scale, to the non-bank public. Some quoted
stocks are issued as well as marketable short-term bonds and
important sums are raised as short-term loans from banks and
other financial institutions. The larger local authorities
are entitled to issue 91-day bills and these count as reserve
assets for the banking system.

The borrowing of the public corporations is, as we have
seen, done largely through central government. The only
exceptions to this are foreign currency borrowing and a small
amount of bank finance.

In Germany the main means of public sector borrowing is
by direct loan from banks but a number of other important
sources of finance exist. As in the UK there is a mixture of
assets aimed at the small saver, marketable bonds and
discountable short-term paper. In the first category come
Federal bonds and Federal savings bonds: the former, first
issued in 1979, earn a fixed rate of interest and have a
five-year maturity; the latter, of longer standing, have an
increasing rate of interest which is compounded and paid at
maturity, normally after a term of either 6 or 7 years.
Federal bonds are marketable and can be held by all residents;
Federal savings bonds are not marketable but can be resold to
the Federal Debt Office after they have been held for at least
one year; they may be held only by resident persons and
charitable institutions.

The Federal government does receive an automatic credit
in respect of increases in holdings of coin but unlike the UK
government does not receive such a credit for increases in
holdings of bank notes. There is some indirect credit in that
the Bundesbank, the issuer of the notes, does lend to the
Federal government as well as to the Länder governments, but
the sums involved are small. At 31st. August, 1980, when
bank notes in circulation amounted to nearly DM 81m., total
lending by the Bundesbank to both levels of government was
less than DM 13m.

As in the UK the sale of fixed interest bonds is an important source of funds. These bonds of initial terms to maturity usually between 6 and 15 years are sold by the Federal government, the Länder governments, the Bundesbahn, the Bundespost and, to a small extent, the local authorities. Interest is determined by market conditions: there is no restriction as to ownership. All of the above institutions also issue fixed interest medium-term notes with maturities from one to four years.

No ordinary Treasury bills have been issued since the early 1970's though there have been a few special issues described in Chapter 8. The Federal government sells significant quantities of discountable Treasury bonds which are similar but which have maturities of 6, 12, 18 or 24 months. These assets are also sold on a smaller scale by the Länder governments and the Bundesbahn and Bundespost. Discountable Treasury bonds have not been redeemable on demand since 1974, but they are highly liquid assets and many of them are held within the banking system.

The main interest of this Chapter is in the monetary implications of public sector borrowing so we shall now consider to what extent the finance of the public sector has, in each country been provided by the banking system. Tables 7.4 and 7.5 give this information for the UK and for Germany respectively, in both cases for the years 1965-1979. For the UK we have presented figures for the whole of public sector borrowing: for Germany, in view of the greater autonomy of the public corporations, we have distinguished between borrowing by general government and borrowing by the Bundesbahn and Bundespost. The amounts listed as borrowed from the banks include the credit to central government in respect of the increased holding of coin (both countries) and of bank notes (the UK) as well as any lending by the central bank.

TABLE 7.4: PUBLIC-SECTOR BORROWING FROM THE BANKING SYSTEM 1965-1979
UK

| | Public-sector borrowing | | |
| | Total | From banks | |
		Amount	Per cent
1965	1,208	613	50.7
1966	964	279	28.9
1967	1,860	695	37.4
1968	1,295	181	14.0
1969	- 445	- 227	(51.0)
1970	- 4	1,234	-
1971	1,403	1,939	138.2
1972	2,050	- 531	- 25.9
1973	4,191	2,300	54.9
1974	6,433	1,410	21.9
1975	10,484	4,195	40.0
1976	9,127	1,098	12.0
1977	5,995	3,363	56.1
1978	8,331	914	11.0
1979	12,564	1,752	13.9
		Overall percentage	29.4

NOTES: The figures include increases in public holding of notes
and coin.

Source: National Income and Expenditure (Blue book) 1977-1980, Bank of
England Quarterly Bulletin.

TABLE 7.5: PUBLIC-SECTOR BORROWING FROM THE BANKING SYSTEM 1965-1979 : GERMANY

| | Borrowing by general government | | | Borrowing by the Bundesbahn and the Bundespost | | |
| | Total | From banks | | Total | From banks | |
		Amount	Per cent		Amount	Per cent
1965	10,029	6,563	65.4	1,982	1,393	70.3
1966	9,557	6,863	71.8	1,201	1,090	90.8
1967	15,279	14,345	93.9	1,247	2,115	169.6
1968	9,122	9,484	104.0	1,433	2,083	145.4
1969	948	2,242	236.5	2,084	2,100	100.8
1970	8,362	6,948	83.1	5,012	3,071	61.3
1971	15,254	10,464	68.6	7,895	5,268	66.7
1972	16,033	9,132	57.0	6,392	4,748	74.3
1973	15,321	13,513	88.2	4,793	3,128	65.3
1974	24,869	18,974	76.3	7,113	5,638	79.3
1975	64,806	51,587	79.6	2,613	5,039	192.8
1976	42,329	28,835	71.5	1,582	- 691	- 43.7
1977	32,322	25,939	80.3	- 540	- 632	(117.0)
1978	42,695	36,330	85.1	- 2,890	- 1,269	(43.9)
1979	43,558	27,830	64.5	- 2,448	- 1,637	(66.9)
Overall per cent			76.7			83.9

Notes: The figures for borrowing by central government include increases in public holding of coin

Source: Deutsche Bundesbank, Monthly Report

The greater reliance of the authorities in Germany on bank finance is immediately apparent. In the 15 years covered by Tables 7.4 and 7.5 over 75 per cent of borrowing by general government in that country was met by the banking system and in only one year out of the 15 did the banks provide less than 60 per cent of general government borrowing. This may be contrasted with the position in the UK where in only one year in the 15 did the banks provide more than 60 per cent of public sector borrowing and where on average the banks met less than 30 per cent of this borrowing. Table 7.5 also shows that the two Federal German public corporations have met their borrowing needs from the banking system to an even greater extent than has German government.

It is interesting to consider the behaviour of the different parts of the public sector. As far as the UK is concerned most of the public sector borrowing from banks is accounted for by the central government; the local authorities have borrowed irregularly from the banks although in some years the absolute amounts have been large; recourse to bank finance by the public corporations has been erratic but has usually been relatively small.

Prior to 1971 both central and local government relied heavily on the banking system for their borrowing needs, subsequently both levels of government relied on the banks much less relative to non-bank finance. In 1972 the banks, enjoying a new freedom over their asset portfolios following the monetary policy changes of the previous year, substantially reduced their holdings of government bonds; and whilst subsequent years saw large absolute amounts lent to both central and local government these sums represented on average a smaller proportion of government borrowing than in the years to 1971. (See Chapter 1.)

In Germany all three tiers of government continued to rely heavily on bank borrowing throughout the 1970's. In the case of the Länder and the local authorities this was particularly marked in the decade of the 1970's when just over 80 per cent of all borrowing by the Länder was from the banks whilst for the local authorities total bank borrowing exceeded their total borrowing requirement allowing re-payment of other debt. The share of Federal government borrowing in the same period accounted for by borrowing from the banking system was 61 per cent.

It should be pointed out that much of the bank lending to the Länder and to the local authorities comes from savings banks many of which are owned by local authorities and all of which are connected to regional Landesbanken-Girozentralen which are partially owned by the Länder.

It is clear there is a significant difference here in government finance in the UK and in Germany. In the former in recent years there have been strenuous efforts to limit official borrowing from the banking system with the consequence of high (nominal) rates of interest and the complete crowding out of private firms from the long-term bond market.[1] In Germany the authorities, faced with smaller relative deficits, have been content to rely heavily on the banking system. This has occurred without any expansion of the money supply that would be considered large by UK standards. The reason for this can be put simply: the German banking system, as is shown in Chapter 2, is the dominant part of the German capital market, its liabilities (of which there is a much broader range than in the UK) are much larger as a share of total financial sector liabilities and as a proportion of GNP than is the case in the UK. The consequence is that large absolute increases in these liabilities are compatible with small percentage increases in the money supply.

---

1.   This would also be due to the uncertainty caused by high and variable rates of inflation.

That bank liabilities in Germany are so much larger
relative to GNP than in the UK and that public sector borrowing
is that much smaller relative to GNP than in the UK means that
the problem of the finance of the public sector is much less
in Germany: the demands of the public sector are less, the
capacity of the banking sector to meet these in a non-
inflationary way is much greater. We have already seen
(Tables 7.2 and 7.3) the difference in borrowing by the
public sectors in the two countries, the difference in
relative size and importance of the two banking systems can
be shown simply. In the five years 1975-1979 total resident
liabilities of the UK banking system averaged 35.3 per cent
of GNP: in Germany the comparable figure was 108.3 per cent.
This means that the scope for credit creation by banks without
any rapid growth in the money supply is roughly three times as
great in Germany as it is in the UK. What has actually
happened is shown in Table 7.6 which shows the amounts of
bank credit granted in both countries for the years 1964-1979
and expresses these amounts as percentages of gross national
product. It can be seen that over the period total domestic
lending by German banks averaged 8.3 per cent of GNP whilst
such lending by UK banks as a percentage of GNP averaged only
just over half as much. And this was over a period when the
money supply was growing slightly faster in the UK than in
Germany. (See Chapter 9.)

The proportion of total bank lending accounted for by
lending to the public authorities in the two countries was
not too dissimilar although it was larger in Germany. In the
years 1964-1979 lending to general government accounted for
25 per cent of all lending to resident non-banks in Germany.
Over the same period lending to the public sector in the UK
absorbed just under 20 per cent of all lending to resident
non-banks in that country.

It is evident then that it is the greater size of the
German banking system which permits it to provide more credit
both to government and to private sector without this

TABLE 7.6: BANK LENDING IN THE UK AND GERMANY

	UK : total domestic lending		Germany : total domestic lending	
	Amount £m	Per cent of GNP	Amount DM.m	Per cent of GNP
1964	608	1.8	31,224	7.4
1965	936	2.6	34,606	7.6
1966	272	0.7	27,911	5.7
1967	1,204	3.0	32,224	6.5
1968	854	1.9	42,064	7.9
1969	224	0.5	52,808	8.8
1970	2,228	4.3	50,771	7.5
1971	3,522	6.1	69,680	9.2
1972	5,408	8.4	88,482	10.7
1973	8,823	11.9	65,180	7.0
1974	5,372	6.4	61,246	6.2
1975	3,503	3.3	78,889	7.6
1976	3,675	2.9	96,307	8.6
1977	7,085	5.0	95,800	8.0
1978	5,500	3.3	122,589	9.5
1979	10,436	5.5	140,905	10.1
Average per cent		4.6		8.3

Notes: GNP is GNP at market prices

Source: UK, Financial Statistics; Germany, Monthly Report of the Deutsche Bundesbank

entailing large increases in the money supply. But it is not only a question of size: banks in Germany have a much broader range of liabilities than do those in the UK and in consequence, they are less dependent on the growth of strictly monetary liabilities.

This difference is sufficiently marked that it is worth looking briefly at the ways in which German banks raise funds. The largest single source is savings deposits: these may be ordinary savings deposits or premium savings deposits attracting an interest bonus from the Federal government. The former are, in principle, subject to notice of withdrawal, typically three or six months, but in practice can usually be withdrawn quickly although possibly at some cost in interest. The latter must normally be held for a period of six to seven years. Another important source of funds is the sale of savings certificates of deposit with maturities of not less than four years and savings bonds with maturities of five to twelve years. Also the savings banks and the Landesbanken-Girozentralen finance some of their lending to general government through the issue of Treasury bonds; these have maturities of one to four years.

Time deposits are issued as in the UK, but unlike such deposits with UK banks which are mostly at seven days notice those with German banks are mostly for a period of several years. Officially classified sight deposits account for little more than 10 per cent of all liabilities to non-bank residents. All this stands in sharp contrast to the UK where the vast majority of liabilities, other than a small amount of capital and reserves, are at sight, at seven-days notice, or, in the case of certificates of deposit, with an initial maturity of three months.

Finally, it is worth noting that the borrowing by the authorities from their domestic banks involves the banks acquiring different assets in the two countries with different consequences for their future ability to create credit. In the UK where monetary control has involved the use of a reserve asset ratio comprised - directly or indirectly - to a large extent of public sector assets, borrowing by the public authorities has provided the reserve assets necessary. The issue of Treasury bills and short bonds is particularly important here. This is not to say that it has been the availability of reserve assets which has caused the expansion of bank lending in the UK in some mechanistic textbook way: the UK authorities have recently denied that they have sought to control the banks directly through control of their reserve assets.[1] However, the supply of reserve assets has not been without all consequence: the authorities state that, for most of the 1970's, they have relied on variations in interest rates to discourage excessive bank lending, and their ability to bring about the interest-rate levels they wished has depended in part on the reserve assets that it was profitable for the banks to obtain. Hence, there was some necessity to try to limit these, hence the need for funding and the regular fluctuations in rates of interest to encourage bond sales.

In Germany the position is very different: there the Bundesbank controls the banks through a cash ratio[2] and hence sales of assets by the public authorities to the banks do not, of themselves, create any easing of credit conditions for the banks: rather it is the reverse, in times of high demand for credit lending by the banks to the public authorities means less lending to private borrowers. Thus logically - much bank lending in Germany to the public authorities is just classified along with other bank loans

---

1.   Green Paper on Monetary Control, Cmnd. 7858, March 1980.

2.   The means of control is termed the Central bank money stock and is defined as banks' required reserves (calculated as the sum of different proportions of different types of liabilities) less the minimum reserve requirement on external liabilities plus currency with the non-bank public. (See Chapters 2 and 9).

and does not create any specific assets. Admittedly some
loans are provided to both the Federal government and to the
Länder by way of the purchase of short-term re-discountable
bonds, and the re-discounting of these does provide the banks
with extra cash. However, banks are each subject to a limit
on the quantity of such assets they can re-discount at the
central bank so any increase in the issue of such assets is
of limited importance for monetary policy. It is worth
noting that in 1975 far from causing a problem borrowing by
the public authorities from the banking system was seen by
the Bundesbank as having been a good thing: the bank stated
that:

> "in a situation like that of 1975 monetary policy
> would have been unable to achieve a specific
> monetary growth without the help of fiscal policy".

The demand for credit by private borrowers was low:
without public borrowing the increase in the money supply
would have been below target.

In conclusion we can state that public sector borrowing
has very different monetary effects in the UK and in Germany.
In the former it is seen as a problem, in the latter it has
not generally been thought of as such. This difference
stems from three things. In Germany the need to borrow
(related to GNP) is much less. In Germany the ability of the
banking system to provide non-inflationary credit is that
much greater. And finally, the methods of monetary control
in Germany mean that government borrowing from the banking
system does not have any implications of making the banks
better able to expand lending to the private sector.

CHAPTER 8:   THE BANKS AND CAPITAL MARKETS
By E. Victor Morgan

1.   INTRODUCTION

Strongly contrasting features of the UK and German
systems are the role of financial markets in the economy,
and the role of banks in the markets. The greater importance
of direct bank lending in Germany obviously implies a smaller
role for financial markets, though it is impossible to say
whether direct lending acquired its present position because
of the relative weakness of markets, or whether the direct
facilities provided by banks (and their close relations with
customers) inhibited the growth of markets. The development
of short-term markets has also been influenced, as will be
shown below, by differences in structure and operations
between the Bank of England and the Deutsche Bundesbank.
The London short-term markets are far larger and more
sophisticated than those of Germany or any other European
country, and are dominated by the banks. Long-term
markets are also relatively more important in the UK, though
the difference in scale is much less marked. There are,
however, big differences in organisation and in the role of
the banks. German banks play a central part in both the
primary and secondary markets for long-term securities, but
the operations of UK banks in these markets are much more
limited.

2.   UK SHORT-TERM MARKETS

As noted in Chapter 1, the short-term sterling markets
involving UK banks are:-

- The money market.
- The market in bills of exchange.
- The inter-bank loan market.
- The market in sterling certificates of
  deposit (CDs), and
- The market in short-term local authority debt.

The very large markets in CDs and in short- and medium-term loans in foreign currencies are outside the scope of this study.

Direct loans between local authorities and between companies are also arranged through brokers. Little is known about these markets, but they are generally believed to be small. They are of some relevance to the banking system, since they provide an alternative to bank deposits for large lenders, and an alternative to overdrafts (or term loans) for borrowers. The fact that the markets have remained small is largely due to competition among banks, which has kept down the margin between borrowing and lending rates in large transactions. However, the existence of direct markets, at least as potential competitors, imposes an additional constraint on bank margins.

The money market

The money market is a market in very short-term loans, mostly at call. The lenders are banks and the borrowers, discount houses and "money brokers" on the stock exchange (see below). Traditionally the London clearing banks were the dominant lenders but other banks have increased their participation and now provide about half of all loans. The Bank of England influences the amount which other banks have to lend by various types of open-market operations, but does not come directly into the money market except as "lender of last resort". Loans are secured by the deposit of bills or short-term government bonds as collateral and are still arranged largely "face-to-face", with representatives of the discount houses calling on the lending banks.

When a clearing bank makes a loan in the money market, the borrower receives a draft on the lending bank's account at the Bank of England. The lending bank's balance with the central bank is thus reduced automatically by the amount of the loan. When the lender is a non-clearer, there is a reduction in its balance with its clearing bank and an equal reduction in the clearer's balance with the Bank of England. The market is thus essentially one in balances at the Bank of England, though the fractional reserve principle operates here as elsewhere, and loans in the market are approximately ten times the amount of banker's balances at the central bank.

The discount houses act as intermediaries between the banks and the central bank. Unlike German banks, UK banks do not normally borrow directly from the central bank. Instead, as described in Chapter 1, they replenish their balances at the Bank of England, when necessary by calling in loans from the money market, the discount houses seek to meet these repayments by borrowing from other banks and, if they fail, go to the Bank of England as lender of last resort.

The market is the focal point for Bank of England operations. Any payment into the Bank, whether as a result of its own operations or of transactions between the private sector and the government, reduces bankers' balances, reduces the supply of money market loans and raises interest rates; any out-payments from the bank have the opposite effect. The rates actually prevailing can thus fluctuate considerably during the working day but are normally below the Bank of England's minimum lending rate (MLR).

The bill markets

Prior to the growth of the markets in inter-bank loans, certificates of deposit and local authority debt (often called "parallel" markets) the discount houses employed the funds that they borrowed in the money market in discounting Treasury bills and commercial bills of exchange, and in holding short-term government bonds. The discount houses have now extended their activities much more widely, but the bill markets are still those most closely related to the money market.

The bill markets operate both as "primary" and "secondary" markets. The sale of new bills is a source of finance for the Treasury, to a limited extent for local authorities, and for private industry and trade. Treasury bills are issued by tender with the discount houses "covering the tender", as described in Chapter 1. Commercial bills may be discounted initially either by a discount house or by a bank.

The main holders of both Treasury bills and commercial bills are banks and discount houses, and the secondary market consists mainly of transactions between these institutions. The discount houses act as "market makers", being prepared to deal either way. There are, however, significant amounts of bills held outside the banking system and these holdings can go up sharply when bank lending is restricted as it was, for example, by the operation of the "corset" during the first half of 1980.

The Inter-bank and CD markets

These markets can be considered together. The difference between an ordinary deposit and a CD is that the latter provides the lender with a certificate that can be sold, at an appropriate discount, if cash is required before it matures. Because of this extra liquidity, CD rates tend to be fractionally below those on inter-bank deposits of the same maturity, but the two move very closely together. Deposits traded in the inter-bank market range in maturity from overnight to two years, though much the greater part are for less than a year. CDs have a minimum maturity of three months. The inter-bank market is a "primary" market only since deposits once made, cannot be sold but must be left with the borrowing bank until they mature. There is an active secondary market in CDs with the discount houses acting as market makers.

These markets originally developed among the non-clearing banks, and especially the overseas banks which were coming to London in large numbers during the 1960's and early 1970's. The clearers have now come to participate on a substantial scale but they still provide less than a third of inter-bank loans, compared with half of call loans in the money market (Table 8.1). Unlike the money market, the inter-bank market is entirely a telephone market and loans are unsecured. Each bank, however, has limits on the amount of credit that it is prepared to extend to each other bank in the system, depending on size and status.

The figures in Table 8.1 are gross, i.e. they show each bank's lending to other banks, but not its borrowing from them. Individual banks will be net borrowers if the total of their deposits from other sources falls short of the loans they wish to make, and vice-versa. They may be both borrowers and lenders if they wish to improve the maturity "match" between their assets and liabilities (see below). Table 8.2 shows the net position of the major groups. The London clearing banks and Scottish banks are large net lenders, the Northern Ireland banks, American banks, "other foreign" and consortium banks are net borrowers, while the accepting houses and other UK banks are roughly in balance.

The Bank of England does not operate as lender of last resort in the inter-bank or CD markets, so there is nothing to prevent rates from rising above MLR. Normally the gap, in either direction, is not very great but in times of exceptional stringency overnight rates can rise to very high levels. Rates of up to 200 per cent per annum were occasionally paid for overnight money during 1980. High rates in the inter-bank market can give rise to the anomaly known as "round tripping". Bank base rates are usually the same as, or very close to MLR, and very large companies can get overdrafts at 1 percentage point above base rate. Hence, if inter-bank rates go much higher than one per cent above MLR it pays such companies to borrow from one bank on overdraft

TABLE 8.1: UK BANKS' HOLDINGS OF STERLING MARKET ASSETS, JUNE 1980.

£m.

	Call Money	Treasury Bills	Other Bills	Inter-Bank Loans	CDs	Local Authorities	Other Market Loans	TOTAL
London clearing banks	1,854	487	1,015	6,253	529	361	76	10,575
Scottish and Northern Ireland banks	307	150	100	722	46	78	92	1,495
Accepting houses	202	57	133	1,397	428	512	209	2,938
Other UK banks	591	157	367	6,693	1,338	1,175	679	11,000
American banks	275	250	156	1,486	495	355	233	3,250
Japanese banks	46	8	2	214	-	9	7	286
Other foreign banks	431	78	148	2,410	165	612	365	4,209
Consortium banks	41	11	17	397	116	164	52	798
TOTAL	3,747	1,198	1,938	19,572	3,117	3,266	1,713	34,551

Source: Bank of England, Quarterly Bulletin, September 1980.

TABLE 8.2: STERLING INTER-BANK LOANS AND CDs. (AMOUNTS OUTSTANDING, JUNE 1980)

£m.

	INTER-BANK MARKET		CD MARKET	
	Deposits with Other Banks	Deposits from Other Banks	CDs Held	Own CDs Sold
London clearing banks	6,253	3,195	529	183
Scottish & Northern Ireland banks	722	720	46	326
Accepting houses	1,397	1,369	428	123
Other UK banks	6,693	6,694	1,338	883
American banks	1,486	3,448	495	1,244
Japanese banks	214	418	-	8
Other foreign banks	2,410	2,931	165	401
Consortium banks	397	553	116	29

Source: Bank of England, _Quarterly Bulletin_, September 1980.

and re-lend, through another bank, in the wholesale market.
This practice, when it occurs, creates an artificial increase
in the rate of growth of the money stock ($\pounds M_3$)

Local authority debt

Local authorities borrow in this market for periods
ranging from overnight to a year. From the point of view of
the lender, these loans are very close substitutes for
deposits of similar maturity and so rates follow closely
those in the inter-bank market. Lenders are mainly banks,
but some industrial and commercial companies also use the
market as a way of holding temporary surpluses.

Operation of the system

The existence of this large volume of short-term assets
traded in active markets has important advantages for the
banks but also poses some problems for the monetary authorities.

The banks have a number of very convenient vehicles for
holding of "second-line" reserves, i.e. reserves that are not
cash but can very easily be turned into cash. Any individual
bank can thus easily maintain a highly liquid position. It
can hold assets that mature overnight yet still earn interest;
it can choose the maturity structure of its portfolio since
there is a plentiful supply of assets maturing on every
working day for a year or more ahead; and if, in spite of
this, it should run short of cash it can easily sell CDs or
borrow in the inter-bank market.

The system also offers the individual bank the
opportunity of "matching" the maturity dates of assets and
liabilities. For example, any bank that felt the average
maturity of its assets was too long in relation to its
liabilities could sell, say, six month CDs and lend the
proceeds overnight in the inter-bank market. This is, of

course, only one of a number of transactions that would produce the same effect.

However, neither of these effects of the operation of short-term financial markets apply to the system as a whole. The maturity pattern of assets and liabilities of the banking system as a whole vis-a-vis the rest of the community is determined by transactions between banks and non-banks, not between one bank and another. It is one of the functions of a banking system to lend at longer term than it borrows and, so long as the degree of "mis-matching" is not too great this can be done quite safely. Active markets in short-term assets can increase the amount of "mis-matching" that the system as a whole can safely undertake by reducing the chance that "excessive" mis-matching by an individual bank could produce losses or default that would shake public confidence in the system and so endanger other banks.

Similar reasoning applies to liquidity. The ultimate means of payment in the whole economic system are notes and coin and balances with the Bank of England. At any point in time the stock of these assets is fixed and the only source of an increase is the central bank. By providing alternative assets that an individual can quickly turn into central bank money, the financial markets economise on the holding of such money and so increase its velocity of circulation. They also ensure that, when individual needs arise, they are quickly met and this again contributes to the stability of the system as a whole. However, if the system as a whole became seriously short of cash, assets that are normally readily saleable would cease to be so, and only the Bank of England could ease the situation.

There is thus a risk that the very efficiency of the market system could endanger stability either by encouraging banks to hold assets that were too long in relation to their liabilities, or by building too large a pyramid of credit on too small a cash base. The "secondary banking" crisis of 1973-74 gave a warning of these potential dangers and led to closer supervision over solvency and liquidity as described in Chapter 10.

The size and efficiency of the markets also poses problems for monetary policy. Under the system that has operated since 1971, banks are required to hold 12.5 per cent of their "eligible liabilities" in a specified group of "reserve assets", (see Chapter 1). Reserve assets include call money, Treasury bills and (subject to some restrictions) commercial bills, but not CDs, inter-bank deposits or short-term local authority debt. Hence, for example, if a bank lends call money to a discount house which then buys CDs, the total amount of reserve assets is increased. There are a number of ways in which this kind of transaction can impair the central bank's control over the total volume of reserve assets, and this is one of the reasons why the Bank of England has made little use of the reserve base as a control instrument, and why proposals for change are now being discussed.

A solution to this problem that has been widely canvassed is that the Bank of England should, like the Bundesbank, concentrate on controlling the stock of central bank money. An argument against such a policy that has been put forward by the Bank of England is that the liquidity of the system depends, as already noted, on the Bank's presence as lender of last resort. Unlimited availability of "last resort" loans would impair control over the stock of central bank money, while if the facility were restricted, as it is in Germany, it is feared that the stability of the markets might be undermined. Another school of thought maintains this dilemma is illusory, and that unlimited last resort facilities can be reconciled with control over the stock of central bank money provided that the bank follows its traditional policy of keeping MLR above the money market rate. Holders of this view believe that the existence of broad and active short-term markets is positively helpful in that the effect of central bank actions is quickly transmitted to a great volume of borrowing and lending transactions.

3.   GERMAN SHORT-TERM MARKETS

The main components of German short-term financial
markets are borrowing and lending transactions between banks,
other than the Bundesbank, and transactions between the
Bundesbank and other banks in a number of short-term
obligations generally known as "money market paper". The
two markets are closely connected, as are the money market
and the bill market in London, and in German literature
they are often discussed together under the common name of
"the money market". They are, however, conceptually
separate and, when we need to distinguish them, they will
be referred to here as "the money market" and "the paper
market" respectively. Dealings between banks, other than
the central bank, in money market paper are only on a small
scale. There are also some transactions between banks in
bills of exchange, short-term bonds and "Schuldschein" notes.
Finally, it should be noted that the central institutions of
the savings banks and co-operative banks provide their
members with facilities for short-term borrowing and for the
investment of surplus funds that are a substitute for those
provided by markets. (See Chapter 2).

The evolution and operation of the German market has
been influenced in several ways by the structure and policy
of the Bundesbank. Here, three differences between the two
countries should be noted. Firstly, the Bundesbank has
branches in all the lander capitals and in a number of major
cities, which provide a clearing service for the commercial
banks, provide re-discount and lombard facilities, and
conduct open-market operations. The German market is thus
much less centralised than the UK, and there is less need
for inter-bank transactions. Secondly, the Bundesbank does
not operate the kind of multiple reserve system that is
operated by the Bank of England; bank reserves have to be
kept in balances with the central bank and, since 1974, the
Bundesbank has set targets for the rate of growth of the
central bank money stock, and it regards these targets as a
key element in its monetary policy. Thirdly, the Bundesbank

restricts its obligations as lender of last resort by
imposing rediscount quotas on the banks.   These
are fixed in relation to bank size but are varied "across
the board" from time to time as an instrument of policy.
Lombard loans are made available at the discretion of the
Bundesbank.

The money market

In principle the money market is open to any
bank, but in practice only about 200 deal on any
significant scale.   Tne "big three" commercial banks
play an important role;   all three have money market
departments in Frankfurt and Düsseldorf, and the Dresdener
Bank and Commerzbank also operate in Hamburg.   The larger
regional and private banks also have strong positions but
many of the smaller banks make little use of the market for
several reasons.   Some of them keep accounts with larger
banks and can meet short-term fluctuations in their deposits
or their lending by building up or running down balances in
these accounts.   The legal provisions restricting the
maximum size of loans in relation to a bank's capital are an
impediment for very small banks, since money market
transactions are in multiples of DM 1m.   In other cases,
lack of technical expertise may prevent a bank from entering
the market.

The mortgage banks are prominent in the market as are
the Girozentralen of the savings banks.   The Girozentralen
offer fixed rates for deposits from the member banks (though
some of the larger ones are able to negotiate) and savings
banks normally deposit their surplus funds with their
Girozentrale. Loans from Girozentralen to member banks have
shown a tendency to rise but are much smaller than the inflow
of deposits so the Girozentralen are large investors on the
money market.   The co-operative banks, many of which are very

small, deposit surplus funds with their Zentralkassen, but do
not borrow from them; the Zentralkassen, in turn, deposit
with the Deutsche Genossenschaftsbank in Frankfurt, and it
is through this bank that the surplus funds of the
co-operative banks enter the market. The Kredidanstalt für
Wiederaufbau is in a special position since it is used at
times by the Bundesbank to channel central bank funds into
the market as an alternative to direct open-market operations.

Both day-to-day loans (Tagesgeld) and time deposits
(Termingeld) are traded in the market. Day-to-day loans may
be either strictly overnight or for fixed periods of up to
thirty days (terminiertes Tagesgeld). Time deposits are
generally for periods of one month to a year, though some
deposits are for longer periods. Both types of deposit are
normally traded in multiples of DM 1m. The market is entirely
by telephone (though with written confirmation) and operates
for only a short period (normally 10.0 to 11.30) each working
day. Loans are unsecured when made between institutions of
equal standing, though security may be required by a large
bank depositing with a smaller one. As in the London inter-
bank market, banks have limits on the amounts they will lend.
Nevertheless, some banks incurred substantial losses in the
collapse of I.D. Herstatt KGaA in 1974 and this led to a
re-assessment of credit risks.

The German money market combines some of the functions
of the money market and the inter-bank market in London.
Since all transactions are settled through the Bundesbank
clearing system, the market redistributes the stock of
central bank money. Transactions at the short end are made
primarily for this purpose, with banks that have "free"
reserves lending to those which are having difficulty in
meeting their reserve requirements. At the same time the
market offers individual banks the opportunity of correcting
"mis-matches" between the maturity structure of assets and
liabilities, and of meeting differences between the inflow

of deposits and the demand for loans. There are no statistics of the scale of operations in the market[1] but it is known that the mortgage banks and the central institutions of the savings banks and co-operatives banks are net lenders. The "big banks" are believed to be in a roughly balanced position, while the regional and private banks tend to be net borrowers.

The paper market

The market in "money market paper" is a primary market for the finance of public authorities, and also the vehicle through which the Bundesbank conducts its open-market operations. As already noted, transactions are almost all between the Bundesbank on one side and individual banks on the other; inter-bank transactions are only small.

The most important assets traded, in terms of amount outstanding, are Unverzinsliche Schatzanweisungen (generally known as U-Schätze). The name is translated by the Bundesbank as "Treasury bonds", though they are in fact book entries in a Bundesbank register; the holder does not receive any certificate of title. They are issued by the Bundesbank on behalf of the Federal Ministry of Finance, the railways and the post office. At times in the past, they have also been issued on behalf of Länder and other public authorities. They are normally issued in multiples of DM 100,000 and with maturities of 6, 12, 18 or 24 months.

Treasury bonds are of two kinds, one of which carries an automatic re-purchase obligation by the Bundesbank, the other not. Bonds carrying the re-purchase obligation are shown in the Bundesbank statistics as, "included in the market-regulating arrangements", and carry a somewhat lower

---

1. The Bundesbank publishes figures of inter-bank deposits but these include many deposits that are not traded in the market.

rate of interest. Since the adoption of targets for the
central bank money stock in 1974, the Bundesbank has tried
to get rid of automatic re-purchase obligations, and this
type of bond is now issued mainly to public authorities who
are not likely to demand re-payment. The Bundesbank has
stated that bonds with automatic repurchase obligations are,
"on principle, not made available to banks". Nevertheless
no significant market in Treasury bonds has developed apart
from direct dealings between banks and the Bundesbank.

When bonds are sold, the account of the purchasing
bank with the Bundesbank will be debited and that of the
public authority credited. However, the reverse occurs when
the proceeds are spent so that issues of bonds have only a
very temporary effect on bank reserves.

Statistics of Treasury bonds include Finance Bonds
(Finanzierungschätze), which are sold only to non-banks in
units of DM 1,000 to DM 100,000, and which are not traded in
the market. They are, therefore, excluded from the figures
given in Table 8.3.

Treasury bills were an important component of money
market paper in the 1950's but ordinary bills have not been
issued since 1973. Bills are still issued as "mobilisation
paper" (see below), mainly to foreign central banks. Very
short-term bills with maturities of four to ten days are
also offered to domestic banks at times when the Bundesbank
wishes to mop-up surplus funds in the money market.

The constitution of the Bundesbank does not allow it
to issue paper in its own name and at times problems have
arisen from a lack of sufficient paper for the conduct of
open-market operations. In 1957, the bank came to an
arrangement with the government under which it could convert
a claim on the government dating from the 1948 monetary

TABLE 8.3: MONEY MARKET PAPER IN CIRCULATION[a]
(DMm. at end of year)

Year	Treasury Bills	Treasury Bonds [b]	Mobilisation and Liquidity Paper	Treasury Notes [c]
1960	199	1,624	5,203	(1,308)
1961	182	1,296	5,292	(972)
1962	187	1,283	3,769	(1,595)
1963	344	1,146	4,690	(1,556)
1964	400	1,297	2,599	(2,241)
1965	875	1,547	1,064	(2,609)
1966	1,452	3,185	878	(2,420)
1967	205	8,633	2,245	4,905
1968	151	9,129	2,534	5,983
1969	200	3,060	2,029	5,659
1970	300	2,400	7,532	5,227
1971	0	2,274	6,477	5,550
1972	100	2,038	4,465	5,914
1973	300	1,425	9,860	(5,399)
1974	0	6,291	8,867	(5,395)
1975	0	13,242	4,173	(8,543)
1976	0	8,106	6,476	(13,017)
1977	0	7,732	5,366	(21,450)
1978	0	7,333	13,205	(26,261)
1979	0	5,928	6,687	(21,872)

NOTES: a Excluding bills of exchange, prime acceptances, etc.

b Excluding Federal financing bonds.

c Data are in brackets for those years in which Treasury notes were not officially money market paper, even though the Bundesbank traded in them as part of its open market operations in the capital market.

Source: Deutsche Bundesbank, Monatsberichte, various issues.

reform into money market paper up to a maximum of DM 8.1bn. These issues are known as "mobilisation paper" (Mobilisierungspapiere). A law of 1967, authorised an additional facility of the same kind for DM 8bn., known as "liquidity paper" (Liquiditätspapiere). Both mobilisation and liquidity paper can be issued either as Treasury bills or Treasury bonds but, apart from the special uses of bills noted above, issues have normally been in bonds. Though issues are technically on behalf of the government, the proceeds are not transferred to government account and then disbursed, like those of ordinary Treasury bonds; instead, they are retained by the Bundesbank. Hence, new issues withdraw central bank money from the market and re-payment of maturing issues has the opposite effect.

Medium-term Treasury notes were also used as money market paper from 1967 to 1972. Even when they have not been officially classified as money market paper, the Bundesbank has used them in market operations. Table 8.3 shows the circulation of these assets at the end of each year from 1960 to 1979. The importance of mobilisation and liquidity paper is clear, especially at times when the volume of bond issues is low.

Various kinds of bills of exchange also serve as market paper. A consortium of banks, including the Bundesbank, have established a company, Privatdiskont AG, for the purpose of dealing in high quality bills, mostly originating in international trade. Bills eligible for re-discount by this company are known as Privatdiskonten, translated by the Bundesbank as "prime acceptances". The Bundesbank has established a special re-discount quota for Privatdiskont AG which at the time of writing stood at DM 2.5bn. A bank which is a shareholder in the company and which holds prime acceptances can either sell them to the Bundesbank (against its own re-discount quota) or sell them to the company. Sales to Privatdiskont thus enable banks to acquire central bank money without using up their re-discount quota. Privatdiskont in turn can re-discount with the Bundesbank,

though subject to a re-purchase obligation, which the
Bundesbank occasionally enforces. The Bundesbank also
re-discounts ordinary bills of exchange that satisfy its
eligibility conditions.

The operation of the system

In principle there is no reason why any bank that has
a re-discount account with the Bundesbank should not trade
in money market paper, but there is no necessity for all
banks to do so. In practice savings banks and co-operative
banks do not deal, though their central institutions do.

The Bundesbank uses open-market operations in money
market paper in essentially the same way as do other
central banks. Purchases of such assets increase, and sales
reduce, the stock of central bank money in the hands of the
banking system; this directly affects short-term interest
rates in the money market and, indirectly, the cost and
availability of bank credit and the growth rate of the money
stock. The technical details of these operations are,
however, influenced by the structure of the market already
described and by the other control instruments that the
Bundesbank uses. These include re-discount and lombard
(short-term loan) rates; variable reserve requirements, and
re-discount and lombard quotas for individual banks,
(see Chapters 2 and 9).

Since 1977 new issues of Treasury bonds have been made
by tender but, with this one exception, the Bundesbank
announces the rates at which it is prepared to buy or sell
various types of paper and leaves the banks to determine the
amounts in which they will deal. The Bundesbank tends to use
a combination of open-market operations and other instruments
that keeps the rate for loans at call in the money market a
little above its discount rate but lower than Lombard rate.
At times when the market is very liquid (often because of an
inflow of foreign capital) the call money rate may fall below

discount rate but then the Bundesbank usually sets a "floor"
by offering very short-term paper at attractive yields.
Conversely, when liquidity is very tight and re-discount and
Lombard quotas have been heavily used, the call money rate
may rise above the Lombard rate, and this has frequently
happened during the past three years.

4.   UK LONG-TERM MARKETS

The primary market in gilt-edged

The primary market in government securities is
organised by the Bank of England. Securities (often called
"stocks")usually carry a fixed rate of interest ("Coupon")
per £100 of nominal value, though recently there have been
a few issues of variable rate stocks with interest linked to
the discount rate on Treasury bills. Maturities are usually
in the range of five to twenty five years, though both
longer and shorter maturities are occasionally issued.
Issues are normally made at a fixed price, commonly at par
but sometimes at a discount. Another recent innovation has
been the offer of stock by tender, subject to a minimum price.
Issues are usually made in blocks of £500m. to £1,000m. and
sometimes more. The whole amount is rarely sold on the
application date and the unsold balance is taken into one of
the official funds (usually the Issue Department of the Bank
of England) and then sold off gradually on the Stock Exchange.
Issues which the authorities are selling-off in this way
are known as "tap stocks".

The main purchasers of new government issues are non-
bank financial institutions. In the past, when banks held
a much higher proportion of their assets in government

securities than they now do, they would take up significant
amounts of new issues. During the seventies, however, their
holdings have been reduced, and they now consist almost
wholly of stocks within a few years of maturity, which are
bought on the secondary market.

The primary market in company securities

There are a number of different kinds of company
securities but the main categories are debentures, preference
shares and ordinary shares. The first two both carry a fixed
rate of interest and are often grouped together as "fixed
charge capital".

The primary market in company securities is in the
hands of "issuing houses", (most of the largest of which are
merchant banks) and stockbrokers. Shares in very small
companies are occasionally issued without a stock exchange
listing but the general practice is that, where a company
does not already have a listing, it should obtain one at
the time its shares are issued to the public. Where a
listing is sought, a broker must be involved in order to
ensure that the listing requirements of the Stock Exchange
are met. There is no compulsion to also employ an issuing
house, but it is usual to do so.

The most common methods of making a new issue are:-

Public issue: A prospectus is published and the
general public is invited to apply for shares at
a fixed price. The merchant bank or broker acts
only as an agent.

Offer for sale: The issuing company sells the
shares "en bloc" to the issuing house or broker,
who then re-sells to the public.

Placing: The issuing house or broker acquires
the shares as with an offer for sale, but sells
them to a small group of clients, mainly non-bank
financial institutions.

Rights issue: This is the cheapest method, and the one most commonly used, by companies that already have a listing and want to increase their capital. Shareholders are offered the right to buy new shares in proportion to the number they already hold. New shares are usually offered at below the current market price and shareholders who do not wish to exercise their rights can sell them in the secondary market.

Issues made by all these methods except placings are underwritten; the issuing house or broker agrees with a group of institutions to take up any unsold balance at an agreed price in return for a commission. Underwriters are generally non-bank institutions, particularly insurance companies and pension funds.

In its evidence to the Wilson Committee, the Stock Exchange put the cost of a typical rights issue to raise £2m. at 4 per cent. The main elements were a tax of 1 per cent, issuing house commission of 0.5 per cent, underwriting commission of 1.25 per cent and broker's commission of 0.25 per cent. The balance was made up of the cost of circulars and share certificates; fees to lawyers, accountants, registrars and receiving bankers; and a Stock Exchange listing fee of £1,200. For a public issue or offer for sale the tax and fees to issuing house, broker and underwriters are the same but other fees are higher and expensive advertising is necessary. This put the estimated cost up to 7.5 per cent of the proceeds.

It will be apparent from this brief description that the merchant banks play a very important part in the primary market for company securities. Besides their role in relation to listed securities, some of them will also find buyers for unlisted securities of small firms and, to a limited extent, make a market in shares of companies that they sponsor. Other banks, however, play only a very small part, mainly in receiving subscriptions and acting as registrars, both of which functions are extensively undertaken by the clearing banks.

The secondary markets

The secondary markets in both gilt-edged and company securities is very much concentrated in the Stock Exchange. There are a few outside dealers, mainly offshoots of US and Canadian broking firms; the members of the Accepting Houses Committee have set up ARIEL (Automated Real-time Investments Exchange Ltd.) to deal in company securities on behalf of its members, though turnover in the year to March 1979 was less than 0.5 per cent of that of the Stock Exchange; and M.J.H. Nightingale & Co. has recently started a very small "over the counter" market in unlisted securities.

During the nineteenth century stock exchanges were established in a number of provincial towns, though they were very much smaller than the London Exchange. During the 1960's the exchanges formed a federation and in 1973 they joined with London to form a single Stock Exchange. Trading floors continue to operate in Brimingham, Dublin, Glasgow, Liverpool and Manchester and brokers have offices in about a hundred towns and cities.

The Stock Exchange has a number of characteristics that are different from Germany, and most other countries. The most important are the following:

i.   The Exchange is an independent organisation electing its own members and governed, through an elected Council, by its members. Though members combine in partnerships or companies for trading purposes, they are elected as individuals.

ii.   Members are prohibited from engaging in any other trade or profession, so that it is impossible for banks to become members.

iii.   The Stock Exchange operates on the principle known as "single capacity". Members are either brokers or jobbers. Apart from a limited range of transactions, mostly international, the rules require that jobbers should deal only with brokers, and that brokers should execute all orders received from their clients through jobbers. Jobbers deal on their own account as principals, and make a market by being prepared to deal either way in securities in which they run a "book". Brokers act only as agents, receiving orders from the public and executing them on the best terms they can get from the jobbers. Jobbers make their profit from the difference between the average prices at which they buy and those at which they sell, while brokers are remunerated by commission.

iv.   The operation of the jobbing system is helped by the operations of "money brokers". Six broking firms are allowed by the Bank of England to borrow in the money market, and this money is on-lent to jobbers against the security of stock that they are carrying. These firms also have arrangements with institutions; largely insurance companies and pension funds, to borrow stock, which they can then lend to jobbers who have sold "short". The system thus reduces the amount of stock which jobbers need to keep on their books, and helps to provide them with finance.

The direct participation of British banks in the secondary securities market is thus confined to lending to jobbers, through the agency of the money brokers, in the money market, and to providing overdraft facilities to broking firms. The latter is not of major importance because the agency business conducted by brokers does not require very large amounts of working capital. Otherwise, the influence of the banks on the market is only as transactors and investment advisers.

The only sector of the market in which the banks are large traders on their own behalf is short-dated government securities. At the last analysis of holdings of the National Debt by the Bank of England (31st. March, 1979) banks held £2,658m. of government stocks and discount houses, £698m. These holdings amounted to 6.5 per cent of all securities outside official hands. However, more than 91 per cent of these holdings were in stocks with less than five years to maturity. These securities are bought in the secondary market; there are active dealings in them in response to small differences in yield during the rest of their lives; and they are often sold back to the government broker when

they get very near to their redemption date. This technique
of buying back stock in the market as it nears redemption is
used by the Bank of England to avoid the inconvenience of
having to transfer very large sums of money on a single day.
These features of the UK system are responsible for the very
large turnover in short-dated government stocks in London.

As shown in Chapter 5, the banks have only very small
holdings of company securities on their own account, and
most of these are subsidiaries and trade investments. They
do, however, manage large funds arising from other activities
including executor and trustee services for customers; the
operation of unit trusts and life assurance subsidiaries;
and the management services provided, particularly by the
merchant banks, for pension funds, charities and wealthy
individuals. The size of these funds and the way in which
they are operated has been discussed in Chapter 5.

It is also common for personal investors, particularly
those with relatively small fortunes, to seek advice from
their local bank manager and to transmit orders to the Stock
Exchange through their bank. The rules of the Exchange
allow brokers to share with banks their commission on
business brought to them in this way. A 1974 survey by EAG
showed that 44 per cent of those questioned had made their
last purchase or sale of equities through a bank[1] though
since banks are used predominantly by small investors the
proportion of personal business coming through banks would
be much smaller.

5.   GERMAN LONG-TERM MARKETS

The primary market in public debt

German public authorities make more use than their
UK counterparts of medium-term non-market assets, with

---

1.   Personal Savings and Wealth in Britain, EAG and
      Financial Times, 1975.

maturities of one to seven years, which are issued directly
to the personal sector. German practice also contrasts
sharply with that of UK in that government bonds traded in
the stock exchange are all no more than medium-term.
Federal bonds (Bundesobligationen) are issued by tender by
the Bundesbank, and there is a small market in them on
the stock exchanges. They have also at times been classified
as money market paper and, even when not so classified, are
used by the Bundesbank in open-market operations. Treasury
bonds (Bundesobligationen), not to be confused with
the Treasury bonds of the money market, were first issued
in 1979. They have a five year maturity and are originally
sold only to natural persons resident in Germany and to
charities. However, they can be re-sold to anyone except
foreigners and there is an active market in them. (See
also Chapters 1 and 9).

The primary market in company securities

The right to issue shares is confined to two types of
company, the Aktiengesellschaft (AG) which corresponds very
closely with the UK public limited company and the
Kommanditgesellschaft auf Aktien (KGaA) which must include at least one
owner with unlimited liability. The former are much the
more common. In principle, bonds can be issued, though only
with ministerial approval, by any company but in practice
they are issued only by the larger ones and mainly by
shareholders' companies. A difference between UK and German
practice is that both bonds and shares in Germany are usually
bearer instruments. As shown in Chapter 2, the bond market
is very much larger than that for shares, in terms of amounts
outstanding. Nearly three quarters of all outstanding
domestic bonds are issued by banks. Issues of industrial
companies accounted for 12 per cent of outstanding bonds,
in 1960, but the proportion had fallen to only 1.2 per
cent in 1979. Foreign issues have grown in importance rapidly
over the past decade.

There is also a difference in the listing procedure for new companies. In Germany a listing is granted only after an issue has been made. A minimum requirement is the publication of at least one year's financial results, but most listing committees have more stringent standards; for example, Frankfurt requires that a company should have shown a satisfactory profit trend over five years and have paid dividends for at least three consecutive years.

Whether an issue is of bonds or shares it is almost always made through a bank, or a consortium of banks in the case of large issues. The bank or banks carry out the functions that, in the UK, would be divided between stock-broker, issuing house, underwriter, receiving banker and registrar. They organise the issue, they prepare the prospectus and are jointly responsible with the company for any misleading statements in it; they receive subscriptions, pay dividends and make arrangements for listing. The bank or banks may acquire the whole issue, as in a UK offer for sale, and take any unsold balance into their own portfolio. Alternatively, unsold shares may be retained in the name of the company and used by the bank in accordance with the company's instructions. It is common for banks to make sales or purchases both in the name of the company concerned and on their own account in order to smooth fluctuations in share prices. We were told in interviews that companies "expect" their "house-bank" to support them in this way during difficult times.

Where established companies wish to increase their capital the usual method, as in the UK, is a rights issue. New shares are issued at a discount compared with the current market price and rights are usually, though not always, marketable.

There is a tax of 1 per cent (the same level as in Britain) on new share issues. For a rights issue of DM 20m. other charges, including banks' commission, legal

and accounting fees, printing and publicity, and listing
fees are estimated to absorb rather 4 per cent of the
proceeds, giving a total cost of rather more than 5 per
cent. Bond issues are slightly cheaper, with a total cost
of about 4 per cent for an issue of DM 20m.

The secondary markets

There are seven stock exchanges in West Germany at
Frankfurt, Düsseldorf, Hamburg, Bremen, Munich, Hanover and
Stuttgart, and one in West Berlin, but those of Frankfurt
and Düsseldorf are much the largest and account for around
70 per cent of all business. The exchanges operate
independently under a constitution laid down by a law of
1908. This law provides for the appointment of official
brokers by the Länder governments, but other members are
elected and the exchanges enjoy a considerable degree of
autonomy. As a result, there are some differences in rules
between them, e.g. on listing requirements.

There are three classes of members: banks; official
brokers (amtliche Makler); and free brokers (freie Makler). The
official brokers act as specialists each in a limited range
of securities admitted to official dealing allotted to him by
the state government by which he is appointed. Orders from
the general public come to the exchanges entirely through banks,
so that brokers have no contact with the public and the function
of the free broker is simply as an agent between the banks
and the official brokers. Prior to 1968 it was common for banks
to 'match' buying and selling orders from their own customers,
but since that time all orders have been brought to the
exchange.

Orders may be left with limit prices or simply "at
best". During a trading session the official brokers collect
buying and selling orders, with limit prices if any, either
from bank dealers or free brokers, and then announce an
official price that will maximise the volume of transactions.

All orders "at best", all buying orders at or above and selling orders at or below the official price are then executed at this uniform price. Others are either cancelled or held over, according to client's instructions. Prices are fixed in percentages of nominal value with a minimum variation of one percentage point. Hence, the volume of buying and selling orders at the official price may not exactly coincide. In that case official brokers are allowed to make up the difference by dealing on their own account. Free brokers fix prices in securities not admitted to an official listing, and may deal on their own account.

Besides this official market, there is a telephone market outside business hours that is important in international securities; a semi-official market in some unlisted securities; and a fairly active options market. Some banks also operate an over-the-counter market in securities not traded on the exchanges.

A substantial telephone market in bonds has also grown up between banks, many of which use bond transactions (often involving a sale and repurchase agreement) as an alternative to transactions in money market paper for managing liquidity.

German banks are clearly much more involved than their UK counterparts in the secondary market. They deal from their own portfolios for ordinary investment purposes; they carry out smoothing and support operations, both from their own portfolios and on account of the companies concerned for securities of companies for which they act as house-bank; they are the only channel through which orders from the general public reach the official market; and they act as advisers to their customers. It is impossible to know for certain whether this last function is more important in Germany than in the UK, but the widespread practice of depositing shares with German banks and completing proxy forms suggests that the role of the German banks is the more influential.

6.   CONCLUSIONS

The markets described in this Chapter are very different
between the two countries. Each are the result of a long
period of evolution and adaptation, with the functioning of
markets influencing the economic environment, and the
environment reacting on the evolution of markets. It is
difficult to form any strong conclusions either about the
causal relationships involved in these inter-actions or about
the respective merits of the two sets of institutions.

There is no doubt that short-term financial markets in
the UK are very much broader than in Germany. Transactions
between banks other than the central bank are very much
larger, and direct transactions between individual banks
(including discount houses) and the central bank are smaller.
Market transactions between banks and non-banks are limited,
even in the UK but they are still far larger than in Germany.

The markets provide individual UK banks with
opportunities for balancing the inflow of deposits and the
demand for loans, and for matching the maturity of assets
and liabilities far greater than are available in Germany;
and this contributes to stability by reducing the chances of
individual banks running into difficulties. However, the
greater average length of German banks' liabilities reduces
their need for matching in the market, and they have
alternative means of equating the supply and demand for loans,
e.g. transactions between savings and co-operative banks and
their central institutions.

As noted earlier, there is a risk that the very
efficiency of UK markets from the point of view of individual
banks may encourage the system as a whole to lend too long,

TABLE 8.4: LISTED ORDINARY SHARES, DOMESTIC COMPANIES, 1979.

	UK	GERMANY
1. Number of companies with listed ordinary shares	2,395	458
2. Market value, end-year £m.	66,933	36,612
3. Turnover during year £m.	12,053	6,734
4. Ratio of 3:2 (%)	18.0	18.4

Source: The Stock Exchange Fact Book, March 1980, Appendix 5.

or to erect too big a pyramid of credit on a given cash base. The Bank of England believes that the operation of banks in the market creates problems for monetary control but this is a matter of controversy and it can be argued that there is also an advantage in that the effect of central bank actions is transmitted very quickly to a wide range of borrowing and lending activities. There is no doubt that the Bundesbank has at times found the relatively small volume of money market paper a handicap as is witnessed by its use of mobilisation and liquidity paper, and by its extension of open-market operations into medium-term notes.

In the medium- and long-term capital market, it is clear that, by almost any measure, the UK market in company securities is more important than that of Germany. Table 8.4 shows the number of companies with listed ordinary shares at the end of 1979, the total market value of these shares and turnover during the year. The UK had more than five times as many companies with listed ordinary shares, and both market value and turnover were nearly twice as high.

TABLE 8.5: NEW ISSUES OF ORDINARY SHARES

Year	UK (£m.)		GERMANY (DMm.)	
	Listed	Unlisted	Listed	Unlisted
1971	537	–	**2,928**	**1,806**
1972	1,040	5	2,422	1,707
1973	202	12	2,292	1,292
1974	96	6	1,475	2,049
1975	1,373	29	3,659	2,249
1976	1,070	10	2,743	3,341
1977	730	–	2,004	2,364
1978	834	–	3,972	1,516
1979	932	–	3,635	1,880

Source: Financial Statistics and Statistical Annex, Series 2 to
monthly reports of the Deutsche Bundesbank.

It has been shown in Chapter 4, that the proportion of
shareholders' funds in the balance-sheets of companies is
markedly lower in Germany than in the UK. The contrast is
rather less clear in relation to new issues. Corporate bond
issues have been small in both countries in recent years
(see Chapter 4). Equity issues are shown in Table 8.5. The
totals are larger than those of Chapter 4 as they include
financial as well as non-financial companies. The value of
unlisted issues in Germany is much greater than in the UK,
which may be partly due to the difference in practice over
listing noted above, and partly to the fact that listing fees
are higher in Germany. The ranking of the two countries in
terms of the value of listed issues varied from year to year.
Issues in the UK were very low during the stock exchange
slump of 1973-74, but over the average of 1975-79, new
listed issues in the UK were about 25 per cent higher than
in Germany, despite the much lower level of investment.

The relatively small role of equity capital in German corporate finance may be partly due (as is often claimed in the UK) to the efficiency of the banks in providing alternative sources of long-term capital, and partly (as German critics sometimes argue) that banks discourage their customers from going to the market. It seems likely, however, that taxation has played a major role; before 1976 the German tax system discriminated heavily against equity finance; most of this discrimination was removed in 1976 but equity finance is still rather more expensive than loan finance giving a similar post-tax yield.

Though listing fees are higher in Germany, the total costs of new equity issues seem to be broadly similar in the two markets. It is not possible to compare the costs of dealing in the secondary market, since there is no way of measuring the average difference between jobbers buying and selling prices.

The process of price formation in the secondary market is very different. In London the price of any given security is likely to vary from deal to deal according to the state of jobbers' books and their assessment of supply and demand. In Germany all deals on the official market are done at the official price of the day, except for a small number of the most actively traded shares that are admitted to "continuous quotation". It is almost certain that the London system enables some deals to be done that could not be done in Germany. For example, if the official price of a German security was fixed at 100, both a buying order at 99 and a selling order at 101 would be impossible to execute on that day. London operates on finer price intervals than one percentage point and prices can fluctuate during the day so it is quite possible that deals of this kind could be under-taken at some time during a day.

TABLE 8.6: SHARE PRICE CYCLES, 1964-1977

	UK		GERMANY	
	Number	Average Amplitude %	Number	Average Amplitude %
Five per cent cycles:-				
upswings	9	48.8	7	33.2
downswings	8	19.8	7	16.0
Ten per cent cycles:-				
upswings	5	86.6	4	53.5
downswings	4	36.2	4	22.5
Twenty per cent cycles:-				
upswings	3	111.8	2	80.2
downswings	3	42.0	2	32.2

Source: E.V. Morgan and R.L. Harrington, Capital Markets in the EEC, London. Wilton House, 1977 and unpublished EAG research.

There is some difference of opinion as to whether a high volume of dealing in security markets is desirable. A widely accepted view is that high volume helps to create conditions in which large deals can be made without wide changes in prices, and to create a market that is technically 'efficient' in the sense that prices are adjusted quickly to reflect all changes in relevant information. It has been argued, however, that the UK market is "over-active". This criticism is based partly on a technical misunderstanding. The jobbing system in London means that transactions that would be recorded only once in other countries are recorded twice - once when the jobber buys and again when he sells. If allowance is made for this, turnover in the London gilt-edged market is still high, mainly because of the large transactions in stocks approaching maturity that were described in Section 4. Equity turnover in relation to volume is very similar in the UK and Germany. The 1979 ratio of turnover to end-year market value was 18.0 per cent for the UK and 18.4 per cent for Germany. (Table 8.4)

The UK market has also been criticised for its volatility. As with turnover, it is not clear how much volatility is desirable. Prices should not react to changes in irrelevant circumstances or over-react to relevant ones but they should reflect fully all relevant information. It can be argued that the large and frequent changes in interest rates, inflation rates, exchange rates and government policy in the UK justify high volatility in equity markets. The measurement of volatility is a difficult matter and a full investigation would be outside the scope of this study. In some earlier EAG work on this subject using data from 1964 to 1977, price cycles were identified with minimum amplitudes between peak and trough of 5, 10 and 20 per cent. The results are summarised in Table 8.6. The number of upward and downward movements do not differ greatly though where differences occur the German figure is always lower. The amplitude of cycles is, however, consistently and markedly smaller in Germany. This greater stability of prices in Germany could be partly explained by the kind of smoothing and support operations by banks described in Section 5. Assuming that banks also advise customers to behave in a similar manner, the high proportion of German shares deposited with banks could also be a contributory factor, but there is no way of assessing the importance of either.

Differences between the two markets reflect many differences in the respective economies besides the differing role of the banks. In particular, differences in government borrowing, the relatively larger role of life assurance in the UK, and differences in the funding of pension rights have obviously influenced the evolution of long-term capital

markets. We can say, however, that our evidence offers
little support for the more common criticisms of UK markets,
and still less for the idea that they could be improved by a
closer involvement of the banking system.

CHAPTER 9:   MONETARY POLICY AND INFLATION
By Richard L. Harrington

1.   INTRODUCTION

Over the past two decades inflation rates in the UK
have been consistently among the highest of Western
industrial countries while inflation rates in Germany have
been among the lowest. The object of this Chapter is to
examine the extent to which this contrast can be explained
by differences between the two monetary systems, and in
the policies of the monetary authorities. Section 2 shows
the course of inflation in the two countries as measured
by index numbers of prices and earnings, and Section 3
gives a brief account of economic theories on the
relationship between monetary expansion and inflation.
Section 4 presents the statistical evidence on the growth
of the money stock, and Section 5 considers the respective
attitudes towards monetary policy in the two countries,
and the instruments used. The contrast between the UK
and Germany in these matters is strikingly illustrated by
the reactions to the 1973-74 oil crisis and these are
discussed in Section 6. Finally, our conclusions are
contained in Section 7.

2.   PRICES AND EARNINGS

The main facts about inflation are contained in
Table 9.1 for the UK and Table 9.2 for Germany. Both
Tables give for the years 1960-1979 indices of retail
prices, wholesale prices (of industrial products) and the
national income deflator. In the UK all three series show
very similar average rates of growth over the whole period
although there are divergences within sub-periods: in
Germany wholesale prices have usually increased less than
retail prices which in turn have usually grown less than
the average price of all goods and services as measured
by the national income deflator. The relatively low rate

TABLE 9.1: UK PRICE INDICES

	Retail Prices	Percentage Change	Wholesale Prices	Percentage Change	GDP Deflator	Percentage Change
			(1975 = 100 all indices)			
1960	36.5	1.1	39.8	1.5	35.5	2.0
1961	37.7	3.3	40.9	2.8	36.6	3.1
1962	39.3	4.2	41.8	2.2	37.8	3.3
1963	40.1	2.0	42.2	0.7	38.7	2.4
1964	41.4	3.3	43.5	3.3	39.9	3.1
1965	43.4	4.8	45.1	3.8	41.5	4.0
1966	45.1	3.9	46.3	2.8	43.1	3.9
1967	46.2	2.5	46.8	1.0	44.3	2.8
1968	48.4	4.7	48.7	3.9	45.6	2.9
1969	51.0	5.4	50.5	3.9	47.3	3.7
1970	54.2	6.4	54.1	7.1	51.0	7.8
1971	59.3	9.4	59.0	9.1	56.5	10.8
1972	63.6	7.1	62.1	5.3	62.3	10.3
1973	69.4	9.2	66.7	7.4	67.3	8.0
1974	80.5	16.1	81.8	22.6	78.7	16.9
1975	100.0	24.2	100.0	22.2	100.0	27.1
1976	116.5	16.5	117.3	17.3	113.5	13.5
1977	135.0	15.8	140.5	19.8	127.4	12.2
1978	146.2	8.3	153.3	9.1	141.7	11.2
1979	165.8	13.4	172.0	12.2	159.6	12.6
	Average Rates of Change					
1959 - 1979	7.9			7.7		7.9
1959 - 1969	3.5			2.6		3.1
1969 - 1975	11.9			12.1		13.3
1975 - 1979	13.5			14.5		12.4

Memorandum Item: annual growth rate of real GNP 1959-1979, 2.6 per cent

Source: Economic Trends, annual supplement 1980;

National Income and Expenditure, 1980.

TABLE 9.2: GERMAN PRICE INDICES

	Retail Prices (1976=100)	Percentage Change	Wholesale Prices (1970=100)	Percentage Change	GDP Deflator (1970=100)	Percentage Change
1960	55.3	1.6	87.7	1.2	70.5	
1961	56.6	2.3	89.0	1.5	73.7	4.6
1962	58.1	3.1	89.9	1.1	77.2	4.6
1963	59.8	2.9	90.3	0.4	79.6	3.1
1964	61.2	2.3	91.3	1.1	81.8	2.8
1965	63.2	3.3	93.5	2.4	84.7	3.5
1966	65.4	3.5	95.1	1.7	87.8	3.7
1967	66.5	1.7	94.3	-0.8	88.8	1.1
1968	67.6	1.7	93.6	-0.7	90.2	1.6
1969	68.9	1.9	95.3	1.8	93.4	3.5
1970	71.2	3.3	100.0	4.9	100.0	7.1
1971	74.9	5.2	104.3	4.3	107.7	7.7
1972	79.1	5.6	107.0	2.6	113.7	5.6
1973	84.6	7.0	114.1	6.6	120.6	6.1
1974	90.5	7.0	129.4	13.4	128.9	6.9
1975	95.9	6.0	135.5	4.7	137.6	6.7
1976	100.0	4.3	140.8	3.9	142.0	3.2
1977	103.7	3.7	144.5	2.6	147.4	3.8
1978	106.5	2.7	146.3	1.2	153.1	3.9
1979	110.9	4.1	153.6	5.0	159.0	3.9
	Average Rates of Change					
1959 - 1979		3.6		2.9		4.3[1]
1959 - 1969		2.4		1.0		3.2
1969 - 1975		5.7		6.0		6.7
1975 - 1979		3.7		3.2		3.7

Memorandum Item: annual growth rate of real GNP 1959-1979, 4 per cent.

[1] 1960-1979.

Source: Monthly Report of the Deutsche Bundesbank.

of growth of wholesale prices reflects above average growth
of productivity in industry. It is not a reflection of
import costs of food prices, both of which rose over the
whole period at a rate similar to that of wholesale prices.

In both Tables we have shown the average rates of
price increases for the whole period and for three sub-
periods: the decade to 1969, the six years to 1975 and the
four years to 1979. The first sub-period shows the
relatively low rates of price increase experienced prior
to the surge in inflation in both countries in the early
1970's - a surge which, as the figures show, may have been
exacerbated by the oil price rises of 1973/4, but which had
begun well before these. The second sub-period shows this
surge in prices and the third shows the divergent
experience of the two countries since then.

If the upsurge in prices in the early 1970's is one
similarity shown by the two Tables the most obvious
difference is that throughout the period the rate of
inflation has been much greater in the UK: over twice as
great when measured by the retail price index. This
difference is maintained in the three sub-periods but on
the evidence here the gap between the two countries has
been widening. Whereas in the 1960's retail prices in the
UK were rising by about 1 per cent more than in Germany,
and the average change in the national income deflator was
very close, by the late 1970's retail prices in the UK
were rising nearly four times as fast as in Germany with
similar discrepancies in other indices.

Indices of wage rates, earnings and unit labour costs
are given in Tables 9.3 and 9.4. They are given for the
same period and sub-periods as the price indices with the
exception of the UK series of average earnings which was
not compiled before 1963. Several points are worthy of
note. Over the period as a whole, money earnings were
rising at a faster rate in the UK than in Germany and given
the difference in productivity growth in the two countries
this meant a large discrepancy in the change in unit labour

TABLE 9.3: UK, WAGE RATES, EARNINGS AND LABOUR COSTS

	Weekly Wage Rates (manual workers) All Industries and Services (July 1972 = 100)	Percentage Change	Average Earnings, Production Industries and Some Services (January 1970 = 100)	Percentage Change	Wages and Salaries Per Unit of Output Whole Economy (1975 = 100)	Percentage Change
1960	48.1	2.6			34.0	0.9
1961	50.1	4.2			35.8	5.3
1962	51.9	3.6			37.3	4.2
1963	53.8	3.7	64.3		37.5	0.5
1964	56.4	4.8	69.2	7.6	38.7	3.2
1965	58.8	4.3	74.1	7.1	40.2	3.9
1966	61.5	4.6	79.0	6.2	42.2	5.0
1967	63.9	3.9	81.8	3.6	42.9	1.7
1968	68.1	6.6	88.2	7.8	43.7	1.9
1969	71.7	5.3	95.2	7.8	45.3	3.7
1970	78.8	9.9	106.7	12.0	49.6	9.5
1971	89.0	12.9	118.7	11.3	54.3	9.5
1972	101.3	13.8	134.0	12.9	59.1	8.8
1973	115.2	13.7	152.1	13.2	63.4	7.3
1974	138.0	19.8	179.1	17.8	77.7	22.6
1975	178.7	29.5	226.6	26.5	100.0	28.7
1976	213.2	19.3	261.8	15.6	110.7	10.7
1977	227.3	6.6	288.5	10.2	121.4	9.7
1978	259.3	14.0	330.2	14.5	134.9	11.1
1979	298.1	15.0	381.7	15.6	155.4	15.2
Average Rates of Change						
1959-79		9.7		11.8[1]		7.9
1959-69		4.3		6.8		3.0
1969-75		16.4		15.6		14.1
1975-79		13.6		13.9		11.7

NOTE: 1. 1963-1979, this series is not calculated for years prior to 1963.

Source: Economic Trends

TABLE 9.4: GERMANY, WAGE RATES, EARNINGS AND LABOUR COSTS

(1970 = 100 all series)

	Hourly Wage and Salary Rates Whole Economy	Percentage Change	Average Earnings Whole Economy	Percentage Change	Wages and Salaries Per Unit of Output Whole Economy	Percentage Change
1960	49.5		44.6		68.4	
1961	53.8	8.7	49.2	10.3	72.3	5.7
1962	58.5	8.7	53.7	9.1	76.4	5.7
1963	61.9	5.8	57.0	6.1	78.7	3.0
1964	65.9	6.5	62.1	8.9	80.2	1.9
1965	71.0	7.7	67.8	9.1	83.3	3.9
1966	76.0	7.1	72.7	7.3	88.0	5.6
1967	79.1	4.0	75.1	3.3	88.1	0.2
1968	82.2	4.0	79.8	6.2	87.9	-0.3
1969	88.0	7.0	87.1	9.2	90.6	3.1
1970	100.0	13.6	100.0	14.7	100.0	10.4
1971	114.1	14.1	111.8	11.8	108.8	8.8
1972	125.0	9.5	121.8	9.0	115.0	5.7
1973	138.3	10.6	136.4	12.0	124.0	7.8
1974	156.2	13.0	151.9	11.4	135.9	9.6
1975	170.7	9.3	162.8	7.2	144.0	6.0
1976	180.9	6.0	174.1	7.0	146.2	1.5
1977	193.4	6.9	186.1	6.9	151.7	3.8
1978	204.4	5.7	195.7	5.2	155.7	2.6
1979	214.5	4.9	206.5	5.5	159.2	2.2
Average Rates of Change						
1960-79		8.0		8.4		4.5
1960-69		6.6		7.7		3.2
1969-75		11.7		11.0		8.0
1975-79		5.9		6.1		2.5

Source: Monthly Report of the Deutsche Bundesbank and Statistical Supplement No. 4.
OECD Main Economic Indicators: Historical Statistics, 1960-1975.

costs. During the 1960's things were different with money
earnings rising faster in Germany and with unit labour costs
rising only slightly less than in the UK. In the early
1970's, there is the upturn in inflation in both countries
that we have already noted and this predictably involves
a sharp jump in the growth of money wage rates and earnings.
The increase in the UK on all measures is greater than in
Germany.

The third sub-period is perhaps the most interesting
as it is here that the experience of the two countries
differs most. The rates of increase in all three series in
Germany drop not only from the high levels of the early
1970's but become lower than rates of increase in the
1960's. That is to say, faced with increasing import costs
- notably oil - the Germans have managed to get the growth
of the main domestic cost - labour - down lower than at any
time for twenty years. This helps to explain the
relatively good performance as regards prices that we noted
earlier. Meanwhile in the UK the experience has been very
different: wage rates and earnings have declined slightly
from the growth rates of the early 1970's but have remained
far ahead of anything experienced in the 1960's. Aided by
a fall in the growth of real output unit labour costs in
the late 1970's were still rising nearly four times faster
than a decade earlier.

In summary there are three main features of this
factual survey which stand out: the persistently higher
inflation in the UK; the upsurge in inflation in both
countries in the early 1970's; and the divergent behaviour
of the two economies since then.

3.   THEORETICAL APPROACHES TO INFLATION

By way of introduction we would stress that modern
theories of inflation are complex and one tends to find
the same or similar factors being cited in more than one
theory. Also we must not lose sight of the fact that

inflation is a process affecting economic behaviour in many different ways; and the forces that maintain inflation in being may be different from those that initiated it.

This being said it is still useful to distinguish those theories which stress primarily excess demand as the cause of rising prices from those which stress exogenous rises in costs of production - primarily labour costs. We shall take the former group of theories first. These theories stemming, in our own time, from an adaptation of Keynesian theories of aggregate demand have as their main idea the notion that just as in one market, prices will rise, fall or remain constant as demand is in excess of, less than, or equal to supply, so in the aggregate economy - the aggregate of all markets - prices will rise, fall or remain constant as the sum of all demands exceeds, falls short of or equals the sum of goods and services supplied. The government is seen as having the ability to control aggregate demand and hence ultimately inflation. However, given that governments are largely dependent on influencing demand in the aggregate and given that in any modern economy the pressure of demand for the products of different industries and regions will vary, governments cannot necessarily achieve low or zero inflation at the same time as achieving other goals such as full employment. There is likely to be a short-run policy choice between limiting demand to curb inflation and expanding demand to reduce unemployment.

This theory was widely held in the 1950's and 1960's and appeared to apply to both the UK and Germany as well as to other developed economies. The remedy for inflation lay in the use of fiscal and monetary policies. During the 1960's, however, experience suggested to an increasing number of people that of these two policies monetary policy was more important. This approach, known as monetarism, did not deny that demand was the immediate cause of inflation but argued that rising demand was caused by - and in the long run could only be caused by - an expanding money supply. Fiscal policy had appeared powerful because (due to government financing) when expansionary it had been accompanied by an above-average rate of growth of money and when contractionary by a below-average rate of growth of the money supply. If this link between fiscal policy and money supply were to be broken then an expansionary fiscal policy would be accompanied by high interest rates, necessary to permit the government to increase its share of the limited credit available, and in consequence private sector expenditures would be discouraged or, as often put 'crowded-out'. Expanding government expenditures would largely displace private expenditures with the result that the net impact on aggregate demand would be low: fiscal policy alone was not very powerful.

On the contrary, according to the monetarists, monetary policy was powerful. An expanding money supply meant both an expansion of bank credit and an expansion of purchasing power. And whilst in the short-run persons and firms might choose to vary their immediate holding of purchasing power (their demand for money) in ways that could not be predicted, in the long run we would expect demand for money to be sufficiently stable so that large increases of purchasing power would be reflected firstly in increased spending and subsequently in higher prices. On the other hand, without an increase in money there would be no reason to expect any sustained increase in aggregate demand or prices.

This monetarist approach to inflation then saw the money supply as being both the cause and the measure of increased demand for goods and services. Increased demand would not be harmful insofar as it met increased supply, hence a growth in the quantity of money in line with the growth in the productive capacity of the economy would be a sound policy. Growth of money could be varied either up or down insofar as there was evidence of a trend demand for money to hold above or below the trend rate of growth of output but apart from this the rate of growth of the money supply should match the trend rate of growth of capacity to produce. This would be non-inflationary. Hence from

this theoretical standpoint, it stood to reason that the
explanation for past inflation was excessive monetary
expansion. And it is this theory which has grown in
influence until control of the money supply has become an
important part of economic policy in most developed
countries. Today explicit monetary targets are in use in
both the UK and Germany.

But no country is an island in economic terms and money
created in one country can easily flow to others, so it is
necessary for any monetary explanation of inflation to take
account of both international and domestic influences on the
money supply. Prior to August 1971 and for brief periods
shortly thereafter, most countries practised systems of
fixed exchange rates - albeit with occasional rate adjustments.
For a government to fix an exchange rate, it is necessary for
it to stand ready to buy or sell its own currency whenever
there is excess supply of or demand for it at the fixed rate.
This commitment to supply one's own currency in exchange for
foreign money was an important limitation on the power of
governments to control their own money supply. It was keenly
felt in Germany, as shown in Chapter 2.

More generally, international trade and capital
movements meant that an expansionary monetary policy in one
country would not be limited in its effects to that country.
An increase in money in one country could flow abroad
directly in capital transactions in which case the country
in question would see its balance of payments deteriorate
and the country receiving the capital inflow would see its
balance of payments improve and its money supply increase.
Alternatively, an increase in money in the one country by
influencing aggregate demand in that country could be
expected to increase the demand for imported goods - both
directly and as a consequence of relative-price effects
when the increased money supply caused the prices of
domestically produced goods to rise. Either way an increase
in the quantity of money in one country would not all stay
in that country - some would flow abroad. Thus monetary

policy in a regime of fixed exchange rates would be
expected to influence not only the domestic inflation rate
but also the balance of payments.

The monetarist approach is thus made more general and
can be made to explain inflation at the level of the world
as well as that of the nation. Put simply, the theory at a
world level says the existing stock of money will be spread
among nations in proportion to their respective demands for
money. If any one nation initiates an increase in the
quantity of money this extra will, in time, get spread
around other nations: world demand being increased, the
initiating nation having a balance-of-payments deficit and
other nations having surpluses. Given fixed exchange rates
no one country can contract out of world inflation: those
who successfully control the domestic creation of money may
nonetheless find their money supply expanding due to inflows
from abroad.

In practice the theory can only be an approximation
to reality: exchange rates are never immutably fixed;
capital movements are seldom totally free; governments can,
and do, influence and/or offset many movements of funds.
However, the experience of the world in the years prior to
the abandonment of fixed exchange rates seemed to many to
be in accord with the predictions of the monetarist theory.

Since 1971 the world has mainly operated under a
regime of floating exchange rates - although within this
regime some countries, including Germany, have chosen to
join a group of countries all holding intra-group exchange
rates stable whilst allowing the currencies of all the
group to fluctuate freely against outsiders. At the time
of writing (November 1980) the Deutschemark fluctuates
only marginally against the currencies of other member
countries of the European Monetary System[1] but freely
against the US dollar and the pound sterling.

---

1.   Belgium, Denmark, France, Ireland, Italy, Luxembourg
     and the Netherlands.

Under floating exchange rates the effect of domestic monetary increases is different. Again these are likely to lead to a desired outflow of money whether it be on capital or current account. But now there are no longer central banks ready to facilitate all such transactions at existing exchange rates. An increased supply of domestic money and demand for foreign monies on a free money market will merely push down the value of the domestic currency. At the end of the day supply must equal demand - therefore no net amount of money will flow across the exchanges. In these circumstances, those countries which initiate monetary expansions will feel the full effect domestically whilst their exchange rates will depreciate. Countries who control their own domestic monetary expansion need no longer import money from abroad provided they are prepared to allow their exchange rate to appreciate.

Whilst initially one would expect the chain of events to be from an increase in the quantity of money to an increase in aggregate demand to a rise in demand for imports and thus to a fall in exchange rate, once those dealing in foreign currency get used to this sequence of events, their anticipation will speed up the whole process. If everyone expects a rapid growth in the money supply to lead to a fall in the exchange rate then anticipatory dealing will bring about this result very quickly. So much did this appear to be happening in the UK in the mid-1970's that some economists proposed this as the main way in which money affects prices: an increase in money leads to a fall in the exchange rate which leads to a rise in the price of imported goods.[1]

Whatever the exact importance of the various possible linkages, the main predictions of the monetarist school for a world of flexible exchange rates are that those nations

---

1. The Bundesbank has recently denied that any such mechanism has applied in Germany. See the Memorandum by the Deutsche Bundesbank in Memoranda on Monetary Policy, Vol II, House of Commons Paper 720 II, HMSO, 1980.

which permit relatively fast rates of monetary growth will
have both high rates of inflation and depreciating currency:
those which achieve relatively slow rates of monetary growth
will have relatively low rates of inflation and an
appreciating currency.

We have touched on expectations and anticipatory
behaviour. Such behaviour in the foreign exchange market
is only one example of an important and widespread
phenomenon: the ability of people to learn and to forestall.
This phenomenon has been incorporated into first the
monetary theories of inflation and then into all theories.
Once people get used to prices rising they will expect
this to continue and come to anticipate it in ways which
will be self-justifying. Firms will plan to review prices
regularly, wage negotiators will demand, or be prepared to
concede, higher nominal increases, borrowers will take on
higher nominal commitments; all in the knowledge that
money receipts, money payments, monetary assets and
liabilities are all subject to erosion in real terms. Such
behaviour will collectively be self-justifying: inflation
will acquire its own in-built momentum.

The main tenet of the monetarist belief is still
there. It is, in the long run, due to excessive expansions
in the money supply that inflations occur and are
sustained; but once rising prices become the norm,
widespread anticipatory behaviour will add its own short-
term impetus to inflation and make it that much harder to
stop. The correct policy is still to curb the growth of
the money supply but this now will only be effective if it
can reduce expectations. The process is likely to be
drawn out and will involve some not inconsiderable loss of
output and employment.

This then is the monetarist school of thought. It
has been stated briefly and has thereby in all probability
acquired a greater degree of precision than it should have.
Monetarists usually stress the existence of time-lags,

imperfections in market economies and the inevitable shocks, mistakes and fluctuations of economic life. Control of the supply of money is not seen as preventing all movements in the price level but it is seen as being a necessary condition for ending the sustained inflation of the last forty years.

Monetarism has not entirely superceded other aggregate demand explanations of inflation: there are still some commentators who argue that whilst excessive demand will cause inflation, increases in money are neither the main cause nor the measure of increased aggregate demand. It will be convenient, however, to leave this view on one side until we have looked at the other main theoretical approach to inflation: that stressing exogenous changes in factor costs.

Whilst in principle, and at times in practice, import costs may be important, this approach has, in the main, focussed on labour costs and has argued in essence that modern trade unions are powerful enough to push up pay independently of market forces. Most firms, faced with powerful unions, will find the cost-minimising strategy is to pay wage increases beyond increases in productivity and pass on the extra costs in higher prices. Most exponents of this theory would not deny any connection between union strength and market forces - unions are in a stronger position in times of high demand for labour - but they would claim some measure of independence for trade unions such that levels of pay can be pushed up even in times of slack demand for labour.

This theory, like the monetarist theory, accepts that people will learn and anticipate, and that in consequence union pressure for large increases in money earnings will be a consequence of inflation as well as a cause. It also accepts that monetary expansion is a necessary concomittant of the inflation otherwise caused so it starts to appear that the two theories are likely to be difficult to distinguish sufficiently in practice to permit any

conclusive test. However, in principle, there is a clear
difference of view as to ultimate causation. Monetarists
see this as an over rapid rate of growth of the money supply
which leads to price expectations and hard bargaining by
trade unions. Labour market theorists see causation lying
with trade union behaviour in the labour market which then
obliges the authorities to allow increases in the money
supply to prevent too-high real wages from causing
unemployment. The third view that we have touched upon
which believes in aggregate demand but not that the money
supply is an adequate indicator of this is very much an
eclectic view. High demand for goods and services (shown
by a low level of unemployment) will cause rising levels of
pay, but low demand for goods and services (and high
unemployment) will not prevent pay rises as here trade
unions' pressures will become dominant. This latter view
seems to be the view of the British National Institute for
Economic and Social Research.

All views have in common that monetary expansion is a
necessary part of any continuing inflation. Any
investigation of inflation must start here.

4.   THE GROWTH OF THE MONEY STOCK

There are many possible definitions of money just as
there are many different measures of price and output
changes. We have no desire to offer any lengthy taxonomy
but we cannot avoid looking at several different measures.
In both the UK and Germany, official publications give
figures of the money supply on three different definitions.
The narrowest definition in each country is M_1 which
comprises currency in the hands of the public plus private-
sector sight deposits. One would expect such an aggregate
to be correlated with a measure of economic activity such
as nominal GNP, since it must approximate to transactions
balances. The problem is that any such correlation would
tell us little about the influence of money on activity as

one would expect this aggregate to be largely endogenous.
Monetary authorities do not control M_1 directly, nor in the
UK or Germany do they set targets for it. The largest
component of it - sight deposits - is a part of total bank
deposits and can be altered at the will of bank customers
by their switching from one type of deposit to another.

The other two definitions of money used in the UK
are closely related. There is M_3, defined as currency in
the hands of the public plus all resident bank deposits in
sterling and foreign currencies; and sterling M_3, defined
as currency in the hands of the public plus all resident
bank deposits in sterling but excluding foreign currency
deposits. The latter definition has the advantage that it
is not affected by changes in the exchange rate: it is
also the one used by the British government in which to
express its monetary targets.

It is worth mentioning that both M_3 and sterling M_3
include all bank deposits irrespective of term to
maturity. This is in contrast to broad definitions of money
in Germany (see below) as well as to the UK definition of
eligible liabilities, i.e. bank liability subject to the
official reserve requirement, which excludes all deposits
with an initial maturity in excess of two years. In practice
most bank deposits in the UK are very liquid and only a very
small percentage have an initial term to maturity as long
as two years. (See Chapter 1).

The two broad definitions of money used in Germany
differ from each other substantially: M_2, which
approximates to the UK M_3, covers currency in the hands of
the public plus all resident sight and time deposits plus
other funds raised by banks on terms of less than four
years to maturity; M_3 covers the same plus savings
deposits at statutory notice. These latter are in principle
subject to three months notice of withdrawal but this can be

waived on the acceptance of a certain loss of interest. German M_3 is a much wider measure than the UK M_3 but it is regarded by the Bundesbank as the single most reliable measure of monetary policy; both M_1 and M_2 being affected by shifts between different categories of (effectively liquid) bank liabilities due to movements in relative interest rates.[1]

We give in Table 9.5 both M_1 and sterling M_3 for the UK and in Table 9.6 all three of the German monetary aggregates. Money-supply figures for the UK are not published for the years prior to 1963 so for the sake of comparability both Tables are limited to the years 1963-79. Figures that are available for the German monetary aggregates show that their growth in the three years 1960-63 did not differ greatly from the average growth over the decade of the 1960's and a similar conclusion in the case of the UK monetary aggregates can be inferred from data on bank deposits.

At first sight the most striking feature is the similarity in the rates of monetary growth in the two countries: over the whole period, M_1 grew at an average rate of 8.5 per cent in Germany and 8.9 per cent in the UK; German M_2 grew at a rate of 9.6 per cent whilst UK M_3 grew at a rate of 10.8 per cent. Looking at different sub-periods we can see that all the German aggregates were growing faster than those in the UK in the 1960's, but that the position was reversed in the 1970's. Another point worthy of note is that the German monetary aggregates showed only slight changes in their growth rates in the different sub-periods shown. This is quite different from both the UK measures which show a rate of monetary growth in the 1970's well over that of the 1960's.

In seeking to analyse these figures several points must be borne in mind. First, as was shown in Tables 9.1

---

1. See the section on monetary policy in the 1979 report of the Deutsche Bundesbank.

TABLE 9.5: UNITED KINGDOM MONETARY AGGREGATES

End of Period	M_1 Amount Outstanding	Change	Percentage Change	Sterling M_3 Amount Outstanding	Change	Percentage Change
1963	7,210			11,210		
1964	7,450	249	3.5	11,860	653	5.8
1965	7,610	179	2.4	12,640	805	6.8
1966	7,600	-3	0	13,060	440	3.5
1967	8,180	670	8.8	14,380	1,248	9.6
1968	8,640	481	5.9	15,490	948	6.6
1969	8,660	27	0.3	15,820	350	2.3
1970	9,420	830	9.6	17,300	1,541	9.7
1971	10,710	904	9.6	19,530	2,308	13.3
1972	12,240	1,508	14.1	24,720	4,927	25.2
1973	13,040	813	6.6	31,450	6,702	27.1
1974	14,470	1,437	11.0	34,670	3,255	10.3
1975	17,220	2,018	13.9	36,980	2,331	6.7
1976	18,950	1,787	10.4	40,280	3,565	9.6
1977	23,090	4,176	22.0	44,340	4,130	10.3
1978	26,940	3,871	16.8	51,080	6,767	15.3
1979	29,660	2,729	10.1	57,910	6,733	13.2
Average Rates of Change						
1963-79			8.9			10.8
1963-69			3.4			5.9
1969-75			10.8			15.1
1975-79			14.7			12.1

Source: Bank of England Statistical Abstract and Financial Statistics.

TABLE 9.6: WEST GERMANY MONETARY AGGREGATES

End of Period	M₁			M₂			M₃		
	Amount Outstanding	Change	Percentage Change	Amount Outstanding	Change	Percentage Change	Amount Outstanding	Change	Percentage Change
1963	67,453	4,407	7.0	94,391	5,962	6.7	149,910	13,379	9.5
1964	72,952	5,399	8.2	100,818	6,427	6.8	163,648	14,133	9.2
1965	78,525	5,573	7.6	106,921	6,103	6.1	180,400	17,234	10.2
1966	79,619	1,094	1.4	113,389	6,498	6.1	194,942	14,960	8.1
1967	87,921	8,307	10.4	127,574	14,190	12.5	217,639	23,350	11.6
1968	93,466	5,531	6.3	145,327	18,150	14.2	245,964	29,140	13.0
1969	99,429	5,963	6.4	156,875	14,548	10.0	268,205	22,881	9.0
1970	108,219	8,690	8.7	173,383	16,408	10.5	291,517	23,982	8.7
1971	121,522	13,243	12.2	198,595	24,967	14.4	330,735	38,713	13.3
1972	139,298	17,546	14.4	232,330	33,505	16.9	378,449	47,144	14.3
1973	142,862	2,572	1.8	265,861	31,943	13.7	416,749	33,996	9.0
1974	158,432	15,500	10.8	279,603	13,682	5.1	452,205	35,176	8.4
1975	179,898	21,396	13.5	279,318	-395	-0.1	490,890	38,425	8.5
1976	186,852	6,884	3.8	298,180	18,922	6.8	532,027	41,007	8.4
1977	208,076	21,094	11.3	331,812	33,472	11.2	591,473	58,946	11.1
1978	237,909	29,743	14.3	375,408	43,496	13.1	656,595	64,782	11.0
1979	247,869	9,860	4.0	406,492	30,954	8.2	696,213	39,248	6.0
Average Rates of Change									
1963-79			8.5			9.6			10.1
1963-69			6.7			8.8			10.2
1969-75			10.2			9.9			10.7
1975-79			8.3			9.8			9.2

Source: Monthly Report of the Deutsche Bundesbank.

and 9.2, the growth of real income has been appreciably
higher in Germany throughout the period in question.   Since
one would expect the growth in the demand for money to
increase in line with income, all other things equal, this
would mean that the rate of monetary growth compatible with
price stability would have been higher in Germany than in
the UK.

That, in the event, monetary growth was slightly higher
in the UK could be taken as a partial explanation of the
higher rate of inflation in that country. But, at best, it
is only a partial explanation: even allowing for differences
in growth of output, the difference in the inflation rates
is greater than can be explained by simple comparisons of
monetary growth. What has happened is that, over the
long-run, nominal national income (comprising changes
in both real income and in prices) has risen faster than the
growth of the monetary aggregates in the UK and more slowly
than the growth of the monetary aggregates in Germany. Put
another way, velocity has risen in the UK and fallen in
Germany. Thus in the former the ratio of GNP to $£M_3$ which
averaged 2.8 in the mid-1960's stood at over 3.2 in the
late 1970's, while the ratio of GNP to M_1 changed over the
same period from an average of about 4.8 to about 6.3.   In
the latter, the ratio of GNP to M_3 fell from about 2.6 to
about 2.0 over this period and that of GNP to M_2 fell from
about 4.2 to 3.5. The ratio of GNP to M_1 also fell, but
only by a small amount.

In the UK the changes in velocity are partially
accounted for by the upward trend in interest rates, but
only partially. In spite of the various econometric studies
that have been made, the demand for money in the UK in the
1970's has yet to be satisfactorily explained. In Germany
there has been no clear trend in interest rates, levels
were similar in the late 1970's to those of the early
1960's and here,too, velocity changes have proved hard to
explain.[1]

---

1.   See for instance the annual report of the Deutsche
      Bundesbank for 1978, p. 36.

Another possible explanation of the trend rate of increase of velocity in the UK is the generally weak competitive position of the banking system in that country and the growth of near-monies. This has generally been seen as something influenced by (to put it no higher) a monetary policy which has all too often sought monetary restraint by imposing non-competitive behaviour on the banking system. Over the years 1963-79, when £M_3 grew by an average of 10.8 per cent per annum, shares and deposits of the building socieites grew by an average of 15.9 per cent per annum.

The conclusions of this discussion would seem to be threefold. Over the last two decades, monetary growth in the UK relative to the growth of real output has, on average, been significantly greater than in Germany. Differences in inflation rates have, however, been even greater still and these are associated with divergent movements in velocity in the two countries: upward in the UK, downward in Germany. There are some reasons for believing that the rising velocity in the UK reflects, at least in part, a shift in demand from bank liabilities to the liabilities of non-bank financial intermediaries.

When we look at the sub-periods, we see there is some broad correlation between monetary change and inflation in the UK. Both monetary series show sharply increased rates of growth in the early 1970's with M_3 growing by about 60 per cent in the space of two years. Subsequently, the growth of M_3 fell back, whereas M_1 showed no sign of decelerating until the end of the decade. There is some evidence to suggest that M_3 was artifically depressed in the late 1970's due to the Bank of England's corset control. The abolition of this control in 1980 led to a significant jump in measured £M_3.

In Germany there was an increase in monetary expansion in the early 1970's but it was shorter lived and less marked than in the UK. Looking at the three sub-periods on which

we have focussed up till now only in the case of M_1 are
there appreciable differences between them; M_1 shows a
significantly higher growth rate in the early 1970's and
then a definite deceleration, M_2 after an actual fall in
1975 continues to grow in the late 1970's at rates not
different from those of earlier years. M_3 shows only a
slightly increased rate of growth in the early 1970's and
only a modest deceleration thereafter.

Monetary expansion influences, and is influenced by,
the flow of money across the exchanges as we have seen
above. In the case of the UK this has usually involved an
outflow of money; in the case of Germany it has usually
involved an inflow. The Bundesbank has frequently complained
of the difficulties of trying to maintain a tight monetary
policy when faced with the need to provide large quantities
of Deutschemarks in exchange for foreign currency, either
to maintain a given mark parity, or, more recently, to
prevent the floating mark from appreciating too fast.

The statistical impact of inflows and outflows of
foreign currency on the domestic money supply is usually
shown by the following identity: domestic credit expansion
(total credit granted by the banking system to domestic
residents) less the increase of banks' non-monetary
liabilities plus the increase in net foreign assets equals
the growth in money, broadly defined. The increase in net
foreign assets of the banking system (central bank and
private banks) shows the inflow (or, if negative, outflow)
of foreign currency and hence will be equalled by an
increase in liabilities to residents; domestic credit
creation shows the extent to which liabilities to
residents are created domestically and the total of these
two less any increase in banks' non-monetary liabilities
will, therefore, equal the growth of banks' monetary
liabilities (including currency) or money broadly defined.

It is possible then to break down the changes in the
money supply into a domestic component, i.e. domestic

credit expansion minus the increase in banks' non-monetary
liabilities and a foreign component. This is done for
both the UK and Germany in Table 9.7. In practice, the
two items shown for each country do not always sum to M_3:
there are some small miscellaneous items we have ignored
but they form a sufficiently large part of M_3 (or $£M_3$ in
the case of the UK) to show the relative influence of
internal and external factors on the creation of money in
the two countries. One point that should be noted is
that the deduction of non-monetary liabilities in the case
of UK banks is usually relatively small and is composed
mainly of changes in banks' capital and reserves. In
Germany, banks have very large non-monetary liabilities
comprising time deposits borrowed for periods of four
years and over, bank savings bonds, savings deposits at
agreed notice (minimum six months) and capital and reserves.
In 1979, total lending by German banks to domestic non-
banks amounted to almost DM 139bn. but nearly DM 76bn. of
this was accounted for by the growth of banks' non-
monetary liabilities so the increase in monetary liabilities
was only DM 63bn.

In seeking to interpret Table 9.7 we must bear in
mind that the division of the increase in broad money into
domestic and foreign components is definitional and does not
of itself tell us anything about causation. For instance,
if we have a year in which DCE was low and there was a large
capital inflow we do not know 'a priori' whether the former
caused the latter or vice-versa. So we must be careful in
drawing inferences. This being said, however, the most
striking features about Table 9.7 is the frequency of net
capital outflows from the UK and the frequency of net
capital inflows into Germany. In only four years out of
seventeen, did the UK banking system acquire net external
assets; in only two out of the seventeen years did the
German banking system not acquire net external assets.
Thus, in this respect the predictions of the monetarist
theory are borne out: countries with relatively high
rates of inflation will export money, those with relatively
low rates of inflation will import money.

TABLE 9.7: DOMESTIC AND FOREIGN INFLUENCES ON THE MONEY SUPPLY

	UNITED KINGDOM (£mn)			GERMANY (DMmn)		
	DCE – banks' non-monetary Liabilities	Net External Assets	£M$_3$ (change)	DCE – banks' non-monetary Liabilities	Net External Assets	M$_3$ (change)
1963	946	-249	679[1]	11,376	3,296	13,329
1964	1,421	-768	653	12,273	1,668	14,133
1965	997	-192	805	17,480	472	17,234
1966	658	-218	440	12,303	3,617	14,960
1967	1,743	-495	1,248	18,260	6,281	23,350
1968	2,011	-1,063	948	20,281	10,929	29,140
1969	-155	505	350	27,195	-2,450	22,881
1970	831	710	1,541	22,745	14,231	23,982
1971	773	1,535	2,308	36,403	11,516	38,713
1972	6,022	-1,095	4,927	39,416	8,664	47,144
1973	7,579	-877	6,702	21,903	23,481	33,996
1974	6,252	-2,997	3,255	25,308	13,188	35,176
1975	3,631	-1,300	2,331	23,170	16,840	38,425
1976	6,286	-2,721	3,565	32,090	8,267	41,007
1977	694	3,436	4,130	51,261	10,147	58,946
1978	7,191	-419	6,767	70,563	7,086	64,782
1979	11,143	-2,892	6,733	63,187	-21,836	39,248

NOTE: 1.   M$_3$ as opposed to £M$_3$.   The difference is likely to be small.

Source: UK FIGURES: Bank of England Statistical Abstract and Financial Statistics.

GERMAN FIGURES: Monthly Report of the Deutsche Bundesbank.

5.   MONETARY POLICY

Monetary policy has been a complex affair in both countries: any attempt in the space available to describe and 'a fortiori' to judge these policies is hazardous and must be undertaken with caution. Nevertheless, some comments of a general nature seem desirable.

Policy has taken place in both countries against a changing background both of circumstance and of ideas. In the 1960's, international exchange rates were 'fixed but adjustable', for most of the 1970's they were flexible; in the first period, policy had to take account of the need to maintain the international parity of the currency, in the second it was concerned with limiting movements in the value of the currency when these were considered undesirable. Foreign currency flows were frequently a problem for both countries despite various expedients employed from time to time to restrict or discourage them. The need to finance the activities of government without thereby creating excessive amounts of new money was a continual problem in the UK and one that caused concern at times in Germany.

In what follows, we shall look at the operational targets of policy in both countries as well as the instruments used to try to achieve these. We shall then consider how policy was related to the ultimate goals such as full employment and price stability and consider some particular episodes.

The operational targets of policy have changed in both countries and the means used to achieve these have been subject to shifts in emphasis from time to time. The UK policy was mainly directed towards influencing interest rates (often more for external than domestic reasons) until the late 1960's. In 1968 at the behest of the IMF, the authorities started to control domestic credit expansion and in subsequent years, gradually shifted the emphasis of policy towards 'the monetary aggregates'. In 1976, the

government began announcing annual monetary targets for
sterling M_3; and in 1980 targets were set for a four-year
period.

There were various tools of policy. Given the
continuing need for public-sector borrowing, operations in
government bonds were crucial: at first these were aimed
at limiting interest rate fluctuations in the belief that
this would encourage the long-run demand for government
stock but with the shift of emphasis towards controlling the
monetary aggregates concern shifted to achieving adequate
sales of bonds even if at the cost of greater interest rate
instability. A corollary of the earlier gilt-edged market
behaviour was a reluctance to sell stock if this meant
sharply depressing bond prices and even, at times, a
willingness to buy back stock to support the market. This
led to a periodic need for large borrowing from the banking
system which, in turn, encouraged the use of direct
quantitative limits on the growth of bank lending to the
private sector, in order to keep monetary expansion within
bounds. The monetary reforms of 1971 did away with such limits
following the growing realisation that in the long-run they
would only promote the growth of non-bank credit and non-
bank intermediation.

Special deposits (equivalent to variations in the
reserve ratio) have been used frequently by the UK
authorities over the last two decades and supplementary
special deposits (effectively a tax on increases beyond a
permitted limit in interest-bearing deposits) were in use
for certain periods between 1973 and 1980, until their
distorting effects were also realized. Minimum lending
rate (MLR) or Bank rate, as it was previously called, has
been changed frequently. Until the early 1970's this was
at the initiative of the authorities but was then a change
to a system whereby it fluctuated in line with Treasury

bill rates. But since this only led to the authorities
manipulating Treasury bill rates in order to achieve
desired levels of minimum lending rates there was -
logically - a reversion to the earlier system of official
fixing of MLR.

In Germany the main operational target of monetary
policy during the 1960's was the free liquid reserves of the
banks comprising essentially cash balances beyond required
reserves, together with short-term domestic and foreign assets
changeable into balances at the Bundesbank at the initiative
of the banks. It was observed that free liquid reserves
were maintained in a broadly stable relationship to total
deposits and the Bundesbank sought to influence the supply
of liquid assets to the banks; precise control was frequently
impossible given the then obligation of the Bundesbank to
maintain the external parity of the Deutschemark and to
supply unlimited amounts of domestic money in exchange for
foreign currency.

This obligation was removed when in 1973 the authorities
finally ceased pegging the exchange value of the Mark and thus
rendered possible a more precise control over the banks.
During 1973 and 1974 the Bundesbank took steps to reduce the
free liquid reserves of the banks to a minimum and then,
in 1974, introduced a new system of control based on the
central bank money stock. This is, in effect, control by means
of a monetary base although as explained in Chapter 2, the
exact definition of the base has certain individual features.
It will be recalled that the central bank money stock is
defined as currency with the public plus required reserves
(at the ratios applying in January 1974) against domestic
deposits - reserves which vary according to bank size
and location, and the composition of deposits between demand,
time and savings deposits. This definition differs from the
American concept of the monetary base by excluding reserves
held by the banks against foreign liabilities (regarded as
not being relevant for domestic monetary control) and by
excluding free reserves.

The central bank money stock can be seen as a weighted monetary aggregate with currency with the public given a weight of 100 per cent and demand deposits, time deposits and savings deposits weighted according to their average reserve ratios in January 1974 (16.6 per cent, 12.4 per cent and 8.1 per cent respectively). This particular aggregate was chosen because in the words of the Bundesbank[1] 'it underlines the responsibility of the central bank for monetary expansion, since the central bank money stock.... is the Bundesbank's direct contribution to domestic money creation' and because it was believed to have a relatively stable long-run relationship with nominal national income. Since 1975 the Bundesbank has published annual targets for the growth of the central bank money stock, but no attempt is made to achieve the targets on a month-to-month basis. In fact, this would, at present, be scarcely possible as minimum reserves are maintained with a time-lag: required reserves in any one month being calculated on the basis of bank liabilities on the 23rd and last days of the preceding month and on the 7th and 15th days of the current month. The Bundesbank supplies the banks with such central bank money as they need but does so on terms of its own choosing, and relies on variations in these terms influencing future portfolio decisions by banks. (See also Chapter 2).

Day-to-day operations then are concentrated on influencing short-term interest rates. This can be done in a number of ways. The Bundesbank sets the discount rate (the rate charged for discounting eligible paper), the Lombard rate (the rate charged for short-term, i.e. one month or less, loans against collateral) and its own dealing rate for open-market operations. These rates are closely related: the Lombard rate is usually from 0.5 per cent and 1.5 per cent above the discount rate and dealing rates are usually between the two. Both discounts and loans against collateral are normally subject to quota limits and these quotas have been changed frequently. A penal rate of

1.   Memorandum by the Deutsche Bundesbank in Memoranda on Monetary Policy, H of C 720 II, (HMSO), 1980.

interest (Lombard rate plus 3 per cent) is charged to all
banks who cannot meet reserve requirements by discounts or
advances within quota.

Open-market operations are mainly conducted in short-
term paper but dealings in government bonds do at times
occur. Open-market operations in foreign currency (spot
official sales of foreign exchange to the banks combined
with a forward purchase) have also, at times, been used to
limit the growth of bank reserve assets. The Bundesbank
also has power to shift government deposits between itself
and the private banking system as another means of
influencing bank reserves.

The Bundesbank does not operate "special deposits" or
"supplementary special deposits" as used by the Bank of
England, but it has powers, which it frequently uses, to
vary banks' reserve requirements. Special reserve
requirements against liabilities to non-residents (sometimes
up to 100 per cent) have been used in an attempt to restrain
inflows of foreign capital.

The Bundesbank itself believes that it has sufficient
power to influence quickly the whole spectrum of interest
rates and that by so doing, it can influence within a short-
time (3-6 months) the composition of financial assets
either in favour of, or against, monetary assets vis-a-vis
longer term assets. Over a slightly longer period of time
(6-12 months), changes in interest rates start to effect
decisions to save and decisions to invest.

The German central bank is keen to stress that it does
not pursue rigidly its monetary targets to the exclusion of
all other considerations. Short-run fluctuations are
accepted and even longer-run changes outside the target
range can be permitted if this seems desirable. In 1978
for instance, the monetary target was temporarily
disregarded whilst the Bundesbank sought to curb the rising
external value of the Deutschemark. However, one should not
confuse short-term flexibility with long-term decision:

the Bundesbank has repeatedly made it plain that it regards
control of the money supply as of great importance and that
its targets for the central bank money stock will, over the
medium-term, be adhered to. As shown in Chapter 2 the
growth of the central bank money stock has generally been
higher than the target, but only by a small margin.

When we come to look at the ultimate goals of policy
and the effectiveness of policy in achieving these, we can
only talk in general terms. The pronouncements of the
authorities tend typically to stress the desirability of
meeting all the main policy goals without stating clearly
their priorities and econometric studies (reaction
functions) seldom give conclusive results. However, having
said that, the evidence is of a much greater concern about
inflation by policy-makers in Germany than in the UK - at
least until recent years - and a much greater belief that
this was related to monetary factors than in the UK.

For much of the period, the UK policy was directed
primarily to unemployment and the balance of payments.
This led to the so-called stop-go policies with expansionary
fiscal and monetary policies being aimed at reducing
unemployment being followed by deflationary policies aimed
at improving the balance of payments. Inflation did not
appear to receive a high priority as such - a fact endorsed
by such reaction-functions as have been estimated.[1] For
much of the period much influential opinion was of the view
that inflation was not caused by, or easily responsive to
monetary policy but was primarily the result of trade-union
wage bargaining. This view found favour with successive
governments and resulted in continued attempts at first,
incomes policies and then prices and incomes policies. In
the course of these attempts, the UK has created - and later
abolished - various institutions to implement the policies.
Controls on prices have tended to grow with each successive
policy, until the election of the present government in 1979.

---

1.   See for instance, D. Fisher: The Instruments of
      Monetary Policy and the Generalized Trade-off
      Function for Britain, 1955-1968. Manchester School,
      1970.

Many observers credit these attempts at administrative control of wages and prices with some temporary success, but few are prepared to argue that they have had any effect on the long-run trend of inflation.

As inflation rose in the late 1960's and early 1970's so did concern about it grow along with a willingness to consider the role of monetary factors in causing it. In 1971, there was a reform of monetary policy aimed at producing both a more competitive financial sector and also a shift in the emphasis of policy towards controlling the monetary aggregates (see Chapter 1). The reform was mismanaged and resulted in the rapid monetary growth of 1971-73. The then Conservative Government fell back on an incomes policy. The succeeding Labour Government combined a policy of attempted control of the money supply with a prices and incomes policy with some success in reducing inflation until the latter half of the policy collapsed in early 1979.

Only after the arrival in office of the new Conservative administration in 1979 has there been a clear policy of attempting to control the money supply and the growth of monetary demand without coupling this with a formal incomes policy. The policy has encountered many problems and despite difficulties in achieving the degree of monetary control aimed for it has nonetheless contributed to the sharpest post-war drop in output and an unemployment total of over two million. However, by late 1980, there was clear evidence of a slowing in the rate of inflation.

German policy shows some differences and some similarities. The biggest single difference has been the complete absence of formal incomes policies of any sort. The German authorities believe that such control of inflation as they deem desirable is obtainable through demand management policies and (although budgetary policy has come to assume considerable importance) for much of the post-war period this has meant largely monetary policy.

The main similarity is that Germany, like the UK, and like most other Western nations has had to contend with a cyclical economy and has had to alternate between phases of expansionary and phases of contractionary policy. During the 1950's and 1960's this was mitigated by an under-valued currency which meant that reductions in domestic demand were usually offset by increases in foreign demand; but since the floating of the Deutschemark this has ceased to be true.

If policy has had to alternate between expansionary and contractionary phases as in the UK, the triggers of policy were not the same. Only occasionally has there been a deficit on the current account of the balance of payments and until 1979 such deficits as there were have been short-lived. Registered unemployment was usually very low until the mid-1970's, with the brunt of changes in demand for labour being born by changes in hiring and firing of foreign workers. Since 1974, however, unemployment rates have risen sharply alongside a decline in the number of foreign workers in employment.

Deflationary policies then have not been prompted by balance of payments problems, nor have they until the last six years, had the domestic unemployment consequences of comparable policies in the UK. Deflationary policies have rather been undertaken explicitly to curb inflation. The public statements of the German authorities are full of references to the need to control inflation and most outside observers suggest that such policies would have widespread popular support in a nation which has not forgotten the hyper-inflations of the 1920's and 1940's.[1]

Some examples can be cited. In 1965 and 1966 the authorities pursued a deflationary monetary policy - raising interest rates and reducing rediscount quotas on several occasions and this resulted in a sharp reduction

---

1. For a recent comment to this effect, see OECD: Monetary Targets and Inflation Control, 1979, p.44.

in the growth of M_1 and smaller reductions in the growth of M_2 and M_3. This was in response to a position of perceived excess demand with low unemployment, high (relative to then recent German experience) inflation rates of over 3 per cent, and in 1965 a deficit on the current account of the balance of payments. It could be argued that the motivation for the restrictive policy was, at least partly, the balance of payments position but it is noteworthy that the restrictive policy was maintained and tightened (interest rates were raised and rediscount and Lombard quotas reduced in May 1966) even after the current balance was clearly moving into surplus. The explanation given for this tightening of policy was that prices were still rising rapidly in the early part of 1966.[1] The result of this policy allied with a deflationary budgetary policy was to bring about the then worst post-war recession with a complete halt to growth in 1967.

In the early 1970's, Germany experienced renewed inflationary pressures with the retail price index rising by over 5 per cent in each of the five years 1971-1975. The growth of real GNP which had shot up after the depressed years of 1966 and 1967 remained high until 1973. The current account of the balance of payments was in surplus throughout. Unemployment rose slowly until 1974 and rapidly thereafter. There were persistent attempts at curbing demand both by monetary and fiscal policy, but in the years 1970-1973, monetary policy was hampered, if not wholly offset, by massive inflows of foreign capital; this was in spite of revaluations of the Deutschemark in 1969 and 1971 and was the cause of the temporary floating of the Deutschemark during 1971 and its permanent floating after March 1973. The continual influx of funds from abroad meant that attempts to raise domestic interest rates were counter-productive and at times the Bundesbank chose to reduce short-term rates in the hope of discouraging inward

---

1.   See OECD: Monetary Policy in Germany, 1973, p.50.

movements of capital. Further, bank reserve requirements
were, at times, eased for reasons connected with the value
of the Deutschemark. In general, however, the trend of
reserve requirements was up in this period and in addition
supplementary reserve requirements were imposed on foreign-
owned liabilities. Rediscount and Lombard quotas were
steadily reduced with the latter being temporarily
suspended in June 1973.

All policy could do, however, was to reduce the effects
of the influx of foreign currency. It was only after the
final unpegging of the Mark that the authorities could begin
to get the rate of inflation down. This, however, is dealt
with in the next section.

The German willingness to use monetary policy to
control inflation shows a clear difference of view to the
UK where, until relatively recently, the money supply was
regarded as little more than a useful indicator reflecting,
rather than causing, trends in wages and prices. Another
clear difference between the two countries already noted
is the attitude of the German authorities to incomes policies.
Germany has had no formal incomes policies at all. This,
however, does not mean an absence of concern about wage
bargaining or the trend of incomes.

Throughout, there has been a realization - made explicit
in frequent statements - that an important function of
published monetary targets is to signal to economic agents
just what the likely growth of monetary demand would be - and
among the most important such agents would be wage
bargainers. It has been regularly stressed that if wages
grew too fast, this would be at the expense of output and
employment. And whilst on occasions the authorities have
taken the view that wages have grown too fast, there have
also been frequent examples of the authorities praising the
realism of those netotiating on behalf of organized labour.
In its annual report for 1979, the Bundesbank referred to
'the sense of economic responsibility shown by management

and labour in the recent wage negotiations'. More recently Count Otto Lamsdorf, the German economics minister, stated that the German trade unions deserved high praise for wage moderation - in particular, in not insisting on an extra bonus to make up for the rise in energy costs.[1]

When the British Government in 1980 began talking about the need for moderate wage settlements, this was immediately described by many commentators as a retreat from monetarism and a form of a back-door incomes policy. It clearly is not: limitation of the growth of monetary demand requires the limitation of the growth of monetary earnings, if unemployment is not to result. This has been realized in Germany for a long time.

6.   THE REACTION TO THE 1973-74 OIL-PRICE RISES

Oil-price increases - more than quadrupling the price of oil - were announced late in 1973 and early in 1974: the first of these two years had already seen a remarkable 50 per cent increase in world commodity prices. These events indicated not only an increase in inflationary pressures as the prices of finished goods were adjusted to take account of higher raw material prices, but also the prospect of a drop in world demand to the extent that the oil producers were slow to spend their increased incomes. The policy reaction in the UK and Germany was very different.

The UK, it must be said, was in a particularly bad situation even before the rises in oil prices. In the two years 1972 and 1973, sterling M_3 had risen by almost 60 per cent; under the incomes policy many wage contracts were to be automatically adjusted for price rises and hence were set to rise as a consequence of the increased costs of raw materials; inflation by the end of 1973 was already close to 10 per cent per annum and rising fast and sterling had already lost 15 per cent of its December 1971 value.

---

1.   Financial Times, 9th September, 1980.

The predictable consequences of the monetary explosion occurred: prices rose at average rates of 16.1 per cent and 24.2 per cent in 1974 and 1975 respectively, whilst average earnings grew by 17.7 per cent and 26.7 per cent. Government policy reflected more concern about recession than about inflation; government expenditure both on goods and services and on transfer payments rose rapidly; the public-sector borrowing requirement rose from 5.7 per cent of GNP in 1973 to 7.6 per cent in 1974 and to 10.0 per cent in 1975. Domestic credit expansion remained high in 1974, 1975 and 1976 but with a substantial current-account deficit on the balance of payments, the rate of growth of the money supply was reduced in 1974 and 1975. Minimum lending rate which had been 13 per cent at end-1973 was reduced, albeit with some fluctuations, to 5 per cent by October 1977. Perhaps not surprisingly, M_3 was again growing at increasing rates after 1976.

Thus, in the years following the oil crisis, the UK showed a reluctance to take measures to curb demand on any large scale - rather the emphasis was on not adding to the world recession and on accepting a large balance-of-payments deficit. Monetary policy remained easy by any normal standards. The main means of checking inflation was again through an incomes policy and whilst there was a deceleration of average earnings in 1976 and 1977, these rose again thereafter: price inflation did fall to just over 10 per cent in 1977 but it was back to 14 per cent in 1978 and on a rising course.

Germany was in a better position to face the effects of the oil crisis and it pursued somewhat different policies thereafter. As we have seen, the Deutschemark was allowed to float in March 1973 after another period of large inflows of foreign currency. This was a signal for a stabilization programme: fiscal measures were taken in May 1973, while the Bundesbank raised bank reserve requirements, temporarily suspended all Lombard credits and raised short-term interest rates to very high levels; these monetary measures being taken between March and June. Thus the inflationary pressures in the German economy were being faced before the oil crisis and although the inflation rate remained high in 1973 and 1974, it began to fall rapidly from the second half of 1975. The growth of the money supply as measured by M_2 fell sharply in both 1974 and 1975.

Some of the May 1973 fiscal measures were rescinded after the oil-price rise, but in general the German reaction was cautious and reflected concern about both inflation and recession. Some modest measures of fiscal stimulation were introduced in 1974 but the Bundesbank did not cut its discount rate from the high level of 7 per cent until the last quarter of the year by when it was clear that real national income was already falling. Budgetary policy was definitely expansive in 1975 (although not sufficiently so to stop unemployment growing more than threefold between 1973 and 1975) and the general government borrowing requirement rose to 6.3 per cent of GNP. However, this was contemplated as a strictly temporary measure. During the course of 1975, cuts in future government spending programmes were announced along with delayed tax increases. The general-government borrowing requirement was down to 3.6 per cent of GNP in 1976 and to 2.7 per cent in the following year. The Bundesbank had a series of annual targets of 8 per cent growth in the central bank money stock although in several years it allowed these to be exceeded by 1-2 per cent. Monetary policy remained relatively tight: although required reserve ratios were reduced from the exceptionally high levels of 1973, they remained high by past standards. Short-term interest rates were reduced in stages throughout 1975 and were again reduced in 1977 - to very low levels - when once again the Bundesbank was becoming concerned about the rising external value of the Deutschemark.

In general, the policy appears to have been very successful. There was no attempt to escape the adjustments imposed by the oil-price rises but there was an attempt to mitigate the worst effects of these by a temporary expansionary fiscal policy. Monetary policy remained tight in the years 1974-76, although some easing occurred there-after due to concern about the external value of the Mark. Inflation which had been 7 per cent in 1973 and 1974, declined steadily to 2.7 per cent in 1978 before turning up again in 1979. Increases in nominal earnings which had averaged nearly 12 per cent in 1973 and 1974 declined steadily to 5.2 per cent in 1978, also turning up again in 1979.

Throughout the period of the middle and late 1970's, the Bundesbank had continued to stress the need for monetary policy to be kept tight so as to minimize the scope for price rises. Monetary targets were set which would leave scope for the growth of real output but if, and only if, prices did not rise greatly. When import costs were rising this was not seen as a reason for a more accommodating monetary policy but rather the reverse: it increased the need for tight money in order to limit the scope for passing on these extra costs in higher prices. Nor was this policy seen as being inimical to the growth of real output; it was repeatedly stressed that in the long run stable prices would be conducive to the growth and efficiency of economic activity.

7.   CONCLUSIONS

The experience of inflation in the two countries in recent years could hardly be more different: the UK, although having reduced inflation from the high levels of the mid-1970's, is still struggling with annual rates of over 15 per cent; the Germans who also had high inflation (by their own standards) in the mid-1970's have since reduced this to levels not much above those of the 1960's.

In 1980, the UK consumer price index is expected to rise by about 16 per cent, the German index by less than one-third of that amount.

It would be idle to attribute this difference to any one simple factor. However, the evidence is that economic policy and particularly monetary policy has been different in the two countries and that this is an important part of any explanation. Monetary policy in Germany - like budgetary policy - has consistently given a higher priority to the limitation of inflation than has been the case in the UK. The main constraints on monetary policy have been external: large inflows of foreign money or large rises in the international value of the Deutschemark.

At the technical level of the operation of monetary policy the authorities of both countries have relied heavily on influencing short-term interest rates but in Germany this has, for a long time, been seen as a means to controlling monetary growth and credit creation; in the UK such an approach emerged during the 1970s. For a long while, the operational target of the UK policy was the level of interest rates per se. In general, despite disavowing any rigid or slavish adherence to its monetary targets, the Bundesbank has consistently focussed on the money supply to a greater extent than has been the case in the UK.

In this it has been helped by having fewer problems arising from the need to finance the deficits of government. As shown in Chapter 7, these have generally been smaller in Germany than in the UK. But even more important, their financing by the banking system was arranged in a way that did not add appreciably to bank reserves. In the UK, banks' holdings of medium- and long-term bonds have steadily declined and their lending to government has been concentrated more and more in the form of highly liquid assets. Further, the way the German banks' range of liabilities spans the whole range of short-term, medium-term and long-term makes them able to provide long-term finance to government as well as to the private sector, without this giving rise to excessive monetary expansion.

The very different UK capital market with its sharp
divide between institutions offering short-term assets (banks,
building societies) and those offering long-term assets
(insurance companies, pension funds) has meant that the
authorities have often faced the restricted choice of either
selling long-term bonds to the latter group of institutions
or of providing more short-term assets to the banks. Now
it would be wrong to see the large amount of long-term
saving in the UK as a disadvantage to the authorities: it
can only appear so insofar as the authorities have not
suited their borrowing techniques to their market. In
Germany, the authorities appear to have done this with much
of their borrowing being at medium- and long-term from
banks financing themselves similarly. In the UK, a
restricted range of assets with highly volatile capital
values and rates of interest frequently negative in real
terms have been offered to the insurance companies and
pension funds. Not surprisingly the latter have become
increasingly concerned with the need to avoid capital losses
or make capital gains and their demand for government stock
has ebbed and flowed according to short-term expectations of
interest-rate movements. The Bank of England has been faced
with the choice of either resorting to bank finance or
bringing about even larger yields on government stock,
each choice likely to make the long-term problem worse.
Only recently has there been much thought of getting out of
the dilemma by widening the range of assets on offer; both
marketable and non-marketable.

It is not that the German capital market is inherently
any more efficient than the UK one: it is that the
authorities appear to have better tailored their policies
to their market.

German policy has been more consistent and, if
exception is made of the various devices that have been
employed to try to discourage unwanted inflows of capital
from abroad, it has relied less on short-term expedients.
Just as the Federal Government has conspicuously not

attempted to use prices and incomes policies so the
Bundesbank has never resorted to administrative methods of
credit control believing that these will only lead to
disintermediation,[1] whereas, the Bank of England, in the
years prior to 1971, frequently imposed quantitative limits
on bank lending to the private sector and in the years
subsequent to 1971 often relied on the equally discriminatory
mechanism of supplementary special deposits. It is unlikely
to be coincidence that for much of the post-war period
velocity has been on a rising trend in the UK and on a falling
trend in Germany.

In as far then as one can compare different circumstances
in the two different countries it appears that monetary policy
in Germany has been more consistent and more effective than
policy in the UK and with fewer adverse side effects on the
allocation of resources within the financial sector. This
may, in part, reflect a greater technical efficiency but it
is probable that technical efficiency is itself more a
reflection of a much clearer view of the ultimate objectives
of policy and an unwillingness to be long swayed from these
objectives by short-run political factors.

The German authorities have persistently stressed the
need for stable prices even at the cost of short-term losses
of output in the belief that in the long-run price stability
will help rather than hinder the growth of real output. The
defence by the Bundesbank of its not having promptly acted
to prevent the sharp drop in output and employment in 1974
is worth repeating:

> '... not even earlier or more massive resort to an
> expansionary policy in Germany could have done more to
> delay the downswing; it could not have prevented it,
> as shown not least by the example of those countries
> which adopted such a stance. In the absence of a
> stabilization policy the exaggerated expectations both
> about the scope available for passing on cost
> increases to customers and about wage rises would have
> been preserved, and a return to more price stability
> would have been deferred to the distant future.
> Nevertheless, real adjustment in Germany to the new

---

1.   Memorandum by the Deutsche Bundesbank, op.cit.

conditions prevailing in the world economy, and
particularly to the fact that owing to the higher
oil prices a much larger part of domestic production
has to be transferred abroad and domestic incomes
have to be reduced accordingly, would have been
unavoidable. Countries which tried to evade this
correction of their income distribution and production
structure only postponed the problem, and at the same
time they had to contend with rising inflation rates
at home, persistent deficits in their balances of
payments and in some cases, the depreciation of their
currencies. In the event of such delays the overall
costs of this adjustment process were ultimately
much higher than in the Federal Republic of Germany
and other countries which accepted the domestic
consequences of the new conditions on world markets
and were thus able in the external field to respond
quickly to the opportunities afforded by trade with
the oil-producing countries and at home to counteract
a decline in demand without having to fear that this
would lead to a new flare up in inflation.'[1]

Whilst the emphasis on price stability has been greater
in Germany this has been carried into action purely by
budgetary and monetary policies. There has been no resort
to formal incomes policies; rather there has been a belief
that sound monetary policies would bring about sensible
adjustments in incomes: the Germans were the first to
announce monetary targets and did so precisely on account
of their expected effect on wage and price setting.

One can argue, and many do, that such policies in
Germany have the support they do due to memories of the two
hyper-inflations of this century. This may well be true,
but it is also the case that their continuance does provide
its own support through the general expectations of
relative price stability. The UK, in 1979, embarked on
policies not dissimilar from those followed in Germany, but
with expectations attuned to the failure of previous anti-
inflationary policies and based on past high rates of
inflation. Quick success seems unlikely but without firm
monetary policies any success in reducing inflation in
the UK would seem impossible.

---

1.   Report of the Deutsche Bundesbank for 1975.

CHAPTER 10: BANKING SUPERVISION
By E. Victor Morgan and K.H. Hennings

1.   INTRODUCTION

The two principal aims of banking supervision are the
protection of depositors from default by banks, and the
protection of the banking system as a whole from weakness
which may develop in parts of it. Since 1945, and
particularly in the current decade, banks have expanded
the range and complexity of their business, in parallel with
the growth of new domestic and international financial
markets. This has led to increasing interdependence within
and between national banking systems, so that the second
aim of supervision has become more important. There are some
similarities, but also a number of differences between the
way in which these problems have been tackled in the two
countries. Germany has had a formal system of supervision
since 1934 but the UK is only now setting one up as a result of
the 1979 Banking Act. The Bank of England has long kept an
informal watch over other banks, and this was so effective
that no major failure has occurred since 1878. Nevertheless,
the events of 1973-4, together with the experience of other
countries including Germany, have convinced the authorities
that old methods are inadequate to meet the new situation
described above.

In Germany, supervision was entrusted to a separate
authority, the Bundesaufsichtsamt für das Kreditwesen (KAB),
which is independent of, though working closely with, the
Bundesbank. In the UK the Bank of England continues its
supervisory activities though in a more formal manner and
with greater statutory authority. One consequence of this
is that in Germany there has always been a clear distinction
between requirements imposed on banks for prudential
reasons and those imposed so that the central bank might use
them as tools of monetary policy. In the UK, this distinction
has not always been clear in the past, e.g. in the reserve
assets ratio discussed in Chapter 1.

Both countries have imposed or are imposing rules
governing capital adequacy, liquidity and foreign exchange
exposure. Since the UK system is only in a formative stage
detailed comparisons are not possible. It seems, however,
that while neither country uses ratios that are mandatory on
a day to day basis, the German system sets more store than
the UK's on adherence to published norms. Also, the German
authorities impose a number of rules on large individual
loans, which have no counterpart in the UK.

Finally, Germany has recently developed, and the UK will
shortly introduce, measures for the protection of depositors.
Again, there are differences of approach. The UK scheme will,
in effect, insure deposits against the failure of the bank
that holds them. The German schemes (which differ somewhat as
between commercial banks, savings banks and co-operative
banks) do not protect deposits but provide for mutual help by
banks in order to prevent failure.

2.   SUPERVISION IN THE UK

The most important Acts were the Exchange Control Act
1947, which gave rise to a list of institutions permitted to
deal in foreign exchange ("the authorised" banks) and the
Companies Act 1948, where the associated list consisted of
those institutions granted certain accounting disclosure
privileges in relation to hidden reserves (the "Schedule 8
banks"). Nearly all UK registered banks which were "authorised"
were also "Schedule 8 banks", so that two lists served to
distinguish fully-recognised and hence supervised banks from
other deposit taking institutions. During the 1950's and
1960's, there were a few cases of failure of non-supervised
deposit-taking institutions, but until 1963, there was no
restriction on any company advertising for deposits and
calling itself a bank. The Protection of Depositors Act
1963 resulted in a third list, later incorporated into the

Companies Act 1967 as "Section 127 banks", which were exempt
from the prohibition then placed on the use of the words,
"bank", "banker" etc. in advertising for deposits. The Bank
was consulted in the construction of the exempt list and
based its recommendations on the two previous lists.

Despite the unsatisfactory legal background to the
definition of a bank, no institution could hold itself out to
be a bank without fear of a challenge, unless it came under
the supervisory area of the Bank, until the advent of the
"Section 123 banks". The Companies Act 1967 provided under
this section for institutions to be exempt from certain
provisions of the Moneylenders Act 1900, where they could
show that they were carrying on a "bona fide banking
business". The test, however, was a purely functional one,
and had no bearing on the reputability of the business, the
quality of its management, or the prudence with which it
operated. As with "Section 127 banks" the Department of
Trade has no powers to supervise the business of "Section
123" certificate holders. (The list of "Section 123 banks"
was effectively closed in 1978 pending the repeal of the
licensing provisions of the Moneylenders Acts and their
replacement by the licensing sections of the Consumer Credit
Act 1974.)

In the late 1960's and early 1970's, the effect of
the statutory provisions just described was to restrict the
coverage of banking supervision to those members of the
banking community whose reputations and standing had
resulted in their being fully recognised by the Bank. The
machinery of supervision varied between groups of banks,
but all of the following groups were covered:
the clearing banks, members of the London Discount Market
Association, of the Accepting Houses Committee, other UK banks
holding Section 127 exemption, and foreign bank subsidiaries
who were authorised, and consortium banks similarly
authorised. This coverage basically corresponded to the
statistical list of banks whose returns have been used to

provide aggregate information on the operations of the
banking sector, except that authorised foreign branches are
included in the list but are not formally supervised.
Becoming a listed bank thus represented the highest degree
of recognition within the banking community, while also
implying since 1971, an undertaking to participate in the
Bank's administration of the macro-economic policy of
aggregate credit control. (See Chapter 1.) Listed banks
are thus also those accepting the requirement to maintain
"reserve assets' at a mimimum of 12.5 per cent of "eligible
liabilities" while honouring any calls from the Bank for
special deposits. While additions to this group were made
from time to time as the progress of individual banks
justified it, in general those deposit-taking institutions
which did not qualify for full recognition were also not
supervised. This state of affairs continued until the Bank
took major steps to extend its supervisory coverage in the
summer of 1974, in the aftermath of the secondary banking
crisis of 1973-74 and the consequent establishment of the
support operation, familarly referred to as the "Lifeboat".
At that time, about 80 deposit-taking institutions which had
not before been supervised accepted supervision voluntarily,
including all except the smallest section 123 banks and the
members of the Finance Houses Association. The companies
then coming under supervision comprised all those known to
the Bank to hold sizeable deposits from the public. At the
same time, the machinery of supervision was radically
revised.

With the coming into force of the 1979 Banking Act,
statutory powers have been conferred on the Bank to
determine which institutions may legally operate as deposit-
taking businesses. Such institutions are divided into two
categories, "recognised banks" and "licenced deposit-taking
institutions". The Bank of England has the sole power to
grant recognition or a licence, and may revoke either. The

main criteria for recognition as a bank laid down in the
Act are:

i.   High reputation and standing in the financial
       community.

ii.   The provision of a wide range of banking services
       (or a highly specialised service).

iii.   Business carried on with integrity and prudence
       and with appropriate professional skills - implying
       that it will be under the direction of fit and
       proper persons.

iv.   At least two individuals to direct the business.

v.   Minimum net assets.

vi.   Net assets and other financial resources commesurate
       with the scale of operations.

The Bank of England's current list of recognised banks
contains nearly 300 names, and corresponds closely with
the list of contributors to banking statistics described
in Chapter 1.

The detailed interpretation of items iii and vi as
set out by the Bank make it quite clear that continuation
of recognition (or a licence) will require the acceptance of
supervision, which thus acquires effective statutory backing
for the first time. Legal deposit-taking authority can be
revoked on the grounds that the institution concerned has
failed to satisfy the prudential criteria set out in the
Act.

Machinery of Supervision

Prior to 1974, superivsion was in the hands of the
Discount Office of the Bank but, following the "secondary
banking crisis", a new Banking Supervision Department was
created, with a considerably enlarged staff. The Bank also
set up a joint working party with the London and Scottish
Clearing Banks to consider matters relating to the adequacy
of capital and liquidity, and its report was published in

1975.[1] Between the publication of this report and the passage of the 1979 Banking Act, the Bank of England extended the coverage of statistical returns required from banks and developed procedures for regular consultation with them. The 1979 Act was followed by the publication of three consultative documents entitled The Measurement of Capital, The Measurement of Liquidity and Foreign Currency Exposure. Consultations on the first of these have been completed and a paper setting out the principles that the Bank will apply has been issued.[2] At the time of writing (December 1980) discussions on the other two were still continuing. The main points of the three documents will be summarised below, but first we note some general features of the UK system of supervision.

The Standing Committee of Bank Supervisors of the "Group of Ten" countries and Switzerland (often known as the Basle Committee) has agreed that national supervisory authorities have a responsibility for the whole activities, domestic and foreign, of banking groups that have head-quarters in their country. Accordingly, the Bank of England will supervise the overseas branches and subsidiaries of UK banks. However, foreign banks operating in the UK will also be required to conform to UK standards in relation to their British opeations.

The Passage of the 1979 Act and the developments arising from it will give supervision more formality than it has had in the past but the intention is to retain two basic principles of the traditional system, flexibility and consultation. Flexibility implies the recognition of differences between different types of bank and differences between individual banks within any type and the avoidance, wherever possible, of ratios applied, "across the board".

---

1. The Capital and Liquidity Adequacy of Banks. Bank of England Quarterly Bulletin, September 1975.

2. The Measurement of Capital. Bank of England Quarterly Bulletin, September 1980.

Consultation implies a two-way exchange of views between the
Bank and the banks, so that the views of the supervisory
authority may be modified, as they have been in the past,
by representations from those whom they supervise.

Capital adequacy

The September 1980 paper states the objective of
supervision of banks' capital as:-

> "(a) to ensure that the capital position of an
> institution is regarded as acceptable by its
> depositors and other creditors, and
>
> (b) to test the adequacy of capital in relation to
> the risk of losses which may be sustained".(1)

For this purpose, it defines an "adjusted capital base" and
sets out two tests, a "gearing measurement" and a "risk
measure".

The "capital base" is made up of:-

Paid up share capital.

Fully subordinated loan capital with a minimum
maturity of five years, and normally amounting
to not more than a third of the total.

Minority interests, and

General reserves and provisions (but not provisions
against specific bad debts).

The "adjusted capital base" is derived by deducting from the
"capital base" the following items:-

Investments in subsidiaries and associates.

Goodwill.

Premises (for the "gearing measurement" only).

Equipment and other fixed assets.

The "gearing measurement" is simply the ratio of the
"adjusted capital base" to deposits and other non-capital
liabilities. The denominator for the "risk measure" is more
complicated. The starting point is the recognition that

1. Bank of England, Quarterly Bulletin, September 1980
p. 324.

some assets carry a credit risk, some a forced sale risk,
and some a combination of both. Ordinary commercial advances
have a weight of 1. Assets with neither a credit risk nor a
forced sale risk (e.g. notes, coin and deposits with the Bank
of England) have a zero weight. Assets with little or no
credit risks but some forced sale risk have weights ranging
from 0.1 (e.g. Treasury bills) to 0.5 (e.g. government
securities more than 18 months to maturity). Unquoted
investments have a weight of 1.5 and property, 2.0.[1] The
"risk measure" is the ratio of the "adjusted capital base"
to the weighted total of assets.

The Bank will monitor these ratios and discuss them
with the banks concerned, taking account of the circumstances
of each, but "for neither ratio is any specific numerical
guideline established". In the Bank's view, the publication
of numbers would allow insufficient flexibility and might
also impair banks' ability to raise new capital when needed.

Liquidity

As already noted the Bank's proposals on liquidity are
still under discussion. The situation has been changed
considerably as a result of the rapid growth of short-term
markets described in Chapter 8 and of the associated practice
of "liability management". As a result liquidity may be
needed not only to meet a sudden withdrawal of deposits or a
sudden rise in the demand for loans, but also as a
precaution against an unforeseen rise in financing costs, as
a result of "borrowing short and lending long" in financial
markets. The Bank proposes a new distinction between
"primary liquidity" and "secondary liquidity", and a new
test of liquidity needs related both to the amount of
"maturity uncertain" liabilities (e.g. ordinary retail

---

1.   A full list is given on page 329 of the September
        1980 _Quarterly Bulletin_.

deposits) and to the net liabilities arising from "mis-matching" of assets and liabilities of fixed maturity (e.g. borrowing and lending at fixed term on the inter-bank market).

Primary liquid assets are cash and assets which the Bank of England will purchase or accept as collateral for loans in its capacity as lender of last resort, and comprise the following:-

Notes and coin.

Balances with the Bank of England (other than special deposits).

Call money with the discount market.

Treasury bills.

Local authority bills and bank bills eligible for discount at the Bank.

UK government securities with less than a year to maturity.

It is proposed that the following should be recognised as secondary liquid assets:-

- Market loans to banks up to 1 month.
- Secured call money with gilt-edged jobbers and "money brokers".
- Loans to local authorities up to one month.
- Non-eligible bills up to three months to maturity.
- Certificates of deposit up to three months.
- British and Northern Ireland government securities with one to five years to maturity.
- Marketable securities of local authorities and public corporations with less than a year to maturity.
- Gold.
- Irrevocable stand-by facilities from other banks.

Required liquidity would be calculated by reference to:-

1.   A proportion of 25 per cent to all gross "maturity uncertain" liabilities, and

2.   A proportion of net liabilities in respect of mis-
matched assets and liabilities with fixed maturity.
The proposed proportions range from 100 per cent
on market deposits from banks up to one month to
5 per cent of net liabilities over a year to maturity.

It is proposed that these requirements should apply
both to sterling and foreign currency business. In respect
of their sterling business, banks would be required to hold
40 per cent of their total liquidity in the primary assets
listed above, all of which are denominated in sterling;
otherwise, requirements could be met by assets in the
designated categories in either sterling or foreign currency.
The paper stresses that all ratios are norms, not requirements
that must be met on a day-to-day basis.

The liquidity proposals have aroused a lot of
controversy in the banking world since they were published
in March 1980. On November 24th., the Bank issued a
statement that discussions were still continuing; when
they are completed, a scheme would be implemented and the
present reserve asset requirements (see Chapter 1) would
be discontinued. It is possible, however, that the scheme
that is eventually introduced will differ significantly
from the proposals outlined above.

Exchange exposure

Until October 1979, banks "positions" in foreign
currencies were limited by exchange control. With the
abolition of exchange control it has become necessary, on
prudential grounds, to limit the losses that a bank may suffer
from fluctuations in exchange rates. Potential losses arise
both from the "structural position" of a bank (i.e. the
relationship between the currencies in which it holds its
capital and reserves and those in which it operates) and
from dealing activities. The Bank proposes to cover the
former by periodic discussions with banks, and the latter
by limiting the size of open positions. It is proposed that

uncovered liabilities (both spot and forward) in all currencies taken together should not exceed 10 per cent of a Bank's "capital base" as defined in the paper on the measurement of capital, with a similar limit of 3.5 per cent in any one currency. Again, the proposals are still under discussion and the limits eventually adopted may differ from those proposed.

Protection of depositors

The 1979 Banking Act also provides for the first formal deposit protection scheme in British banking history. The scheme will apply to all banks and licenced deposit-taking institutions unless exempted by Treasury order. It will provide for repayment, in cases of insolvency, of deposits of less than £10,000 except for secured deposits; deposits with an initial period of more than five years to maturity; and deposits made after an institution has ceased to be licenced or recognised. The scheme will be administered by a Deposit Protection Board composed of the Governor, Deputy-Governor and Chief Cashier of the Bank of England (ex-officio) together with bankers and members of the staff of the Bank appointed by the Governor. It will be financed by contributions (pro-rata to deposits) from all the institutions covered. The Board is required to fix an initial contribution at a rate that will raise a total fund of not less than £5 million or more than £6 million which will be lodged with and invested by the Bank of England. If the fund falls below £5 million, the Board may, with the approval of the Treasury, levy an additional contribution at a rate that will restore it to between £5 million and £6 million. The Board will also have powers to raise special contributions and to borrow if such actions are necessary in order to meet its obligations. These provisions of the 1979 Act will come into force from a date to be fixed by Statutory Order but, at the time of writing, the order had not yet been issued.

3. SUPERVISION IN GERMANY

Supervisory authorities

The Kreditwesengesetz (KWG, Banking Act) of 1934 has
recently been amended in answer to a number of spectacular
crashes in the early 1970's.[1] In its present form it
establishes a general public supervision of all banking
business in Germany. Thus the Bundesaufsichtsamt für das
Kreditwesen (BAK) in Berlin has to give permission before
any firm can engage in banking business; the KWG prescribes
legal requirements that must be fulfilled before permission
can be given. There must be at least two experienced owners
or managers, the firm must have sufficient capital resources,
and must, in many cases, be incorporated. The permission
can be granted on conditions only, can be denied, and can
be revoked. In order to be able to pursue its task of
"containing abuses in the banking sector which endanger
the security of the funds entrusted to banks, or which impede
the orderly conduct of banking business, or which could lead
to considerable disadvantages of the economy as a whole"
(KWG, art. 6(2)), the BAK has the power to ask banks for all
kinds of information, to order special audits, or to interfere
with the conduct of business; this includes the power to
order the immediate cessation of all business. Banks have to
inform the BAK of all changes in their legal status, or in
those empowered to represent them; they also have to report
their monthly balance sheets as well as their annual accounts
to the Bundesbank (whence they are transmitted to the BAK).
The BAK has to be informed of particularly large loans, of
loans to any of the bank's directors or managers, and of
loans to subsidiaries. There are also limits to the size of
loans. Finally, the BAK can issue rules about liquidity and
asset ratios in consultation with the Deutsche Bundesbank.[2]

1. For the text of the Act, see Möller und Consbruch
    (1977); an unofficial translation has been published
    by the Deutsche Bundesbank; another can be found in
    Schneider et. al. (1978). For an analysis, see
    Möhring und Nirk (1976) and IBRO (1978), Chapter IV.
2. The rules applying to loans, or limiting them, as well
    as requirements pertaining to liquidity and asset
    ratios, will be discussed in Chapter "X" of this study.

The KWG also empowers the Federal Minister of Finance
to issue, after consultations with the Deutsche Bundesbank,
rules about the conditions, terms, and maximum interest rates
applicable to borrowing and lending by all banks. Up to
1967 such rules were in operation, but in 1967 it was decided
to abandon them. Since then the banking associations have
been issuing guidelines for their members which, however, do
not have the binding character the rules had before 1967.

In addition to the KWG, the banking sector is subject
like all other businesses to the cartel legislation (Gesetz
gegen Wettbewerbsbeschränkungen, GWB). But Art. 102 GWB
exempts banks from the general ban on cartelization; hence
guidelines issued by banking associations are legal. Nevertheless banks are still subject to the general supervision
of the Federal Cartel Office (Bundeskartellamt) in Berlin as
regards any abuses that hinder or impede competition.

Banking supervision is the responsibility of the BAK,
the Bundesbank has only a supporting role. De facto, however,
the Bundesbank's position is quite strong, as most of the
reports go first to the Bundesbank, and are then transmitted,
often with a commentary or recommendation, to the BAK.
Nevertheless, it is the BAK which decides on sanctions, or
orders special investigations (which are conducted either by
the BAK, or the Bundesbank, or an outside firm). Some
reports banks are obliged to give also go directly to the BAK,
as, e.g., reports about mergers between banks. The division
of labour between the BAK and the Bundesbank is further
exemplified by the fact that none of the various rules to
be discussed below are instruments of monetary policy: they
are elements of the institutional framework within which
banks pursue their business (and the Bundesbank its monetary
policy). To be sure, there have been changes in these rules,
but they have typically been changed in response to banking
crises and bank crashes rather than the necessities of
monetary policies. Thus the crash of the Herstatt Bank in

1974 (which had little to do with monetary policy: and much
with unguarded and apparently unsupervised foreign exchange
dealings by an over-ambitious dealer) led to several changes
which all had the effect of tightening up the rules and
strengthening the supervisory framework. Apart from those to
be mentioned below, surprise investigations of banks by the
BAK have become routine.

Capital and liquidity

Article 10 of the Kreditwesengesetz (KWG hencethforth)
stipulates that banks "shall maintain adequate equity
capital". While the act is quite explicit about what is to
be reckoned as capital, there is no formal definition of
what is considered to be "adequate". Instead, the act
provides that the BAK shall formulate principles according
to which the adequacy of equity capital will be judged.
Similarly, article 11 KWG requires banks to maintain a
"sufficient" level of liquidity, and again requires the BAK
to formulate principles as to what will be deemed
"sufficient" liquidity.

Four such principles have been formulated.[1] For
historical reasons they are numbered I, Ia, II and III.

Principle I requires that total lending plus participations do not surpass 18 times the amount of equity capital.
Bills discounted and guarantees are included in the total
amount of lending. Long-term mortgage loans, guarantees,
loans to non-banks guaranteed by a public agency, and loans
to foreign banks are only counted with half their value,
while lending to domestic banks is counted only with one-
fifth of its value. Lending to public agencies other than
banks is not to be included in total lending.

---

1.   The text of the Grundsätze über das Eigenkapital und
die Liquidität is regularly published in the
Bundesbank's annual report. An unofficial translation
is provided in Appendix I to this Chapter.

Principle Ia (which was included in October 1974 as a reaction to the crash of the Herstatt bank) formulates three different requirements:

(i)   the difference between assets and liabilities denominated in foreign currencies (and, since February 1980, between holdings and liabilities in gold, silver and platinum) shall at the end of each business day not exceed 30 per cent of the amount of equity capital. The principle applies to the sum of the net positions in each currency and each metal; it is not possible, therefore, to offset a positive net position in (say) dollars with a negative net position in (say) pounds sterling. No distinction is made, however, between different terms to maturity.

(ii)   The difference between assets and liabilities as defined in (i) above which fall due within any one month shall not exceed 40 per cent of the amount of equity capital.

(iii) The difference between assets and liabilities as defined in (i) above which fall due within any calendar half year shall not exceed 40 per cent of the amount of equity capital either.

Taken together, these rules limit the amounts of open positions banks can take on foreign exchange markets and on the markets for gold, silver and platinum.

Principle II requires that long-term assets do not exceed long-term liabilities. Long-term assets include lending with maturities over four years, holdings in securities not traded on stock exchanges, participations and holdings of land, buildings and equipment. Long-term liabilities include equity capital, deposits other than saving deposits from banks and non-banks with a maturity of four years or more (plus 10 per cent of all such deposits with shorter maturities), 60 per cent of all savings deposits, bonds outstanding with a maturity of four years or more (plus 60 per cent of those with shorter maturities), 60 per cent of reserves for pension liabilities, and, in the case of the central institutions of the savings institutions and the co-operative banks, 20 per cent of all deposits from either savings banks or co-operatives with a maturity of at least six months.

Principle III, finally, formulates a similar requirement with respect to short-term assets and liabilities: certain short-term liabilities shall not exceed certain short-term assets. The short-term assets include: 20 per cent of all lending to banks with maturities of at least three months, but less than four years; lending to non-banks with maturities of less than four years including lending on the basis of bankers' acceptances; and listed shares and investment certificates. The short-term liabilities comprise 10 per cent of liabilities to banks with a maturity of less than three months; 50 per cent of liabilities to banks with maturities of three months and more, but less than four years; 20 per cent of all savings deposits; and 20 per cent of all bonds issued in circulation.

It should be noted that these principles are not absolutely binding in the way asset ratios will be. Failure to satisfy the rules only creates a presumption that the bank does not have "adequate" equity capital or "sufficient" liquidity. It may justify its actions, and the BAK may accept the justification. When it does not, it can only take action after asking the bank concerned to satisfy the rules within a given period. The ultimate sanctions include prohibitions on entering in new business transactions, or the order to cease trading as a bank altogether. It is not surprising, therefore, that as a rule most banks satisfy these rules; Table 10.1 shows that the number of banks which did not was small in recent years.

Of the various principles, principles Ia and II are those which have restricted banks most in recent years. Principle III has been restrictive for some banks, particularly commercial banks. Principle I seems to give least trouble.

Because of the increased activity of a number of German banks in the markets for gold, silver and platinum, these metals were included, early in 1980, in Principle Ia,

TABLE 10.1: NUMBER OF BANKS WHICH DID NOT SATISFY EQUITY AND LIQUIDITY PRINCIPLES[a] (ANNUAL AVERAGES)

Year	I	Ia[b] (i)	Ia[b] (ii)	Ia[b] (iii)	II	III
1973	93				125	291
1974	61				40	149
1975	37	7	5	4	5	59
1976	41	4	3	2	6	77
1977	35	3	2	1	3	89
1978	41	3	3	2	10	83
1979	46	3	1	1	11	122

NOTES: a All banks reporting excluding branches of foreign banks, hire purchase banks, and public mortgage banks. The total number of banks varies, but has been above 3,000 in all years.

b Introduced only in October 1974. Only some 400 banks report whose total net open positions exceeded 100,000 DM.

Source: Deutsche Bundesbank, Geschäftsberichte 1978, 1979.

which originally only covered foreign exchanges. Some of the banks concerned are also heavily engaged in foreign exchange business. It is, therefore, likely that Principle Ia will restrict them more than it did in the past, unless some of their dealings in either precious metals or foreign exchange is moved to foreign subsidiaries.

By way of conclusion it should be mentioned that there is one further rule which is absolutely binding. Article 12 KWG stipulates that a bank's permanent investments in land, buildings, ships and participations shall not exceed the amount of equity capital at its disposal. As the amount of such investments is on the whole small, this rule is not as a rule restrictive even though the share of equity capital in total liabilities tends to be small. Again, however, the situation may well be different for individual banks.

Lending rules

Rules which relate to bank lending cover three different
types of loans. There are rules about "large" loans
(Grosskredite), rules about lending to any one person or
company in excess of one million DM (Millionenkredite), and
rules about loans to directors, employees and other related
persons and companies (Organkredite),

Rules about "large" loans (Grosskredite): Article 13
KWG defines "large" loans as loans which exceed 15 per cent
of a bank's equity capital, provided they exceed 50,000 DM
(unless they exceed 75 per cent of a bank's equity capital).
Such loans have to be decided upon by a unanimous decision
of all directors, and have to be reported to the Bundesbank,
which passes on the information to the BAK. Since 1976,
no single "large" loan shall exceed 75 per cent of equity
capital; the five largest "large" loans must not exceed
three times the amount of equity capital; and the sum of
all "large" loans must not exceed eight times the amount of
equity capital. For the purpose of these rules, loans
include credit lines; credit guarantees given and loans
extended by purchase of bills of exchange are also included,
but only 50 per cent of their total amount is reckoned as
a loan. In 1979, the Bundesbank received more than 130,000
reports on "large" loans.

Statistics about the extent to which these rules have
reduced the growth of lending are not available, but it is
well known that they have been restrictive for some banks.
There is no question that they are one reason for the rapid
growth of foreign subsidiaries of German banks, particularly
those in Luxembourg, where no such rules are in force.
Moreover, it is common knowledge that two groups of banks in
particular suffer from the restrictions imposed by these
rules: private bankers, and savings banks (Sparkassen).
Private bankers have all the well-known difficulties of
small firms in obtaining additional equity capital; after
all, they are the small firms of the banking sector. The

disappearance of private bankers, and the relatively large numbers of mergers involving them, has something to do with this. The problems encountered by savings banks exacerbate some structural differences found in a banking system which consists of private and public banks. While private banks can obtain additional equity capital on the capital market (at least in theory), public banks cannot. As the equity capital of savings banks is provided by the local authorities (cities or counties) in which they operate, savings banks have often found it difficult to increase their equity capital, particularly in local authorities which depend heavily on grants from their Land.

In the discussion which followed the publication of the Gessler Report on the structure of banking,[1] the saving institutions have proposed to deal with this problem by arguing that a similar procedure should be applied to them as is applied to credit co-operatives. By law, members of co-operatives can be called upon to provide additional equity capital; this uncalled liability is usually limited to their share in the co-operative, but can also be unlimited. To take account of this, the rules on equity capital and liquidity provide that the paid-up equity capital of co-operatives is, for the purpose of these rules, to be increased by an amount which reflects these uncalled liabilities (and which is agreed upon by the co-operatives and the BAK after consultation with the Bundesbank). The savings banks now argue that they are guaranteed by their local authority, and that therefore their capital resources are larger than the equity capital they have at their disposal: hence they should be allowed a similar addition to their equity capital. Naturally enough, private banks have opposed this proposal. They have been irked already by the "fictitious" capital addition allowed to credit co-operatives (which never once made use of their members' uncalled liabilities). To extend this priviledge to savings banks would in their eyes further aggravate this element of unfair competition, and would also further increase the

1.   See Bericht (1979).

advantage savings banks already have because of their public status. Because of this, the Gessler Report opposed such proposals, and also proposed that the credit co-operatives' priviledge be reduced gradually. Whether this recommendation is followed, or whether the savings institutions get some of their proposals accepted, is uncertain. What is certain, by contrast, is that savings banks are restricted in their lending by the rules on equity capital and liquidity because they cannot obtain additional equity capital as easily as other banks.

Rules on loans of more than DM 1 million: According to article 14 KWG all banks have to report at bimonthly intervals all persons or companies who hold loans exceeding one million DM from that bank; no matter whether from that bank alone, or from that bank together with other banks. Article 2(2) KWG extends this reporting obligation to insurance companies and social security agencies. The act stipulates further that the Bundesbank has to match these reports from banks and other financial institutions, and has to notify all lenders involved if any person or company has such loans from more than one bank of the total amount of loans, and the number of banks involved. Guarantees and bills of exchange bought are to be included in the total amount of lending, but have to be listed separately.

As Table 10.2 shows, this category of bank lending has grown quite rapidly in recent years: some commercial banks reported more than 5,000 recipients of such loans in 1979. One reason for this is the inflation of monetary values and the fact that the limit of one million is unchanged since the 1930's.[1] Again in 1979, banks and insurance companies received notifications about more than 95,000 persons and companies which had received loans exceeding one million from more than one source. 34 companies had received loans exceeding one billion DM at the end of November 1979.

It should be noted that there is only the obligation to report: there are no limitations in the rules other

1.   See Deutsche Bundesbank (1978).

TABLE 10.2: LOANS EXCEEDING ONE MILLION DM

Year[a]	Total Amount of Loans (Billion DM)	Number of Loans Reported	Number of Reporting Banks	Number of Reporting Insurance Companies
1962	77	31,672	527	331
1967	121	42,990	897	378
1972	291	80,237	1,728	350
1973	325	88,187	1,858	347
1974	367	94,985	1,964	350
1975	416	100,338	2,043	344
1976	462	115,481	2,120	357
1977	516	127,751	2,197	407
1978	566	142,656	2,330	435
1979	609	164,215	2,507	442

NOTE: a   All data relate to the end of November of the year given.

Source: Deutsche Bundesbank, Geschäftsbericht 1979, p. 73,; and Deutsche Bundesbank (1978), p. 26.

than those applying to "large" loans, or those arising out
of other rules such as the principles discussed above.

Rules about loans to related persons or companies

(Organkredite): These rules, contained in articles 15 to
17 KWG, stipulate that loans to related persons and companies
must be decided upon unanimously by all directors of the bank
concerned, and have to be approved by supervisory bodies if
they exist. In most cases, they also have to be reported
to the Bundesbank (and thus the BAK). Related persons and
companies include among others:[1]

- owners, directors, managers and employees of a bank
  as well as their wives and children, if the loan
  exceeds a certain limit;

- members of any supervisory body and their wives and
  children;

- representatives acting on behalf of those mentioned
  already;

- companies which have as a director or owner or member
  of a supervisory body a director, owner, or member
  of a supervisory body of the bank (except when the
  person in question is a member of a supervisory body
  only of both the bank and the company);

- companies if 25 per cent or more of their equity
  capital is owned by the bank;

- companies which own at least 25 per cent of the
  equity capital of the bank.

Again, the act provides only for an obligation to report;
there are some civil law liability rules if the rules are
not kept, but no sanctions that could be applied by the
Bundesbank or BAK.

Some 25,000 such reports were received in 1979 by the
Bundesbank. While this includes a large (and undisclosed)
amount of inter-company lending, quite a few of these reports
are due to loans given to employees, mainly for house buying
or house building purposes.

1. The rules about these loans are too complex to be
   discussed here in detail. Reference to the relevant
   articles of the KWG must suffice. An English
   translation is available, e.g., in Schneider, Hellwig,
   Kingsman (1979), pp. 88-92.

Deposit Security Schemes (Einlagensicherung)

There is no general deposit insurance scheme in
Germany which is comparable to, say, the American Federal
Deposit Insurance Scheme. Instead, there are what may be
called deposit security schemes (Einlagensicherung):[1]
arrangements which do not insure deposits, but which ensure
the security of deposits. Indeed, these schemes go further,
because they ensure the security of other liabilities than
deposits as well, and in many cases ensure the very
existence of a bank. Three features characterize these
schemes: most of them are of fairly recent origin, there
are different schemes for different groups of banks, and
they are all combined with more or less compulsory
supervision schemes operated by banking associations.

After the banking crisis of 1931 the co-operative
banks created a small deposit scheme the main function of
which was to help credit co-operatives which were in
difficulties. No other group of banks had similar
arrangements. It was only in 1959 that the association of
Bavarian private bankers started a similar scheme which was
meant to "support private bankers which have liquidity
difficulties, with a view to secure deposits and to prevent
the public from losing trust in private banks".[2] In 1966
the association of German banks (Bundesverband deutscher
Banken) started a scheme along the same lines by creating a
fund (Gemeinschaftsfonds) which again combined help for
private banks in difficulties with the aim of preventing a
loss of trust in private banks. A government report,
published in 1968, examined (among other things) these
schemes, and found them wanting.[3] As a result, the
association of German banks improved their scheme, and the

---

1. Even the name is different: the German for deposit
insurance is Einlagenversicherung, not Einlagensicherung.
The similarity of these terms is, of course, intentional.

2. Article i of their statutes. See Ronge (1979), p. 227,
where the statutes were reprinted along with those of
other schemes.

3. See Deutscher Bundestag (1968).

savings institutions introduced a scheme of their own in
1969. The collapse of the Herstatt bank in 1974 demonstrated
that these were still insufficient, and the government
proposed a public deposit insurance scheme, but suggested
that they might be persuaded to abandon their plans if the
banking sector came up with an acceptable proposal of its
own. The Bundesverband deutscher Banken responded in 1975
by refurbishing the Gemeinschaftsfonds into a Einlagensicherungsfonds which proved acceptable to the government and the
BAK, and was formally included in the framework of banking
supervision by some clauses in the Kreditwesengesetz which
refer to it. At about the same time both the savings
institutions and the co-operative banks refurbished their
schemes along the lines suggested by the government, so that
today there exist three different schemes side by side for
private banks, for savings institutions, and for co-operative
banks.

As mentioned, these schemes are given official blessing
and are integrated in the framework of banking supervision.
Thus their reports, both general ones, and those which result
for special investigations of individual banks, have to be
transmitted to the BAK and the Bundesbank (article 26(2) KWG).
Again, the powers of the BAK are stayed when one of the funds
undertakes to ensure the security of deposits of a bank in
difficulties (article 46a(1) KWG).

Because they differ somewhat from each other, these
schemes will be discussed separately below.

Finally, it should be mentioned that again as a
consequence of the Herstatt bank crash the Bundesverband
deutscher Banken, at the behest of the Bundesbank, and with
their active support, created the Liquiditätskonsortialbank
in Frankfurt which is also meant as a self-help institution
of the banking sector for banks in difficulties, and which
will also be discussed below.

The co-operative banks' scheme: In its present form the
Garantiefonds of the co-operative banks is part of their
supervisory scheme (Prüfverband). Every co-operative bank
has to be a member of this scheme, which regularly examines
their books and annual reports, and also conducts special
investigations when necessary. Submission to all this is a
necessary condition of membership in the co-operative
movement. The scheme is organized regionally, and the
Garantiefonds is administered by the relevant regional
associations. Every credit co-operative (as well as their
central institutions) contribute an annual levy of 0.05 per
cent on most deposits as well as some loans. The fund thus
accumulated is used to help member banks which have got into
difficulties by way of either guarantees, or loans, or direct
support (which has to be paid back if the operation proves
successful and the bank is nursed back to profitability).
Help is given long before the troubles become public: and
has to be given when there is a danger that open reserves
(those published in balance sheets as distinct from those
resulting from undervaluing assets, etc.) have to be
diminished. The aim is clearly to prevent the difficulties
becoming public knowledge. In all cases a special
investigation will follow, and continued membership of the
co-operative movement is dependent on implementation of
whatever recommendations result from it. In many cases,
credit co-operatives in difficulties have been merged, and
their management changed. As far as is known, there is no
case since 1945, in which the members of the credit
co-operative were asked to pay up the uncalled liability;
nor is there a case of a credit co-operative leaving the
movement.

In addition to the Garantiefonds, there is what is
called a Garantieverband: basically an association of
(almost) all credit co-operatives which gives guarantees
for loans or deposits when there are signs of difficulties.
This is thus a first line of defense as compared with the
Garantiefonds. It is financed by contributions which are
called when needed.

<u>The savings banks' scheme:</u> For a long time the savings
banks did not see the necessity to worry about a deposit
security scheme. As they are legally guaranteed by their
local community (city or county) or, in the case of the
Landesbanken-Girozentralen, by the relevant Land, there
seemed to be no reason, in particular as there is in law, an
obligation on the part of the public authorities guaranteeing
them to provide them with whatever funds are required to
adequately pursue their business. However, it was always
feared (realistically as it turned out), that local
authorities would be slow if not unwilling to live up to this
obligation, Hence, the savings banks were prompted, as
mentioned above, to set up their own additional scheme which
would ensure rapid help with no danger of moves getting
bogged down in the quagmires of local politics.

The construction of the Sparkassenstützungsfonds
resembles that of the co-operative institutions, only that
this scheme is not as closely tied up with the savings'
banks supervisory scheme as that of the co-operative
institutions. Twelve regional funds for Sparkassen are
linked by a network of mutual guarantees: a fund specifically
for the Landesbanken-Girozentralen is also integrated with
them. Decision making is regional with central assistance,
except that the central decision making body can dispose of
15 per cent of the funds in emergency cases of national
importance. The funds are financed by a levy of 0.03 per
cent on all loans, and are supposed to accumulate approximately
910 million DM, half of which is planned to be an uncalled
liability. There can be special levies up to 0.06 per cent
per annum if the funds are deemed insufficient. As in the
case of the co-operative banks, the aim of the scheme is to
provide help long before the difficulties of a bank have
become public knowledge. Loans may be repayable or not,
but are in any case granted only on condition that the
recommendations of a special investigation are followed.
In practice this has often meant merger with other savings
banks, or a restructuring of the bank concerned together
with a change in managers.

Two cases have become known in which savings institutions have been helped by the Stützungsfonds. One is the Hessische Landesbank-Girozentrale in Frankfurt which got into difficulties in 1974-1976 because of incautious foreign exchange transactions, and at the end of 1976 was found to be in need of approximately 2 billion DM. According to the structure of ownership, half of this sum had to be contributed by the Land (Hessen), and the other half by the Sparkassen in Hessen. The latter acknowledged their obligation, but found the sum too large for them, and accordingly asked their local authorities to contribute. The local authorities refused, arguing that the troubles stemmed from the Landesbank part of the bank, and should, therefore, be borne totally by the Land. When it became clear that any help for the bank would become enmeshed in protracted bickering between local authorities and the Land, with the possibility of long drawn-out legal court cases, the association of German savings institutions (Deutscher Sparkassen- und Giroverband) agreed to pay 300 million DM out of central funds which were financed by a special levy on all savings banks (some of which had to ask the Stützungsfonds for help). The remaining 700 million DM were eventually paid by the Sparkassen in Hessen, many of which were again forced to seek the help of their Stützungsfonds, which in turn had to negotiate a special loan on the capital market to bring together the funds required. In the meantime, the Hessische Landesbank, restructured, and under different management, is working profitably again. The profits have been used to replenish its own reserves, but will be used, from 1979-80 onwards, to repay the help received from the various institutions involved.

The other known case concerns the Stadtsparkasse Witten in Westphalia. This bank was found in 1976 to be in need of some 60 million DM, about three times its equity capital. Again the guaranteeing local authorities refused to bear the loss. After lengthy negotiations the town of Witten contributed a loan of 15 million DM. The rest was guaranteed by the Westdeutsche Landesbank which thus saved the bank from being closed down by the BAK. At a later stage, the Stützungsfonds was asked to contribute as well.

Both cases indicate that local authorities may be unwilling, and certainly are slow, to help. Both also show that the savings institutions movement is prepared to shoulder quite substantial losses in order to prevent one of their member banks from going bankrupt, even if there is (understandably) some bickering about who is going to contribute how much. The Stützungsfonds can be seen as instruments for quiet and quick help which does not depend on prior agreement about the distribution of the burden.

In both cases, too, the supervisory agencies (Prüfverband) of the savings institutions played a prominent part.

It should not go unmentioned that when the government suggested that the savings institutions devised their own deposit security scheme they had not only the speediness, efficiency, and noiselessness of help in mind. The government was also concerned with the issue of unfair competitition. Not only can savings banks advertise the fact that they are guaranteed by local authorities: they also did not incur any costs for their deposit security. By asking them to fund a scheme, the government thus at least forced them to incur costs comparable to those incurred by other banks, especially private ones.

By way of an appendix it should be added that other public banks, particularly public mortgage banks, still have the advantage that they do not contribute to any deposit insurance scheme.

The private banks' scheme: The schemes operated by both the co-operative banks and the savings institutions are in a sense an extension of the fact that they are common groups; they are characterized by a strong element of mutuality. There is much less common interest among private banks, which after all compete against each other incomparably more than do either co-operative banks or savings institutions. Although constructed along similar lines, their deposit security scheme is centred much more on non-bank deposits, and much less on the continued existence of the whole business activity.

The scheme consists of a fund (Einlagenfonds) which is administered by the Bundesverband deutscher Banken (which represents all banks, not just private ones). According to its statutes,[1] its aim is the same as those of the other schemes: helping a bank in difficulties in the interest of those who kept deposits with it in order to prevent a loss of trust in private banks. However, while the fund can extend help to save the bank as a whole, the only part of a bank's business which is expressly safeguarded are its non-bank deposits (sight, time and savings deposits, and savings bonds). Up to 1976 there was a limit of 20,000 DM per deposit holder: on the prompting of the government, this has been replaced by a much more generous limit - 30 per cent of the bank's equity capital. As there will be few deposits which exceed 30 per cent of a bank's equity capital one can safely assume that practically all non-bank deposits are safeguarded by this scheme (in particular as one would expect a depositor to diversify his holdings if they approach this limit). For obvious reasons, deposits by directors, owners, or members of the bank's supervisory board, their wives and children and their representatives are excluded.

There is thus a significant difference between the private banks' scheme and the scheme operated by the savings institutions and the co-operative banks. While the latter attempt to safeguard the business as a whole, the former will explicitly safeguard only non-bank deposits. The Einlagenfonds may attempt to safeguard more, but need not. It has indeed been argued[2] that as a rule the Einlagenfonds will not be able to do more than to safeguard

1. Reprinted in Ronge (1979), pp. 234-246.
2. See Schmidt (1976a), and Ronge (1979).

non-bank deposits: and that the bank itself will be allowed
to fold up its business. One reason for this is that it
would be ironic if a bank which got into difficulties were
baled out by its competitors; another is the fact that
private banks which are in difficulties will be closed by
the BAK, and that after such a closure there is little left
but ceasing to trade altogether. The only case in which a
bank was closed by the BAK occurred too recently (a small
private bank in Frankfurt, Hassel & Co., was closed earlier
in 1980) to say whether this presumption is borne out or
not.

It could be argued, however, that this is one reason
why the Bundesbank was keen to establish the Liquiditäts-
Konsortialbank: for this institution (to be discussed below)
can be seen as an attempt to provide help before the BAK finds
it necessary to intervene.

There are other differences between the private banks'
deposit security scheme and those of the savings
institutions and the co-operative banks. While in the latter
membership is compulsory, membership in the private banks'
scheme is voluntary, and not all private banks are in fact
members. Moreover, the Bundesverband deutscher Banken has
the right to vet applications, and the statutes of the fund
lay down rather stringent conditions for membership:
"sufficient" equity capital according to the principles
laid down by the BAK; at least two directors who can be
trusted to pursue business policies which do not endanger
the security of their deposits; satisfactory profits and
sufficient liquidity; and membership in a supervisory scheme
operated by the Bundesverband deutscher Banken. These
requirements may be reasonable, but they are more stringent
than those laid down in the KWG as pre-conditions for the
licensing of a bank by the BAK. The Bundesverband deutscher
Banken will, therefore, not accept any private bank;
moreover, it has the power to exclude one if it holds that
it no longer satisfies the requirements. This, together
with the requirement that a bank must be a member of a
supervisory scheme has led to fears that the Einlagenfonds

will have a discouraging effect on outsiders, and may indeed amount to a cartel regulating entry into the banking industry.[1] It is perhaps too early to judge whether such fears are justified or not, but it should be pointed out that a member bank has no claim to be helped: the Einlagenfonds can help, but need not. While a similar provision is written into the statutes of the other schemes in operation in order to prevent the funds concerned to be classified as insurance companies (which would seriously hinder their activities), there is a danger that help will be made dependent on "satisfactory" behaviour which in turn will be judged by a bank's competitors. Such fears have also been aroused by the fact that the Einlagensicherungsfonds is administered by a committee of nine, three representatives each of the Big banks, the regional banks, and all other banks. In practice, therefore, the three Big banks are all represented, while all other banks have to elect representatives. Experience has shown that these tend to come from the larger banks, who thus dominate the committee.

The Einlagensicherungsfonds is financed by a levy of 0.03 per cent on all deposits which are safeguarded by it. If the fund is deemed insufficient, the levy can be raised to up to 0.06 per cent. It can also be lowered if the fund is deemed to be sufficiently large.

As in other schemes, if any payments are made to a bank, or on its behalf, they are repayable if the bank continues to exist or is taken over by another bank. In addition, however, there is a special clause concerning subsidiaries. They have to contribute as if they were independent banks: but any payments to them have to be guaranteed by their institutional parent(s), and are thus repayable by them.

So far no cases have become known in which the Einlagensicherungsfonds has become active, so that little can be said about the experience with this scheme. It is known, however, that the Bundesverband deutscher Banken was

---

1. See particularly Ronge (1979).

involved when the business of two small private banks which
had been closed by the BAK was liquidated. Private (non-bank)
depositors were paid according to the rules of the
Einlagensicherungsfonds, and the required funds lent first
by the Bundesverband, and then from the Einlagensicherungsfonds (which at that time was not yet officially in
existence). If this is anything to go by, the Einlagensicherungsfonds will indeed not safeguard all business of
a bank, but only its deposits.

The Liquiditäts-Konsortialbank was founded in
September 1974 under the direct impression of the crash of
the Herstatt bank by the Bundesbank, which holds 30 per
cent of its equity capital, together with the Bundesverband
deutscher Banken and some other banking associations. Its
equity capital amounts to 250 million DM, but there is an
uncalled liability of a further 750 million DM. In
addition, the Bundesbank has granted a special rediscount
quota of 500 million DM, so that total funds available
amount to 1.5 billion DM.

Its purpose is to help banks which are in temporary
liquidity difficulties but are otherwise solvent by
entending loans, normally by bills of exchange or bankers'
acceptances. In a sense, therefore, the Liquiditäts-
Konsortialbank is there to give help before the
Einlagensicherungsfonds or any of the other schemes become
involved or the BAK finds it necessary to intervene.

Next to nothing is known about its activities. As it
is legally in the form of a limited liability company,
there is no need to publish an annual report, or annual
statements. Moreover, the very nature of its purpose
implies that little became known about its activities.
What is known is that the Liquiditäts-Konsortialbank is
co-operating with the deposit security schemes discussed
above. Thus it was involved both in the baling out of the
Hessische Landesbank (by helping savings banks in Hessen
to finance their contributions), and the liquidation of the
Pfalz-Kredit-Bank, one of the private banks mentioned above.

SELECT BIBLIOGRAPHY

ENGLISH LANGUAGE

Baker, J.C. The German Stock Market. Its Operations,
Problems and Prospects. Praeger. New York, 1970.

Bank for International Settlements. Payments Systems in
Eleven Developed Countries. Basle, 1980.

Bank of England. The Measurement of Liquidity. London
1980.

Bank of England. Quarterly Bulletin, London. Quarterly.

Bank of England and H.M. Treasury. Monetary Control.
Cmnd. 7858. HMSO 1980.

The Banker. London. Monthly.

Baring Bros. & Co. Ltd. Merchant Banking Today.
London. 1970.

Bayliss, B.T. and Butt Philip, A.A.S. Capital Markets and
Industrial Investment in Germany and France.
Lessons for the UK. Farnborough: Saxon House 1980.

Bockelmann, H. Notes on Courakis. Zeitschrift für die
gesamte Staatswissenschaft 136, 1980.

Branson, W.H. Halttunen, H. Masson, P. Exchange Rates in
Short Run: The Dollar-Deutschemark Rate. European
Economic Review 10, 1977.

Bundesverband Deutscher Banken eV., The Banking System
of the Federal Republic of Germany. Köln:
Bundesverband 1978.

Cameron, Rondo. ed., Banking and Economic Development.
New York: Oxford University Press 1972.

Central Statistical Office. Financial Statistics.
HMSO. London. Monthly.

Central Statistical Office. National Income and Expenditure
of the UK. London. HMSO. Annual.

Channon, D.J. British Banking Strategy and the International
Challenge. Macmillan. London 1977.

Committee of Inquiry on Small Firms. Report. Cmnd 4811.
HMSO. London 1971.

Committee of London Clearing Bankers. The London Clearing
Banks. Evidence to the Wilson Committee. London.
1977.

410.

Committee on the Working of the Monetary System (Radcliffe Committee). Report. HMSO. Cmnd 827. London 1959.

Committee to Review the Functioning of Financial Institutions. (Wilson Committee). Report 2 Vols. Cmnd. 7937, HMSO. London 1980. The Financing of Small Firms. Cmnd. 7503. HMSO. London, 1979. Evidence on the Financing of Industry and Trade. 8 Vols. HMSO, London 1977-78. Second Stage Evidence 5 Vols. HMSO, London 1979-80.

Committee to Review National Savings (Page Committee) Report. Cmnd. 5273. HMSO. London. 1973.

Courakis, Anthony S., Monetary Thought and Stabilization Policy in the Federal Republic of Germany, 1960-76 in Frowen, S.F., Courakis, A.S., Miller, M.H. (eds.), Monetary Policy and Economic Activity in West Germany. New York: Wiley 1977.

Courakis, Anthony S. On Unicorns and Other Such Creatures: The Case of the German Central Bank Money Stock. Zeitschrift für die gesamte Staatswissenschaft 136, 1980.

Crockett, A. Money. Nelson. London. 1974½

Gerschenkron, A. Economic Backwardness in Historical Perspective. Cambridge, Mass.: Belknapp Press of Harvard University Press 1966.

Herring, R.J. and Marston, R.C. Sterilization Policy: The Trade-Off between Monetary Autonomy and Control over Foreign Exchange Reserves. European Economic Review 10, 1977.

Inter-Bank Research Organisation, The Regulation of Banks in the Member States of the EEC. Alphen aan Rihn: Sijthoff and Noordhoff, 1978.

Irmler, H. The Deutsche Bundesbank's Concept of Monetary Theory and Policy. K. Brunner (ed.), Proceedings of the First Konstanzer Seminar on Monetary Theory and Policy. Kredit und Kapital: Beiheft 1. Berlin: Duncker and Humblot, 1972.

Johnson, Christopher. Anatomy of Finance, 1970-75. Longman, London. 1977.

Lehment, Harmen, Exchange-Market Interventions and Monetary Policy: The German Experience, in Kiel Working Papers 111. Kiel: Institut für Weltwirtschaft 1980.

Morgan, E.V. and Harrington, Richard. Capital Markets in the EEC. Economists Advisory Group. London 1977.

Morgan, E.V., Personal Savings and Wealth in Britain. Financial Times. London, 1975.

Morgan, E.V., Harrington, R.L. and Zis, G. Banking Systems and Monetary Policy in the EEC. Financial Times. London. 1974.

National Economic Development Office. Finance for Industry. HMSO. London, 1975.

OECD, Capital Markets Study (I: General Report, and Statistical Appendix: II: Formation of Savings: III: Functioning of Capital Markets: IV: Utilisation of Savings) 4 Parts. Paris: 1967-68.

OECD, Monetary Policy in Germany. Paris. OCED 1973.

Pringle, R. Banking in Britain. Methuen. London 1973.

Revell, J.R.S. The British Financial System. Macmillan. London, 1973.

Richter, Rudolf and Teigen, Ronald L. Commercial Bank Behaviour and Monetary Policy in an Open Economy: West Germany, 1960-1979. Saarbrücken 1980.

Roskamp, Karl W. Capital Formation in West Germany. Detroit: Wayne State University Press, 1965.

Samuels, J.M. and McMahon, P.C. Saving and Investment in the United Kingdom and West Germany. Westmead, Farnborough: Wilton Publications, 1978.

Schlesinger, H. and Bockelmann, H. Monetary Policy in the Federal Republic of Germany. In: Karel Holbik (ed.) Monetary Policy in Twelve Industrial Countries. Boston: Federal Reserve Bank of Boston 1973.

Schlesinger, Helmut Recent Developments in West Germany Monetary Policy, in S.F. Frowen, A.S. Courakis, M.H. Miller (eds.), Monetary Policy and Economic Activity in West Germany. New York: Wiley 1977.

Schneider, Hannes, Hellwig, H.J. and Kingsman, David J. (eds.) The German Banking System (Texts). Frankfurt: Knapp 1978.

The Stock Exchange. The Stock Exchange Fact Book. London. Quarterly.

Strümpel, B. Saving Behaviour in Western Germany and the United States. American Economic Review (Papers and Proceedings LXV, 1975.

Tamari, M. Some International Comparisons of Industrial Financing. A Study of Company Accounts in the UK, USA, Japan and Israel. Stonehouse: Technicopy 1978.

Thorn, Philip and Lack, Jean M. Banking and Sources of Finance in the European Community. The Banker. Research Unit. London.

Vittas, D. (ed.) Banking Systems Abroad. Inter-Bank Research Organisation. London. 1978.

Willms, M. Controlling Money in an Open Economy, the German Case, in Federal Bank of St. Louis Review, 4, 1971.

SELECT BIBLIOGRAPHY

GERMAN LANGUAGE

Albach, Horst et. al. Probleme der Sparförderung in der OECD Untersuchungen über das gesamte Spar-, Giro- und Kreditwesen Reihe A, Band 70. Berlin: Duncker und Humblot, 1973.

Anon., Vermögensbildung der Arbeitnehmer. Das 624-DM-Gesetz. Stuttgart: Deutscher Sparkassenverlag 1976.

Bank-Betrieb, Bundesverband Deutscher Banken, Köln, monatlich.

Bärmann, Johannes (ed.), Europäisches Geld-, Bank- und Börsenrecht. Teil I: Bundesrepublik Deutschland. Berlin: Duncker und Humblot 1974.

Becker, W.D. und Falk, R. (eds.), Unternehmensfinanzierung bei geänderten gesamtwirtschaftlichen Finanzierungsstrukturen. (Schriften des Verbands öffentlicher Banken Heft 1). Göttingen Schwartz, 1977.

Bericht der Studienkommission "Grundsatzfragen der Kreditwirtschaft" (Schriftenreihe des Bundesministeriums der Finanzen. Vol.28). Bonn: Stollfuss 1979.

Bonsels, Johannes, Vermögensbildung und Sparförderung. Eine Darstellung des dritten Vermögensbildungs- gesetzes sowie des Spar- und Wohnungsbau-Prämiengesetzes. Neuwied und Berlin: Luchterhand 1970.

Brehmer, E. Struktur und Funktionsweise des Geldmarkts in der Bundesrepublik Deutschland seit 1948. (2nd Edn.) Tübingen: Mohr 1964.

Bundesverband Deutscher Banken eV., Der zentrale Kapital- marktausschuss ZKMA 1957-1979. Köln: Bundesverband 1979.

Büschgen, Hans Egon, Das Universalbankensystem. Frankfurt: Knapp 1971.

Büschgen, Hans Egon, Einführung in die Banketriebslehre. 2 Vols. Frankfurt: Knapp 1977.

Caesar, R., Die Rolle der Mindesreservepolitik im Rahmen der Geldbasiskonzeption der Deutschen Bundesbank. Jahrbücher für Nationalökonomie und Statistik 191, 1976.

Delorme, H. und Hoessrich, H.J., Konsortial- und Emissionsgeschäft. Frankfurt: Knapp 1971.

Deutsche Bundesbank Monatsberichte, Frankfurt, monatlich.

Deutsche Bundesbank, Revidierte Ergebnisse der Finanzierungsrechnung für die Jahre 1950 bis 1960. Frankfurt:
Deutsche Bundesbank, 1978.

Deutsche Bundesbank, Währung und Wirtschaft in Deutschland
1876-1975, Frankfurt: Knapp 1976.

Deutsche Bundesbank, Die währungspolitischen Institutionen
und Instrumente in der Bundesrepublik Deutschland.
2nd. Edn. Frankfurt 1971.

Deutsche Bundesbank, Zahlenübersichten und methodische
Erläuterungen zur gesamtwirtschaftlichen
Finanzierungsrechnung der Deutschen Bundesbank
1950 bis 1974. Frankfurt: Deutsche Bundesbank,
1975.

Deutsche Bundesbank, Zahlenübersichten und methodische
Erläuterungen zur gesamtwirtschaftlichen
Finanzierungsrechnung der Deutschen Bundesbank
1960 bis 1977. Frankfurt: Deutsche Bundesbank
1978.

Deutscher Bundestag, Bundestagsdrucksache V/3500, 1968.

Deutsche Bundestag, Bericht über das Ergebuis einer
Untersuchung der Konzentration un der Wirtschaft.
Drucksache IV/2320.

Dickertmann, D. und Siedenberg, A. Instrumentarium der
Geldpolitik. 3rd edn. Düsseldorf: Werner-
Verlag, 1979.

Duwentag, Dieter, Kreditwesen in der BRD. II. Überblich.
Handwörterbuch der Wirtschaftswissenschaften
12. Lieferung 1979.

Engels, Wolfram, Börsen und Börsengeschäfte. Handwörterbuck
der Wirtschaftswissenschaften, 15. Lieferung 1979.

Erhard, Ulrich, Statistische Untersuchung der Zusätzlich-
keit der Kapitalbildung aufgrund gewährter Sparprämien.
Dissertation Marburg 1968. (= Zusätzliche Kapitalbildung durch Sparprämien? Eine statistische Analyse.
Marburg: Elwert 1968).

Exo, R. Die Entwicklung der sozialen und ökonomischen
Struktur der Ersparnisbildung in der Bundesrepublik
Deutschland Berlin: Duncker und Humblot 1967.

Frehsee, G. Berechnung und Erklärung der Sparquote der
privaten Haushalte in der BRD von 1950-1970.
Universität Bonn, Institut für das Spar-, Giro-,
und Kreditwesen. Diskussions-papier Nr. 8.

Fricke, D. Das Sparverhalten der privaten Haushalte in der Bundesrepublik Deutschland. Eine empirische Überprüfung der Sparfunktion. Berlin: Duncker und Humblot 1972.

Giese, Hans E. Sparen mit Sparprämie. 5., Überarbeitete Auflage. Stuttgart: Sparkassenverlag 1976.

Gösecke G, und Bedau, K.D., Verteilung und Schichtung der Einkommen der privaten Haushalte in der Bundesrepublik Deutschland, 1950 bis 1975. Berlin: Duncker und Humblot 1974.

Gruhler, Wolfram, Eigenkapitalausstattung - Bestandsaufnahme und Folgerungen. Beiträge zur Wirtschafts- und Sozialpolitik, Institut der Deutschen Wirtschaft, Nr. 34. Köln 1976.

Grunwald, J.G. und Jokl, S. Wettbewerb und Eigenkapital in der deutschen Kreditwirtschaft. Berlin: Duncker & Humblot 1978.

Hartmann, M. Einlagensicherung in der Bundesrepublik Deutschland. Bonn: Institut für das Spar-, Giro- und Kreditwesen an der Universität Bonn 1976.

Hein, M. und Flöter, H., Macht der Banken - Folgerungen aus der bisherigen Diskussion. WSI Mitteilungen 7/1975.

Herrmann, A. Die Geldmarktgeschäfte. Frankfurt: Knapp 1979.

Hettlage, Karl M. Steuerliche und andere staatliche Massnahmen zur Vermögensbildung, In:Helmut Schlesinger et al. Vermögensbildung, Vermögensverteilung und Kapitalmarkt. (Schriftenreihe des Instituts für Kapitalmarktforschung. Frankfurt am Main, Kolloquien-Beiträge. Frankfurt: Knapp 1974.

Hielscher U. und Laubscher, H.D., Finanzierungskosten. Kostenbestandteile, Kostenvergleiche und Usancen der Industriefinanzierung. Frankfurt: Knapp 1977.

Höhnen, Wilfried, Die vermögenspolitischen Gesetze und Massnahmen in der Bundesrepublik Deutschland. Köln: Bund-Verlag, 1968.

Immenga, U. Beteiligungen von Banken in anderen Wirtschaftszweigen. Ulrich Immenga. (Aktualisierte Fassung einer Studie im Auftrag der Generaldirektion Finanzinstitutionen und Steuerfragen der Kommission der Europäischen Gemeinschaften) Baden-Baden, Nomos Verlag, 1978. (Studien zum Bank- und Börsenrecht).

Jahrbuch Für Nationalökonomie und Statistik, Fischer, Stuttgart, jährlich.

Janberg, Hans (Hsg.), Finanzierungs Handbuch. Wiesbaden: Gabler 1964.

416.

Kaiser, W. und Zerwas, A., Die Struktur des Sparens in der Bundesrepublik Deutschland von 1950 bis 1967. Statistisches Material und methodische Erläuterungen. Berlin: Duncker & Humblot 1970.

Klörgmann, Bernhard, Ratgeber für die Einkommensteuer 1979. Stuttgart: Sparkassenverlag 1980.

Kredit und Kapital, Duncker und Humblot, Berlin, viertel jährlich.

Krümmel, H.J., Wettbewerb und Konzentration im deutschen Bankwesen. Bonn 1977.

Krümmel H.J. und Erner, G. Konzentrationsgrade im deutschen Kreditgewerbe und ihre Veränderung, 1961-1975. Bonn 1978.

Laux, Hans, Das dritte Vermögensbildungsgesetz. 5. Auflage. Heidelberg: Verlagsgesellschaft Recht und Wirtschaft 1972.

Leifert, H., Finanzierungs-Leasing in Deutschland. Berlin: Schmidt 1973.

Lipfert, H., Der Geldmarkt. Frankfurt: Knapp 1962.

Lipfert, H., Der Geldmarkt mit Euro-Geldmarkt (8th edn.). Frankfurt: Knapp 1975.

Lipfert, H. Wandlungen von Kapitalstruktur und Finanzierungs-formen deutscher Industrie-Aktiengesellschaften. In: Fritz Neumark (Hsg.), Strukturwandlungen einer wachsenden Wirtschaft, Bd.2 (Schriften des Vereins für Sozialpolitik, NF Bd. 30/II. Berlin: Duncker & Humblot 1964.

Lütje, Berndt und Wieners, Klaus, Das Bankwesen in der Bundesrepublik Deutschland. In: Rudolf Regul und Herbert Wolf, Das Bankwesen im grösseren Europa. Baden-Baden: Nomos 1974.

Möhring, Philipp und Nirk, Rudolf, Das Kreditwesengesetz. 6th edn. Frankfurt: Knapp 1976.

Möller, Annemarie und Consbruch, Johannes, eds., Bankrecht. München: dtv 1977.

Moesch, Irene und Simmert, Diethart B., Banken: Strukturen, Macht, Reformen. Köln: Bund-Verlag 1976.

Monopolkommission, Hauptgutachten 1973/75: Mehr Wettbewerb ist möglich. Baden-Baden: Nomos 1976.

Mülhaupt, Ludwig, Strukturwandlungen im westdeutschen Bankwesen. Wiesbaden: Gabler 1977.

Mülhaupt, L. und Wielens, H. Unternehmensfinanzierung heute. Neue Chancen für die Aktie. Frankfurt: Knapp 1978.

Müller, K. Die Stellung der Banken im Wirtschaftssystem der BRD - Ihre potentiellen und faktischen Einflüsse auf Nichtbankunternehmen, Institut für das Spar-, Giro- und Kreditwesen an der Universität, Bonn.

Münker, D. Das langfristige Kreditgeschäft der Grossbanken. Analyse eines Grundproblems in der deutschen Kreditwirtschaft. Stuttgart: Poeschel 1967.

Neumann M.J.M., Konstrukte der Zentralbankgeldmenge. Kredit und Kapital 8, 1975.

Pohl, Manfred, Kreditwesen in der BRD. I: Geschichte. Handwörterbuch der Wirtschaftswissenschaften, 12. Lieferung 1979.

Prost, Gerhard, Das Kreditwesen in der Bundesrepublik Deutschland. Frankfurt: Knapp 1975.

Richebächer, Kurt, Börse und Kapitalmarkt. Frankfurt: Knapp 1963.

Richebächer, Kurt, Rapporteur's Report. In: OECD (1967-1968), Vol. III.

RKW, Kapitalstrukturuntersuchung der Unternehmen des verarbeitenden Gewerbes in Schleswig-Holstein. Kiel: Rationalisierungskuratorium der deutschen Wirtschaft 1974.

Ronge, Volker. Bankpolitik im Spätkapitalismus. Frankfurt: Suhrkamp 1979.

Sachverständigenrat, Jahresgutachten 1979/80 Bonn: Heger 1979.

Schmidt, D. Der Einlagensicherungsfonds des privaten Bankgewerbes. Sparkasse 1976.

Schneider, M. Praxis der Bankaufsicht. Frankfurt: Knapp 1978.

Sombart, Werner, Die deutsche Volkswirtschaft im neunzehnten Jahrehundert. Berlin: Bondi 1909.

Sparkasse, Deutscher Sparkassen und Giroverband E.V., Bonn, monatlich.

Statistisches Bundesamt, Bevölkerung und Wirtschaft 1872-1972. Wiesbaden: Kohlhammer 1972.

Statistisches Bundesamt, Volkswirtschaftliche Gesamtrechnungen: Konten und Standardtabellen 1978. (Fachserie 18, Reihe 1). Stuttgart und Mainz: Kohlhammer 1979.

Stein, Dietrich, Wettbewerbspolitik und Geschäftbanken-system. Bochum: Brockmeyer 1975.

418.

Stützel, Wolfgang. Banken, Kapital und Kredit in der zweiten Hälfte des 20. Jahrhunderts. In: F. Neumark (ed.), Strukturwandlungen einer wachsenden Wirtschaft. Vol. II. (Schriften des Vereins für Sozialpolitik NF 30 (II)). Berlin: Duncker & Humblot 1964.

Timmermann, Vincenz. Lieferantenkredit und Geldpolitik. Berlin: de Gruyter 1971.

Torklus, Rüdiger von. Analyse der Kapitalausstattung der deutschen Unternehmen auf der Grundlage der Einheitswertstatistik. (DIW-Beiträge zur Strukturforschung Heft 8) Berlin: Duncker & Humblot 1969.

Vormbaum, Herbert. Finanzwirtschaftliches Gleichgewicht und ausländische Investitionen in der Bundesrepublik Deutschland. In: Karl Alewell (Hsg.), Betriebswirtschaftliche Strukturfragen. Festschrift zum 65. Geburtstag von Reinhold Henzler. Wiesbaden: Gabler 1967.

Vormbaum, Herbert. Finanzierung der Betriebe. 5th Edn. Wiesbaden: Gabler 1977.

Wagner, Kurt., Die deutsche Kreditwirtschaft. Frankfurt: Knapp 1970.

Weber, Adolf. Depositenbanken und Spekulationsbanken. Ein Vergleich deutschen und englischen Bankwesens. Leipzig: Duncker & Humblot 1902.

Wirtschaft und Statistik, statistiches Bundesamt, Stuttgart und Mainz, monatlich.

Wissmann, B. Die Zinsempfindlichkeit der deutschen Sparer. Berlin: Duncker & Humblot 1960.

Zeitschrift für die Gesamte Kreditwesen, Knapp, Frankfurt, zweimal in Monat.

Zeitschrift für die Gesamte Staatswissenschaft, JCB/Mohr, Tübigen, monatlich.

LIST OF WORKING PAPERS BY PROFESSOR K.H. HENNINGS

1. Investment and Saving in the West German Economy
   Since 1950.
   (revised, May 1980)

2. The Share of Non-Corporate Firms in the German
   Business Sector.
   (May 1980)

3. Private Household Saving Behaviour in Germany.
   (May 1980)

4. Notes on Financial Assets. I. Financial Assets
   Typically Available to Households.
   (May 1980)

5. The Promotion of Savings in Germany.
   (May 1980)

6. The Asset Structure of German Firms.
   (June 1980)

7. The Flow of Funds to Industry and Commerce.
   (July 1980)

8. Notes on Financial Assets. II. Financial Assets
   Typically Used to Finance Business.
   (August 1980)

9. How do Banks Decide on Loan Applications?
   (August 1980)

10. German Capital Markets.

Photo-copies of these papers may be obtained on application
to Economists Advisory Group Ltd., World Trade Centre,
52, St. Katharine's Way, London E1 9LB.

EAG regrets that it will have to charge the cost of
reproduction and postage.